The Batsford
ENCYCLOPAEDIA OF CRAFTS

The
ENCYC
OF

Batsford
ENCYCLOPAEDIA
CRAFTS

H E Laye Andrew

B T BATSFORD LTD · LONDON

*For my four children, Henry, Martha, Claude, and Felix, who are blessed
with that special form of creativity, a sense of humour, which is, perhaps,
the root of all other forms of creativity.*

© *Laye Andrew 1978*
First published June 1978
Second impression October 1978
Third impression 1979
This hardback edition 1988

ISBN 0 7134 6249 3

*Set in 9 on 10 pt. Monophoto Plantin by
Servis Filmsetting Limited, Manchester
Printed by The Anchor Press Ltd
Tiptree, Essex
for the Publishers B T Batsford Limited
4 Fitzhardinge Street, London W1H 0AH*

Introduction

This encyclopaedia concentrates on the techniques of the various crafts as opposed to describing how to make a single item in a given craft. This is because I believe that what a person makes is of value only when it is a personal expression of their own ideas. The most stumbling declaration of love is more valuable than the most beautifully declaimed expression of love written by another man for another woman.

Given the right equipment, most crafts are very simple to do; to become expert requires practice, but no more practice than is involved in making anything else. When you have acquired a skill, you will not be satisfied with copying someone else's ideas; above all, do not underestimate yourself, for there is an enormous reservoir of untapped talent and ideas in everyone.

The book covers as many traditional crafts as possible, as well as the more modern media: plastics and resins, for example, have opened up very interesting new areas, and have their own techniques and processes which are well worth exploring. Some crafts have been thought of as purely children's activities, such as french knitting, but *all* crafts are as interesting and as full of potential as the person practising the craft.

A list of museums in the appendix gives information on the crafts in which they are particularly strong; it is hoped that, when you have experimented with a technique yourself, you will look on both historical and contemporary products of art and craft with respect and understanding, instead of bemused awe. Every artefact which surrounds us has been designed by human beings – this book will help you to look at everyday objects in a new way, and consider how you would have tackled the problem, or how you would improve it.

Learn to look at objects, plants and animals really closely; the artist's and poet's capacity for detailed observation is not a rare capacity, but only a capacity rarely used – a capacity we all have. Always remember, the artist is not a unique person – rather, each person is a unique artist.

Acknowledgement

My thanks are due to all the people in the village of Pembrokeshire where I was born and in which I grew up, who encouraged curiosity, learning, excellence, and indulged and delighted in all forms of idiosyncracy. My roots lie there, and without that environment this book would never have been written.

My thanks also go to Thelma Nye and William Waller of B.T. Batsford for their encouragement and support; to my friends for their interest and help; to my dear friends Angela and Brian Compton-Carr for their concern and firmness when my spirit flagged; and last, though by no means least, my thanks to Alan.

I am deeply indebted to the following authors who have kindly allowed me to reproduce examples of their work: Elizabeth Aaron, Beryl Ash, George Aspden, June Barker, Alan Barnsley, the late Dora Billington, George Borchard, Germaine Brotherton, Pierre Bruandet, Marie Campkin, Robin Capon, Jean Carter, the late Geoffrey Clarke, Peter Coker, John Colbeck, Paul Collins, Valerie Conway, John Crawford, Ian Davidson, Alastair Duncan, Anthony Dyson, Jane Elam, Warren Farnworth, Francis and Ida Feher, Peter Fraser, Peter Gooch, Peter Green, Rolf Hartung, Virginia Harvey, Pat Holtom, Helen Hutton, Suzy Ives, Tony Jolly, Anthony Kinsey, Dietrich Kirsch, Jutta Kirsch-Korn, Dieter Klante, John Lancaster, Klares Lewes, Marjorie Murphy, Frederick Palmer, Nora Proud, Ernst Rottger, Evelyn Samuel, Lettice Sandford, Herbert Scarfe, Bonny Schmid-Burleson, Mary Seyd, Phyl Shillinglaw, Eirian Short, Caryl and Gordon Simms, Brigitte Stoddart, Ann Sutton, Alice Timmins, Heinz Ullrich, Joy Wilcox, and Gerald Woods.

My thanks are also due to the firms who were so generous in supplying materials to explore – Rowneys, Dryad, and E.J. Arnold.

AUTHOR'S NOTE

The terms and brand names used throughout this book relate predominantly to the British market. Where applicable, the American equivalent is given afterwards in brackets.

Liquid measures are given in UK imperial units, thus 1 pint = 20 fluid ounces. Since the American pint equals 16 fluid ounces, American readers may wish to make the following conversion, 1 pt (UK) = 1.0321 pt (USA), to obtain complete accuracy.

Contents

Adhesives

GLUES

Glues have been used since prehistoric times, probably the natural waxes and gums such as rosin, rubber, shellac, and beeswax that were still being used up until the 1930s. These are all exuded either by trees or insects. Animal and casein glues were used by the early Egyptians in the construction of furniture and the application of decorative veneers, and both are still widely used in the furniture trade. Animal, casein, and vegetable glues were replaced to a large extent by the rapid development of synthetic plastic resins in 1935, which meant that for the first time metal, glass, and plastic could be bonded.

Starch used as an adhesive was found on documents in Egypt dating from 3500 BC. Starch was used for paper sizing very early in the development of papermaking in China, and its use spread until the fourteenth century, when it was abandoned. In England its use was mainly in laundering for stiffening clothes, its use as such first appearing in the reign of Elizabeth I. Dextrine was discovered in 1830, when someone noticed that partially burnt starch dissolved very readily in water forming a thick very adhesive paste. It was commercially produced in Germany in 1860.

There are three types of glue made from natural materials: animal, vegetable and mineral.

Vegetable glues

Vegetable glues are based on starch, which is present in many plants, particularly in the tubers, roots and seeds, e.g. potatoes, corn. Potatoes produce farina, which is widely used on the Continent; cornflour is made from corn or maize; tapioca comes from manioc or cassava (cassava paste is the resist used in traditional indigo dyeing in Africa), and sago comes from certain palm trees. From these products are made many of the glues commonly used in schools and in the home. Gloy, for example, is made from farina. Although the way in which the starch is extracted from the plants varies considerably, in the main they are steeped in water, then mashed up to release the starch, centrifuged, and the fibrous waste separated. The pulp remaining is washed to remove the gluten and the starch is filtered off and dried.

When heated with certain catalysts, dextrines or soluble starches are formed, and these are the bases of many industrial glues, such as those used in book-binding and box-making, and the stiffening put into cheap cloth known as 'dressing'. Flour itself, mixed with water, was used as a paste in the home for sticking down newspaper cuttings and the like before pastes and glues became generally available and cheap. There are still some wallpaper pastes on the market which are made from a processed mixture of flour and starches. Another traditional glue was the white of egg that was left in the shell after the egg had been broken and used in cooking.

Animal glues

Animal glues include those made from skins, bones, fish scales, the swimming bladder of fish, and whey.

Bone glue Scrap bones of all sorts are treated with a solvent to remove the remaining fats. The bones are then washed and coarsely ground, then subjected to high-pressure steam and boiling water in succession, the steam breaking down the bone structure, and the boiling water dissolving the glue. The glue liquor is concentrated and cast into 'cakes'.

Casein This is made from whey (separated milk) treated with acetic, hydrochloric, lactic, or sulphuric acid. The resulting 'curd' is dried, the acid washed out, dried again, and ground. This is a glue much used in furniture making.

Fish glue This is made from the bones, skin, scales, and heads of fish, treated with hydrochloric acid. The glue liquor is not cast into cakes after being concentrated.

Hide glue From abattoirs and tanneries come the heads, ears, and unusable scraps of hide which have all fatty matter leached out with dilute lime water. They are then washed and boiled, and the glue liquor is concentrated and set in 'cakes'. The *premier cru* from this distillation is gelatine (gelatin), used in the confectionary trade.

Isinglass This is a curiosity rarely used, but comes (along with caviar) from the sturgeon: from the inner lining of the swimming bladder.

Mineral glue

This is known as sodium silicate, which, depending on the proportion of silica to sodium oxide, can vary in viscosity from a thick gel to the thin and watery. It has an almost universal and exclusive use in the production of corrugated cardboard.

SYNTHETIC RESIN ADHESIVES

Thermosetting types (i.e. those which undergo a chemical change on hardening).

Epoxies These are the most versatile, giving excellent adhesion to porous and non-porous surfaces, including metal. When made without solvents there is almost no shrinkage on hardening. They are normally sold in two parts, one tube containing the resin, the other the catalyst. They are mixed in small quantities immediately before use, and the speed with which they harden is known as their 'pot life'. This varies from seconds to half an hour, so that the pot life of the epoxy being used must be known before work is begun. Epoxies can be modified to cure quite hard or with slight flexibility.

Phenolics are sold as liquids which cure by evaporation of the solvent. For the strongest bond, both surfaces are thinly coated with the adhesive and allowed to 'dry', i.e. the solvents evaporate, and are then joined together. Once the two surfaces are pressed together, there is no adjusting them. Very good on wood, phenolics are not suitable for metal or glass.

Ureas work best on porous materials – but a related group of resins, the polyurethanes, are among the best adhesives for glass and metal and porous materials.

Polyester resins are used as binders for glass fibre. Like the epoxies these harden chemically so there is no shrinkage. The curing (hardening) of resin can be accelerated by heat.

Silicones These adhesives are the synthetics with the highest temperature resistance. They have a high moisture resistance and are used in electrical insulation.

Resorcinol resins are excellent on wood and porous materials: not so good on glass or metal. They have a high water resistance.

Thermoplastic synthetic adhesives do not retain their bond at high temperatures.

Vinyl resins are the most commonly known adhesives in this group. Vinyl acetate, vinyl chloride, and vinyl butyral all give good adhesion to metal and glass.

Cellulose derivatives, especially cellulose acetate and cellulose nitrate, are the all-purpose school and household adhesives which are mixed with water and although they are excellent for paper, they are no use on metal, glass, or cloth.

Acrylic The most transparent synthetic resin, though not with the best adhesive qualities, with the exception of a rapid-cure cyanoacrylate formula which has excellent metal and glass adhesion.

USING GLUES AND ADHESIVES

White glue or PVA (Elmer's Glue-All) is resin-based, and made in two strengths. The 'heavy duty' is suitable for wood construction and veneering. The 'general purpose' is ideal for card constructions, balsa wood models and polystyrene. It is wasteful to use on paper collage, but if a stronger bond is needed than can be achieved with wheat or wallpaper paste, dilute PVA glue with water. The one paper it is useful for is tissue paper, as it does not cause the paper to bleed. If you dilute by more than a third with water, even PVA will make tissue bleed. When it is dry it is completely transparent which makes it perfect for colour-mixing experiments using tissue. Arnold Tissue Paste (Sisk Tissue Collage Glue) is specially made for tissue. Diluted PVA can be painted over models to make them waterproof, though it does leave the surface shiny, and can also be used as a medium to mix with powder paints. Glue sticks (Pritt) are handy to use when gluing paper.

Wash all brushes immediately after use. They can be washed out very easily in water while the brushes are still wet, but only with difficulty if the glue dries on fabric, brushes, or any absorbent surface.

Gloy Children's Glue and Arnold Classroom Glue (Elmer's or Ross School Glue) can be washed easily out of clothes, even when the glue has dried. The Arnold is one of the few glues that will stick polythene (transparent plastic film). Another Arnold speciality is Albagum, which is specially designed to glue metallic papers. Sandford's Grippit (USA) is an excellent glue for paper, as it can guarantee no wrinkling effects.

A splendid latex glue the consistency of milk is Gripsotex. It makes a superb bond on leather, and is flexible. The same firm also makes Gripsotite, a neoprene cement, and Gripsoplast which will glue PVC. Copydex is another latex glue, which, if used as an impact glue on expanded polystyrene, is very effective.

Evostik manufacture many adhesives; Evostik Impact is good for those difficult non-porous surfaces such as stone and metal; Evostik Clear is a useful domestic choice, that will stick most things, with the exception of foam polystyrene, which it dissolves. Both Evostiks will glue metal foil. UHU is another all-purpose glue which will glue anything with the exception of polythene and polystyrene.

The two-part epoxy resins are the really powerful adhesives for the really difficult materials like stone and metal. Araldite is the well-known and trusted one, but new adhesives are coming onto the market all the time. The American firm of Dow Corning produce some excellent glues, with very specific properties. Their Urethane Bond is a one-tube glue of remarkable strength, but if it accidentally gets onto anything it is almost impossible to remove even if you treat it at once. This even applies to hands! Throw-away gloves should be used when working with it, and any excess should be wiped off immediately with a rag dipped in turpentine. This glue is not for children.

Borden make a very rapid setting two-part epoxy which sets in 5 minutes and is heatproof and waterproof. Some one-tube glues have also been produced recently which will stick all kinds of metal, and harden in 4 hours.

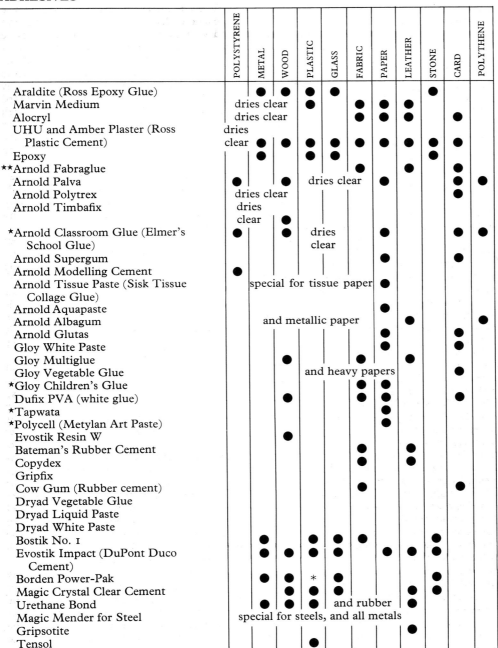

	POLYSTYRENE	METAL	WOOD	PLASTIC	GLASS	FABRIC	PAPER	LEATHER	STONE	CARD	POLYTHENE
Araldite (Ross Epoxy Glue)		●	●	●	●				●		
Marvin Medium		dries clear		●		●	●	●			
Alocryl		dries clear				●	●	●		●	
UHU and Amber Plaster (Ross Plastic Cement)	dries clear	●	●	●	●	●	●	●	●	●	
Epoxy		●		●	●			●			
**Arnold Fabraglue						●				●	
Arnold Palva	●		●	dries clear			●			●	●
Arnold Polytrex		dries clear								●	
Arnold Timbafix		dries clear	●								
*Arnold Classroom Glue (Elmer's School Glue)	●		●	dries clear			●			●	●
Arnold Supergum							●			●	
Arnold Modelling Cement	●										
Arnold Tissue Paste (Sisk Tissue Collage Glue)		special for tissue paper					●				
Arnold Aquapaste							●				
Arnold Albagum		and metallic paper					●	●			●
Arnold Glutas							●			●	
Gloy White Paste							●			●	
Gloy Multiglue			●			●		●		●	
Gloy Vegetable Glue						and heavy papers	●			●	
*Gloy Children's Glue						●	●				
Dufix PVA (white glue)			●			●	●			●	
*Tapwata							●				
*Polycell (Metylan Art Paste)							●				
Evostik Resin W			●								
Bateman's Rubber Cement						●		●			
Copydex						●					
Gripfix						●					
Cow Gum (Rubber cement)							●			●	
Dryad Vegetable Glue											
Dryad Liquid Paste											
Dryad White Paste											
Bostik No. 1		●		●	●	●			●		
Evostik Impact (DuPont Duco Cement)		●	●	●	●			●	●		
Borden Power-Pak		●	●	*	●				●		
Magic Crystal Clear Cement		●	●	●	●				●		
Urethane Bond		●	●	●	and rubber			●			
Magic Mender for Steel		special for steels, and all metals									
Gripsotite									●		
Tensol				●							

★ Washes out of clothing even when dry.
★★ Will not wash out of clothing when dry.

*rigid plastic

There are lots of two-sided tapes which vary in strength from very fine ones which can be used for thin papers, to others which are extremely strong. 3M is the firm producing some of the most interesting of these double-sided tapes, and a very useful one has a magnetic strip on the outside which is available in a wide range of widths. Blick in the UK manufactures small double-sided pieces of 'tape'. Twin-Tak Adhesive (Dick Blick) and Scotch Double Coated Tape are good double-sided tapes available in the USA. Trendymend repairs torn plastic. Invisible tape can be used on paper and still be written over.

Blu-Tack (Plasti-Tak) is very useful for temporarily mounting posters and drawings, and can be re-used again and again. Do not leave it up for long periods, because it will eventually mark both the paper and the wall.

A big breakthrough has come with the

manufacture of spray-on adhesive. 3M make Spraymount and Photomount. Spraymount opens up a whole new world in the area of tissue paper, because the very fine spray deposits an incredibly thin layer of adhesive which does not distort the paper by wrinkling, and there is no bleeding. Perfect for illustrations, its potential has not been seized by the public because of the comparatively high cost; however, unlike most aerosols which are used up in a very short space of time, these cans last a long time.

Airbrush

The airbrush was invented by an American called Burdick in about 1891. They were called Aerograph de Vibliss, from the name of the man who pioneered their manufacture. One of the earliest users of aerograph or airbrushes amongst artists was Man Ray. They were very expensive pieces of equipment, and although they were widely used in photographic studios for touching up, it was not until the invention of the aerosol can and with it a source of compressed air that its use for the artist craftsman become possible.

An airbrush is a tool rather like a fountain pen to hold, which has a hose connected to it leading to the compressed-air canister, and attached to it underneath, a small glass jar in which the paint is held. On the top (of the simplest model) is a valve which one presses with the forefinger, and a fine spray of paint is released from the airbrush. With the simplest brush that is the only manual control one has, so that to make a fine line one has to hold the brush near to the paper (or model), and to make wider strokes one moves the brush further away. With the more expensive models, one can control the width of the line by a more sophisticated control on the top of the brush. There are also models with a small cup attached to the brush (to one side) instead of the glass jar underneath, and if one is doing a lot of graphics this is a great advantage, because it is very easy to wash out and change to another colour.

Aerosol cans can be rather expensive to run if one does a lot of airbrushing, because these are precision instruments and must be very carefully cleaned after use and between each colour, and to clean them using either water, if the paint has been water based, or the appropriate solvent, one is also using up precious compressed air to force the water, etc. through. An electrically operated compressor is sold which will last for ever, and is equal roughly to the cost of 30 cans of compressed air. Another long-term supply of compressed air is from a car tyre (attached to a wheel), for which a small adaptor is sold which is fitted to the tyre valve. To replenish the compressed air, take it to the nearest garage and have it inflated.

The advantage of an airbrush is that it gives a very even layer of paint to a surface, without any brush marks. It is excellent for using with stencils, especially where there is very fine detail in the cutting, or where you want to use several colours on one stencil. The edge of the sprayed area (when not using an internal stencil) is very distinctive, for it achieves a gradation of colour virtually impossible by any other means.

Almost any paint can be used as long as it is thinned down to the right consistency by the appropriate thinner; if the paint is very difficult to thin to an even consistency, try straining it through a pair of nylon tights.

Always hold the surface to be sprayed as near to the vertical as possible. If you try to spray onto a horizontal piece of paper there is a likelihood of the paint forming too-large droplets, and there would be a very uneven finish to the work.

Animation

Today one thinks in terms of animated cartoons when animation is mentioned, but attempts relying in the main on 'Persistence of Vision' were made to animate drawings since 1825, when John Ayrton Paris, the President of the Royal College of Physicians, invented the 'Thaumatrope'. This was a disc onto which two drawings were made, e.g. of an empty cage on one half, and a parrot on the other half, and when the disc was spun rapidly by two strings attached to the disc, the parrot appeared to be inside the cage.

In 1832 two inventions following through this idea appeared. One, the 'Phenakistiscope' invented by M. Plateau, was a large disc with many drawings towards the edge, which was fitted into a holder which had a series of slits all around the edge. The drawings faced outwards, and the machine was held up facing a mirror, and spun rapidly. By looking through the slits at the mirror one had the impression of the figures actually moving. The other invention that year was the 'Zeotrope', by W.H. Horn, of Bristol. The slits in this were placed all round a drum which could revolve very freely, and inside which the strip of paper with the drawings in various positions was fitted. The slits were in the upper half of the drum, and the drawings were fitted into the lower half. The changes in position between one figure and the next in sequence are exactly the same as used by animated cartoonists today.

A more sophisticated version was produced in Paris in 1878 by M. Emile Reynaud, called the 'Praxinoscope'. This used a fixed background onto which, by means of mirrors, the animated figures could be superimposed, thus appearing in an appropriate setting.

A similar technique is used in the making of 'flip-through' books. At the bottom of each page is drawn a figure, each drawing being slightly different in position from the previous one, so that when the leaves of the book are flipped through the figure appears to be moving. It requires a lot of patience, and the slighter the difference between one drawing and the next, the smoother the movement will appear. The same is true of animated films, where each drawing is made on a separate piece of paper, and photographs are taken one frame at a time by a fixed overhead cine camera. Two holes are punched in the bottom of the piece of paper on which the drawing is to be made, and the paper is slotted onto two matching pegs. This ensures accurate registration of each drawing. Drawings are made over a lightbox, so that the previous drawing is laid down first and the blank piece of paper is laid on top and traced through, alterations in movements being made to those parts which need it, and so on.

Drawings can be made either on paper or on sheet acetate, which has the added advantage of being used in conjunction with a strip of background which can be moved underneath the figure, frame by frame, to give the illusion of the figure moving through the background.

In addition to drawn figures, one can use jointed puppet figures, pantins and shadow puppets (see section on puppetry), and objects, e.g. matchsticks, coins, pencils, plasticine, etc.

FURTHER READING
GODFREY, R. AND JACKSON, A., *Do-it-yourself Film Animation* BBC Publications

Art Protis

This technique was developed at the Wool Research Institute in Brno, Czechoslovakia.

Dyed, carded (but unspun) wool is laid on a backing. The arrangement is then fed into a textile machine which fastens the loose fibres onto the backing with a virtually invisible series of threads.

Sign of Heaven by Ivana and Zybněk Siaviěceks (courtesy the International Wool Secretariat and the Wool Research Institute, Brno, Czechoslovakia).

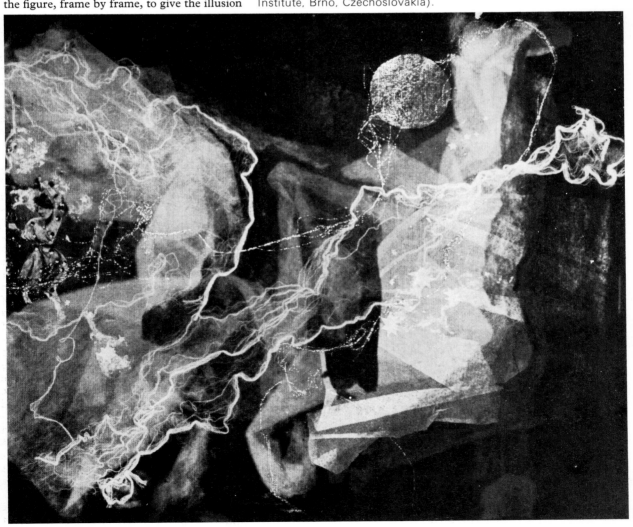

Assemblages

Assemblages are collections of objects arranged in either an aesthetic relationship, or a curious juxtaposition which explores some particular idea. Although the name normally applies to such collections in two dimensions, it can also apply to three dimensions.

Duchamp had been the forerunner in this field in 1921 with his 'Why not sneeze?', the title being a typical Dada non sequitur. It is a birdcage filled with sugar lumps, a cuttle-fish bone, and a thermometer. Only when it is lifted does one realize that by the weight, they cannot really be sugar lumps. In fact they are made from white marble. He takes the illusion, and then mocks it.

The arrangement of objects was not one which required special technical knowledge or much skill, and the making of assemblages by people quite outside the art world (for these assemblages relied on puns or were simply arrangements of objects with private associations) became the vogue amongst intellectuals in the 1930s.

The frequently illustrated fur cup, saucer, and spoon by Meret Oppenheim was made at this time. This odd juxtaposition of materials and purpose was utilized by Dominguez when he upholstered a wooden barrow with lavish red satin. This piece achieved great popularity, and many copies were made of it.

Surrealist dioramas were made by the American Cornell in the 30s. The boxes were treated as stage sets, and were combinations of space and illusion, similar to the theatrical setting of de Chirico's paintings. Notable amongst Cornell's boxes is his 'A Pantry Ballet for Jacques Offenbach'.

In 1938 in Paris a very large exhibition of Surrealist art and objects was held. It was to be the last, for with the war many artists went into hiding while others left for America. The exhibition was arranged in such a way that it created a total surrealist environment. (Though the idea of total environment, and the wish/intention to shock the visitors out of their complacency had been done first by Duchamp in 1920.) Dali's main contribution was in the foyer, where he had erected a very large decaying taxi. In it were two dummies, a driver, and a female passenger. Ivy trailed in and out of the car windows and struggled to get in at the door. Inside, showers of water sprayed down intermittently over the two occupants. The female passenger looked quite demented as live snails crawled all over her, and up the windows and all over the inside of the cab!

A series of shop mannequins had been 'dressed' by such artists as Arp, Mirò, Masson, Man Ray, Dali, Ernst, Tanguy, and Duchamp. One of the most disturbing was that of Masson.

Humour, wit, and ingenuity are sadly not considered worth fostering in the work of children, which is a great loss. Puns and a fiendish delight in the incongruous are a major part of children's creativity, from very early years. The four-year-old who offered me a bunch of daisies surrounded by 'leaves' of wriggling worms found my reaction hilarious, and this incident is common to children left to their own discovery. Their drawings at home are often full of wit and curious subject matter. 'Man holding back leg of a giraffe' was the subject matter not of a Dada painter, but a solemn four-year-old girl.

(Below) 3-D assemblage using junk materials. (Below right) The exploitation of commercial packaging is a typical assemblage technique.

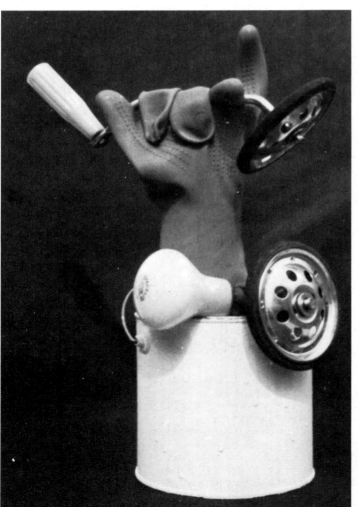

Batik

HISTORICAL

Batik is the technique of applying hot wax to cloth and subsequently immersing the cloth in a cold-water dye. The origins of this craft are similar to those of tie-and-dye. By the thirteenth century it was regarded as a pastime suitable for Javanese noblewomen. The fashion then spread throughout the whole of that society and was soon being exported. The batiks were (and still are) mostly dyed in blue and brown. Europe tried to imitate the technique industrially (first, in England) but the cost of the dyes themselves made it very expensive. The source of all dyes up until the nineteenth century was either plants — lichens, roots, bark, and berries — or rocks, mud, and, to obtain a purple colour, crushed murex shells. (See section on Shells.) In 1856, however, Henry Perkins accidentally discovered a purple dye while trying to extract quinine from aniline. Since then aniline, which itself is oily and colourless, has become the source, along with other coal tar derivatives, of most dyes.

The fashion in batik was at its height in Germany at the turn of the last century, and curtains as well as clothes were made using the technique. The wax was sometimes left in the curtain fabric to simulate stained glass even more effectively. In Africa the resist is made from cassava flour paste. The random crackle pattern of batik was especially hard to reproduce mechanically but the batiks made in England today for export to Africa are very convincing imitations of real batik.

EQUIPMENT AND MATERIALS

For applying the wax to the cloth

a domestic deep fat fryer (portable) or double boiler; paraffin wax; tjanting or brushes, hog or bristle; wooden frame.

The *deep fat fryer* eliminates the need for lots of equipment to melt the wax safely. It has a thermostat so that the temperature can be adjusted at will: it will hold either a little wax, or as much as 3 litres. If you are seriously doing batik, or have it permanently in a syllabus, this is the equipment to get.

The wax can be melted in other ways, though. A tin can which has been opened at each end can have holes punched all round it so that air can circulate. A nightlight (slow-burning candle) can be used inside that as a source of heat. A larger can is stood on top and some paraffin wax or candles put in it to melt. This method does not get the wax very hot, and must be kept right next to the person using it. It must also have a sheet of asbestos under it.

Alternatively melt the wax in a double boiler on an electric ring (hot plate). The wax is put in the top and water in the bottom is kept just on the boil. If there is no boiler it can still be done with a saucepan to hold the water and a can in the saucepan to hold the wax.

Resin or beeswax can be added to the paraffin wax, though it is in no way essential: it makes the wax less brittle. If you would like to try it, the proportions are one part resin/beeswax to four parts paraffin wax. If you have not got paraffin wax, melt down some white candles.

The *wooden frame* is useful if you are making a picture. It keeps the material nice and taut, but one can work without it. An old wooden picture frame would do.

One needs something to apply the wax to the cloth; *pipe cleaners* can be bent into all sorts of shapes, and the cotton on them holds quite a lot of wax. Hoghair *brushes* are good, but the traditional tool is the *tjanting*. This holds a small quantity of wax in the reservoir in the 'nib', out of which leads a small tube. The hot wax comes out of this in a fine trail and this tool is excellent for very fine work.

For dyeing

Rubber gloves If you do not wear these when you are dyeing, then you will have to wear cotton ones afterwards to hide your hands! One can use bleach to get rid of dye on skin, but it stays in the cuticles very stubbornly, and under the nails.

Plastic or enamel bowls, or old baby bath For the dye liquid, and for catching the drips when the fabric is hung out to dry.

Plastic measuring spoons For accurately measuring the dye powder, salt, and soda. You might like to guess later, but to begin with measure everything.

Bowls or screw-top jam jars For mixing dyes.

Plastic or pyrex measuring jug

Lots of old newspaper Used when ironing off the wax.

Dyes Dylon cold water dyes (and salt and soda), or Procion 'M' dyes (and salt and soda). Rit dyes are available in the USA.

Detergent For washing off the wax, and a supply of hot water. Domestic detergent will do, but Lissapol is used for Procion.

Iron For ironing out the remnants of wax in the cloth.

Cloth onto which one applies the wax and dye

Cotton; silk; silk and cotton mixture; linen. Man-made fabrics require special dyes, and often do not take the dye colour as well as natural fibres. The result is more successful if one can apply heat to the dye solution, but for batik the dye solution must be cool or cold when used.

METHOD

Before you start work on fabric, experiment on paper so that you really understand the concept behind the craft. When you understand *why* you are doing something you do not make stupid mistakes and you are far more likely to make some useful discoveries.

To understand the concept, one needs only a candle, some clean paper, and two colours of ink.

Light the candle, and let the wax drip onto the paper. In spots, lines – it does not matter. With the lightest-colour ink, say red, cover all the paper. Where the wax is on the paper the dye cannot penetrate, so it stays white under the wax.

Let the ink dry, and add a lot more drips of hot candle wax. Now cover the whole paper with some black ink (covering all the red paper). Let it dry. Scrape off the wax with a knife, and you will see white spots and red spots on a black background. Iron off remaining wax between sheets of old newspaper. It is in fact the same 'stencil' concept which acts as the basis for so many crafts.

In schools, Brusho (Putnam) dyes are excellent for doing paper batik, and practice with all the tools, the tjanting, pipe cleaners, rolled-up rag, etc., and the real wax, can be had without the expense of working on cloth. Although the concept of batik can be understood with candle and ink as described above, it is more difficult putting that concept into practice when faced with a design, so it really is important to experiment with more than one and preferably three colours on paper first. When using yellow as the first colour and blue as the second, where the blue is painted onto areas coloured yellow it will change to green, but one needs to know what *sort* of green. If it is not what one wanted, then a different blue or a different yellow is going to have to be used until one gets the right colour. When a third colour is used, more adjustments might have to be made.

Experiment Use the techniques from one craft and see if they can be applied to another. You might not think that enamelling has much to do with batik, but the technique of cloisonné is one well adapted to batik. Make the 'cloison' of wax by drawing a circle of wax on the paper, or lots of circles. In enamel this would be of copper and filled with powdered enamel, but you can fill the wax ring with dye. Each ring can have a different coloured dye in it.

Try putting a thick coating of wax on the cloth and drawing into it with a pin: mix batik and tie and dye; try making 'blot' pictures with hot wax; use the fold-and-dye method of decorating tissue paper, etc.

A man's plain white handkerchief is useful for a 'set piece'. It is small and there is no problem of finishing off for little children.

Transferring the design to the cloth

One can either draw with a soft 4B pencil or charcoal directly onto the cloth, or, if one is using a frame, lay the stretched fabric over the prepared design, and draw the design which can be seen through the cloth.

N.B. All cloth should be washed first to remove any 'sizing'. This is a sort of starch used to stiffen the cloth, and some have a lot on, some none, but if it is left on it will act as a resist to the dye and the cloth will dye unevenly. The washed cloth must be dried and ironed before use.

Applying the wax to the cloth

The wax must penetrate *right through the cloth*. If it sits on top of the cloth, when the fabric is dyed the dye will creep under the wax from the other side, and there will be no design left on the cloth. When the wax penetrates the cloth, the cloth changes colour: it becomes darker, and is transparent. When it sits on top of the cloth it is an opaque white.

To penetrate, *the wax must be hot*. The wax can cool on the way from the pan to the cloth, so one must have the wax immediately next to the cloth being waxed.

The traditional tool for applying the wax to cloth is the tjanting. This consists of a wooden handle with a copper reservoir which has a fine spout at the end. This tool is used for fine lines. When large areas are to be covered, a brush is called for. Keep the tjanting in the hot wax before using to heat up the copper. This will keep the wax in it hot longer while you are drawing with it. As soon as the wax gets cool, it will block up the spout. Put the tjanting back in the hot wax then and it will heat the copper up once more. Continuous flowing lines are the most suitable to make with the tjanting because once the wax has started pouring out of the spout it will not stop until the reservoir is empty. Practice on some paper is essential when using this tool.

To heat the wax, either switch on the deep-fryer, or melt wax in the top of a double boiler, or in a can in a saucepan of water on an electric ring. Once the wax has been melted it can be kept hot in a tin over a nightlight (see p. 18).

Another method of applying wax is with pipe cleaners. The furry part of the cleaner holds enough wax for two or three prints with one dipping, and is especially good for decorat-

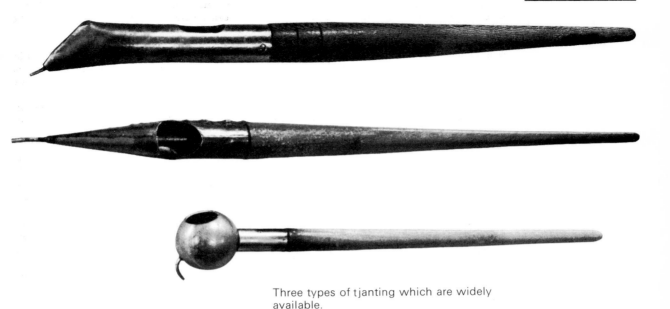

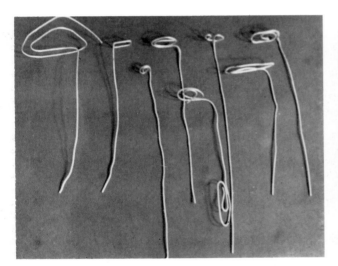

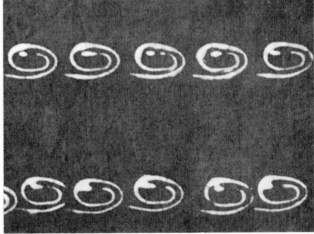

Three types of tjanting which are widely available.

Bent wire stamps and the patterns they form

ing small objects like puppet and dolls' clothes, soft toys, etc. Other stamps can be made out of a tightly rolled strip of linen (this will make a dot, the size depending on the size of the bundle); a strip of thick felt tied round a fat stick (this will make an O); cloth tied round a square section piece of wood will make a rounded-off square, etc. Invent your own stamps: metal is very good for making stamps, brass tubing is specially good.

If when one has finished the waxing one finds that there are parts where the wax has not penetrated, turn the cloth over, and paint those parts with fresh hot wax. If the cloth is on a frame then it is a simple matter. If you have been working on clean unprinted newsprint, you will have to pull the cloth off the paper because the wax sticks to the paper. It is better to use greaseproof (waxed) paper, to which it is less likely to stick. Do not use newspapers because the ink in the newsprint can penetrate the cloth through the hot wax.

17

The simplest items in which to heat the wax. On the portable hot plate is a saucepan of water and standing in it are two cans holding the molten paraffin wax, or melted candles. To the right is the punched tin surrounding the nightlight (candle) keeping the tin above it hot.

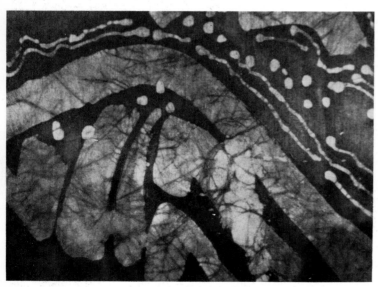

Example showing the different effects achieved by using a brush or a tjanting. Note that small dots can also be made with the tjanting.

Cracking the wax

Cracking in the waxed areas is an inherent quality in batik work. It is one of the main ways in which one can recognize a piece of batik. The cracking can be completely random, or it can be controlled up to a point. If the wax is cold, the lines will be fine. In hot weather it is a good idea to run it under a cold tap for a while to make it quite cold before cracking the wax.

To control the cracking, one can push a stick or back end of a brush into the waxed cloth, and fold it round the point, crushing it as one does so. One can use the same technique around a bottle, ruler, marble, etc.

Dyeing the cloth

Use either Dylon cold-water dyes which are available in most general stores, or Procion 'M' dyes.

Dissolve one small tin of Dylon cold-water dye in 1 pint of warm water. Put in a large bowl and add sufficient cold water to cover the cloth to be batiked completely. Directions on the tin will give instructions on how much dry weight of cloth will be dyed by one small tin. In another small bowl, dissolve 4 heaped tblsps salt and 1 tblsp of washing soda in 1 pint of hot water. Add to the dye bath.

Put the cloth into the dye bowl, making sure that there is no part of the cloth above the surface, and make sure that none pops up during the dyeing process. It must stay in the dye for 30 minutes, but turn it occasionally to make sure that all the cloth is being dyed evenly. Lift out of the bath, and dry.

Re-wax the cloth in those parts that you wish to stay the colour of your first dye. Dye the cloth in the next colour. Lift out and dry. Re-wax again, if you choose. When the dye is complete, rinse the cloth to get rid of all surplus dye. When the water is running clear, put the cloth into a clean polythene bowl, and pour some boiling water and detergent over it. This is to release the wax. If the water is left to get cold, the wax will float to the surface of the water and form a solid sheet, which can be lifted out and used again.

Lift out the cloth and hang up to dry. Any remaining wax can be ironed out between sheets of old newspapers.

Procion 'M' dyes are a range of very clear dyes which come in intense colours. They are really permanent, very easy to use, and dye silk, cotton, and linen very well.

FURTHER READING

PROUD, N., *Simple Textile Dyeing and Printing* Batsford

SAMUEL, E., *Introducing Batik* Batsford

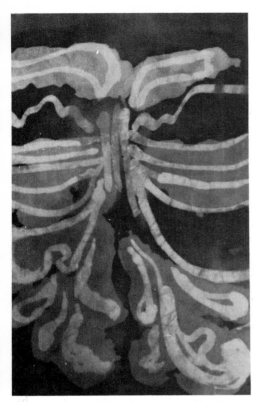

A two-colour print using wax applied by the tjanting for the first colour, and a brush before the second colour.

POSSIBILITIES WITH BATIK

Categories of design

free pictures; abstract shapes; direct onto a predetermined shape, e.g. soft toy, doll, bag, etc.

Patterns organized into

all-over patterns; border patterns; radial patterns.

Patterns made with

a brush; drips from a candle; pipe cleaners or other stamps.

Things to make with batik

bow-ties, ordinary ties; pictures/panels; cushions; skirts; bags; roller blinds; lamp-shades; dolls, and doll's clothes; scarves; tablecloths; pillows; blouses; soft toys.

Wax applied to

fabric; paper; wood; leather; pottery.

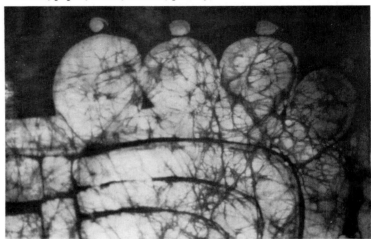

Typical 'cracking' that is inherent in batik. The wax on the cloth cracks when handled in the dye, and dye seeps through the cracks down to the fabric, leaving a fine cobweb of lines.

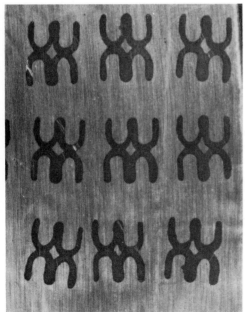

How the wax looks on cloth before dyeing. The pattern should always appear darker than the cloth.

The same pipe cleaner shape (arranged in a different organization) after dyeing the cloth and ironing off.

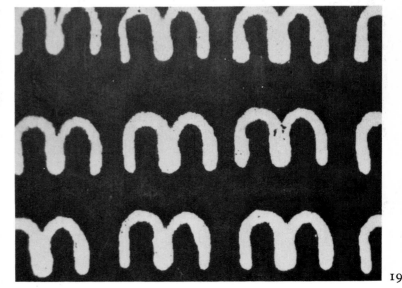

Beads

The urge to wear objects which apparently have little survival value but which give the wearer great pleasure seems to be a much more significant difference between man and other animals than some of those the scientist selects.

HISTORICAL

The most desirable stone in early times was the turquoise. First found in the Sinai peninsula, it was later mined in Nishapur in Persia, in central Asia, and in New Mexico – all bleak desert areas. It is not surprising that the turquoise became the chosen stone to protect travellers. The name turquoise incidentally comes from the name Turkey. The earliest known manufacture of glass is in Georgia in the USSR in about 3000 BC. One thousand five hundred years passed before glass was made in Egypt. The manufacture of glass is very important in the history of beads, because for all those people who could not afford semi-precious or precious stones, and found the wearing of seeds and shells too unsophisticated, glass beads gave a quality of richness that was not obtainable any other way.

Amentophis II established glass works in Thebes, and blue glass beads were made at Deir-el-Belni in 1400 BC, and his son Akhenaton established the glass bead works of Tell el-Amara.

Faience, which was also known as *fake Malkat* (Malkat was the place in Sinai where the turquoise was first mined), and glass beads were made to imitate turquoise, lapiz, and carnelian. Before glass was discovered, faience beads were made by heating a bead of quartz in a little lime and colouring – copper to make blue, manganese for black and purple. There is little difference in manufacture between faience and glass. In fact, faience heated with a little soda becomes glass.

The peak of Cretan bead technology in metal was 1600 to 1300 BC, their knowledge of gold techniques being very extensive. They knew how to 'granulate' gold, the technique of granulation being the process of attaching tiny gold spheres to flat metal.

At Sidon, around 300 BC the technique of making millefiore beads was being used. The principle is that used in making seaside rock. Molten glass is pulled out into very thin 'canes'. A bunch of these canes are held together to form another thick cane and dipped into molten glass fusing them all together. The cane is then sliced up as one slices a cucumber, and dropped onto a molten glass bead.

Beads made by the Venetian method are made as follows. A large 'bubble' of glass is blown, in the colour required, and a helper pulls the opposite side of the bubble out into a long tube, sometimes up to 100 ft long. The original bubble becomes the hollow of the tube, and when the tube is cut up into short lengths, the hollow becomes the hole in the bead. When the tube is cut into lengths of $\frac{3}{4}$ in. or more, they are called bugle beads.

To round the edges of the beads, which are still sharp at this stage, they are put in a drum of finely pulverized sand and ashes. The metal drum is rotated and heated, just enough to soften the glass which rounds the edges of the bead. The mixture of sand and ashes prevents them sticking together, and is washed off when the drum is cooled.

Another method of making coloured beads is by having the colour on the inside of the bead only, the outside being made of clear glass. This is done by making the original bubble of coloured glass, and then dipping it into clear molten glass. When pulled out into a tube it produces the beads described above, but they look cheap and gaudy next to opaque body colour glass beads. Good quality beads are of an even size, and when doing any beadwork it is important to use these. Irregular beads spoil the look of the finished product.

Millefiore beads spread with trade all over Africa, and this technique, elaborated, was used and still is by the Venetian glassworkers, as beads and inset into paper weights, where they look like ornate multi-coloured daisies.

Glass 'eye-beads' were made near Athens around 2000 BC, to celebrate some cult, but the Phoenicians perfected their manufacture. Later a flourishing glass industry was set up in Alexandria by Alexander the Great to make trading beads. The tradition continues to this day and in Aleppo and in Turkey the making of beads, and in particular the making of Fatima Eyes, flourishes.

The beads most prized by the Greeks were those made of amber. To obtain this, they established mule-pack routes, all the way from the Aegean to the Baltic, where amber occurs naturally as a fossilized pine resin. The Romans preferred gold jewellery, later setting it with rubies, emeralds, diamonds, and sapphires.

Millefiore beads are known in Africa as 'aggrey' beads. The use of these beads as currency was still being carried on by the Portuguese explorers, as they encircled Africa looking for a route to India, and they poured shipload after shipload of beads into Africa, in exchange for gold, ivory and slaves.

Beads made out of shell and called 'wampum' were used by American Indians for money. The strings of shell, cut and shaped rather like a sequin, were strung together and made up as belts, the loose beads being used as small change by the white settlers.

The Spaniards traded beads in the southwest of North America as early as 1540, and by 1750 English, Dutch, and French traders were bringing beads to the eastern coast of North America. Beads were not available to the plains Indians until about 1800.

By 1650, the Dutch had founded their own

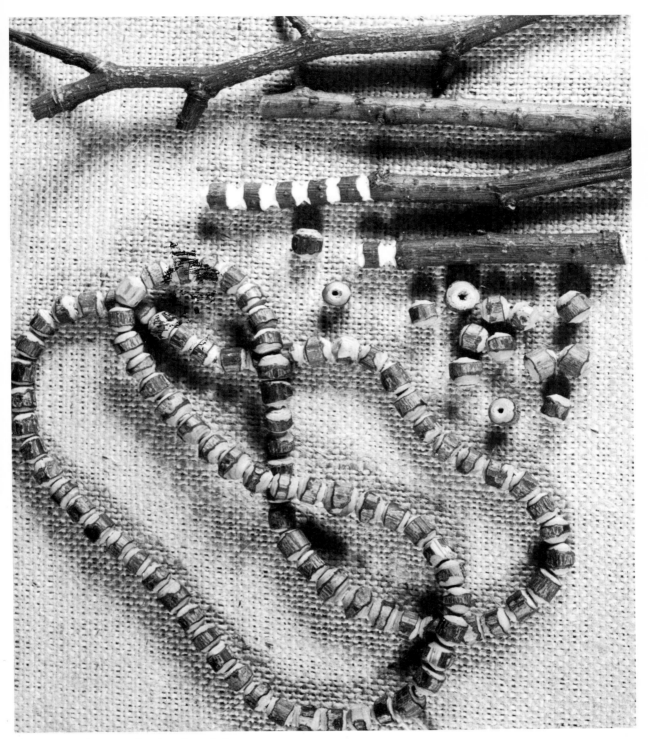

Beads made from a twig, showing all the
stages from the twig to the finished
necklace.

bead factories near Amsterdam. Cambay, in India, is an important centre today for the production of trade beads, and it is claimed that it has been so without interruption for 7000 years.

In Armenia in the third century AD, glass beads, mosaics, and even window panes were being made. And although the remarkable Tamurlane brought glass craftsmen to Samarkand in Tajikistan, Peter the Great still had mica in his windows.

Heavily beaded clothes had two heydays in England, the first in Elizabethan times, and the second in Victorian England. Beads were used to make jewellery, and to decorate clothes, accessories, and many domestic articles such as purses, kettle and teapot stands, fire screens, bell-pulls, etc.

Modern beads

Most of the beads available in schools today are either of wood or plastic, and what they lack in colour, they compensate for in the wide variety of sizes and shapes. The beads one finds in shops are very limited in size and colour, and if one wants beads, then a visit to a shop that sells only beads and sequins is the answer because the variety that is made is quite extensive, and also less expensive than those bought in local shops. However, it may be found that it is sometimes cheaper, weight for weight, to buy beads which are made up as necklaces, especially in the cheap chainstores or in street markets.

Do not forget when buying glass beads that you *must* buy a special bead needle at the same time, and a patent needle threader is a good idea too, because the eye of a bead needle is very small.

American Indian moccasin, totally beaded. The thread used is animal sinew, and the points at which the lengths of beads are sewn down form the lines around the moccasin. (Collection Dr A.A. Black.)

Beads are threaded onto cotton before being caught down. In order to make a regular pattern, the beads have to be carefully counted, especially in this case where the shape is constantly increasing.

The beads which decorate this headdress were first sewn onto a thread and then stitched onto the shaped base.

BEAD MAKING

Beads can be made out of *pips and seeds* simply by making a hole in them when they are fresh and before they have dried out. Pips such as orange and apple, and seeds like melon are suitable. *Fruit stones* are rather more difficult to deal with and have to be drilled. Dates are simple to drill, being fairly soft, but the stones of plums, apricot, and cherry need a little more patience when drilling. *Acorn cups* can be drilled, as can the dried halves inside. *Shells* can be drilled by placing on a lump of plasticine to hold them steady. *Pebbles* cannot be drilled, but they can have bell caps glued to them, or string and leather thonging. (See section on Pebbles.)

To make beads from scratch, one can use clay, salt and flour dough, and papier mâché.

Clay

This can be pressed into moulds, or rolled into spheres, discs, cylinders, etc. The variety of shapes is endless. Remember to make a hole in the centre before firing. Beads can be fired in a simple sawdust kiln, pit kiln, dustbin (garbage can) kiln, or even a well-stoked-up domestic fire if the beads are put in the hottest part. Leave until the fire has gone out.

Flour and salt dough

One cup flour mixed with 2 tblsps salt and enough water to make a stiff dough. Do not add too much salt, or the dough will never dry out. Powder paint can be added to the flour before being mixed, or the beads can be painted when they are dry. Make holes in them before putting them on the radiator to dry. To make marbled beads, make up two or three different loads of dough each coloured with a different powder colour. Press each colour on top of another ball, and roll the whole lump into a long sausage. Cut up into slices, about $\frac{1}{4}$ in. thick, and you will discover that each slice is marbled. Make a hole, etc., or try rolling out like pastry, and cut up into various shapes. Press beads or seeds into them, paint and use for Christmas tree decorations. When dry, they can be coated with some varnish to lengthen their life. If they are painted with colour mixed with Marvin glue, or with acrylic paint such as Cryla colour, they will not need varnishing.

Papier mâché

For making small things like beads or pendants, it is more satisfactory to use instant papier mâché, to which one only has to add water.

Laminated paper

Roll up long triangles of paper coated with Polycell (wallpaper paste) around a knitting needle to form beads that are fat in the middle; strips of paper make cylinders. Decorate with paint and tissue papers.

Wire and tissue paper

Using white glue, paste tissue paper over a simple flat shape of thin wire, then trim when dry. Leave a loop of wire free for threading. Paint with nail varnish to strengthen. (See section on Tissue Paper.)

SEWN BEADS

In Nigeria there is a unique use made of beads: to decorate the crowns or ceremonial head-dress of the Iba. The technique used is the same as that used by the American Indians on their moccasins, pouches, etc. The beads are threaded on a long string and this is sewn onto a base either to make a pattern or to cover the whole surface, as in the moccasins and the headdress. The unique aspect of the illustrated headdress is in the treatment of the birds. The birds, including their wings, are modelled, and the beads are laid in rows on this model until the whole is covered.

Detail from an antique American Indian bag which uses beads threaded onto cotton. (Collection Dr A.A. Black.)

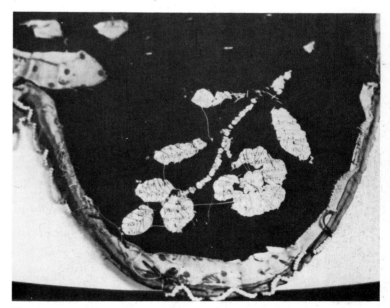

The reverse of the antique American Indian bag, showing the use of paper to give the decoration more rigidity. (Collection Dr A.A. Black.)

23

Some of the sequins available. Specialist shops offer a wide variety of shape, size and colour.

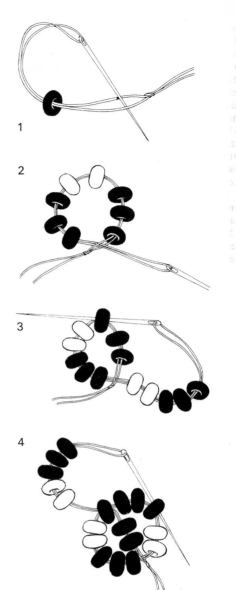

1

2

3

4

The finished zigzag braid.

The Mexicans do a similar thing with coloured wool stuck onto clay shapes until they are completely covered.

Beads strung on long lengths are also made into curtains, and there are some very lovely Chinese ones appearing on the market. These are usually of floral subjects or birds, but the Victorian fringes round lamps used the same idea, though these were usually geometrically patterned.

Beads were also appliquéd onto detachable ornaments which were worn on dresses in Victorian England.

Wire can also be used for threading beads, and this means that the beads can be arranged into free-standing structures. The Victorians generally made bouquets of flowers, the most magnificent of which would be arranged in a vase and kept under a glass dome. Smaller sprays were used as brooches. A leaf spray can be made by threading all the beads needed for each spray on to a long piece of fine wire, and by bending the wire round into a loop and twisting it. Continue doing this until 12 leaves are made, twisting the wire after each leaf, and then bend the leaves to alternate sides. The flowers are made by threading up one long (bugle) bead, three round beads and another bugle bead. This forms one petal. Make five, wire them all together, wire a large bead in the centre, and the flower is complete.

STRINGING BRAIDS

Use 'Rocaille' beads, size 2/0 or 3/0, in two or more different colours. Bugle beads or oval wooden beads can also be worked into a braid for a pleasing effect. Use a bead needle (size 10), and synthetic thread, or shirring elastic if the braid needs to be expandable. The thread should be coated with beeswax to make it stronger and easier to work. Children may find it easier to thread fine nylon gut (as used by anglers) through the beads without having to use a needle at all.

Zigzag braid

The thread is always used *double*, so cut a *long* piece, and pull it across the cake of beeswax. Knot the two ends together about 2 in. from the end. Thread one bead on and slip the needle between the threads as shown, that is, between the knot and the bead. That is to secure the bead, and make sure it does not slip off.

To make the braid, thread 2 black, 2 white, and 3 black. Slip the needle between the threads above the knot and below the first bead you put on. Then follow step 2 and 3, and repeat stages 2, 3, and 4 until the braid is as long as you want.

Adding new thread

When you need a new length of thread, leave the needle dangling, and take a *new* needle and thread up and wax as before and always. Do not make a knot: starting two or three rows before the point at which you ran out of thread, run your needle through two beads (there is one or possibly two threads in the hole already, so it will be a little stiff to push through). Leave a 2-in. tail at the side, and make a buttonhole stitch (slip knot) between the 2nd and 3rd beads, thread through the next bead, do another buttonhole stitch, and follow the route of your previous thread. You will inevitably come out where you finished, and you are all ready to continue.

Note, the change in colour of the thread in the diagram is only to show where the thread goes more clearly. It is *not* a different thread.

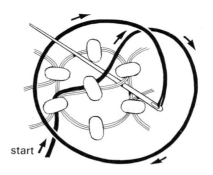

start

The slip knot

Joining up the two ends to make a circular necklace.

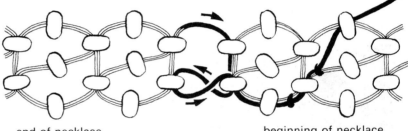

end of necklace

beginning of necklace

Attaching new threads.

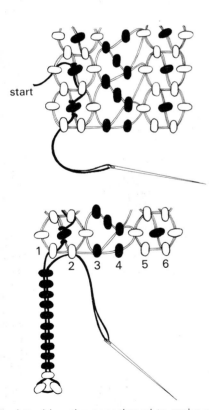

start

1 2 3 4 5 6

Attaching the new thread to make a bead fringe. Note that the fringe is made by threading the beads twice, and at the bottom one has to add one, two or three beads: whichever number, these are only threaded once, and form the end which stops all the other beads falling off.

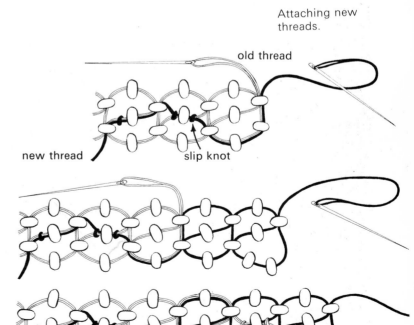

old thread

new thread

slip knot

old thread cut

25

BEADWEAVING

Equipment

Loom A loom can be made by using an old picture frame, with tacks hammered into two opposite sides – but you will be limited to length. A loom with rollers, like the one illustrated, is very simple, and because there are rollers at each end, quite long lengths can be woven, and the ridged bars at either end ensure that the warp does not slip.

Needle Use a bead needle (size 10). The hole in the centre of beads for bead weaving is very small, and the needle also needs to be quite long.

Materials

Beads 'Rocaille' beads, size 2/0 or 3/0.

Thread For the warp, linen thread or a synthetic button hole thread. Shirring elastic if you are making pony-tail bands or bracelets.

For the weft, any synthetic. It is stronger and more resilient than cotton. Coats' Drima is good. Quite a lot of the weft shows, so choose a colour appropriate to the colour of the beads you will be using.

Beeswax To make the thread stronger and less likely to get knotted.

Method

Setting up the warp Decide how long you want the beadwork to be, add 14 in., and that will be the length of each thread of the warp. The number of threads will be the number of beads wide in the pattern plus one.

Hold the threads in a neat bunch and knot them all together at each end. Divide roughly into two, and slip the knot over the stud on one roller. Slacken off the wing nut and roll up the warp (the bunch of threads) until the other knot will just slip over the stud on the other roller.

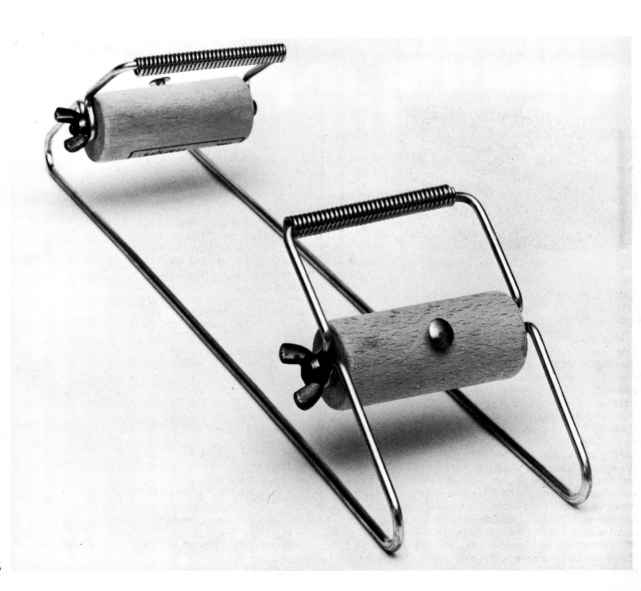

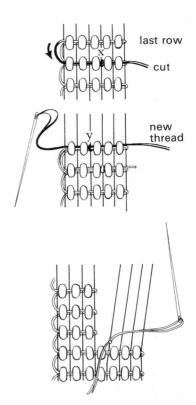

last row

cut

new thread

Method of attaching new thread.

Tying the new thread onto the second side of the necklace. The tail is threaded through the lower beads.

Left A bead loom, and *above* the bead loom set up, showing the point at which the necklace divides.

Now place the threads in the hollows of the ridges on the crossbars, one in each hollow. Do the same at the other end and you are all ready to start. Check that the warp is good and tight, and start at the end without any warp rolled onto the roller, not as in the photo. If you are doing a long length, when the warp is filled up, slacken off the wingnut, and roll carefully on to the roller nearest you, until the warp is 'empty' again. Tighten the nut.

Weaving Thread the needle as for making a free braid, and onto the warp thread nearest the edge, and close to the roller, make a slip-knot. Slip the needle *under* the warp to the right-hand side and pick up the required number of beads and *leave them on the needle*. With the needle now pointing to the left, and the needle *under* the warp, lift the needle until there is one bead between each warp thread.

Holding the beads steady with a finger of the left hand, pull the needle through, still holding the beads in place. The needle is on the left-hand side of the work. Push the beads up with your finger until the holes in each are visible above the warp and slide the needle through all the holes *above* the warp this time. The needle is now on the right-hand side. N.B. You do not actually weave – you rather make a sandwich of the warp each time; one way the thread is taken *under* the warp, the other way it is taken *over* the warp.

After your first experiments with pattern arrangements, you will probably want to work out your patterns before you begin. This is done on graph paper, one square representing one bead. It is most important that you experiment for yourself once you have learned the technique.

FURTHER READING

BARRINGTON HAYES, *Glass Through the Ages* Penguin

CROIX, I.A., *Creating with Beads* Little Craft Series, Oak Tree Press

EDWARDS, J., *Bead Embroidery* Batsford

ERIKSON, *The Universal Bead* W.W. Norton, New York

GILL, A., *Beadwork: The Technique of Stringing, Threading and Weaving* Batsford

MURPHY, M., *Beadwork from North American Indian Designs* Batsford

SEYD, M., *Introducing Beads* Batsford

Bois Durci

Bois Durci was a mixture made from sawdust mixed with albumen (white of egg), or gelatine (gelatin) or size, which was put into a steel mould and pressed in a hydraulic press. After being heated by either steam or direct or radiated heat, the mould was rapidly cooled with water. It was generally coloured black.

Invented by M. Charles Lepage of Paris, it was patented in England and France in 1855, and although it quickly became popular in England and on the Continent, by 1887 it was virtually dead.

It was very tough, and could take the finest of details when moulded, and in addition it was non-inflammable. Although the inventor saw his invention as being most suitable for knife handles, pipes, jewellery, furniture, etc., it was most widely used for portraits in low relief on small plaques. The portraits were in profile, and as such were representative of the prevailing interest in silhouettes. The subjects of the profiles were either religious, or members of the European nobility and royal families.

Book Craft

The simplest books can be made without very special equipment by children aged from five to 13. Simple experimenting with folding paper, and sticking paper onto cardboard or stapling paper will be good practice before books are begun. (See the section on Paper for some useful exercises.) Covers are made of card, strawboard covered in paper or cloth (newsboard or binder's board). (Binder's board does not warp.) However, both sides of the strawboard must be glued with a covering, otherwise it will curl, and no amount of pressing will flatten it. If you have different qualities of paper on either side of the strawboard, you might have to have two layers of paper on one side to counteract the pull on the other.

SUITABLE WEIGHTS OF STRAWBOARDS

10 oz – for the small exercises. Easy to cut with scissors by young children.

16 oz – for most of the larger exercises. Can be cut by children of 9–11 with scissors. It is better cut with a knife and straight edge, or card cutter.

24 oz – for very large projects, portfolios, etc. Cut with card cutter/guillotine (paper cutter), or Stanley knife and steel straight edge.

FOLDING AND CUTTING

Paper is folded with a bone tool called a folder. It keeps the paper clean, makes sharp creases on the folds, and is also used for 'creasing' paper. This is when the bone folder is used on edge and is run down the line of the fold on the *inside*, along a rule.

Most cutting can be done with *scissors*: 4-in. round-ended scissors are safest for the youngest, but the 6-in. length with one blade pointed and the other rounded are better for accurate cutting. It is important to buy the best quality scissors possible. For really accurate work, a craft or *Stanley knife and a steel straight edge are essential*.

A *thick piece of strawboard* of the 32-oz weight is adequate to protect the table, and not too damaging for the knife. When trimming with a knife, cut with a pair of scissors to near the edge to be finally cut, leaving a narrow margin to be cut with the knife. It makes the cutting much easier.

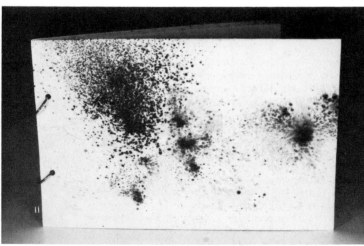

(Above) Small pieces of card were covered in illustrations cut from newspaper/magazine photographs, and glued onto matchboxes.

Two pieces of card (one for the back, one for the front) were covered on both sides. The loose pages and the covers were punched and held together with spring ring clips.

This is an alternative method for loose cut pages, the covers and pages being laced together.

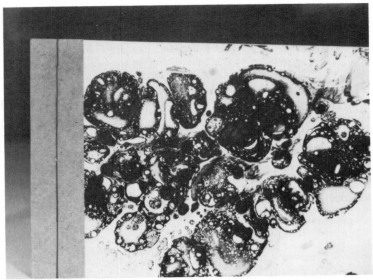

Another loose, cut page book, held together by sewing with strong linen thread at the edge.

For cutting simple books and pads when they are finished, *a trimming press* is invaluable. It compresses the sheets to be cut, thus ensuring a clean trimmed edge, and it holds the steel edge immovable. It is not an expensive piece of equipment.

A card cutter or guillotine is very useful to cut up quantities of paper. An intelligent, steady child of eight upwards can cut with a card cutter without risk *if he is trained how to use it*.
1 Never lower the blade unless the left hand is firmly holding the paper or card on the body of the card cutter.
2 Make sure that the hand is kept well clear of the blade.
3 Allow only *one* child to use the cutter at one time.

Do not attempt to cut more than one piece of card at a time, and no more than six sheets of paper. All the pressure should be put on holding down the paper/card and *not* on the blade.

Cutting the paper for the leaves
Let the size of the paper you have dictate the size of the book you are to make. To decide on the size first, and cut your paper to fit, might well result in a considerable waste of paper.

MAKING THE COVER
Materials
Wallpaper paste, such as *Polycell* is a cheap and effective paste to use. If fabric is being used to cover the outside of the book, then a dilute white glue should be used. *Brushes :* use a large brush – 1-in. flat varnish brushes are best. Wash them out after every session. *Rags :* small pieces of clean rags are essential during pasting, but use them for fingertips only, not for the paper or book. *Newspapers :* these

are needed to lay the materials on while pasting, and for rubbing down after covering the strawboard. They should be torn into quarter- or half-sized sheets, and put in a pile ready for use. Always throw away a piece of newspaper directly it has paste on it. It can be put into a bucket ready for making papier mâché, or have cardboard boxes around the room to collect all the waste that accumulates.

Cutting the paper to cover a piece of strawboard
Lay the sheet of strawboard down onto the piece of paper to cover it. Lay a ruler along the edge, and draw a line along the outer edge of the ruler. Do the same along each edge. Cut along the drawn edges. The corners now have to be 'mitred'. This is to make the corners tidy. The line of the mitre should be outside the corner of the board by the thickness of the card to be covered.

Using the paste/adhesive
Dip only the tip of the brush into the paste. When not in use lay the brush down on a piece of scrap paper at the side of the paste pot. Always put the brush down in the same place. Always brush from the paper onto the newspaper. Never from the newspaper to the paper ; if you do you are very likely to get paste under the edge of your paper. The top three-quarters done, move your fingers to the opposite edge and paste where your fingers were. Do not leave blobs of paste on the paper, or ridges. Make sure that all the paper is covered with paste. Work quickly. Paper, cloth, and card begin to swell and stretch as soon as they are pasted. Always rub down with your fingers covered with a piece of newspaper. Do not handle pasted paper more than you really have to. It is fragile when wet.

Lay the pile of cut newspaper on a table and on top lay the piece of paper to be pasted. Paste the paper: lift it up with one hand, quickly take off the piece of newspaper and lay the pasted piece down on top of the pile again.

Onto the pasted paper lay the piece of strawboard. Centre it carefully. Press it down onto the paper. Hold the strawboard down with the left hand, and with the other hand lift up the piece of newspaper, pull it up and onto the board.

Still pulling the newspaper tight against the strawboard lay it down on the strawboard and press the flap down on the board. Do the same around all the edges. The 'lining' paper, trimmed to the exact size, is pasted and laid on the board, thus covering the edges. This all has to be done very quickly.

The hinge is reinforced before the card is covered.

A hinged cover, which also uses découpage as a decorative feature.

MATERIALS AND EQUIPMENT FOR MAKING AND BINDING A BOOK

THE INSIDE	THE COVER	SUNDRIES
Typing paper	Cardboard (Newsboard)	Linen thread, 16 medium, 25 fine
Pastel paper	Strawboard	Needles (bookbinders')
Cartridge paper	Grey board (Binder's Board)	Long-arm stapler
Frieze paper	Manilla	Brass screw binders
Brush work paper	Cover paper	Brass eyelets
'Cambridge' paper	Libra film	Eyelet tool
'Oxford' paper	Polythene sheeting, .005 in.	Combined punch and eyelet
Brown paper	Gummed cloth binding	Pliers
Home-made paper	Muslin	Glue brush
Collection of scrap	Paper for covering the	Paste brush
papers, experimental	strawboard	Flat hog paste brush
papers, etc.	Paper for the 'end papers'	'Oxford' paste brush
	Cloth in variety	Polycell (wallpaper paste)
		PVA glue (Elmer's Glue-All)
		Metal non-slip rule
		Bookbinders' awl
		Bone folder
		Steel T-square
		Square awl
		Card cutter
		Bookbinders' press

JOINING TWO COVERS WITH CLOTH TO MAKE A HINGE

Between the two covers and the spine must be a small gap, so that the covers can bend freely.

On the inside of the spine, mull is used for additional strength.

The outside of the cover, ready for the outside covering to be glued on.

SEWING A SINGLE SECTION

A section is a number of leaves folded in half. They can be sewn with 2-stitch, 3-stitch, or 4-stitch sewing.

Marking out

The first and last marks should always be set at least ¾ in. from the top and the bottom of the fold. The space between them is divided equally according to the number of stitches. Use a strip of paper and fold to make the positions for the holes. There is no need to use a ruler.

Piercing the holes

It is far easier to sew the pages together if the holes are made first. Use an awl for this. Small paperclips holding the paper steady make this much easier.

Length of thread

The length will be twice the distance between the two outermost marks, plus 6 in. for sewing and tying the knot. Always start from the inside of the section and pass the needle to the outside.

2-stitch sewing

Out at 2, in at 1, down the fold and out at 3, in again at 2, and tie off over the stitch.

3-stitch sewing

Out at 2, in at 1, down the fold and out at 3, in at 4, out again at 3, in again at 2, and tie off over the stitch.

4-stitch sewing

Out at 3, in at 2, out at 1, in again at 2, down the fold and out again at 4, in at 5, out again at 4, in again at 3, and tie off over the stitch.

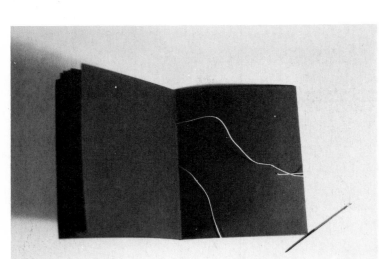

The folded pages, from the inside.

The folded pages from the outside; the final stitch is about to be made in the centre hole.

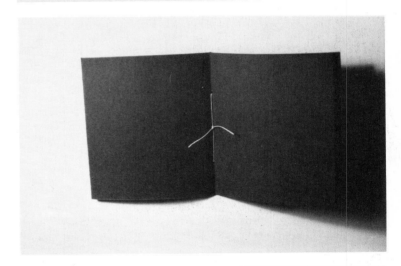

The cut ends of the thread are on either side of the long stitch; a knot is made over it, and the ends are cut to within 1 in. or so of the knot.

The finished tie — seen from the inside.

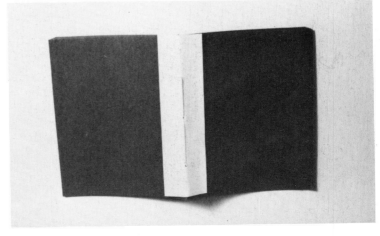

Bookbinding tape can be sewn into the booklet on the outside of the fold for added strength.

SIMPLE BOOKS

Offcut strips too short to be folded in half can be stapled together at one end and used as roughwork books. A scrap of manilla paper folded in half will make an adequate cover, and can be stapled on at the same time as the pieces of paper are folded together. These small covers are a perfect size for practising the different types of decoration.

To make a rather more sophisticated type of jotter, and one which can be re-used, holes are punched (using a 2-hole punch) in the top of a stack of paper all cut to the same size. They can be of different colours and qualities, but they must be trimmed to the same size. Holes are also punched in the top of the piece of stiff cardboard that is to be the backing for the jotter. (This is essential to make the whole thing rigid.) The loose sheets of paper are then attached to the cardboard with paper fasteners. The decorated cover is put on last of all, and glued into place on the cardboard at the back *below* the opened-out ends of the paper fasteners. Use neat (not dilute) PVA (white glue). When all the paper has been used up, the paper fasteners can be undone, and a new pad fastened on.

The cover of the pad which is to be re-filled several times, must be fairly substantial. The card for the cover should be the exact width of the cardboard backing, and the height of the cardboard plus a 2-in. overlap at the back plus the width of the pad of paper.

When the cover is dry, these two points are marked on it, and creases made with a bone folder, so that it will 'sit' neatly when it is glued on. The cover can be protected with a self-adhesive plastic transparent film (matt) to within 1 in. of the end at the back. A $\frac{1}{2}$-in. strip can be pasted with PVA glue and smoothed onto the cardboard backing *below* the fasteners. Alternatively, a strip of gummed cloth binding can be pasted with white glue and smoothed very strong.

Covers can be decorated by wetting the paper, letting all the surplus run off, and gently tapping the side of the container of powdered ink onto the wet surface. Only a minute amount is needed. Papers made in this way are a very useful addition to collage materials. Watching the powder as it spreads into the water is a delight in itself, rather like watching continually moving flames in a fire. Try drawing on the picture when it is dry, exaggerating those parts which are most suggestive to you of trees, waterfalls, landscapes, or whatever you see there. This was a technique much favoured by Leonardo da Vinci for his imaginary landscapes, but it is not so simple as it sounds.

A pocketed container for letters or postcard collection.

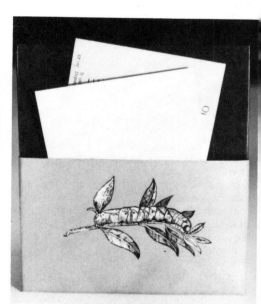

Pockets used to make a note paper and envelope pad.

DECORATED BY	COVERS	BOOKS
Covers	*Shaped*	*Cut sheets*
Potato prints	Apple	Stapled
Stick prints	Letter shapes, etc.	Stitched: Chinese/Japanese
Junk prints		Screwbound
Patterns drawn with:	*Made of*	Laced
felt-tip pens; ordinary	Manilla	Paper fasteners
pens; wax crayons	Coloured card	Hinged rings
Fold and dyed papers	Strawboard	Plastic slides
Marbling	Greyboard	
Wax rubbings	Cover paper	*Folded sheets*
Batik on paper		Sewn, with mull
Splatter prints	Librafilm	Sewn, without mull
Pulled string prints	Sheet polythene, .005 in.	Stapled
Monotypes		Zigzag
Lino prints	*Envelopes for*	
Combed paste	letters	*Books illustrated with*
Cut paper	postcards	Lino prints
Combed, cut crayons	scrap paper	Rubbings
Stencilling	Pleated envelopes	Cut-outs
Embedded leaves, ferns	Slip-on covers	Free drawing
Splatter	Portfolio	Wood engravings
Airbrush	Album: closed back, open	Etchings
	back	Prints (plasticine)
End papers	Board case, with pocketed	Monoprints
Marbling	lining	Wood cuts
Fold and dye	Board case, with large	Collage
Batik	pocketed lining	
Splatter prints		
Pulled string		
Potato prints		
Stick prints		

FURTHER READING

MUIR, D., *Binding and Repairing Books by Hand*
 Batsford

Bottle Cutting

Apart from its fashionable re-cycling aspect, it is an interesting aesthetic challenge: the point at which the bottle is divided so that each part remains aesthetically satisfying, and the problems of fitting two different shapes together so that when they are one new shape, the curves of each bear some relationship to the other.

Equipment
 a bottle cutter (sold in craft shops).

Materials
 empty bottles; wet and dry sandpaper; 2-part epoxy resin adhesive (if you want to construct an article from several parts).

METHOD
Follow the instructions that come with the glass bottle cutter. When the bottle has been scored, the tricky part is to get the glass to part cleanly. Fill the bottle with water that is off the boil. Leave it to stand in the bottle for a minute or so, until the glass is warmed through, then run the cold tap slowly and, holding the bottle firmly, and keeping the scored line underneath the cold water, rotate the bottle slowly. Hold the top of the bottle in one hand and the bottom in the other. This is because when it does break, it does so suddenly, so hold the bottle near the bottom of the sink, in case you jump and drop the bottle in your surprise.

Hog hair bristle brushes for oil painting:
long flat shape, and long filbert shape.

Ox-ear hair brushes
suitable for poster
paint, gouache, etc.
The oblique end is
useful for making
either thick or thin
strokes.

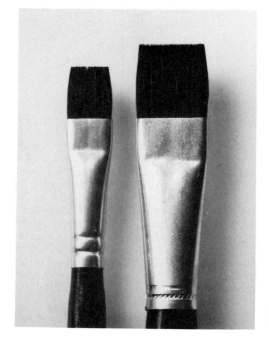

Brushes

Artists' brushes used in painting are usually made from the hair of various animals, such as squirrel, hog, and ox, and each hair-type is used for a different style of work.

Lettering brushes.

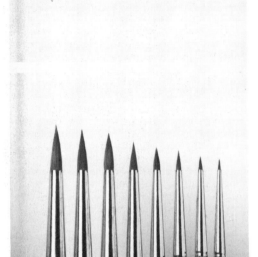

Round spotting brushes, used for very fine detail and miniature painting.

Flat watercolour brush (squirrel). (Photographs by courtesy of Rowney Ltd.)

Designer's brushes, made from sable.

Candle Making

Candlelight seems to have a universal fascination, regardless of the age of the onlooker. Making candles seems to be equally fascinating. The winter is the best time to do them, for it is a warm job, and there will be a heady smell of hot wax in the air, and if you perfume them, that too.

There are three main ways of making candles: *Dipping*, *Pouring*, and *Casting*. The most popular of these is the casting method.

Some could afford the luxury of a candle made from beeswax: it produced little smoke and the smell was of honey. They were made by the POURING process. The beeswax was melted in small quantities at a time, and poured onto a suspended wick. Any that did not stick to the wick was caught in a dish underneath the candle, and re-used. When the surface had hardened, more molten wax was poured over, and so on. This method produces a rather lumpy candle, and this was made smoother by rolling the still-soft candle between two pieces of metal or wood.

These spectacular-looking candles are very simple to make. They are ordinary commercial white candles, which have had spoonfuls of hot coloured wax poured all over them.

Candle made almost entirely from whipped wax. The colour to be seen running through the candle was coloured wax poured on last to fill up all the spaces left by the whipped wax. The result is a marbled quality which looks very attractive when lit.

DIPPING was the traditional one, before the invention of paraffin wax or cotton wicks. The candles were made of tallow, made from the suet of beef, pork, or mutton, and smelly smoky things they were too. The wick was a length of peeled rush; this was dipped into molten tallow, lifted out to cool, dipped again for a moment until another layer was built up, then taken out and cooled again. This process was repeated until the desired thickness was obtained, which was normally about one-third the thickness of our everyday domestic candle.

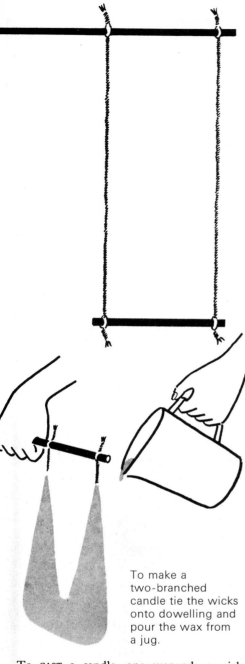

To make a two-branched candle tie the wicks onto dowelling and pour the wax from a jug.

To CAST a candle, one suspends a wick secured at each end in a container, and pours on the molten wax. Tallow could be treated in this way, but not beeswax because it sticks to the sides of the mould. It is possible to make a candle in a tube of cardboard, or a glass, but the simplest method for a beginner without any special equipment is to cast the candle in an empty plastic ice-cream cup, or polythene bottle.

Candles cast in a drinking-glass can look very amusing, especially when they are made to look like a glass of beer with a 'head' on it, but they do not work very efficiently as candles. After the candle has burned down a little way

below the level of the top of the glass, it begins to flicker, and the flicker gets wilder and wilder until it is like a chained spirit trying to shake itself free. This is caused by the rising currents of warm air, and there is nothing to be done about it. Beside which, pushing a wick down into the candle after it has been made and making sure that it is absolutely central is no job for a beginner.

The wick is a very important part of the functioning of a candle. It has to be right in relation to the diameter of the candle. And luckily, this is how it is sold. If the wick is too small for the candle, the flame will be small, and unable to melt the wax to the edge of the candle, so that it burns a hollow in the centre of the candle, and after a while it will go out through lack of oxygen.

If it is too thick, the flame will be too hot, and the molten wax will soon overflow the edges of the candle, and burn down very quickly. It will be seen, therefore, that it is not possible to choose an appropriate wick for a conical candle. It will start off by running down the sides because it is too big, and soon after halfway down the candle it will go out because by then it will be too small! Concentrate on a candle shape that burns efficiently, and indulge your creativity in the areas of colour and pattern.

The swirling technique.

These candles are exquisitely detailed: the patterns are like frost on a window pane on a wintry morning. They are two-coloured candles, and before the wax is really set, a needle is inserted down the side of the mould, and wiggled very slightly from side to side. The top colour (bottom when the candle is finished) runs down making these lovely patterns.

CAST CANDLES

Equipment

Thermometer A culinary one will do, but the temperature at which one does the various processes is vitally important, and not even experienced candle makers use guesswork. Wax at high temperatures is very dangerous, and can burst into flame.

Old saucepans and cans for melting the wax. This is best done in a tin can standing in a pan of boiling water. Make sure it never boils dry, and keep your eye on the temperature.

Moulds There are lots of special candle moulds available now, in rubber, metal, glass, etc., but empty small plastic moulds and yoghurt cartons are perfectly good for children to start with. The sort of plastic they are made of has excellent release qualities. Metal moulds can easily get scratched, and any marks on the inside will be visible on the candle, so take care. Rubber moulds are peeled off the candle like a banana skin off a banana. Rub the outside of the mould with talc so that it will slide over itself easily as it peels off.

Wash your moulds in hot soapy water. It is important to have the moulds quite clean when you use them. Store them in a large paper bag.

Scales for weighing the ingredients.

Measuring spoon for the dye powder.

Materials

Wax is available in large blocks from specialist suppliers and some craft shops. A good candle burns steadily and lasts a long time, and produces little smoke. A wax with a low melting point will burn down fairly quickly, one with a high melting point will last a long time, but is more likely to crack. The best all-purpose wax is one with a melting point of 145 °F (63 °C). Low melting point waxes are very useful when you want to make candles by the dipping process. Their adhesion is very good.

In their natural states, paraffin waxes can look very different: some are a translucent white, and although the colours look a little darker when they are not lit, once lit the light penetrates the whole candle; and some are quite opaque white. These take the dye very well and look very bright when cold. If you have no access to paraffin wax, ordinary household candles can be melted down and used in just the same way.

Stearin This comes in a powder-like state, and should be added to the paraffin wax in proportion from 5% to 30%. It will improve the brightness of the candle, strengthen the wax, and give a glossy finish; however, it is expensive.

Micro-crystalline wax This is added in the proportion of 2–3% to improve the burning qualities of the candle and increase its life.

Wick Buy the real thing from a craft shop. String, wool, or cotton will not do.

Mould release This is essential to coat the inside of the mould before the wax is poured in, otherwise the candle will not come out.

Dyes Special dyes are available for wax. They come in powder form or as a solid cake. Try both to see which you prefer.

Perfume Special perfume can be added to candle wax when it is molten, but although the candle smells gorgeous while you are making it, its smell will be rather fugitive unless you keep it in an enclosed bottle.

Wicking the candle

Putting the wick in after the candle has been made is essential in some processes, but it is more efficient as a practical candle for burning if the wick is fitted in as the candle is made.

The thickness of the wick has been covered (see previous page). Cut a length of wick which is the height of the candle plus 3 in. The extra length is for the knotting. Make a hole in the bottom of the mould with a hot needle. Do not make the hole too large or the wax will pour out at the bottom as you pour it in at the top. Thread the wick through this hole, and tie a knot on the *outside*. *Dip the knot in some hot wax.* This seals both the knot and the hole. It is important to seal the knot, because the mould is cooled in a bucket of water, or it can be, and if the wick is not sealed it will become wet.

To fasten the other end of the wick, lay a pencil across the top of the mould, and tie the wick to that. Move the wick around until it is central. This is how the wicking is always done, whatever method you use to fill the mould.

Stand the mould up, and pour the hot wax into it, to the top. Leave it to cool for an hour, by which time the wax will have shrunk and there will be a hollow in the top. Prick the crust on the top of the wax with a pencil because under the crust is an air pocket which has appeared during cooling. This has to be filled up with more hot wax. On a large candle, the topping-up process might have to be done as many as three times. When the candle is quite cold, the wick around the pencil can be cut off as close as possible to the wax.

Turn the mould the other way round *but do not cut the knot off*. This is the wick that is lit. Crack the wax off and undo the knot. The candle can now be slid out of its mould.

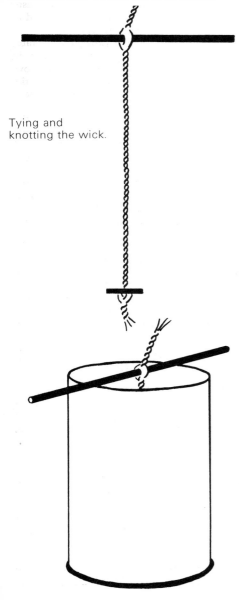

Tying and knotting the wick.

Striped candles

Wick the candle as described above, and coat with mould release if needed. Melt three lots of wax, and add colour to two. To the other one add stearin to make the white opaque (or make as many different colours as you like).

Micro-crystalline wax is useful to add to other wax when making striped candles. It is a 'stickier' wax, and prevents layer separation. It dyes well, and is very translucent.

Pour the first layer to a depth of about 2 in., and put the mould in water to cool it. The stage at which you pour the next layer on is a tricky one to gauge, for the following reason: if the wax of the first layer is too cool, then when the next layer is poured on it will not 'stick' to it, and when the candle is turned out it will be in two parts. If on the other hand it is not cool enough when the next layer is poured on, instead of forming a separate layer it will mix with the previous one and instead of a white stripe and a red stripe you will have one pink stripe. The wax must be warm, but the film on top must be firm when you prod it with your finger. Experience is the best teacher in this. Fill the whole candle up with different layers allowing each one to cool before going on to the next. Striped candles look especially good if you add mottling oil (see below) to the wax.

Zigzag striped candles

These are made by tilting the candle mould when you pour each layer. You can change the angle at which the mould is set with each layer. For the last layer, of course, the candle must be standing upright.

Mottled candles

To make these one must have some mottling oil. When this is added to molten wax, as it cools small crystals rather like snowflakes are formed. No mould release is needed for these candles. The candle must be allowed to cool slowly for crystals to form: do not try to speed the cooling by putting in a bowl of water. The dyes used for colouring also affect the mottling; certain colours only allow small crystals to form.

Oil is added in the proportion of 3 tblsps of oil to 1 lb of wax. This proportion can be varied; for more mottling add more oil. When the wax has reached a temperature of 160 °F (71 °C) add the oil and immediately pour into the mould. To slow the cooling down, put a paper bag over the mould.

These candles are especially attractive when layered and tilted.

Hurricane candles (shells)

These are not candles at all but candle shells. Small nightlights or 'votive candles' are lit and the shell is placed over them. The light glows through the wall of the shell or hurricane candle. These last until they are accidentally broken.

The mould *must* be wide, more than 4 in. Block up the wick hole, there is no wick in these

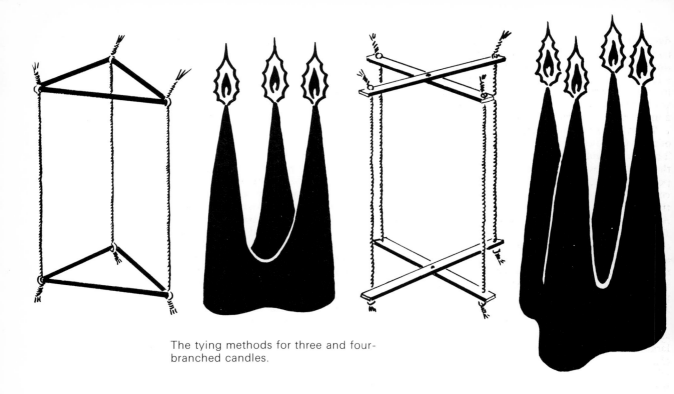

The tying methods for three and four-branched candles.

shells. Melt enough wax to fill up the moulds to the top. To make the shell stronger, add 1 tsp plastic additive per 1 lb wax and bring up the temperature of the wax to 190 °F (88 °C).

Fill the moulds to the top, and cool in a bucket of water. Watch the wax carefully and when the wax at the outside of the mould has hardened to about $\frac{1}{4}$ in. (you will see a change in colour as it cools and hardens), lift the mould out of the water and pour it back into the saucepan. Put the mould on one side now, for the shell remaining in the mould to harden.

Swirling technique

This produces very lovely candles but they are not easy to make. The technique is similar to that used for making hurricane candles. Melt a small amount of coloured wax in two containers, one colour in each container. Make the dye very strong. Coat the inside of the mould with mould release. Heat the wax to 160 °F (77 °C) and pour it into the mould. Turn the mould in your hand, letting the wax trickle in rivulets around the mould as you do so. Do the same with the other colour. Cool the mould in water.

Heat some wax to which you have added some stearin, to make the white very opaque, and pour a little into the mould. Swirl this around the mould until the whole of the inside is covered. Before the final filling up of the mould takes place, there must be none of the coloured wax showing at all. This is important, because if there is some showing when the hot wax is poured in to make the candle, the heat from it will melt all the carefully swirled pattern that was on the outside (inside of the mould).

Sand-cast candles

Damp some sand with water until when some sand is squeezed in your hand it will retain its shape when your hand is opened. Fill a poly-thene washing-up bowl with the sand and pack it down firmly. Press a shape into this sand with a small bowl, bottle or lump of wood.

A sand candle has a thick layer of sand around it when it is finished, which does not disinte-grate because the grains of sand are welded together with wax. Making this outside case is a little tricky, and not a technique for children.

Three points are important: the sand must be well packed down; the sand must be of the right consistency; the temperature of the wax when it is poured is crucial. *This technique is potentially dangerous and maximum precautions must be taken.* The wax is heated up to 300 °F (140 °C), a temperature far higher than for any other method. The wax used must have a melting point of 145 °F (63 °C) or above. Check with your supplier about the melting temperature of the wax, and do not attempt to make these candles unless you know precisely what sort of wax you are dealing with, and have a thermometer. Watch the thermometer in the wax like a hawk, and do not be frightened if the wax starts cracking and popping. That is the water being evaporated off. It may also smoke. When it reaches 300 °F (140 °C), pour it into the hollow in the sand. Pour it into a spoon, held near the bottom of the hollow, to spread the wax as it fills the mould and prevent it from making a hole in the base of the sand. Fill the hollow up to the top. There will be more noise as the wax goes into the sand because that is damp. The level of the wax in the sand drops a lot because it is seeping into the surrounding sand and forming the crust or case. While it is still malleable, poke a hole in the middle with a long thin knitting needle, and insert some wire-cored candle wick. Leave a piece about 2 in. sticking up above the top of the sand.

When the wax is cold, dig around the edge of the candle (not too near) and gently lift it up. There will be a band of sand above the level of the top of the wax. Into this gap you will now pour some more ordinary wax which is coloured. Dye colour turns muddy if put into the first very hot wax.

Aluminium foil used as a mould
Pack a polythene bowl with some sand. Hollow out a pit in the middle. Do not worry about the shape: exploit the irregular shapes one can make with this technique. Lay some foil in this hollow. Heat some wax to 195 °F (91 °C) and pour into the foil. Use one colour or several. Allow to set.

To fit a wick in, heat a metal knitting needle, and poke a hole down the centre. Make it larger than the wick, because it is filled up afterwards with liquid wax anyway. Push a wired wick down the hole, with a fine knitting needle. Top the hole up with hot wax. Peel off the foil when the candle has set completely.

OTHER METHODS OF CANDLE MAKING

Hand-formed candles
The feel of warm wax is the most delightful sensual sensation, and this can be indulged in when making hand-formed candles. It is best done with the wax that is left in a saucepan from another process and is useless because it has cooled too far.

Scrape it out, and squeezing it in both hands, play with it until you have a shape you like. If it gets too hard before you are satisfied with the shape, put it in a cool oven on a linen towel until it has warmed enough to be malleable again. Do not worry about the towel. The wax comes off quite easily, and any left will come out in a hot wash. Fit in the wick as in the aluminium foil method above.

Chunk candles
The chunks are made in the same way as the shapes for appliqué (see below). The only difference is that the wax is an inch or so deep. Use wax with a high melting point, 145 °F (63 °C). Heat it to 195 °F (91 °C), colour it, and pour into the tray. When it has cooled a little, mark it out into squares as if you were making fudge. Let it cool completely and cut through. Tip out the squares, and do the same again until you have piles of several different colours. Pile these squares into prepared moulds, and pour clear wax of a lower melting temperature onto the chunks. Because it is of a lower melting point, when it is poured over the chunks they will not melt and lose their shapes.

Branched candles by the pouring method
Equipment
a small saucepan (or double boiler) in which to melt the wax; a dish to catch the drips; a small jug; thermometer.
Materials
2 ft candle wick; 10 in. by $\frac{1}{4}$ in. dowelling rod; 3 lb candle wax; a level tsp dye.
Method
Cut the dowel rod and the wick as illustrated (spaced about 4 in. apart). Melt the wax and dye in the saucepan and set aside to cool. When it is at 160 °F (71 °C) pour off some into the jug, and the pouring process can start. Pour slowly and carefully over the dish. Wait until the wax has cooled a little before starting on the next layer. When the pouring is finished, cut the wicks at the top so that $\frac{1}{2}$ in. sticks out. Cut the bottom off flat. The lower dowel is completely embedded.

Making wax tapers
These are a variation of the dipping process. The wick is drawn through a trough of molten wax slowly so that it gets a good coating. The temperature should be 125 °F (52 °C) for best results. One needs to use a thin wick and a hard wax, melting point 140° to 150 °F (60° to 65 °C). Wicks can be used singly or twisted together in various ways.

Branched candles by the dipping method
Attach the wick, as illustrated, to a length of dowelling. Dip repeatedly in a pan of molten wax until they are as thick as you want them. The size of the candle will depend upon the size of the container for the molten wax; e.g. if you have a pan 12 in. deep, and 8 in. wide, it will need about 16 lb of candle wax to fill it, 40-in. candle wick, 8 in. of sewing thread, a 7-in. length of $\frac{1}{4}$-in. dowelling rod from which to suspend the wicks, and one dessertspoonful of candle dye.

DECORATING CANDLES

Candles decorated by fusing powder dye to the exterior
Make a candle with 5 tblsps of stearin added to the wax. This makes a particularly white candle, and will make the colours appear much brighter. It is easier if you begin with a candle that has flat sides rather than round. Lie the candle down flat, and on the top surface sprinkle some powdered dye: one colour, or two. Using a small gas (propane/butane) torch, with the flame at its smallest, run the flame lightly over the area where the dye is. The wax will melt, and the dye run into it. By moving the torch around one can make the dye go in the direction of your choice. Keep the torch moving around, and move it fairly quickly. One can either cover the whole candle in this way or save the colour for one particular place.

Wax appliqué
Shapes of a contrasting colour can be applied to a candle quite simply. Using a shallow tin tray, pour on dyed wax to a depth of $\frac{1}{8}$ in. If

you cover the tray with mould release first, the wax will come out that much easier.

Let the wax cool, and then with a knife cut out some freehand shapes: you can use pastry cutters (the smallest) or any improvised cutter. Pop out the shapes, and attach them to a candle with some melted wax on a small brush.

If you would like the shapes to be raised up from the surface, leave the shapes on waxed or greaseproof paper on a plate over a saucepan of hot water. This will soften the wax enough for the shapes to be modelled with the fingers before applying them to the candle.

Whipped wax

Pour the liquid wax into a bowl, and with an egg-beater or whisk, whip until it becomes frothy. It cools fairly quickly, so you have to move fast. If it does solidify, put it back in the pan, melt it down and whip again. Spread the wax all over a spherical candle, and you have a snowball: use it to top candles made in a glass: or make complete candles. Apply to the outside of a candle with an old knife.

Painting with wax onto a candle

Melt several small amounts of wax (microcrystalline) in some tin cans. Add a different colour dye to all but one; add plenty. Using a

1-in. household paint brush, dip in the undyed wax and paint onto the candle. As the wax on the candle cools, 'scumble' it with the brush, i.e. disturb the layer of wax by continuing to brush it as it cools. This gives the surface a texture onto which the coloured wax is now brushed. Do not put too many layers of coloured wax on, or the texture will build up too much and the surface become covered in a lot of lumps.

For this technique to be effective, it must be done on a fat candle. Its special quality is lost on a tall thin one. Try it on a hand-formed candle.

Glow-candles

These are white candles which have been dipped in coloured wax. Hold a made candle by the wick and dip the candle up to the wick in a pan of hot wax of any colour. Lift out, cool, and dip again. Cool and dip again. Set on one side to cool completely. When these candles are lit, the light will glow through the shell.

FURTHER READING

COLLINS, P., *Introducing Candlemaking* Batsford

Candlemaking Leisurecraft

STERLING, G., *The Tall Book of Candle Crafting* Oak Tree Press

CANDLES

ALTERING THE SURFACE WHEN FINISHED (COLD)	SERENDIPITOUS MOULDS	PURCHASED MOULDS
Hammering	(once only)	Rubber
Carving	Sand	Tin
	Crumpled tinfoil	Glass
Applied decoration	Vinyl embossed wallpaper	
Leaves, ferns	Cardboard	
Ribbon, beads, sequins	(limited life)	
Tinfoil flowers	Yoghurt cartons	
Cut and applied wax	Jelly (gelatin) containers	
	(cut to release)	
	Polythene bottles	
	(long life)	
	Plastic drainpipe	
	PVC corrugated sheeting	

Card

Making objects in card poses an advanced problem in design. Although the finished result might look simple, it is the simplicity that hides great skill. The problem set here is to construct an animal or house or other subject, and only by cutting and folding to make the designs 3-dimensional and stable, without the addition of other pieces.

In order to design in this way, some experience is needed in paper sculpture, and methods of fastening paper. Paper sculpture is usually not painted, relying purely on the forms created. However, models in card may be decorated, but the colouring must be handled very carefully. The more complicated the

original shapes in the design, the simpler should the decoration be.

Materials

Card If buying from a printer, ask for 5-sheet thickness. If buying from an art shop, choose some thicker than a postcard, but not too thick. If the card is too thin it will bend and cockle on being painted. If no card is available, then use the thickest cartridge possible. These are for the final model. The trials can be made in any stiffish paper. Use a good pair of scissors.

Paints Designers' gouache paints are excellent but one can decorate in other ways too: coloured sticky paper shapes, areas of coloured paper, coloured photographs from magazines, stencilling, airbrush, pen lines, brush lines, potato printing, stick printing, etc. If any large areas are to be pasted and stuck with paper, leave to dry overnight if possible, with a weight on, and do it before the model is made up.

Simple animals, like the tiger, could be tried first. Fold a piece of paper in half, and with some animal in mind (preferably have a book with good photographs of the animal in it) exaggerate some part of it and simplify the rest. Again, if the animal is to be decorated, make the shape strong but simple. When you are satisfied with the shape, trace it off or draw round the original onto the final stiff paper or card. Decorate it before it is folded, using any of the methods suggested above. Do use photographs to give yourself plenty of information to work from. Few people have perfect pitch, and even fewer have a perfect visual recall.

The basic fact to remember when designing animals like this, is that the fold line down the centre of the back must be straight. Concentrate on a bold initial shape, and bold decoration.

The tiger, folded and cut out.

FURTHER READING

ALTON, W., *Making Models from Paper and Card* Batsford

ASPDEN, G., *One Piece of Card* Batsford

GERLINGS, C. & IVES, S., *Noah's Ark in Paper and Card* Batsford

KÄLBERER, G., *Cardboard* Batsford

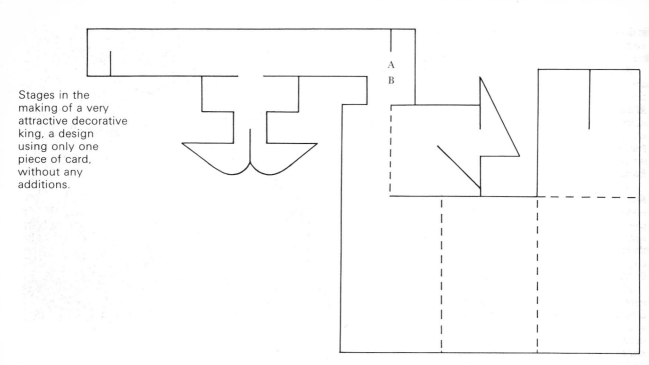

Stages in the making of a very attractive decorative king, a design using only one piece of card, without any additions.

A
B

Casting

CASTING – PLASTER

The casts in the following examples are made in plaster: superfine *dental plaster*, not the pink or brown rough plaster builders use. All art suppliers stock it, some large chemists do, and some denture repair shops will let you have some. It must be kept dry if you are storing it. If the plaster has 'gone off' it will never set. Plaster has a great affinity for water, and if it is kept in a damp place, the moisture in the air will be absorbed into the plaster, and once the process has started it is irreversible.

Do not make the plaster up in too large a quantity. It is set hard in 8 minutes, but it is too stiff to pour in 4 minutes, and you cannot pour a bucket of plaster into 20 small moulds in 4 minutes!

Mix the plaster in a 1-pint polythene bowl. Fill it three-quarters full with water. Into the water start sprinkling the plaster, and go on sprinkling until it appears at the top of the water. At this stage, it starts floating on the surface, so stop. Immerse your hand in the liquid, and stir around, making sure there are no lumps. Then pour into the mould or moulds. If there is some left over, do not pour it down a sink. Leave it in the plastic bowl. In 10 minutes or so, it will have set hard, and can be squeezed out and used for shallow carving.

Whatever happens, do not put plaster down the sink. It blocks the drains and someone will have an almost impossible job clearing them. If doing this in schools, see that the children's clothes are well protected. It is enough for one child to be mixing the plaster, and getting her hands messy. A bucket of water should also be available for washing the wet plaster off your hands.

As the plaster is setting it gets quite warm. Do not become alarmed; it will cool again as soon as it has set. If it does not get warm, the plaster has already 'gone off', and it never will set. If the cast is large, say the size of a polythene washing-up bowl, leave it a day to really dry out, but if it is a small one, up to 1 ft square, it can be released in 10 minutes.

If only a small cast is being made, another method of mixing the plaster can be used. Fill a small yoghurt pot with dry plaster, and lower it into a bucket of water. When the bubbles stop rising from it, it has absorbed all the water it can. Lift it out of the water, and stir it with a stick. This makes a thinner mixture than the traditional method, but it works well, and takes fine detail.

When taking casts in the garden, or of small imprints in plasticine, place a 'wall' around the mould to contain the plaster while it is setting. A very simple method is to cut up a ring wall can be used over and over again. rings. Press this into the plasticine around the imprint, or into the ground around the imprint in the garden, and into this pour the plaster. After 10 minutes, the polythene ring can be taken off, and the plaster cast pushed out. The polythene can be used over and over again.

Casting from a mould made in damp sand

It will be found practical to contain the sand in something. A polythene washing-up bowl is ideal, either a square or a circular one. Ordinary builders' sand is poured into this, until it is one-third full, or less. Water is poured on until the sand is damp enough to keep its shape when it has been squeezed.

Flatten the surface with a block of wood, or a brick, or even your hand. Into this smooth surface, press any piece of 'junk': toy bricks, pieces of wood, polythene bottle tops, fingers, knuckles, pencils, etc. It is a good idea to see how many different marks one object can make, depending on which part is pressed in, or how far it is pressed in, or at what angle. When the possibilities are exhausted, pour in the wet plaster of Paris. This size will take a little over half a bucketful of water which makes nearly three-quarters of a bucketful of plaster. Leave for a day to really dry off, then lift out the cast and dust off the sand.

Making a mould in plasticine

Plasticine can be pressed onto many objects to make a record of their surface. It does not leave

Casting in clay. The slab of clay which has the impressions made in it has a 'wall' of clay fastened all round to contain the plaster of Paris while it sets. Note the consistency of the plaster as it is poured in.

When the plaster has set, the clay wall can then be peeled off. Hold the plaster in your hand, and peel off the lower piece of clay. The pattern will be on the underside of the plaster and in reverse.

a mark on a surface it has been pressed on, and takes very fine detail. The undersides of leaves can be pressed into plasticine, as well as feathers, buttons, lace, medals, coal-hole gratings, shells, shallow carvings, etc.

A 'wall' is placed around the plasticine and

Plaster cast in a
polythene bag.

VINAMOLD

This is a useful material for taking casts because it is flexible (hot-melt vinyl chloride) and can be peeled off the finished cast. Plaster or resin can be used to make a cast. The Vinamold has to be melted and poured while liquid over the object you wish to take a cast of, so there must be some retaining wall around it. This could be corrugated cardboard, allowing enough to go twice round the object to be cast. Leave a gap between the object and the retaining wall which must come 3 in. or so above its top. Seal the base of the retaining wall around the outside with plasticine.

Equipment

scientific thermometer (reading to 140 °C); saucepan; asbestos mat; thick gloves; large spoon; pair of scissors.

Feathers gently pressed into the surface of clay and the impressions filled with plaster. Note the extremely fine detail one can obtain with this method of casting.

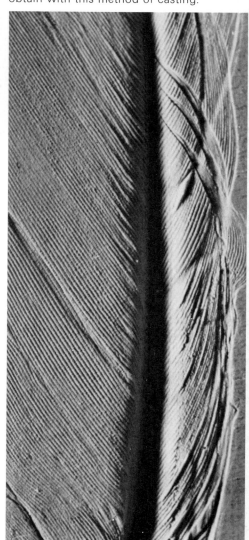

plaster poured in, and in 10 minutes, the plaster replica will be complete.

Lino blocks, when they are of no further use, can be brushed with oil, or vaseline, and have plaster of Paris poured into them, after a 'wall' has been fitted around the lino block. The plaster will be set in 10 to 15 minutes.

Clay

Clay can be used in exactly the same way as plasticine is used. The disadvantage of clay is that it dries out and becomes unusable until it is wetted down again. The surface has to be prepared by brushing with liquid soap, detergent or vaseline before the plaster can be poured onto it to ensure an easy release. It also leaves marks on the surfaces of carvings or whatever it is used on.

Plaster stamps

These can be used for impressing into clay when making pottery. Patterns can be pressed into a piece of rolled-out plasticine. A wall 3 or 4 in. high this time is fitted around it, again cut from polythene bottles. The plaster is poured into this, and released in 10 minutes. These stamps can be used for decorating slab, coiled, or thrown pots, or tiles.

Larger stamps can be made using a tin can for the walls. If you have a wall can opener, the tops and bottoms can be cut out of a can as with this type of can opener the edges are not sharp.

Materials

Vinamold; corrugated cardboard; dental plaster (to make the cast); plasticine; wire to make a loop for hanging, if the object cast is to be a plaque (an opened-up paper clip will do).

Method

Cut up the Vinamold into small chunks and put a handful into the saucepan over a *moderate heat*. Begin stirring as soon as it melts and continue adding a handful at a time until it is all liquid. This is quite a slow process, and it can take up to an hour to melt 2 lb. When the temperature reaches 280 °F (140 °C) take it off the heat, and when it has cooled to 240 °F (120 °C) pour it over the object from which the mould is being made. Pour in a continuous stream beginning at the outside edge, allowing the liquid to fill the middle as it flows. Continue until there is a thickness of 2 in. or so above the top of the object from which the mould is being made. Leave to harden overnight.

Do not let children do this unsupervised: the temperature to which the Vinamold has to be heated is considerably higher than boiling water, and the smell is rather unpleasant. If you can do it out of doors, so much the better.

Remove the retaining wall, and take out the object from which the mould has been taken. Turn over the mould so that the hollow into which the resin or plaster is to be poured is on top. The flexible mould has to be supported in some way while the plaster is poured in. Support it by holding it in a bowl and filling the space between the Vinamold and the bowl with sand, then pour in the plaster. When cold and hard, remove the Vinamold mould from the sand and carefully peel it off the plaster cast. If the cast was made in resin, one does not have to be so careful. Try not to break the Vinamold, because one can take several casts from one mould.

CASTING RESIN

(For full details on Resin techniques, see that section.)

Polyester resin (available in most craft shops) is stored in two parts, which are mixed in specific proportions immediately before pouring into the mould. Although they are supposed to have a life of six months, it is best to buy it when you need it. Some suitable moulds are pottery, polyurethane, glass, metal, silicone rubber, and plaster of Paris.

The liquid goes 'off' very quickly once the catalyst has been added. One has to have everything ready and at hand once the resin is prepared. One can tell how far the setting process has gone by the state of the liquid. It changes from liquid to jelly, then to a soft rubbery state, and then to hard and very hard.

Most manufacturers give instructions about how much catalyst to add to 1 lb of resin. They also supply efficient polythene bottles to use as droppers. The amount of catalyst varies with the room atmosphere, temperature, and with how fast you want the resin to set (go off). If you want to make up some resin in small quantities the following table will be useful.

1 ml = 1 cc
5 cc/ml = 1 large teaspoon
10 cc/ml = 1 large dessertspoon
20 cc/ml = 1 large tablespoon

RESIN	CATALYST
5 ml/cc	4 drops
10 ml/cc	6 drops
20 ml/cc	10 drops
30 ml/cc	12 drops
40 ml/cc	14 drops
50 ml/cc	16 drops
60 ml/cc	18 drops
70 ml/cc	20 drops
80 ml/cc	22 drops
90 ml/cc	24 drops
100 ml/cc	26 drops

Setting depends on the following three things:

Air temperature This is assumed to be 68 °F (20 °C). If colder than that it takes longer to set, if warmer it sets more quickly. If it is over 70 °F (20 °C), use less catalyst.

Thickness of the casting The above table is for casts of $\frac{1}{2}$ in. thick. If the casting is thicker, reduce the amount of catalyst; if thinner, increase the amount of catalyst.

If too much catalyst is used, the casting is likely to crack when it is set hard. If too little is used, it does not completely set, just stays tacky.

Accelerator Check that your resin is pre-accelerated. It is always best to buy it that way,

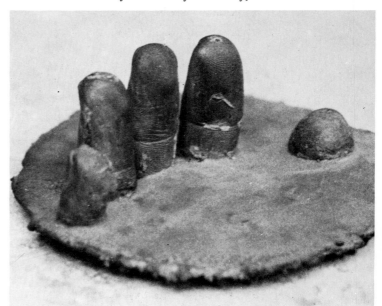

To make a high-relief cast, the clay must be deeper than the depth to which the objects (fingers) are pushed in. A wall must still be made around the mould after taking the object out.

otherwise one has to add the accelerator oneself. *Never mix accelerator and catalyst together*. First add one to the resin, and when thoroughly mixed, add the other. See manufacturers' instructions for quantities to add.

Making sure the cast comes out of the mould easily

One does this by polishing the inside of the mould with a wax. 'Release agents' are the name given to substances which ensure an easy release from the mould. Rub the inside of the mould with wax, and polish to a high shine. Repeat once. (Do not use a silicone wax for this.) PVA water-soluble release is then sponged thinly all over the surface. If you are casting onto wax, none of this is needed, for wax is a release agent itself. Resin will not stick to cellophane, acetate or perspex.

Making the cast rigid

If you are setting a block of resin, nothing will need to be added to strengthen it. On the other hand, if you are taking a thin casting (mats, trays, panels, etc.) with one surface exposed while casting, the resin needs to be reinforced with *glass-fibre mat*. This is available in many weights and widths, and can be cut with a pair of scissors in its raw state. The thickest mat is used for cars and boats; the thinnest, called tissue, and as fragile as tissue paper, is for the finest castings, and where translucency is important. It is laid onto the wet resin, and pressed in with either a stiff brush or a ridged metal roller made for the purpose. Although it is white in its raw state, it becomes almost transparent once it is embedded in the resin.

Cleaner

Always remember to clean your tools very quickly after using them in the resin, otherwise they will be useless, for the resin will set on them. This does not apply to the polythene containers in which the resin has been mixed. The resin can be peeled off the inside of bowls or buckets while it is in the rubbery state quite easily, even when it has set. Acetone will dissolve resin, or you can buy resin solvent from the suppliers of the resin. Clean the brushes and rollers in the solvent, then wash in warm soapy water, rinse and dry. *Do not use these tools again until they are completely dry.* Clean your hands in a cleansing cream and wash well after working with resin and fibreglass. Pour the solvent in which the tools have been cleaned down a drain, not down the sink, because it gives off toxic fumes.

Keeping the mould cool while casting

Like plaster of Paris, resin generates a lot of heat while curing. If a large casting is being made, pour only $\frac{1}{4}$ in. at a time, otherwise the heat will crack the resin.

To reduce the heat, fill a polythene bowl with some cold water, and stand the mould in that. Make sure that the water does not spill over into the resin. One could also stand moulds in a bowl of wet sand.

To estimate the amount of resin needed for a given mould, fill the mould with water: carefully tip the water into a measuring jug. Now you know how much resin you will need. This has to be done well before you start, because the mould must be absolutely dry before any resin is poured in.

Filling the mould

Add the catalyst (hardener) to the resin and stir well. Avoid getting any bubbles: stir gently and continuously, do not stop and start. Resin hardens best when it is *not* in contact with the air. For this reason it is a good idea to cover the exposed area on the top of the mould with cellophane paper, while it is setting. When the resin has set, the cellophane can be taken off the cast (because cellophane does not stick to resin) and there will be no tacky surface.

Removing the cast from the mould

Put the mould in hot water for 10 minutes, completely submerging it now that it is set hard. Then soak it in cold water, upside down, and repeat until the casting drops out. When it is removed from the mould, leave it out in a warm room for a couple of days or more to continue hardening. Leave a week before polishing.

Polyester resin cast in plaster mould

A plaster of Paris mould is an efficient, cheap mould to make if a lot of casts are needed. Put the plaster mould in a tray of water, and soak it well. Into the wet mould pour the resin. Cover immediately with cellophane or cling-film. When the resin has set, lift it out of the mould and peel off the cellophane.

Resin can also be poured into wet (damp) clay. Cover with cellophane for a day or two to cure. It takes longer with this method than normally. Cover the whole thing with cling-film or cellophane, both clay and resin. The clay will still be damp when the time comes to peel it off the resin. This makes it easier to get out of the nooks and crannies in the mould. It is most easily done by putting the whole thing in a bucket of water, and taking off the clay under the water. The surface may still be tacky, and it is possible to use that to advantage by sprinkling glitter onto the surface.

Making a remeltable flexible mould material

For small castings use equal quantities of edible gelatine (gelatin); anti-freeze; water. For a stiffer material for larger castings use (by weight): 1 part water; 2 parts gelatine; 2 parts anti-freeze.

Put in the top of a double boiler, and stir until the gelatine is dissolved. Grease some coffee tin containers with vaseline and pour in the mixture. Cover each container with the plastic cover that comes with it for use when opened. When you need some 'jelly', cut out a piece from the container and melt it in a double boiler.

This 'jelly' is ideal for non-porous materials, such as glass, plastics, metal, stones, plasticine etc.

Casting with the home-made 'jelly'

Place the object to be used for a mould in the bottom of a squat 6-oz tin (the size is not critical), face uppermost. Warm the tin and the object in an oven. Heat the 'jelly' to 140 °F, and pour over the object until it is covered to a depth of 1 in. above the top. Allow to cool slowly. When cold remove from the tin, and take out the object. You are now ready to pour the polyester resin, and take a cast.

You will no doubt have spotted a snag. Polyester resin gets heated on setting, and the jelly' is melted with heat. So, it is important to keep the mould as cool as possible while the resin is curing (setting). To do this, place the mould in a flat-bottomed tray filled with water, and coat the inside of the mould with a thin layer of resin: when it is set give it another thin coat. You can then fill the rest of the mould up with resin. Cover the top with cellophane.

When the casting is hard, carefully peel off the 'jelly'. If you are careful the mould can be used again. It can also be remelted and the jelly' used again.

Moulds from sheet acetate

Make a small version in paper or card first. Cut it in acetate when you are satisfied with it and tape the edges on the outside with masking tape. Paint all the taped edges on the inside with polyester resin, to prevent leakages. This type of mould is easily distorted with the heat of the 'curing', so fill a cardboard box with polystyrene beads or vermiculite, and into this push the acetate mould, carefully. This supports the mould, and prevents distortion. Fill the mould with resin and cover with cellophane. When set, the sheet acetate comes away from the resin very easily.

Casting in a wax mould

The model can be made in wax, clay, or plasticine. When it is completed, the model is brushed with liquid detergent if it is made from wax, or a PVA water-soluble release agent if made in clay or plasticine.

Dip in hot wax until there is a thin coating on the model, then quickly plunge into cold water to set the wax. Dip again in the hot wax, cool again in the cold water. If the wax is too hot, it will melt the wax you have just put on. It has to be liquid and clear.

When the wax is built up to about ¼ in. cut in half with a piece of fine wire or nylon gut. The wax or clay/plasticine model is then removed. The two pieces are fitted together again and the outside sealed with some more hot wax. The shell can be held together with an elastic band (not too tight). Resin can then be poured into the shell, after the inside of the mould has been coated with PVA water-soluble release agent. The exposed resin is covered with cellophane or cling-film. When it is hard, the elastic band is removed and the two parts of the shell parted. If there is difficulty, the wax mould can be warmed in hot water for 15 minutes or so, after which it will come away easily.

If a clear casting is being made, interesting air spaces can be made in the resin by setting lumps of 'jelly' (see above) in the resin making sure that one end of the 'jelly' sticks out of the top of the mould. When the resin is set, the 'jelly' can be pulled out, leaving an irregular empty shape in the cast.

Casting resin between two sheets of glass

2 sheets of window glass (1 ft square); 1½ yd plastic-covered clothes line; 9 bulldog clips; polyester resin; resin colours; mould release; mirror glaze.

Sand the edges of the glass to smooth off the edges. Clean the glass very carefully, with detergent and warm water. Rinse and dry with a clean cloth. Wax both sides of the cloth with mirror glaze wax, and polish immediately. Repeat the waxing and polishing. Sandwich the clothes line around the edges of the glass along three sides. The glass is gripped firmly together by the bulldog clips, three per side. Masking tape is stuck along the two top edges of the glass to make the pouring between the sheets of glass easier. The space between the two sheets of glass is filled with resin. When it is set, the clips are taken off and the glass prised off.

The panel is left to 'cure' overnight. It is cured when a wooden stick cannot be pushed more than an eighth of an inch into the top of the resin. The resin on the top will be sticky, and will remain sticky for a long time. As soon as the glass is removed from the resin, the resin is polished with more mirror glaze wax. (For variations on the technique see the section on Resin.)

Cast intaglio plate

The base is a sheet of Perspex (Plexiglass), a self-releasing surface for resins. The areas are built up with hot micro-crystalline wax poured onto it. The wax can be engraved, and so can the perspex, with a dentist's or similar drill. A wall around the perspex to hold the resin is made with masking tape stuck all round the edge. The resin is then poured onto the sheet of perspex. The wax should be coated with silicone to ensure a good release. For a large plate, it will be necessary to pour three layers of resin onto the perspex, at 5-minute intervals. Leave overnight before peeling off.

Casting resin in wax

Pour some melted paraffin wax into a tin tray (melted-down candles will do just as well). When it is cold, incise the wax with a lino-cutting tool, or a thick needle. Plan the design as for cloisonné, i.e. so that all the lines connect with another line. Also, draw a line all around the edge of the tray. Onto the wax, pour clear catalyzed resin, making sure that it goes into the incised lines. Lay a mat of thin glass fibre in it and stipple well in. Cover with a sheet of waxed paper, or cellophane, and squeeze out all the air bubbles.

When it is hard, pull off the resin sheet. On

the front now is the raised design that was incised into the wax. Each enclosed area can now be filled with transparent colour. It is as well not to fill adjacent areas at the same time, because of leakage. As soon as an area has set, the next one to it can be filled.

Casting from a clay mould

Impress the clay with a design, cover the hollows with oil (mineral oil) and pour polyester resin into it. After the resin has cured, the resin cast and the clay can be parted with ease.

CASTING METAL

Cuttle-fish bone casting

One can cast in metal in a cuttle-fish bone, and although the bone is limited in size, it is cheap, and a fairly easy material to carve. They can be bought in pet shops or jewellers' suppliers, and can sometimes be picked up on the beach. Try to choose as fat a one as possible. This is because you can then cut it in half, carve the design on the inside and bind the two halves together with soft iron wire. Leading from the top of your carved design to the top of the bone, or what will be the top when it is upright, must be a funnel, with the widest part at the top. To prevent air bubbles getting trapped when the hot metal is poured into the carving, escape channels for air must be scratched, leading from various parts of the design (at the side) out to the edge of the bone. If air does get trapped, that part of the design will be missing

when it is taken out. Prepare the area where the casting is to be done by covering it with a sheet of asbestos.

The cuttle-fish bone has to be kept upright while the metal is being poured in and while it is cooling. This can be done by supporting it with some bricks. In a plumber's ladle melt some pewter (this can be done on a gas stove) and pour it in a steady stream into the funnel at the top of the bone. Take the mould apart when it is cool, and release the casting. Aluminium can be also used similarly but first has to be melted by a blow torch.

It is possible to use smaller bones, if each one is rubbed down flat on the side to be carved so that they make a tight fit when put together.

Casting in stone

American Indians use this technique to cast their beautiful silver buckles and bracelets. The design is carved out of a flat pumice stone and the molten silver is poured into the hollow. This mould is permanent and can be used almost indefinitely.

Lost wax process

This process is simple in concept, but until recently has been complicated to practise, although the Benin bronzes were made using this process, as are a great many Indian metal toys made by local craftsmen. The model to be ultimately cast in metal is first made in a special wax. This is suspended in a container and liquid is poured around it which solidifies 'the investment' and covers the wax model completely.

Above is the whole cuttle fish, below, on the left the cuttle-fish bone rubbed flat and on the right, metal still in the bone.

This antique doorstop was made by casting in tightly packed damp sand. (Most man-hole covers are cast in sand.)

A hole (sprue) is hollowed out in the top of the investment until it connects with the wax model. The container, investment, and wax model are then heated at a very high temperature and the wax model melts and because of the intense heat, burns away completely. Other objects which will burn away at high temperatures can also be used, e.g. leaves, pine cones, insects, matches, nut kernels, etc. These are called 'replicas' and are a purely mechanical process, the only aesthetic contribution involved is in the choice of the object itself. Any very fragile areas such as insect legs and leaf stems have to be supported by the application of a spot of wax to the underside where it will not show in the finished casting. Another method of giving some temporary rigidity is by using a strong hair spray.

Molten metal is then poured into the space left by the burned-away model and when it is cooled, the investment is broken away revealing the model that was in wax now in metal.

The advantage of this method is the ability to use a model of any shape without problems of undercutting and making the mould. If you can make it in wax, it can be cast by the lost wax process, providing that it is not too large. The process is mainly used in making jewellery, or very small sculptures. The disadvantage is that you can only make one casting from the model, because the cast is broken up to take the finished cast out. The freedom of design, however, makes it a very desirable method to use.

Until now, equipment for using this technique was strictly commercial, but now there is an excellent piece of equipment used in conjunction with an enamelling kiln, which can be used at home. The firm manufactures the enamelling kilns and the lost wax equipment, and supplies the modelling wax and investment. Full details are given with the piece of equipment, which uses a vacuum to draw down the molten metal into the investment, after the metal pieces have been melted by a propane or similar torch with a fine flame in the sprue at the top of the investment. There is a hole in the bottom of the investment container, to which the wax model is attached by a stem of wax. It is to this hole that the vacuum is attached. The wax stem and the stem connecting the top of the model to the sprue are also filled with molten metal so that when the investment is broken open there will be two 'legs' attached to the model. These are sawn off, and the marks filed and polished away. For the person who already has an enamelling kiln, or who feels restricted after a while with conventional jewellery techniques, this process offers a whole new world.

FURTHER READING

CHOATE, S., *Creative Casting* George Allen & Unwin

FARNWORTH, W., *Creative Work with Plaster* Batsford

NEWMAN, J.H. & NEWMAN, L.S., *Plastics for the Craftsman* George Allen & Unwin

YARWOOD, A., *Plastics, Craft and Design* Nelson

An Indian (modern) candle holder in brass using the lost wax process. The fine detail is made by rolling the wax into fine rolls, and the detail around the head shows the coiling very clearly.

CASTINGS MADE OF

METAL	RESIN	PLASTER
Cuttle-fish bones	Clay	Sand
Pumice stone	Plasticine	Clay
Investment	Incised wax	Plasticine
(lost wax process)	Sheet Perspex (Plexiglass)	Incised wax
	Plaster of Paris	Lino cut blocks
	Remeltable rubber	Remeltable rubber
	Silastomer silicone rubber	Silastomer silicone rubber
	Home-made 'jelly'	Home-made 'jelly'
	Pottery	Pottery
	Metal	Waxed cardboard
	Glass	Glass
	Acetate sheet	
	Wax	

CANDLE WAX	CLAY	
Sand	Plaster of Paris	
Cardboard	'Sand bags'	
Polythene		
Plastic		
Tinfoil		
Vinyl paper		
Metal		
Rubber		
Glass		

RESIN

CASTING	PANELS
From a clay mould	'Stained glass' plus coloured acetate plus glass lumps and epoxy
In a wax slab	
	Cloisonné with black braid
In wet clay	
	Directly onto glass plus gelatine plus glass strips plus acetate
Between two sheets of glass plus colour plus wax	
	Glass 'stuck' to glass
In silicone rubber	
	Onto silver foil
Embedding	
Natural objects	*Intaglio plates by*
Doyleys	Painting onto perspex with medium casting an intaglio plate by using wax to raise up and drilling to lower
Plastic beads	
Junk metal	
	Used as 'enamel'
Three-dimensional	
Polystyrene plus fibreglass	Clear coating onto papier mâché
Fibreglass on chicken wire	
Free-form fibreglass	
Carved polystyrene plus epoxy paint	
As bases for relief paintings	
Carved and stuck onto canvas	
Sheet polystyrene heat-moulded (in oven)	

TWO-STAGE MOULDS	ONE-STAGE MOULDS	ONE-STAGE CASTING
Plaster of Paris Remeltable rubber Silastomer silicone rubber Home-made 'jelly'	Ready-made: metal/rubber/ glass Acetate sheet Two sheets of glass/Perspex (Plexiglass)	Plasticine Clay Sand Lino cuts Cuttle-fish bone Stone Incised wax Sheet perspex

Cellophane

This material tantalizes with its colours, and its quality of transparency and shininess, but to use it is difficult. One can cut it up and use it in a warp in some experimental weaving, but it tends to lose some of its transparency. There is no glue that will stick it to itself or to anything else satisfactorily. It will stick to paper with Polycell (wallpaper paste), but it soon comes off. It can be stuck with some of the newer glues, but only in spots, and often one needs to overlay large areas, and these glues destroy something of the surface as well as being very expensive.

Fish and butterfly mobiles can be made, using Polycell as the paste, with wire between the two sheets to make it stiff. The wire is laid on in the shape the part is ultimately to be, and the whole piece of paper is glued. Lay it carefully on one side to really dry out, and do not handle it too much. When quite dry, cut around the wire, but leave a good ½-in. border between the wire and the edge. Make darker shapes in the wings or fins by placing several layers of other colours between the two outer layers. Any pieces stuck on the outside simply fall off, so do not attempt to add extra details to the surface of the shape.

A folded shape cut out of strong black paper to support the coloured cellophane.

Cellophane stuck together with Polycell and wire embedded between the layers. The rectangular shape is how it is left while the paste sets, the shape is cut round the wire finally leaving a margin of at least ½ in. outside the wire.

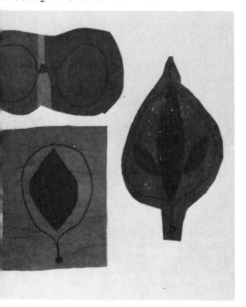

Butterfly with cellophane wings; the body was made around a wired armature.

Chenille

Chenille is a yarn constructed in the same way as a bottle brush, only in chenille the core is cotton rather than wire, and the 'bristles' of the brush are either wool, rayon, or silk.

In Britain it is associated with heavy fringed Victorian tablecloths in deepest maroon and darkest green, but in China they have turned this apparently unpromising material into a highly creative one. The core is of wire and the threads are of silk, and exquisitely coloured. Many different thicknesses of chenille are used, sometimes several in one object, e.g. birds, sometimes, as in butterflies, only one; and when fine details are needed, as in the beaks of birds or the faces of cats, these are carefully cut.

The bodies of birds and cats can be made from one thick length of chenille, while the wings of butterflies can be constructed of 10 or 11 parallel lengths. The bodies of butterflies can be of a thicker chenille, cut to shape.

Chenille is available from E.J. Arnold, Butterley St, Leeds (UK) and Hammett's, Boston, Mass. and Verona NJ (USA).

Contemporary examples of Chinese chenille work.

The butterfly wings are fastened together underneath with a short length of cotton-covered wire.

Collage

The name comes from the French word for glue, *colle*. The inventors of the technique could be said to be Picasso and Braque. Picasso's 'Still Life with Chair Caning' combined oil paint with glued-on oilcloth, but the first to use *papiers collés* was Braque.

The Dada movement, the cult of the anti-art, was an important factor in stimulating interest in this new medium, and it saw the emergence of two major artists in this medium, Max Ernst and Kirt Schwitters. The surrealists also used collage, artists such as Dali, Ernst, Miró, and Magritte. Many refinements of the technique were developed at this time so that they now cover: Assemblage, Fumage, Brûlage, Découpage, Affiches lacerés, Déchirage, Décollage, Froissage, Frottage, Mixed media, Fabric collage, Photograms, Photocollage, Photomontage, Papier collé, and Natural collage.

The ease of the technique prejudices those who believe that profundity has no place with the accidental, but few works of art are entirely without the accidental, and exactly how accidental or how controlled the medium is depends upon the artist and his expertise in that medium.

Materials

Schwitters, the really outstanding artist in this medium, collected everything that had been thrown away: bus tickets, feathers, string, newspapers, envelopes, stamps, shoelaces, soles, old nails, rags, bills, bags, etc. His name for the medium was 'Merz'.

Before anyone can begin a collage one has to have a collection of 'findings' and at the same time some sort of organization.

Equipment

Background: either of hardboard, plywood, chipboard, glass, linoleum, stretched canvas/hessian, cardboard (for the very light objects). Adhesives: see the list of adhesives and their properties, but Evostik UHU, Weldwood, Casco, Copydex, Marvin Medium will provide a selection suitable for anything other than heavy bits of metal. The new acrylic polymers are most useful – quick-drying, they can be diluted with water, can be used on any surface, and bits of paper fabric can be stuck directly onto wet colour. If the background is wood, you can nail anything which is heavy onto it.

All collage should have a protective coating, and the acrylic polymer medium and varnish are splendid. They strengthen the paper while at the same time making it waterproof, and one can choose either a gloss finish or a matt.

DÉCOUPAGE (cut paper collage)

Done with scissors (Chinese ones available from Colletts (UK) in a wide range of sizes are excellent), razor blade, or Stanley knife. Use either:

1 *one type* of paper and *several colours*
2 *many types* of paper and *one colour* range
3 with experience, 1 and 2 can be mixed
4 patterned papers
5 textured papers

When using bought tissue papers remember that the colours fade very quickly in strong light. It is better to buy white tissue and colour wash with artist's water colours which do not fade.

SGRAFFITO

Clip together four or five sheets of paper the same size but using a variety of either texture or colour. Cut through the different layers revealing the ones below through the cut shapes.

PHOTOCOLLAGE

Choose a theme, subject and select photographs and pictures from magazines, etc., which relate to it. Fantasy, satire, and wit are essential to a successful photocollage: one of the most difficult media to work in successfully.

PHOTOMONTAGE

Done with photographs in a dark-room. A new photograph is constructed out of images taken from them.

DÉCHIRAGE (torn paper collage)

Certain papers tear more easily than others. Japanese papers are perfect but very expensive. Acrylic vinyl polymer the ideal glue. Try using torn paper plus printed paper, tinfoils, luminous papers.

DÉCHIRAGE MOUILLÉ (torn paper collage worked into while soft and wet)

Try working with black paper as the background, and apply natural objects (grasses, etc.) and overlay them with white tissue in many layers, the tissue being pressed around the objects and folded while the glue is still wet.

FROISSAGE

Is an extension of the above technique. The paper is deliberately folded and crumpled and sticks, seeds, and grass are stuck on and overlaid with more transparent paper, the effect being much more textural than the previous one.

DÉCOLLAGE (a variation on the sgraffito technique)

Several layers pasted one over the other, and beginning at the top, they are successively torn, revealing the layer below. Peel off while still wet, and cut carefully. This is a very tricky method.

BRÛLAGE (burning)

The paper is dampened so as to be able to control the burning and scorching from the candle flame. Burri set the paper alight, and let it fall onto a prepared plaster ground, later fixing it with PVA medium: this is called *Combustioni.*

FUMAGE (smoke marks)

The smoke from a candle is deliberately used in certain areas and intensity.

AFFÎCHES LACERÉS

Offshoot of Déchirage mouillé, using scraps of torn paper – the backs of old weather-worn posters (Gwyther Irwin), with some of the paper so pasted and kneaded that it has become impasto.

FROTTAGE (rubbings)

A technique much used by Max Ernst, who cut up various rubbings, rearranged them, and sometimes added drawing to the frottage. (See section on Rubbings.)

FURTHER READING

BRIGADIER, A., *Collage; a Complete Guide for Artists* Pitman

CAPON, R., *Paper Collage* Batsford

FARNWORTH, W., *Approaches to Collage* Batsford

SIMMS, C. & G., *Introducing Seed Collage* Batsford

STRIBLING, M., *Art from Found Materials* Crown, NY

(Top) Collage of matchboxes, matches, corrugated cardboard, string, etc. The whole collage was painted white to concentrate the attention on texture, and light and shade.

Collage of sections of dowelling and square-section wood.

APPLY TO	MATERIALS USED

Paper
Card
Hardboard
Glass
Fabric
Wood, three-dimensional (carved)
      two-dimensional
Wood, natural
Metal
Expanded polystyrene
Papier mâché
Laminated paper on chicken wire
  armature
	Glass
	Sheet, broken, moulded, marbles, etc.
	
	Plastic
	Glued, melted, sheet, tube, pre-formed
	
	Fabric
	Net, lace, leather, fur, felt, towelling, old
	  sacks, satin, unravelled knitting, discarded
	  clothes, shoes
	
	Metal
	Sheet, shavings, wire, nails, pins, scrap,
	  mechanical bits
	
	Fabric can be
	Cut, torn, edges burned, pulled apart
	
	Paper can be
	Torn, cut, crumpled, folded, burnt, smoked,
	  rolled, laminated
	
	Types of paper
	All *printed ephemera* of all sorts, tickets,
	  matchbox covers, cigarette packs, food
	  labels, old used envelopes, etc., metal foil
	
	Wax
	Sheet, melted, dribbled, etc.
	
	Natural objects
	Bones, seeds, feathers, wool, wood (natural,
	  twigs), wood shavings, *metal ephemera*

Cork Pictures

Making pictures in cork was a favourite Victorian pastime. A. Ingram, a sailor from South Shields (1855–1935), made pictures in cork in the popular subjects of the time, castles, cathedrals, and ruins. Cork raspings, old bottle corks, and cork sheets were used, on a firm base of wood.

The cork is hollowed either by burning with a hot wire, or with a pointed bradawl. Powdered brick, lichens, and moss can also be added, and oil and varnish can be applied to the finished picture.

Moss and bark were also added to seascapes (rocks in the foreground would have moss stuck to them) and landscapes incorporating ruins would also sometimes have pieces of bark or cork stuck onto the walls. Sometimes dried moss would be used to 'frame' a woodland or other suitable picture.

This small, delightful picture is made of slivers of rough cork and smooth cut cork.

Corn Dollies

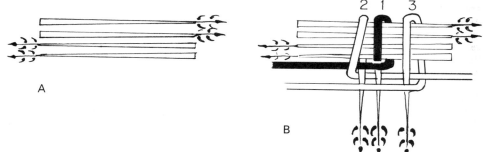

A

B

Arabic cage.

The plaiting of straw into devices with magical attributes, either to placate the goddess of the harvest, or to aid fertility, is known wherever grain has been harvested in olden times, and its origins are lost in antiquity. Made from the last sheaf of wheat standing in the field, and carried on the last cartload home, held by the prettiest girl in the village, the corn dolly became a Christian cross, and crowned the harvest offerings in the church.

Materials
Straws prepared as described in the section on Straw Work.

METHOD
The basic plaits will be found in the section on Plaiting. For really detailed descriptions, see *Decorative Straw Work and Corn Dollies* by Lettice Sandford.

ARABIC CAGE
Variations on this are found throughout the Arabic-speaking world. The handle is not essential and is added at the end. Begin with four straws with heads on. Arrange them parallel to each other (diagram A), with two heads at each end.

Begin at the centre (B). Fold a straw with a head on approximately in half. Hook it over the four horizontal pieces, the half with the head on being on top. Bring the other half down the back, and cross it over the front half, making it lie parallel to the original four. Other straws are added, one to the left, one to the right and so on until only the heads of the original four straws are showing. Cut the ends tidily so that the heads at the top overhang them.

BOUQUET DE MOISSON
The technique is based on the Arabic cage, but instead of single straws, use small bunches of straws. The centre is strengthened by a thick wire cross 16 in. by 19 in. Thread the wire through a length of straw so that the wire is hidden. Tie it into a cross so that the top arm is $5\frac{1}{4}$ in. Keep the centre diamond-shaped, 11 in. at its longest length, 8 in. the other way. The other 5 in. is to form the handle support. The decorative plaits are triangular four-plait with core, and are built up on wire, which is curved to make the particular shapes.

TOPSHAM CROSS (DEVON)
Only one plait is used – the traditional two-plait. The radiating centre is supported by two wire rings (lampshade rings), 8 in. and the other 4 in. The decoration at the top of the cross is made separately, and fastened to a length of wire which is pushed into the top bunch of wheat.

A seven-straw spiral, made without a core, by Anita Dunn.

FURTHER READING
ASHLEY, *The Ashley Book of Knots* Double-day
LAMBETH, M., *The Golden Dolly* John Baker
SANDFORD, L. AND DAVIS, P., *Corn Dollies and How to Make Them* Federation of Women's Institutes
SANDFORD, L., *Straw Work and Corn Dollies* Batsford

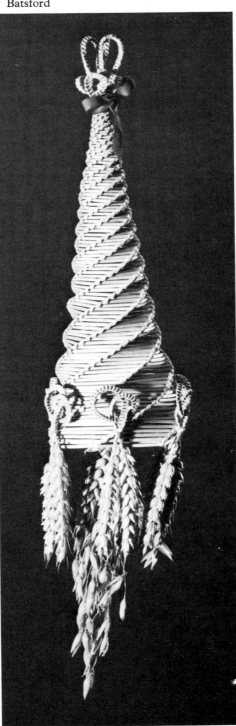

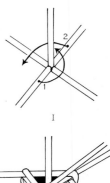

I

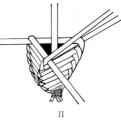

II

One or more straws can be used as a core. Five straws are tied together, and one is left upstanding, the other four are spread out equally around it. Work the straws round, noting that a four plait produces a triangular spiral.

61

Bouquet de Moisson.

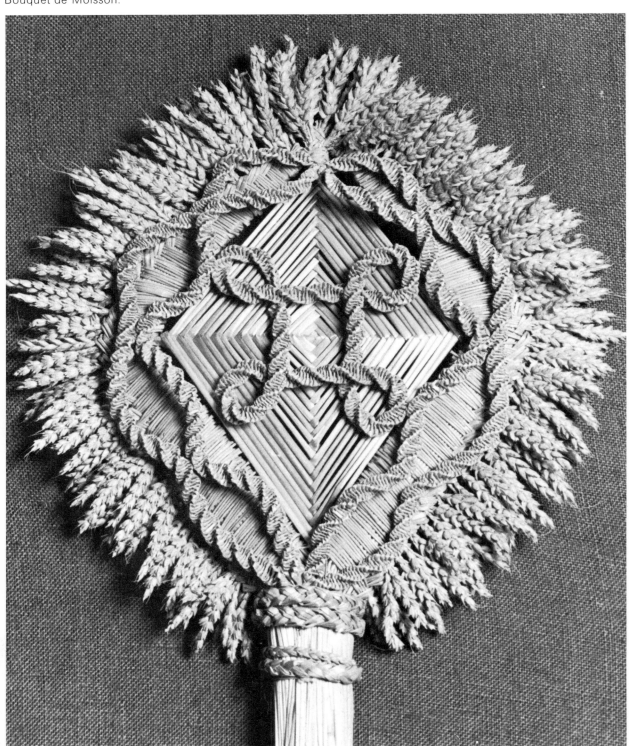

Topsham Cross, Devon.

Worked around a core, the diagrams show the sequence of making a five straw spiral (producing a four-sided spiral).

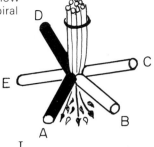

I

Corrugated Cardboard

The following photographs show how to use the qualities which are particular to corrugated cardboard. They also serve to illustrate how such a material can be explored in many ways, without the inhibitions of assumptions as to its potential.

Formalized explorations of the cardboard's folding and bending qualities.

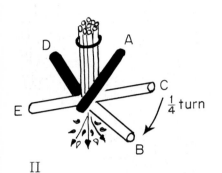

$\frac{1}{4}$ turn

II

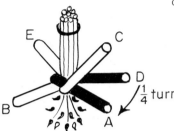

$\frac{1}{4}$ turn

III

V

IV

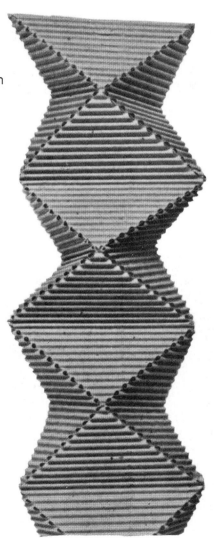

Joining in new straws, either real straw, or art straws, is inevitable. Cut the new straw at an angle, and insert into the hole of finished straw. Do not make two joins in one round if at all possible, as it weakens the structure.

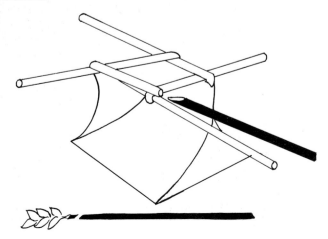

FURTHER READING
HARTUNG, R., *Creative Corrugated Paper Craft*
Batsford

Exploring the grip of the corrugations as well as the flexibility.

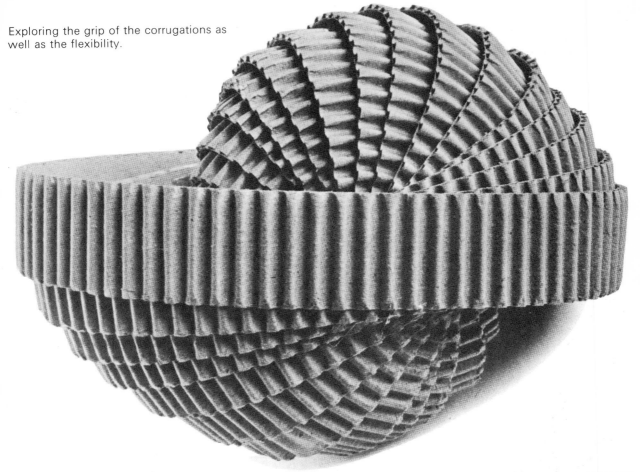

This utilizes the fact that the card is made up of two layers glued together. Parts of the corrugations are torn away leaving amorphous shapes made up of very regular, rigid lines; this creates a great deal of tension between waywardness and rigidity in the same shape.

The corrugations in this edge print (right) have a restless feeling. In sharp contrast, the rigid constant quality of the next edge print (far right) uses the corrugations as lines.

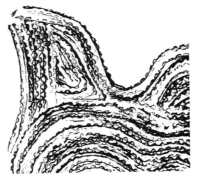

65

Decalcomania

One of the more expensive Victorian crazes, this is a method of transferring prints to glass, porcelain, china, wood, silver, plaster of Paris, ivory, alabaster, or paper. The surface to be decorated must be absolutely clean and grease-free. Glass is probably the easiest surface to start with, or the plain, flat centre of a white plate.

Using the transfer varnish 'Decal-it', which is available from most craft shops, tape the corners of the print, face up, to a piece of waxed paper. Apply six coats of Decal-it to the print, each coat being put on in a different direction. Allow each coat to dry before the next coat goes on (about 15 minutes). Wait 2 hours. Soak in warm sudsy water for 1 hour – longer if necessary. Place the print *face down* on a smooth hard surface. Rub down firmly, until the paper peels from the transfer. Design shows clearly when the paper has been removed. Be careful not to tear or stretch the transfer.

Allow the transfer to dry. If any paper remains, remove with a wet finger. To stick the transfer to the surface, apply one coat of Decal-it, position the transfer, and using a straight-sided drinking-glass, roll it from the centre to each side, removing all bubbles.

A simpler method of transferring pictures from magazines and newspapers onto glass, stone, wood, and fabric, is by using gloss polymer 'medium': if the surface is absorbent, seal it with two coats of gloss polymer 'medium'. Apply a third coat and while it is wet, lay the picture face-down onto it, and smooth flat, removing all air bubbles. Leave to dry overnight.

Soak the back of the picture with water, and when the paper is thoroughly soaked, rub it gently with your fingertips. The paper forms little balls as you rub, and you will see the picture embedded in the medium now attached to the surface you have been applying it to. Any milkiness on the picture disappears after you give it a final coat of gloss medium. Note that the picture will be reversed, so do not use lettering.

(In the United States, Decal-It is available from L.L. Weans Co Inc, Amityville, New York. Crackle-It, Age-It and Protect-It are also obtainable for producing various effects.)

Découpage

The name comes from the French word *couper*, to cut, and the technique involves the decoration of furniture and a wide range of small objects with coloured paper prints/engravings which are stuck onto the wood, and covered with many layers of varnish. At least, that was the traditional way, because initially the craft was developed to produce a cheap version of the very fashionable Chinese lacquer which was very expensive on its appearance in Europe in the eighteenth century. Its origin in lacquer ware is seen in the names by which it is known in Italy, *lacche povere* and *lacca contrafacta*, and in France *laque pauvre* (and sometimes *l'art scribanne*).

The traditional method after gluing down the paper cut-outs, was to put on the varnish coats. This was done both to protect the print but also to embed the print in varnish to make it look more like real lacquer. The final varnishing should leave the surface perfectly flat so that if one ran the fingers over the surface, one could not feel any signs of the cut-out. In order to achieve this, up to 20 coats of varnish were put on, each one sanded down before the next coat was applied.

Materials

Something to decorate A box, bed-head, tray, mirror frame, waste-bin, table top, bottle, chest of drawers, etc. It can be wood, metal, or glass.

Prints These can be collected from colour supplements, catalogues, illustrations from books, prints bought specially for the purpose, or wrapping papers. The thinner the paper the prints are on the better: they take less time to cover with varnish. If the prints are on thick card, soak them in warm water and peel off the backing paper, or use an emulsion called Decal-it to remove the print. Keep the prints organized into classes (in see-through press-together polythene bags), e.g. flowers, birds, trees, faces, boats, all separate. Do not cut them out until you are ready to use them.

Paint You will need it for two purposes, one for painting the object itself prior to sticking on the cut-outs, the other for colouring black-and-white prints. For painting the object, use *emulsion paint* (house paint). Buy two cans, one black, the other white. Black is a good background for many things, but if you want to use other paler colours, add colourizer (these

Wigstand transformed with découpage.

The cut-outs are glued on the inside of the bottle, which is used as a book-end.

are strong stains made for mixing with paints, and available where paint is sold) to get the shade you want. If you want your prints coloured, either use wax crayons, coloured inks, or felt-tip pens. If you use water colours these must be sealed with a dilute PVA (white) glue when they are dry.

Brushes For water colour, a fine water colour brush size 0 is needed. You will also need a $1\frac{1}{2}$-in. brush for the emulsion, and a 1-in. brush for the varnish/polyurethane.

Scissors The scissors need to be small, pointed, and very sharp. A curved pair can be a useful addition for cutting curves. For through-cutting of large areas of paper around the print an old large pair is best.

Adhesive Polycell is very useful; wait until it has thoroughly dried out before you varnish. Dilute PVA glue dries more quickly. (In the USA use Hyplar Gloss Medium & Varnish.)

A pair of tweezers Tweezers are useful for picking up small prints and placing them on the object, but not essential.

Varnish Use polyurethane varnish, which dries much more quickly than the traditional varnish. Do not use matt, which is rather cloudy. Also buy some white spirit (mineral spirits) for cleaning the brush.

METHOD

Paint the object to be decorated with two coats of emulsion paint. If you paint it some colour other than black, remember that it will change slightly when varnished, because the varnish yellows.

Cut out the print Choose a print that has a very simple outline for your first piece. Leave ferns and complicated trees and scrolls until you have a little expertise in cutting. Begin by cutting out the large areas of waste around the print. Change to the fine scissors for the details. Cut right into the corners, and do not worry if you cut the print, as it will not show when it is stuck down. Leave the most fragile parts till the last. There is less chance of their getting damaged that way. If the design is very complicated, the print can be cut up into manageable sections, and reassembled on the object. The joins, if you are careful, will not show. When cutting, feed the paper into the scissors with your left hand (if you are right-handed) keeping the paper as far back into the scissors as possible, using the tips only for snipping into corners.

Glue the back of the cut-outs, and lay them on the background. Press down so that there is no trapped air under the print, and wipe off any excess glue around the cut-out.

Coat the whole design with dilute PVA when it has dried, and if there are any brush marks left when that has dried, rub them away with some very fine wire wool. Dust carefully and apply the polyurethane varnish. Put on as many coats as you can, weighing up your patience against the finish you want. It will probably vary from two coats to ten!

FURTHER READING

NEWMAN, T., *Contemporary Découpage*
    George Allen & Unwin
WING, F.S., *The Complete Book of Découpage*
    Pitman

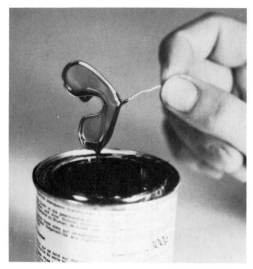

Letting the excess lacquer run back into the tin.

Shapes left to dry in an old potato half.

Dip-it Lacquer

This is a commercial kit which supplies a liquid plastic forming a very thin film when a piece of wire is bent into a continuous shape and dipped in the liquid. The excess is allowed to run off, and the very thin film is left filling the shape made by the wire. It has to be allowed to dry and become papery to the touch. This takes 24 hours before it can be safely handled. Cut an old potato in half, and stick the wet shape into it. Make sure that no two shapes touch while they are drying.

Experiment with various wire shapes, and try bending the wire into three-dimensional as well as two-dimensional shapes. When the shapes are dry, they can be wired into groups to make flowers, butterflies, dragonflies, etc. The quality of the sheen, and the remarkably thin layer of plastic that fills the shape, have a lot in common with the wings of dragonflies. When made to form the body and wings of a light model aeroplane frame, the film can keep the aeroplane gliding on the gentlest of air currents for a considerable time.

The three-dimensional shapes that can be made with this material cannot be made by any other. It needs experimenting with to find out what it is really capable of doing.

Take care to keep the lid very securely fastened on. It is as well to have two people working at the same time to ensure that the whole tin is used up, because once it is more than half empty, the air in the tin will begin the drying process (which is what is relied on to make the material become hard when the shapes are made), and it will be impossible to use.

Pieces arranged to make leaves and flowers.

Discharge Printing

This technique does not have any large-scale application. It uses the reverse of normal printing: instead of printing a pattern in a colour on white fabric, one bleaches a design onto a fabric that has already been dyed. The extent to which the dye can be discharged from the material depends upon the fastness of the colour.

Dyeing the fabric

Dye cotton fabric with a solution of potassium of permanganate (1 tsp to 2 pints hot water). Dip it in the dye, leave it for a moment, but make sure all the cloth is dyed. Take it out, rinse it in cold water, dry it, and iron it.

Lemon juice

If one prints this cloth with lemon juice, sharp white patterns will appear gradually after printing, which look very attractive against the dull yellow ochre of the dye.

Household bleach

A mixture of one part household bleach (sodium hypochlorite) to three parts water can be used as for lemon juice. It is suitable for block-printing only. It is a risky method to use because if the bleach is a little too strong it will rot the fibres of the cloth.

Formosul

Another bleaching agent is Formosul. It has a very unpleasant smell, so take care where you use it. The discharged pattern appears when the fabric is steamed. If you do not have a steamer and you still want to try it, you can use a steam iron, or press with a damp cloth. To make Formosul solution, mix: three parts Formosul powder, one part glycerine, four parts water, 12 parts gum tragacanth thickening.

Gum tragacanth

To make gum tragacanth thickening: soak 1 oz gum trag. chips in 1 pint water for 2 days; simmer for 8 hours in a steam saucepan, stirring occasionally, and adding water to compensate for evaporation; cool and strain.

Commercially dyed fabrics

Discharge printing can be practised on commercially dyed fabrics, except those which are guaranteed fast. Different fabrics will respond in varying degrees; on some the dye will fade completely, on others the colour will merely become paler.

FURTHER READING

PROUD, N., *Simple Textile Dyeing and Printing* Batsford

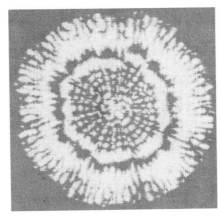

Linen cloth was first dyed in potassium permanganate, then a lino block print was made using lemon juice.

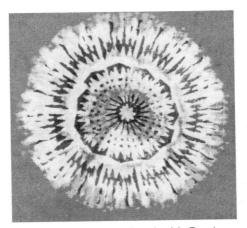

The print was over-printed with Procion dye, then the same lino-block was used, with a lot more lino cut away.

A print made from the block with a P.R. resist.

A block cut from Durafoam (Styrofoam).

Dolls

DRIED APPLE DOLLS
These are American curiosity dolls. The head is made from a peeled and carved apple, which wrinkles as it dries. Eyes are added to the old wrinkled face which is dressed in a bonnet.

DRESSED PAPER DOLLS
These were originally used as fashion plates to spread the latest fashion, but had little special advantage, and they soon became children's toys. An example at the Museum of Childhood in Edinburgh is of Little Fanny, a 3-in. high doll with story and clothes all sold in a pocket-sized wallet.

HOBBY HORSE
This hobby horse is made from two pieces of cloth, stuffed and sewn onto the top of a broom handle.

A strip of cloth is sewn very tightly round the broom handle, and it is to this that the head is sewn. PVA (white) glue applied to the broom handle first will prevent the strip of cloth sliding down the pole. The cloth could have the decoration screen printed, batiked, or embroidered onto it, or the dye could be painted on, or drawn on with fabricrayons.

RAG DOLLS

This pattern is for making a simple rag doll, without any gussets. The shaping is made by darts in the waist and the neck. Sew all round the body shape, leaving an opening at the bottom for putting in the stuffing.

Sew all round the legs and arms, leaving them open at B and C. Turn them inside out, so that the right side is outside, and stuff kapok or acrylic fibre through the openings. Make sure the stuffing is firm, and add a roll of cardboard in the neck to make it really firm. Embroider the features on the face, and sew the arms and legs firmly to the body.

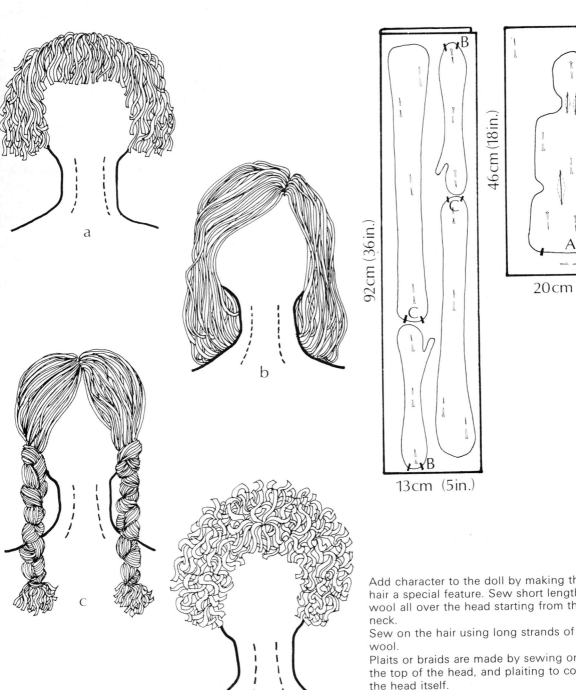

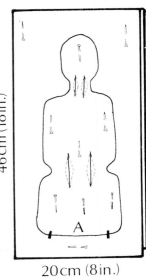

Add character to the doll by making the hair a special feature. Sew short lengths of wool all over the head starting from the neck.

Sew on the hair using long strands of wool.

Plaits or braids are made by sewing only at the top of the head, and plaiting to cover the head itself.

Loops and short unravelled knitting can be used for curls.

The finished rag doll, complete with a Regency style dress.

SIMPLE DOLLS

Simple dolls can be made by children from paper or clothes pegs and fabric.

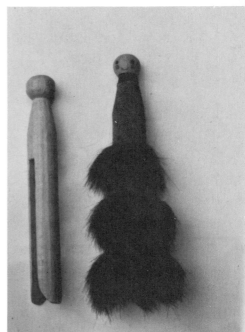

a) Wooden pegs (clothes pins) can have faces painted on the round end, and material glued to the body.
b) Peg dolls dressed in scraps of lace and fur.

Modern painted wooden dolls from India, made from turned shapes.

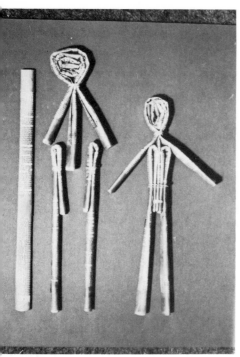

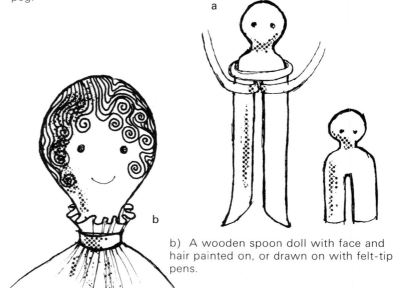

a) Wooden peg dolls, with pipe cleaners wrapped round for arms: 'children' are made by sawing off the lower half of the peg.

b) A wooden spoon doll with face and hair painted on, or drawn on with felt-tip pens.

ightly rolled newspaper, taped with rown sticky paper to stop it uncurling.)n the left is the original length, in the entre are the pieces partly constructed, nd on the right the finished paper doll.

he head is padded out with some otton wool and covered with stretchy rêpe paper, and the paper doll dressed vith dyed crêpe paper.

c) Paper figures, made to stand up by folding down the centre: the arms are slotted through slits. Details are drawn on with felt-tip pens.

d) The simplest of dolls is made by putting a small ball of cotton wool in the centre of a handkerchief and securing it with a rubber band. Unravelled wool could be used for hair either sewn or stuck on, and the features could be drawn on or sewn.

FURTHER READING
GREENHOWE, J., *Making Miniature Toys and Dolls* Batsford
IVES, S., *Dolls for Children to Make* Batsford

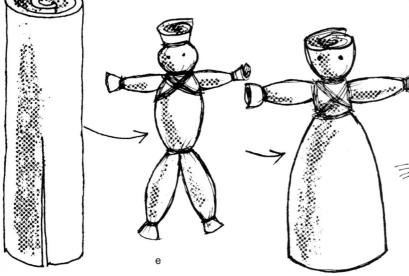

e

f

e) Dolls can be made from a roll of sheet polythene foam, secured with string or rubber bands.

f) Finger puppets can be made from the fingers cut from old gloves, with additional eyes, whiskers, hair, and hats sewn or glued on.

Drawing

This drawing by a child of 10 was drawn from observation, and shows a lively awareness of the possibilities of soft pencil, from tone in a mass, to varied weight of line.

The highlights were drawn first in candlewax. Colour washes were applied, and the whole thing superimposed with an ink drawing. The problem to be solved is one of creating an illusion of form, or a decorative, flat problem which is suggested in the ink drawing which is superimposed.

rying Flowers

me flowers dry quite *naturally* if they are
t standing in water in a warm room until all
e water has evaporated; for example, lark-
ur, golden rod, bells of Ireland, hydrangea,
d delphinium.

Some, such as delphinium, larkspur, heli-
risum, rhodanthe, sea lavender, and Chinese
tern, can be *air dried*. To do this, strip off all
ves and hang up in small bunches in a dry,
ol, airy place. The flowers should be quite
y when they are picked, and not fully opened.
is is especially true of helichrisum, which
st be picked while the centre is still tightly
sed, otherwise the petals will totally reflex in
days after picking, and will be useless. If
ey are picked while the whole flower is still in
d, one will have perfect three-quarters-
ened flowers in a few days after hanging.
e seed heads of all sorts of grasses can be
ed this way too.

Another method, and one which heightens
colour, is to preserve the flowers *in borax*,
t it does make them fragile. For this, you
l need a cardboard box. Put a layer ($\frac{1}{2}$ in.) of
rax on the bottom. On this layer place the
wer heads, stalks down. Very gently, sprinkle
re borax over the flowers, making sure that
borax gets between all the petals. Continue
til they are completely covered, replace the
, and put in a warm cupboard until they are
pery to the touch. This may be in 24 hours,
it may take as long as ten days.

Silica gel crystals weigh much less than
rax, and so are better for very delicate
wers. The method is the same, but the dry-
time is only two or three days. These
wers must be kept in a very dry atmosphere,
ferably under a glass dome. (Silica gel is
tainable from John Bell & Croydon, Wig-
re St, London, W1.)

arrangement of dried flowers and
ssed leaves in a deep box-frame. The
ckground is deep blue velvet.

Dyes—Commercial

'PRIMITIVE' DYES

(Use on cotton, linen, wool, rayon. Always add
the chemicals to the water.)

Potassium permanganate (permangan-ate of potash)

Dissolve $\frac{1}{2}$ tsp crystals in $\frac{1}{2}$ pint warm water.
Paint on the fabric and leave to dry. The colour
changes from pink-red to brown. If it is too
light in colour, do it again.

Iron buff

Dissolve 1 lb ferrous sulphate in 1 gallon of hot
water. Add $\frac{1}{2}$ lb lead acetate (poison) and leave
overnight. Strain off the green liquid, and throw
away the white sediment *immediately*. Immerse
the cloth in the green liquid for 1 hour. Drain,
and dry. Develop in 1 gallon of cold water and
3 oz caustic soda (lye). Steep for 2 minutes,
drain and dry. When it has dried, rinse it
thoroughly and wash in warm water.

Indigo

Fill a large enamel pan/bucket with 1 gallon
warm water. Add $\frac{1}{4}$ tsp of sodium hydrosul-
phite. In a small basin, put $\frac{1}{2}$ pint warm water.
Into this put 3 tsps caustic soda flake, 3 tblsps
indigo grains, and $1\frac{1}{2}$ tsps sodium hydrosul-
phite. Add half this solution to the water in the
enamel pan, and stir gently.

Place the pan on an electric/gas ring/stove;
slowly raise the temperature to 110 °F (45 °C)
but *never above*. In 10–15 minutes the liquid
will turn yellow. Turn the heat off and let the
liquid cool, and settle. Wet the cloth and
immerse in the dye. Leave in for 15 minutes,
then lift out. While the cloth is in the air, the
dye on it is oxidizing. Put the cloth back in the
dye, leave for a while, lift out, and so on.
Gradually the cloth changes colour, and goes a
deeper and deeper shade of blue. The process,
however, takes oxygen into the dye-bath, and
so shortens its 'life'. When the liquid turns a
dull grey, the other half of the solution can be
added to the dye-bath to 'revive' the dye
liquor. Finally rinse the cloth in soft water to
which a cup of vinegar has been added. Wash
as usual.

HOT-WATER DYES

Dylon multi-purpose dyes

Mix $\frac{1}{2}$ tsp dye powder to a paste with some cold
water. Add 1 pint of boiling water, then 4 pints
of hot water. Put in the cloth, and bring to
simmering point, gradually adding $1\frac{1}{2}$ tsps of
salt. Simmer 20 mins at 194 °F (90 °C). Use on
cotton, linen, rayon, nylon, and terylene.

ICI chlorazol direct dyes

Mix 1 tsp dye powder to paste with cold water.
Add 1 pint of boiling water. Add 4 pints of
water, and keep the dye liquid simmering for
20 minutes. 3 tsps salt should be added
gradually. Lift out and rinse; dry. Use on
cotton, linen, and viscose rayon.

Rit dyes
Available in the USA, Rit dyes are excellent for all washable fabrics.

COLD-WATER DYES

Dylon cold-water dyes
Dissolve 1 small tin of dye (or 2½ tsps) in 1 pint of warm water. Stir well. Dissolve 4 tblsps salt and 1 tblsp soda in 1 pint of hot water. Stir well and cool. When the cloth is ready for dyeing mix the two solutions together. The cloth should be wet before it is immersed in the dye. Dye for ½ to 1 hour. Stir from time to time while the material is in the dye. Rinse the material well in cold water, until the water runs clear. Cover with boiling water, add detergent, and leave for 5 minutes. Wash and dry.

Deka dyes (32 colours – for batik)
The colours are fixed when *finished* with a special fixative.

Procion 'M' dyes (good for batik)
The 'fixing' (making the colour 'fast' to light and washing) is achieved by merely hanging the dyed fabric in the air.

For 2 yd of cotton (medium weight), dissolve the dye powder in ½ pint of warm water. For a pale colour ½ tsp will be enough, for a very intense shade up to 5 tsps will be needed. In another bowl or bottle dissolve 5 heaped dessertsps of salt in 2 pints of water. In a third bowl, dissolve 2 heaped dessertsps of washing soda in just enough warm water to actually dissolve it. Add the salt solution to the dissolved dye in the large bowl. Wait until the liquid is cold.

Just before you actually put the cloth into the dye bath, add the soda solution. This must be done *just before* the cloth is put in, because once the soda has been added, a chemical reaction takes place, and even if no cloth has been put in, after 2 hours it will be quite useless as a dye, having no effect upon the cloth at all. So, *immediately the soda has been added, put in the cloth*. Submerge the cloth completely, and keep it submerged for 10–15 minutes. If any is exposed to the air, the 'fixing' process will begin, and the cloth will be unevenly dyed. Stir the cloth gently while it is under the dye, to get an even colour. After 15 minutes, take out the cloth and hang up to drip dry. Make sure that there is a large bowl underneath to catch all the drips.

If doing batik, when the cloth is dry, a second waxing and dyeing can be done. If one is very careful not to crack the wax too much it is possible to do three dyeings in different colours, but to begin with one will probably find that after two dyeings, wax is beginning to come off the cloth. The result of this will be that the subsequent dyes would 'creep' under the wax, and dye the cloth in those places that had been waxed out in order that dye should *not* get there. So that this does not happen one gets rid of all the wax and after the cloth has dried one

starts all over again.

To rid the cloth of wax rinse off in co[ld] water until the water runs clear: pour on bo[il]ing water plus ½ tsp Lissapol (or boil the clo[th] in the water plus Lissapol for a couple [of] minutes). Leave to get cold and take off t[he] sheet of wax. Rinse the cloth in warm soa[py] water, dry, and iron. If a third colour is r[e]quired, wax out all those areas that have be[en] already waxed out, plus those areas which a[re] to be blocked out, before the third colour [is] applied. After the final dyeing, leave for [?] hours to dry then wash thoroughly.

Fibrec dyes
Breen by Fibrec is available in the USA f[or] dyeing natural fibres and rayon.

SCREEN AND BLOCK PRINTING DYES

Printex
Stir well 1 lb of binder (binder CM 18%) a[nd] 1 heaped tsp of pigment. Then fix by ironi[ng.] Use on cotton, viscose rayon, silk, nyl[on,] terylene (*not* wool).

Tinolite (Geigy)
Stir well 1 lb of binder (binder CM 18%) a[nd] 1 heaped tsp of pigment. Fix by ironing. U[se] on cotton, viscose rayon, silk, nylon, teryle[ne] (*not* wool).

The pigment and binder will keep indef[in]itely separately. Once mixed they should not [be] kept more than two weeks. If some is left ov[er] and is too old to be used on fabric, it can still [be] used for paper screen prints. Both tinolite a[nd] printex dyes must have their screens wash[ed] out in *cold* water if there is a halt in the printi[ng] such as break time or lunch time. There is [a] preservative in the pigment which is toxic, [so] very young children should not use the dye. [It] is, however, quite safe to use the ready-mix[ed] dyes.

Helizarin
Mix 1 tblsp of pigment, 1 lb binder, and ¼ t[sp] of Condensol together very thoroughly wi[th] a spoon. Use for both screen printing a[nd] block printing. Keep the mixed dye in a scre[w] top jar. A skin forms very quickly on the dy[e,] once it has gone hard it is useless. Fix by iro[n]ing with a hot iron.

For printing on paper, add pigment [to] binder D. 1 tblsp pigment to ¾ pint binder. A[ll] the colours are intermixable, but the black [is] very strong, much stronger than the oth[er] colours, so take care. Binder R can be used [to] reduce (thin) the mixture.

Oil-bound screen inks
For matt opaque prints, use as supplied fr[om] the manufacturer (after thinning with wh[ite] spirit). For transparent prints, which utili[se] overprinting, add inks to transparent mediu[m,] 1 of ink to 2 of medium. Thin with white spir[it.]

Rowney fabric printing dyes
These are available from craft shops in sm[all] quantities ready mixed. The range of colours

articularly good, and they can be used on otton, linen, silk, dacron, orlon, acrylic, and ylon. The dyes can be used as they are, for creen printing, block printing, stencilling, or ainting. To fix the dye, either iron the printed bric on the reverse side, or place in an electric ven at 316 °F (140 °C) for 3 minutes. Arnold ake fabric dyes which are fixed with an iron, lled Polyprint. These are suitable for sten-lling, screen lino, and block printing.

NEXPENSIVE SCREEN PRINTING YE/INK (on paper only)

olycell and dye powder (Brusho)

tir well half a packet of Polycell and 3 pints of ater, avoiding lumps. The mixture is ready hen it is completely transparent. Fill a 1-pint r with paste. Dissolve $\frac{1}{4}$ tsp dye powder/rusho in hot water. Stir into the paste in the r. It is now ready for printing.

niline dyes

ecipe proportions and method as above. The yes have very bright colours, but they are not st to washing.

yes can be thickened with Paintex (Dylon), Manutex (from Dylon, Mayborn Product), d Polycell.

NSTANT DYES

here are very many dye recipes; some are omplicated in procedure, some are positively angerous: do not smoke or have naked flames hile using them; some give off noxious mes; some use acids/poisons in their in-redients. With others you cannot tell what olour you are printing until the fabric has been rocessed (fixed); some use bleach, which rots e fabric if you add a little too much; some quire the most unlikely equipment such as eam cupboards; some fade quickly and sily. (Even the heat of the iron in some cases ill cause the dye to disappear.) The following, owever, are more or less 'instant' methods of bric printing or applying dye to fabric per-anently, and are easily available in craft ops.

ri-chem (18 colours)

hese are tubes with ball-point tips. Draw rectly onto the fabric: it gives lines rather an areas.

abricrayons (8 colours)

hese crayons give areas or lines. Draw the esign onto paper: place drawing side down on e fabric and iron the paper. The heat of the on permanently fixes the design. Suitable for nthetics only, nylon, terylene, etc.

entel pastel dyes (16 colours)

se directly onto the fabric. Can be washed ut before it has been ironed (useful). Perman-tly fixed by ironing. Suitable for cotton.

olyprint (8 colours – intermixable)

lix binder (Polyprint Cut Clear) with Poly-rint dyes. Fix with ironing. All tools must be cleaned with soapy water. Suitable for screen printing, lino, and block printing.

Deka fabric colours (21 colours including gold and silver)

Paint on with a fine brush. Made fast by ironing.

Aerosol spray paint

This can be used for temporarily patterning fabric. Spray through lace, nets, or a paper doyley, or stencil using paper shapes, leaves, scissors, etc.

Thick wax crayons

These can be used to make a wax drawing on paper, rubbing very hard so that a thick layer is built up. Lay this drawing *wax side down* onto the fabric, and iron the paper. The melted wax is absorbed into the cloth with all the colour. (There is a very pleasant, soft, coloured drawing left on the paper, which one could try using as a base for fine line drawing.) This will not stand washing.

Fabraprint

This is another set of dyes made by E.J. Arnold, which is specially recommended for primary children. They are made in a range of brilliant colours (non-toxic) and can be used for sten-cilling, block prints, etc. To fix the dyes, a special fixer has to be painted over the dyed areas. The cloth is then put into a sealed poly-thene bag and left overnight. The fabric is washed to remove any excess fixer, and then dried. (E.J. Arnold dyes are available only to schools and colleges.)

Ways of identifying an unknown fabric (the fibre) by burning

Wool and silk Difficult to keep the flame alight; yarn where burnt forms black bead; gives off a smell of burnt feathers!

Cotton, linen, and viscose rayon Burns very easily; does not form a bead; smells of burnt paper.

Nylon and terylene Forms a bead; burning nylon smells of celery; Terylene has a pleasant aromatic smell.

Measurements and weights of dyes

It is advisable to buy a set of plastic measuring spoons. They are inexpensive, and give meas-urements of a tblsp, a tsp, $\frac{1}{2}$ tsp, and $\frac{1}{4}$ tsp. They are obtainable at most stores. The contents of the spoon should be levelled with a knife.

Dry measures $\frac{1}{4}$ tsp of dye = 1 g; 3 tsps = 1 tblsp.

Liquid measures 10 fluid oz = $\frac{1}{2}$ pint.

Metric conversion 1 oz = $28\frac{1}{2}$ g; 1 fl oz = $28\frac{1}{2}$ oz; 1 cc water weighs 1 g.

Temperature conversion 10 °C = 50 °F; 20 °C = 68 °F; 40 °C = 104 °F; 70 °C = 158 °F; 100 °C = 212 °F.

FABRIC PRINTING DYES

BATIK	BLOCK/SCREEN	TIE AND DYE	MISCELLANEOUS
Procion 'M'	Helizarin	*Hot*	Trichem
Dylon cold-water	Printex	Dylon multi-purpose	Fabricrayons
dye	Tinolite	ICI chlorazol	Pentel pastel dyes
Indigo	Polyprint	Vegetable dyes	Deka fabric
Deka dyes	Reeves fabric dye		colours
Potassium		*Cold*	Aerosol spray
permanganate		As for batik	paint
Batikit dyes (USA)			Wax drawing (iron)

Dyes — Vegetable

Materials dyed with vegetable dyes have a most distinctive colour range of secondary/tertiary colours, which come as a gentle delight to the eye after the onslaught of raucous colour we have had to accustom ourselves to. Vegetable dyes are obtained from the fruits, flowers, skins, barks, roots, and stalks of various plants and trees, and are used in conjunction with various mordants.

There is a considerable variation in the colours obtained by vegetable dyeing, and if it is proposed to carry out a specific project using these dyes, it is advisable to dye the whole amount at the same time. Even though the identical plant, picked at the same time of year, is used, and all the other ingredients are as similar as possible, it is still unlikely that the resulting dye colour will be exact because of variation in soils and general climatic conditions. However, the variations are part of the fascination of vegetable dyeing. Experiment, and keep a detailed log book so that you may repeat your experiments.

ORGANIZATION OF WORK AREA

A special room in which to dye is ideal, even if it is a tool shed. It should have a sink, and ideally hot and cold water. A large table, three or four shelves, a set of weights, a thermometer, a gallon measure, some large enamel saucepans, two or three pyrex or enamel basins, a chopping board, and a sharp knife will supply all your needs. For the actual dyeing, a gas ring or electric portable ring will be more suitable than the kitchen stove.

A stock of labels (ordinary and poison), notebook and pencil, a pair of scissors, and wooden or glass sticks for stirring the dye and lifting it out of the dyebath should always be near at hand. Glass rods are far better than wooden ones because the wooden ones become impregnated with dye, and if they are used for a light-coloured dye, they can stain it badly. To prevent having permanently stained hands it is essential to wear rubber gloves. On a shelf out of children's reach should be kept the mordants, some of which are poisonous, and they should be clearly labelled 'Poison'. Bulky dyestuffs should be kept in polythene bags or large paper bags and hung on hooks on the wall. On a lo[w] shelf can be kept the pots and pans; these mu[st] be kept scrupulously clean. The pan in whi[ch] indigo is used should never be used for anythi[ng] else. Another large galvanized iron pot (fro[m] a hardware shop) should also be kept separa[te] for washing-out the dyed yarns.

Labelling

This is another very important aspect. It [is] essential to label all jars of chemicals, a[nd] berries, bark roots, etc. Each skein of yarn mu[st] have a tag on it giving the information abou[t] the dyes pertaining to that skein, or a code. Th[is] code can then be written up in full in the lo[g] book.

E.g. on the skein the code 'AA Blackberrie[s] alum'; and in the log book the full informatio[n]

Code	AA
Dye material	Blackberries
Season of collection	Autumn
Mordant	Alum
Fibre	Wool
Date of dyeing	September 1973
Bath number	1

Water

Use rainwater if available, but it is a counsel [of] perfection. It is possible to add a water soften[er] as sold in food chainstores. Or use washi[ng] soda: 1 lb to 1 quart of boiling water. Dissolv[e] the soda in the boiling water. This mixtu[re] will keep almost indefinitely. Use at the rate [of] 2 tblsps to each gallon of dye water.

THE DYE MATERIALS

Not all natural dyes are from plants; cochine[al] comes from an insect, and there are sever[al] clays which give good dyes. Hot, dry summe[rs] are the good years for strong dye material[s]. Always have an illustrated botanist's handbo[ok] while out in the country so that strange plan[ts] may be identified and labelled. Also take [a] collection of old paper or polythene bags in[to] which to put all the gatherings.

Barks and roots Collect in late winter or sprin[g] when the sap is up. *Take only small amounts [of] bark from trees, for they can be killed if a com[plete ring is taken from around the girth of th[e] tree.* So, cut a strip *vertically.* Do not take a[ll] the roots of a plant either, unless it is a weed [or] being thrown out.

Berries Pick when completely ripe. Only th[e]

ark-coloured berries are of use, and not all of
hem.

Blossom Cut when the flower is just reaching
full bloom.

Stalks, stems and twigs These should have two
years' growth. The tips do not dye well. Some
grasses are good if picked in summer or
autumn.

Nuts (hulls and shells) Collect when the nut is
mature, but not when it has been left a winter
in the ground.

Imported dyestuffs

Kermes and cochineal are animal dyes, both
derived from the dried bodies of insects.
Cochineal gives various shades of red, depending on the mordant. Kermes also gives red but
is difficult to obtain.

From various trees are obtained yellow/
orange from Flavine (from the Quercitron
bark); yellows again from Fustic chips (from
Morus tinctoria); browns from Kutch (from
Acacia trees).

Persian berries, depending on the mordant
used, give yellows, from lemon to olive.
Madder (the roots of *Rubia tinctoria*) gives
brownish red, purplish red, or bright red
depending on the mordant.

THE MATERIAL TO BE DYED

Animal (wool) and vegetable (cotton, jute,
hemp) and silk are the most successful fibres to
use. Dye them either raw (e.g. fleece) or in the
yarn. It is possible to dye the fibres when
woven. Try to avoid dyeing any that has been
bleached. The most successful dyeing is done
with yarns in their natural, unbleached condition. Make sure that the skeins are well tied. If
they undo, the untangling can take a very long
time. Unless you want tie dyed rainbow wool,
do not tie too tightly. Where it is nipped with
the string or wool, the dye will not be able to
penetrate, and when it is undone it will still be
white at those points. It is attractive when that
is what is wanted.

THE DYEING PROCESS

Temperature lukewarm = 95–105 °F (35–
40 °C); hot = 145 °F (60 °C); simmering =
180–210 °F (85–95 °C); boiling is 212 °F
(100 °C).

The process of dyeing is undertaken in three
stages: scouring, mordanting, and dyeing.

Scouring

This is a technical term for washing in warm
soapy water until all the oils and grease
naturally occurring in these fibres are removed.
The yarns are immersed in an enamel pan in
warm soapy water to which soda (for softening)
has been added. The pan is then put on the
heat, and simmered for 20 minutes to 1 hour.
Place the lid on the pan so that the room does
not get too steamed up; this also helps to make
sure that the yarn stays below the level of the
water. If the yarn has already been bleached,
it will take only half the time in the scouring

pan. (The argument against bleached yarn is
that it has lost some of its 'life', and does not
have the same 'feel' as an unbleached yarn.)

Let the water in the scouring pan cool, and
then take the yarn out. Immerse in water of
approximately the same temperature and rinse
all the soap away. Rinsing in the same-
temperature water is especially necessary for
wool, for if there is too great a change in the
temperature of the water, there will be shrinkage. While scouring, *animal fibres* should be
kept *below boiling point, vegetable fibres* can be
boiled.

Mordant

In theory, a mordant is a chemical which will
combine with a dye substance to form a fast
(permanent) colour. Alas, some natural dyes
seem to fade whatever one does. One can
mordant either before the yarns are dyed,
while the yarns are dyeing, or before and after
the yarns are dyed. Each has its advantages: if
the yarns are mordanted first, the colours are
clearer, and there is more control over the
mordanting results; if one mordants and dyes
at the same time, one saves time; if one does it
before and after the dyeing, it can make the
colours faster, brighter, and stronger, and can
change the colour.

Mordanting is at least as important as dyeing.
If the yarn is not well mordanted, it cannot be
well dyed. There are some dyestuffs that do not
need any mordant at all: lichens are one of
these, and these are called substantive dyes (see
below). The easiest fibre to mordant is wool,
which has porous fibres. Silk is difficult insofar
as once silk is boiled it is spoiled, so one has to
be extremely careful at all times that the liquid
in which the silk is placed *never* boils. Cotton
and linen have very strong fibres and it is
difficult to get the mordant to penetrate.
Different mordants produce different colours
with the same dyestuffs. When mordanting
remember that too much tin makes the yarn
harsh and brittle; too much chrome impairs the
colour; too much iron (copperas) hardens
wool; too much alum makes it sticky.

Some common mordants are as follows:
Alum Either granular or powdered, it is inexpensive. Store in a dry place, and do not use
too much, or the yarn will be sticky. 1 lb of
alum will mordant 5 lb of yarn, and is most
effective if used before the yarn is dyed. For
1 lb of dry yarn, you need 3 gallons water
(warm) in a 5-gallon enamel pan, and 3 oz alum
(1 oz alum = 1½ tblsps). Dissolve the alum in
the water, and add wet fibres, and simmer for
1 hour. When cool, rinse in warm water and
dye. For vegetable fibres, add 4 oz instead of
the 3 oz for animal fibres and ¼ cup of soda.
Proceed as above.
Blue vitriol (copper sulphate) Comes in either
lump or crystal form, fairly inexpensive: 4 oz
will mordant 1–3 lb of yarn, depending upon
the depth of colour required. Works best on
wool and colours fibres green. Good results

79

from either mordanting process. For 1 lb of dry yarn, you need 3 gallons of warm water in a 5-gallon enamel pan, 2 oz blue vitriol (animal fibres) or 4 oz blue vitriol (vegetable fibres). Dissolve vitriol in water. Add the wet yarn, simmer wool for 1 hour, boil vegetable yarns for two hours. Cool, rinse, and dye.

Chrome (potassium dichromate, or bichromate of potash) Colours yarns in range from tan to orange. Expensive, but a little goes a long way. Very sensitive to light, the granular chrome should be kept in a tin, and the container in which the mordanting takes place must be kept covered. If light gets to the fibres, they will turn green, instead of the yellow that one is trying to get. Chrome is poison. Avoid inhaling the fumes.

Chrome gives best results before the yarn is dyed: good with all fibres, excellent with wool. For 1 lb dry yarn, you need 3 gallons warm water in a 5-gallon enamel pan, 1 tblsp chrome (animal fibre), 1 tblsp chrome for light colour, 2 tblsps chrome dark colour for vegetable fibres. Dissolve the chrome in the water, add wet yarn and simmer wool for 1 hour, boil vegetable yarns for 1–2 hours. Cool, rinse, and dye.

Copperas (ferrous sulphate) Inexpensive, 4 oz will mordant 2 to 4 lb of yarn. It darkens the fibres and produces greens, purples, and blacks, depending on the dye material. Too much can damage the fibres so take care. Poor for silk, very good on wool and vegetable fibres. Light shades are obtained when it is used before the dye bath, darker tones are obtained if used at the same time as the dyestuff. For 1 lb dry yarn, you need 3 gallons warm water in a 5-gallon enamel pan, 3 oz copperas (1 oz copperas = 2 tblsps) (animal fibre), and 4 oz copperas (vegetable fibre). Dissolve the copperas in the water. Then put in the wet yarn. For animal yarns, simmer for 30 minutes, then add 4 tblsps tartaric acid and ½ cup of Glaubers salts which has been dissolved in 1 pint of hot water. Simmer for another 30 minutes. Take out, rinse, and dye.

For the vegetable yarns, add the wet yarn to the liquid (as in the first part of this recipe) and boil for 1 hour. Add the identical tartaric acid and Glaubers salts dissolved as above, and boil again for another 30 minutes. Rinse and dye.

Tannic acid (tannin) Turns fibres tan to brown. Has a tendency to get darker with age. Occurs naturally in some barks, galls, leaves, and twigs especially the Sumach tree. But only the variety with red berries. The variety with white berries is deadly poison. Oxgalls and nutgalls both contain tannic acid, and can be used instead of the powder.

Tin mordant ½ oz tin crystals to 1 lb of wool. Proceed as for alum. It produces brighter colour than the other mordants, and is either used by itself or in conjunction with others to brighten.

DYEING

Vegetable dye baths will ferment very quickly within two or three days for some, so th dyeing should be done as soon as it is mad Whatever the vegetable matter used for makin the dye bath, after 30 minutes a mixture 4 tblsps tartaric acid (or cream of tartar) an ½ cup Glaubers salts dissolved in 1 pint of h water is added to the dye bath, after temporaril taking out the yarn. The Glaubers salts ar used as a levelling agent. It exhausts the colou in the dye bath, and makes for uniform dyeing The tartaric acid (or cream of tartar) is used t make the colours bright and clear. Bot ingredients are cheap, especially when bough in quantity.

The dye bath should be luke-warm when th wet yarn is put into it. Raise the temperature t simmering, and then begin to time the bath For a light colour, leave it in 20 minutes, fe dark shades 30 minutes. At this point, take ou the yarn and pour in the tartaric/Glaube solution. Return the yarn, and simmer or bo (simmer for wool, silk, boil for cotton, etc.), fe another 20 or 30 minutes. If the yarns ar cooled in the bath, it darkens the colour.

Take out the yarn, and rinse it in water of th *same temperature as the dye bath.* Three rinse ending with a luke-warm rinse is usuall enough; by this time, the water should b running clear. Dry the yarn outside if possibl away from direct light and heat. The sam applies if one has to dry it indoors.

A quarter of a cup of vinegar added to th final rinse helps to return the softness to woo

DYE BATH RECIPES

Bedstraw (mordant with alum, chrome) Fe 1 lb wool yarn (already mordanted), boil 1 l bedstraw roots until soft. Cool and strain o liquor. Proceed as above using this dyestuff. makes yellow red with alum, and crimson re with chrome.

Beetroot (with alum mordant) For 1 lb wo yarn (already mordanted) cover 10 lb beetro with about 3½ gallons of water and simm until the beets are cooked. Remove the bee from the pan. These may now be used for foo The remaining liquid is the dye bath. Procee to dye as above. It makes various shades of ta and is fast.

Blackberry tips With iron mordant these gi an almost black colour.

Broom (with alum mordant) For 1 lb wo yarn, use 1 lb broom, and proceed as above. makes a bright yellow.

Chamomile (with alum mordant) For 1 l wool yarn, use 1 lb flower heads, and procee as above. It makes a bright yellow.

Cochineal (with alum mordant) METHOD 1 Fe 1 lb wool yarn (already mordanted), use ½ l powdered cochineal. Twelve hours before yo are ready to do the dyeing, mix the powdere cochineal to a paste with warm water in a bo large enough to allow for the mixture thicker ing. Stir three or four times in this period. Add to the warm water in the enamel pan. Heat and simmer for 10 minutes. Add the wet yarn to the dye bath and simmer for 30 minutes. Cool, rinse until clear, and dry. It makes a purple-red and is fast. METHOD 2 For 1 lb unmordanted yarn, use 4 oz alum, $1\frac{1}{2}$ oz cream of tartar, and $1\frac{1}{2}$ oz cochineal. Dissolve the alum and cream of tartar in the saucepan, bring to the boil, and simmer for 20 minutes. Take out the wool and put in the cochineal. Stir until dissolved, put the wool back in, and simmer for $\frac{3}{4}$ hour. Take out and rinse when cool.

Crab apples (with alum mordant) For 1 lb wool yarn (already mordanted), use 4 gallons red, ripe wild crab apples (or ornamental). Place the crab apples in the 5-gallon container, cover with water and boil until they are soft. Cool and strain. Proceed as above. It makes shades of pink, fairly fast.

Dandelions (with alum mordant) For 1 lb wool yarn (already mordanted), use 3 gallons dandelion flowers. Cover the flowers with $3\frac{1}{2}$ gallons of water, and boil for 45 minutes. Remove the flowers, add the wet wool, and proceed as above. It makes shades of soft yellow and the colour is fast.

Elderberries (with alum mordant) For 1 lb wool yarn, use 4 gallons elderberries. Place the elderberries in a 5-gallon container, cover and boil for 1 hour. Crush the berries as they are boiling to extract as much juice from them as possible. Cool and strain off the berries, and proceed as above. It makes various shades of purple and is fast.

Marigold flowers (with alum mordant) For 1 lb wool yarn, use 4 gallons marigold flowers. Place the marigold flowers in the 5-gallon container, cover with water and boil for 45 minutes. Cool, remove the flower debris, and proceed as above. It makes shades of yellow and is fast.

Onion skins (with chrome mordant) For 1 lb wool yarn (previously mordanted with chrome), use 4 gallons of red, or yellow, onion skins. Place the onion skins in a 5-gallon container. Cover with water, and boil until the skins are almost clear. Cool and remove the skins. Add the wet already-chromed yarn, and simmer for 30 minutes. (Remember to keep the pan in which you are doing the dyeing covered when you are using chrome mordant.) Proceed as above. Red makes a dark-golden colour, and is fast; yellow makes yellow and is fast.

Persian berries (with alum mordant) For 1 lb wool, use 4 oz Persian berries. Put the wool in the mordant bath (alum and cream of tartar) and boil for 20 minutes. Lift the wool out of the bath, put in the well-pounded berries, and simmer for $\frac{1}{2}$ hour. Put the wool back in the dye bath and dye for $\frac{3}{4}$ to 1 hour. It makes shades of yellow.

Pine cones (with alum mordant) For 1 lb wool yarn, use $1\frac{1}{2}$ lb cones. Break up the cones and boil for 3 or 4 hours, then proceed as above. It makes a reddish-yellow.

Tea (with alum mordant) For 1 lb wool yarn, use $\frac{1}{2}$ lb dry black tea leaves. Pour 2 gallons of boiling water over the tea. Steep for 1 hour, and strain. Add the wet yarn, and proceed as above. It makes shades of tan and is fast.

DYEING WITH LICHENS
(substantive dyes)

Harris, Donegal, and Shetland tweed owe their characteristic smell to the boiling lichen in which they have been dyed. It is still used for dyeing wool in those places and Orkney, Skye, Northern Ireland, Sweden, Iceland, Wales, and Norway. There are 40 to 50 lichens which give a dye, but those found growing on stone give a better colour than those growing on trees.

Parmelia omphalodes Also called Black Crottle (Scotland), Kenkerig (Wales), and Arcel (Ireland). Found on rocks, hills and moors. It gives a good warm reddish-brown, and a 'Harris tweed' smell.

Parmelia saxatilis Found on stones and rocks near the sea. It makes a very good shade of orange-brown.

Parmelia parientina This is the bright yellow lichen that one sees growing on old stone walls and old barn roofs. It makes a yellow-brown.

Ramalina scopulotum This is the common grey lichen that one sees growing on old stone walls, especially near the sea. It makes a yellow-brown.

Lobaria pulmonaria Found on trees in England and Scotland. It makes a good orange.

Ochroechia tartarea Found on limestone rocks, in Wales, Shetlands, etc. It makes a red.

Method of dyeing with lichens

Put the lichen in a large pot and fill with water. Bring to the boil very slowly, and simmer for 2 to 3 hours, then let it cool. Next day, put the wet wool in the pot and boil all together until the required depth of colour is reached. *Do not take the wool out until the dye is cold*; then rinse it out: you will find the loose lichen falls off; or put a layer of lichen, layer of wool, layer of lichen, until the pot is full. Fill with water and simmer for several hours until the colour is reached that is required. Let it cool in the water: take out and rinse well. The colour will be very fast.

FURTHER READING

ASH, B. & DYSON, A., *Introducing Dyeing and Printing* Batsford

GOOCH, P., *Ideas for Fabric Printing and Dyeing* Batsford

PROUD, N., *Simple Textile Dyeing and Printing* Batsford

Egg Decorating

PREPARING THE EGG

Either hard boil the egg first for at least half an hour (really hard-boiled eggs will keep indefinitely), or blow the egg to retain just the shell. To do this, make a small hole at each end with a *very* sharp needle, then make the hole large enough to take a darning needle. With the darning needle, poke around inside the egg until you have broken the skin holding the yolk, and stir the mixture. Then put your mouth to the hole, and holding the egg over a basin, blow. If it does not work, put a meat baster over the hole at the flatter end, squeeze the rubber bulb at the end of the tube, and after a few squeezes, a thin stream of yellow liquid will start to come out from the other end.

Materials

eggs (blown or hard-boiled); PVA (white) glue; braid, lace, ribbon, wool; beads; feathers; stands (bases); cold-water dyes, inks, nail varnish, acrylic paint, or felt-tip pens; straw; candles; dried grass, leaves, etc.; tissue paper, etc.

Equipment

needle; meat baster; nail scissors; paint brushes (very fine); small hobby drill (not essential).

MAKING THE PATTERNS

There are many techniques to use: scratched decoration; hot wax; stencils; straw; hot coloured wax; coloured paper shapes; dried petals, leaves, etc.; wool; lace, braid; beads; marbled.

Scratched

Dye the egg a rich dark colour: in this way the fine scratched lines will show up more effectively. Or take the boiled egg out of the boiling water, and dry in a towel, then while it is still hot, colour it all over with wax crayons. The heat of the egg will melt the wax, and the colour will be absorbed into the shell. Hold the egg in a cloth while you do it, because the egg is *hot*. Do not wait until it is cool enough to hold in your hand, because by then it will be too cool to melt the wax. You could use several colours on one egg, one colour on top of the other, starting with the lightest colour next to

The white lines are made with hot wax painted on the egg-shell. The shapes left were coloured with different coloured inks.

Egg decorated with paper shapes cut from tissue paper, and glued on with PVA (white glue) to prevent bleeding of the colour.

the shell, ending up with the darkest colour on the surface. Scratch with a sharp needle through to different layers, and the drawing will appear in several different colours.

Hot wax

This is really batik on eggs. It is a traditional technique in Czechoslovakia and in the Ukraine where it is called 'Pysanky'. It is also practised in Poland and India. The batik tool called a janting can be used, or use the Czech tool called a stuzka. Something similar can be made from a pin stuck into the cork from a wine bottle, or a piece of dowelling, or even a pencil.

To melt the wax and keep it hot, put a large potato, cut in half, flat side down on the table. Bend an old dessertspoon at its narrowest point so that it is at right-angles to the handle. Stick the handle of the spoon into the potato. Under the bowl of the spoon place a nightlight. The flame should be just licking the spoon. Into the spoon put ½ in. wax cut from a candle. If the wax gets too hot (remember wax is inflammable) move the nightlight to one side for a moment. Dip the pin head into the hot wax and drop a blob of hot wax onto the egg shell. You will have to dip the pin into the wax for each dot.

To make shapes instead of dots, use a feather. When the decoration is finished, put the egg in the dye colour. More than one colour can be used (as in batik) and if this is your choice, make the first colour a lighter one than the second, which must be darker. On the first colour, when it is dry, more wax can be added, and the egg dyed again. When all is finished, the wax is removed. To do this, hold the egg against the side of the flame. Do not hold it

over the top or it will be smoked. As the wax melts, mop it up with a paper tissue, held at the ready.

Stencils

Small ferns, or feathery herbs, or small paper cut-outs, are dipped in salad oil, then arranged on the surface of a hard-boiled egg. Tightly wrap a piece of old nylon stocking around the egg, tying the ends tightly to hold the plants or paper very close against the egg. Put it into the dye, and leave it there until it is dyed as dark a shade as required. Then lift out the egg and untie the stocking, taking off the plants or paper. The shapes of the plants will be left on the egg, undyed.

Cut straw

After a 20-minute soak in hot water, split the straw along its length, and open out flat. While the straw is still damp, cut it up into diamonds, triangles, and chevron shapes. Put the glue on the dull side and press onto the egg in an organized pattern arrangement. The eggs should be dyed a strong colour before the gluing starts. Tweezers are useful to place the small pieces.

Hot coloured wax

In a small container, melt some candlewax. To colour this, break up some children's brightly coloured wax crayons (one colour at a time, otherwise you will end up with brown wax). Stir well until the colour is distributed through the candlewax, then, with a pin fixed in the end of a pencil, drop the coloured wax onto the plain undyed egg, until the whole egg is completed.

Coloured paper shapes

Coloured paper shapes have to be quite small,

Small pieces of dried pressed ferns were glued on in a regular arrangement.

Acrylic painted decoration.

This decoration is made by a 'stencil' of fern tied onto the surface of the egg very firmly by an old nylon stocking. The colour on the egg was made by boiling it in onion skins for half an hour.

otherwise the paper will crease as it is pressed around the egg. These can either be stuck onto plain undyed eggs, or onto dyed eggs. If the whole surface is not to be decorated, the remaining shell can look very attractive if a coating of pearl nail varnish is applied.

Dried petals, leaves

These can be arranged and stuck on with cold-setting plastic or clear nail varnish (see section on Enamelcraft). A coating of plastic will seal the whole surface.

Wool

Coat half the egg with a white PVA glue and press on wool in close rows. With one half done, glue can be applied to the other half, and wool applied firmly to that. Lace and braid can be applied in the same way.

Dyeing the eggs

Using vegetable dyes, for yellow, use onion skins and saffron (expensive); for brown, use tea, coffee, and onion skins; for red, use beetroot juice, onion skins, and vinegar; for green, use spinach. For onion skins, spinach, and saffron, put in cold water and add the egg. For yellow, leave in until the egg has turned yellow. Leave in longer for brown. For green, leave until it is the shade you want.

Dylon cold-water dyes can be used as if you were dyeing fabric. Waterproof inks are just painted on with a soft brush. If you rub the dry dyed eggs with a little oil it enhances the colours. Plastic 'medium' can also be used for this purpose.

If the eggs are not to be used as hanging decorations, they can be carefully filled with plaster of Paris, or Polyfilla. Block the other end with Blu-Tack (Plasti-Tak) while setting. The Chinese painted eggs exquisitely, generally with landscapes. These were filled to make them less fragile.

FURTHER READING

NEWSOME, A.J., *Egg Decorating, Plain and Fancy*, Crown Publishers Inc, New York

EGG DECORATING

DECORATION APPLIED TO THE SURFACE	DECORATION ONTO THE SURFACE
Straw	Wax crayons
Sealing wax	Batik
Beads	Etching
Paper cuts (tissue)	Stencilling (using natural objects tied on with old nylon stocking)
Adhesive paper spots, stars, etc.	
Lace motif (appliqué)	Stick printing
Feathers	Felt-tip pens
Wool	Nail varnish
Découpage (photos, drawings)	Cold enamelling
Glued ferns, petals, leaves, etc.	Marbling (dipping method)
Seeds (glued)	Indian-ink drawing
Braid (string) cloisonné	Acrylic paints

Enamelcraft

This is a trade name for specially prepared cold-setting plastic which can utilize the techniques of 'proper' enamelling without the need for a special kiln and sources of heat. It can be applied to a wide range of materials, such as glass, metal, china, plastic, wood, stone, cloth and cardboard, whereas proper enamelling has to be done on gold, silver or copper.

Cloisonné can be produced with this cold-setting resin by laying wires onto a background with some clear plastic. One then fills the spaces with coloured plastic. *Plique-à-jour* is also possible with this material and is much tougher. The wire shapes are laid onto Perspex or Plexiglass to which the plastic will not stick, and the areas are filled with the coloured plastic. When it is quite set, it can be lifted off the Perspex. Instead of wire, one can use leather thonging, braid or cord, which can be stuck onto glass or plastic sheeting. This has the advantage of being thicker, and the thicker layer of plastic is therefore stronger. In this method, the drawing can be placed underneath the glass or plastic sheeting, and one merely follows the lines in the drawing, sticking the thonging to the glass with clear plastic. Copper blanks, normally sold for proper enamelling, can be used to make pendants, earrings, keyrings, etc.

Sparkling translucent effects can be achieved by sticking metal foil (cooking foil) to the surface of the object being 'enamelled'. It can either be stuck down with plastic flat, or crumpled first and then stuck down, so increasing the reflectivity. Cloth, bones, thread, paper, in fact anything which is dry, can be laid into the plastic while it is still wet, and one is still free to add colour, either translucent or opaque, to the surface. There is great scope for experimenting with this material.

The plastic is in two parts: the hardener (a liquid), and the basic liquid plastic. These are mixed by volume, one part hardener to two parts plastic. To this mixture is added the colour, either translucent or opaque. The plastic is workable for up to 3 hours. It then becomes too hard to use.

It is applied with either a paint brush, or a mixing stick. The surface, as always, must be free of grease. Do not use too much plastic or it will trickle over the edge. If one needs a thick layer of plastic, a 'wall' of adhesive tape can be wrapped around the edge of the object, and this will hold the additional thickness until it is quite dry. The tape can then be pulled off. The plastic is not fully dry until after seven days. It is touch dry in 24 hours in a warm room, but it is wiser to leave it longer before handling it. Because plastic will stick to almost any surface, make sure that all surfaces are covered with either newspaper or plastic sheeting.

Materials required for enamelling:
1 Enamels 2 Lump enamel 3 Gum tragacanth 4 Roll of paper 5 Copper blanks 6 Brushes 7 Spatula and sgraffito tool 8 Sieve 9 Screw punch 10 Punch 11 Brass tongs 12 Round-nose pliers 13 Cap sieve 14 Carborundum stone 15 Steel stilts 16 Nichrome wire trivet.

Enamelling

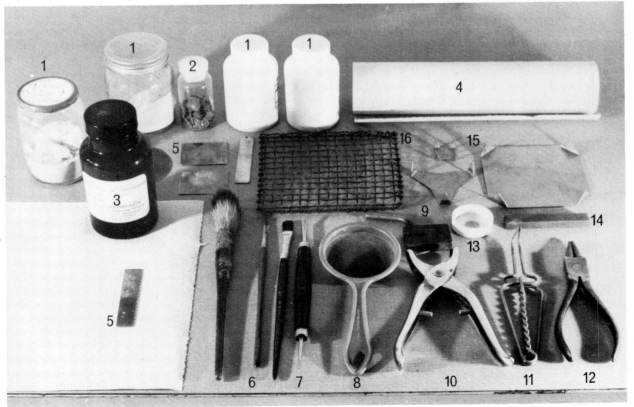

The base of enamel is a clear colourless transparent vitreous compound called 'flux'. This is a composition of minium, potash, and silica. This flux is coloured by the addition of oxides of metals. Enamels are either 'hard' or 'soft', depending upon the amount of silica in the mixture. When it is 'hard', it requires a very high temperature to fuse it. Fine gold or pure copper are the best metals on which to enamel. There are seven methods of enamelling.

Cloisonné This method involves the bending of thin metal strips to form the outline of the pattern. The metal strips are fixed to the metal base by either silver solder or the enamel itself. Into the spaces between the raised outline the enamel powder is laid and then fused in a kiln.

Champlevé The principle is the same as *cloisonné*, only this time to achieve the 'walls' which will separate the different colours of the enamels the metal base is carved away, leaving walls between one trough and another. The enamel powder is then placed in the troughs or hollows between the lines ('walls') as in *cloisonné*.

Basse-taille The metal base is either silver or gold in this style of enamelling, and is carved in low relief. A translucent enamel is then applied to the whole surface and when the metal is fired the carving in the metal shows through the enamel.

Plique-à-jour Similar to *cloisonné* inasmuch as it involves metal strips, but this time they are soldered to each other and not to a base. The wire framework is laid upon a base of platinum, copper, silver, gold, or hard brass, and the areas between the wire walls are filled with enamel powder and the enamel fused in a kiln. When it is cooled, the wire framework filled with what is virtually a stained-glass window is removed from the metal base on which it was laid. It is a very fragile style of enamelling.

Painted enamels Usually done on copper but it

Large front-loading furnace.

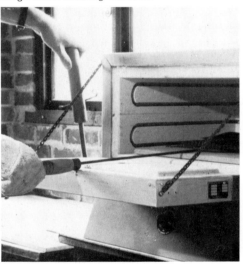

Firing with a butane torch.

Hot plate type of kiln.

Firing equipment. Stilts.

can be done on silver or gold. After cleaning with acid and water, enamel is laid over the entire surface, back and front, and fired. The design is then painted on in enamel and again fired.

Encrusted enamelling refers to the enamelling of jewellery or other small objects, either in the round or in relief.

Miniature enamel painting White enamel is fired on a gold plate (base) and onto this white surface are painted raw oxides to which a little flux has been added.

METHOD

Cut some 1 mm (20 g) sheets of copper or steel into 1 in. by 2 in. rectangles. Clean with methylated spirits (denatured alcohol) or acetone, then with wire wool, water, and pumice powder. Dry. Coat thinly with gum tragacanth solution (or gum karaya). Sift a thin layer of enamel powder over, as thin as possible without leaving bald areas. Dry thoroughly by

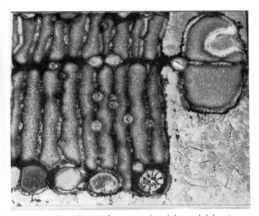

Wet application of enamel with gold lustre. Small panel by Gerda Flockinger.

placing on top of the furnace. The glue must be completely dry before it is put in the furnace. If it is not, it will bubble when it is put in the furnace and the enamel will fly off. When the furnace is 1560 °F (850 °C) (i.e. bright red), place it in the furnace. At first it becomes black, then red hot, then glasslike. This indicates that the enamel has fused. Now take it out of the furnace and put on one side to cool slowly away from draughts. The colours change on cooling; bright red looks black at one stage.

Gum tragacanth solution

Buy the gum tragacanth in powdered form. Dissolve $\frac{1}{2}$ oz of gum in meths. Add slowly 2 pints distilled water. (A few drops of formaldehyde can be added to prevent it fermenting.) Polycell can be used instead: 1 tsp powder sprinkled onto $\frac{3}{4}$ pint water. Stir thoroughly, and wait until all the grains have disappeared. Glycerine thinned with a few drops of meths also makes a good adhesive.

For transparent enamels, one must use copper (or gold or silver). The copper must

still be cleaned very thoroughly (one can use a solution of 3 parts water to 1 part nitric acid, *adding the acid to the water*, and immersing the copper in the solution). Do not touch the surface of the metal. Hold it by the edges. Apply gum solution with a soft brush, sift over with transparent enamel, dry, and fire at 1500 °F (820 °C).

Washing transparent enamels before use Half fill a jar with powder enamel, and fill up the jar with water. Pour off the milky liquid from the top. Repeat until the liquid is clear. Tip out the enamel paste onto some clean paper, and dry out on top of a stove or the furnace. When it has dried out to a powder again put it into an airtight screw-top jar. Or the wet paste can be used for the *cloisonné* technique. Remember, powdered enamel is as powdered glass. When sifting, wear a mask.

Swirling with lid removed to show technique.

VARIOUS ENAMELLING TECHNIQUES

Silver and gold foil

This is sandwiched between two coats of enamelling. The copper is given a first coat, the pieces of foil placed on it, and another layer of transparent enamels is used to enclose it. Special foil has to be purchased, and gold or silver leaf cannot be used because it is too thin. The foils are supplied protected on each side by a sheet of paper. Keep them as they are, never touching the surface of the foil with your fingers. Air can get trapped between the foil and the enamel, and to avoid this, the foil is pricked with a needle through the layer of paper to allow the air to escape.

The foil is cut into shapes before it is laid on the enamel, and to do this, paperclip the paper

Pendant with swirling.

and foil together and draw the design on the top layer of paper. Cut out the shapes with a pair of scissors. Brush gum over the enamel, and using the still-sticky brush, touch the foil pieces, lift them up and place on the gummed enamel base. Smooth the foil down into the gum, brushing towards the edge of the piece. Dry on top of the kiln, then give the piece a short firing, which is merely to let the foil sink into the base enamel. Polish the foil with a glass fibre brush, and dust on a thin coat of transparent enamel, and then a second, after the first has been fired.

Swirling

Unlike other techniques, this is done to the molten enamel in the kiln. A special tool is used which is a length of metal bent at one end at right-angles, with a wooden handle. Place chunks or enamel threads on the piece being decorated (on the base enamel) and when it is molten, using the tool gently, swirl the colours/lines around. After using the swirler lay it down on the asbestos sheet: it is very hot. The blob of enamel on the end is easily broken off when cool.

Transfer designs

Any print which uses an oil based ink can be used to make the transfer. Roll an even layer of ink with a roller over your block (litho plate, potato cut, lino block, polystyrene, etc.). Lay a piece of tracing paper over the block, and rub evenly until an even layer of ink is transferred to the paper. This is then pressed onto the enamel surface. Peel off the paper, dust the oily print with enamel, and fire. Dust it over the whole piece, and gently tap to shake off the excess powder which will only stick to the print. Fire as usual.

Threads

Enamel threads are normally bought ready-made but they can be made in an enamelling kiln. Fill a fireclay crucible (the sort silver-smiths use) with lump or ground enamel, and place on a firing rack. Put it into a cold kiln and allow to heat until molten. Wearing asbestos mitts, and using tongs, remove the crucible from the kiln and place on an asbestos sheet. While one person holds the crucible steady another dips into the molten metal a steel rod which has had the tip heated red-hot in a blow-torch. Lift out the rod, and walk away lifting the rod as you do so. Lifting the rod out is just like taking a spoon out of a jar of syrup. If you hold the rod over an asbestos sheet it forms the scribbles that syrup does on a piece of bread and butter. You can do this, or lift and walk: as you lift, the air cools and solidifies the enamel, making straight threads. Cut the thread with pliers, first at the rod, then at the crucible. The molten enamel in the crucible is cooling all the time, and you will only be able to make three dips, probably only two at first. The thickness of the thread depends on how fast the rod is lifted from the crucible. The faster you lift it, the thinner it will be.

Threads can be applied directly to copper, or onto enamel. They can be bent by holding in a low flame of a gas torch. Arrange threads on a sheet of asbestos, and using a gas torch, heat at the places where the rods overlap until they fuse. The threads can then be picked up as one, but take care: they are very fragile. Paint gum on the copper or enamel and lay the threads down on that. If you decide to work direct on copper, choose thicker threads.

Chunks

These are purchased in a wide variety of colours. When melted and fused they still retain a slightly angular shape, so if you want a pool of colour you have to use enamel balls. Use a pair of pointed tweezers to place chunks on an enamel surface which is painted with gum. Watch the progress of the enamel through the peephole in the kiln, and remove it when you are satisfied with the results.

Sgraffito

In this technique the design is scratched into powdered enamel. The copper is painted with gum and opaque enamel is dusted over. Dry the piece on top of the kiln and when quite dry scratch a design into the powdered enamel, taking great care to hold only the very edge of the piece. Scratch until you see the copper showing through. Tip off all the loose powder

Cigarette boxes decorated with sgraffito.

you have scratched off. Fire as usual. The plain copper will of course have firescale on it, and this is removed by dipping in dilute nitric acid. The piece can then be refired with a second coat of transparent enamel. More *sgraffito* could be done in the second coat while in powder form over those parts which have opaque enamel on them.

Champlevé ring, French.

Stencils

These can be cut from paper, or made from dried leaves, grasses, flowers, or net, lace, string, etc. The stencils are dipped in dilute gum, and using pointed tweezers, lift and lay onto either copper, or an enamel. Spray the remaining surface with gum, or paint gum on, and then dust the surface with enamel powder. Try to keep most of the powder on the surrounds of the stencil, but put enough over the edge of the stencil or it will not show. Any enamel on the stencil is wasted. When the gum is almost dry, remove the stencil with tweezers. Fire as usual. Designs using stencils can be built up over several firings if you use transparent enamels and reposition the stencils each time.

Glycerine

This can be used to hold powdered enamel to the copper as does gum. The glycerine is diluted in a small pot with water, added drop by drop and mixing well. It is dilute enough when the mixture flows easily from the brush or nib if you wish to draw with it. Add a few drops of food colouring to the mixture, otherwise you will not be able to see what you are doing. Paint or draw a design onto an enamelled base. Dust with enamel powder and blow off any excess.

The firing of this technique requires special attention. Place the piece in a kiln for 2 seconds with the kiln door open. Remove and cool. Smoke will be seen coming from the piece: repeat the process of firing for 2 seconds and removing and cooling until no more smoke is given off. Then give it a 'proper' firing, watching through the peephole until the enamel is smooth and shiny. Then remove from the kiln. Only opaque enamels are used for this technique, because the glycerine makes the transparent enamels cloudy. Wash the brush in warm soapy water to get rid of the glycerine.

Inked copper blank ready for sifting with enamel.

Finished piece.

Cloisonné

Prepare the copper shape by counter-enamelling, cleaning the front and coating with gum. Dust on powder enamel (transparent flux), and on this place the bent copper shapes (*cloisons*). Use pointed-tipped tweezers to do so. Dry on top of the kiln, and then fire. Remove, and when cool, clean the copper with a stick of carborundum. Using an eyedropper, add gum tragacanth to powdered enamel until it forms a paste when stirred with a spatula. Allow to dry completely, and fire. The spaces in the wire shapes can be filled with various coloured enamels and all fired at the same time.

Painting with enamels

Buy specially prepared painting colours for this. They are mixed with fat oil and oil of lavender, and applied with a fine brush. It is always done on an enamelled surface, using soft enamels. The firing is a short one.

Applying the enamel wet

First apply a ground coat of transparent flux onto clean copper and fire it. When cool, apply the wet paste in various colours with a spatula or very fine brush. Dry off completely and fire as usual.

Counter-enamelling is enamel applied to the back of a piece. It is essential if doing *cloisonné* or using lumps. When a piece is being counter-enamelled, the stilts on which it is placed should hold it on the edges only – otherwise the stilts can become embedded in the enamel when it melts in the kiln. The same care with the stilts must be taken on each of the successive firings.

Applying the counter enamel.

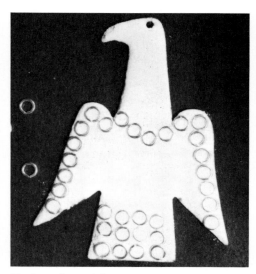

Placing silver cloisons onto powdered base coat.

Filling the cloisons with paste enamel.

Finished pendant.

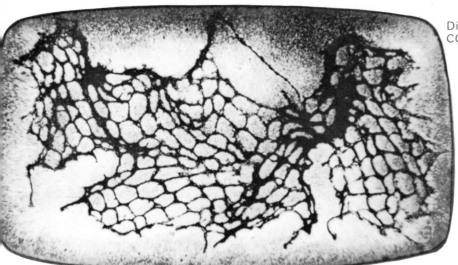

Dish showing net stencil. (Courtesy of COID.)

The outline of the design being scratched in the dry enamel. The tool used is a scriber which is also used in inlay work. For larger areas it is worthwhile making a special tool. A piece of copper wire is hammered flat and cut straight at the end.

After firing, the exposed copper is covered with firescale.

Soft enamels make 'squiggles' when taken out of the kiln but towards the end of the drawing straight threads can be made.

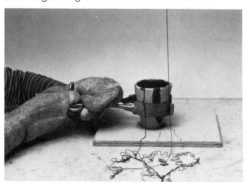

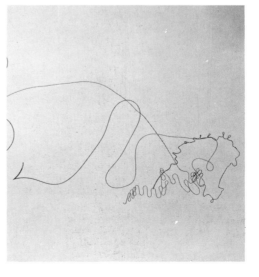

'Squiggles' form natural patterns.

Bending a straight thread with the aid of a torch. The flame should be low, otherwise it will burn through the enamel.

Threads fused on copper.

Metal foil and paper held together with paper clips.

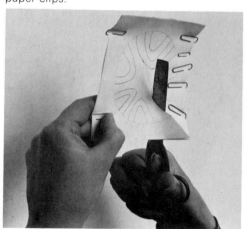

Positioning the foil with a brush.

Polishing with a glass-fibre brush after firing. Transparent enamel over foil gives a real sparkle. Blues go well over silver, and ruby over silver gives the impression of a rich gold.

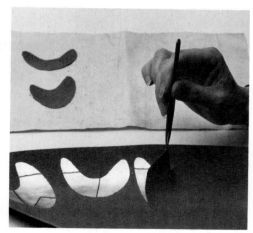

Removing the stencils in a half-dry state by picking up the edge with pointed tweezers.

GAUGES FOR SHEET COPPER

In the United Kingdom, copper sheet is measured by the Standard Wire Gauge (SWG). In the United States of America the Brown and Sharpe Wire Gauge (B&S) is used.

SWG	in.	B&S
24	0·022	23
	0·025	22
22	0·028	21
	0·032	20
20	0·036	19
	0·040	18
	0·045	17
18	0·048	
	0·050	16
	0·057	15
16	0·064	14
	0·072	13
14	0·080	

ENAMELS

TRADITIONAL METHODS	MODERN METHODS
Cloisonné	*Sgraffito*
	Liquid enamel
Champlevé	painted on:
	Mosaic
Basse-taille	Millefiore
	Silver foil/gold foil
Plique à jour	Shot enamel
	Threads
Painted enamels	Cracking enamel
	Swirling/scrolling
Encrusted enamels	
	Stencils
Miniature enamel	Cut paper
painting	Leaves
	Grasses
	Nets/string/lace
	Transfer designs
	Lino paint
	Potato print
	Leaves/grasses
	Screen prints

Etui, enamel on copper, mounted in gilt-metal, painted in colours and gold. Probably made at Birmingham or Bilston, about 1760.

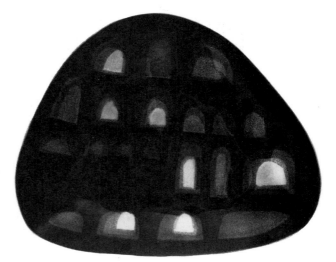

This finished piece shows the use of positive stencils of the same shape but diminishing in size in each application. The last firing was a short overfire to allow the base colour to soften the lines of the pattern.

FURTHER READING

CLARKE, G., FEHER, F. & I., *The Technique of Enamelling* Batsford

93

Encaustic

Hot-wax painting, which became a lost craft during the Middle Ages, is powdered colour added to molten beeswax. This is applied to the canvas, or prepared board, with either a palette knife or a brush.

The palette itself also has to be kept warm, because the wax has to be kept in a malleable state. When the picture is finished, the surface is heated to fuse the wax into a whole, without it actually becoming so soft that it runs. The strong Egyptian sunshine would have been perfect, and it was in Egypt that this craft really flourished. Sometimes Roman frescoes have been mistaken for encaustic painting, because they have a surface coating of wax, but this was applied on a completed fresco in order to preserve it.

One can experiment with encaustic painting by using candle wax instead of beeswax, heated over a nightlight candle in an enamel plate or large tin lid, and powder colour.

Enlarging

There are three simple ways of doing this.
1. Project a film slide of the design onto a wall which has pinned on it either fabric or paper and simply trace around the image.
2. To enlarge a photograph or a drawing, an epidiascope (opaque projector) is used to project the image.
3. The last method is by 'squaring up' the drawing.
The small drawing is divided into halves (by folding) and into halves again. This is done both horizontally and vertically. In a complicated design one might have to divide into sixteenths.

The enlargement has to be the same *proportion* as the original, so pin the original in the bottom left-hand corner of your enlargement paper. Draw a diagonal line from the bottom left-hand corner of the original up to the top right-hand corner and extend the pencil line right across the enlargement paper. At any point along that line one can drop a vertical line, and by extending a horizontal line to the left-hand edge of the enlargement paper one will have a rectangle of exactly the same proportion as in the original small drawing.

Fold the enlarged rectangle into exactly the same number of squares as the small drawing, then draw in the enlargement, working square by square until completed. If one part is very complicated, that particular square might have to be divided into four on the original and the enlargement in order to make the copying easier.

Squaring up the drawing to enlarge the design.

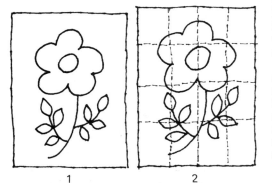

1   2

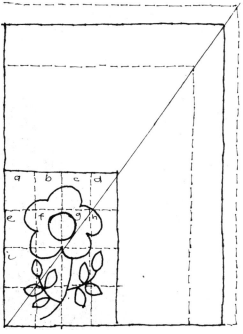

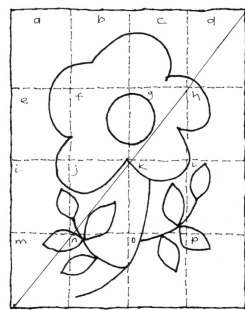

3   4

Etching

Traditionally the plate used for etching was copper. It allows much finer work to be done, but is at least twice the price of zinc. Zinc reacts with the acid faster than copper, and has a pleasing 'tone' on the print. New materials are being experimented with all the time, e.g. aluminium, lucite, masonite, and steel. The advice, as always, is experiment as soon as you have mastered the principle.

HARD GROUND ETCHING
Cleaning the plate
This should be done to clean the surface of all grease, so ensuring that the ground will really adhere to the metal, and not break down while in the acid. The old method was to rub the surface all over with powdered whiting and water. Household ammonia can be used instead of water, and any detergent can be used instead of whiting. Rinse under a tap. A plate is clean when the water forms an unbroken film over the whole surface. Dry on a hot-plate.

The traditional 'ground'
Warm the plate on a hot-plate. Rub the ball of hard ground around on the plate to soften it. (Hard ground is mainly wax, supplied in balls about the size of a golf ball.) Use a special leather-covered roller to roll the warm ground on the plate until there is an even layer all over. Roll in many directions. The desired thickness is only recognized by experience: if it is too thin it does not resist the acid, if too thick it will flake off.

Smoking the ground
This was done because the colour of the wax layer is very similar to that of the copper, and it was difficult to see the line one had cut. To make it easier to see, the wax ground was blackened by the smoke from wax tapers (slender candles). Hold the plate ground-side down, and run the flame across the ground, leaving a sooty black surface when the plate is cool. Do not keep the flame in one place too long, or it will burn the ground.

Asphalt hard ground
Add equal parts of liquid asphalt and turpentine. Stir well. Stand the plate against a vertical surface, and using a large soft-haired brush lay the ground in even layers, one just overlapping the other horizontally. Heat the plate over a stove to allow the solvent to evaporate and form a hard smooth coat.

Drawing on the plate
The object is to scratch away some of the ground, so that when the plate is immersed in the acid the unprotected metal will be bitten by the acid, leaving a line sunk in the metal. It is into this sunken line that the ink will be rubbed, and this is what is printed. A darning needle, old dentist's tool, or something similar can be used if you have no etcher's needle. Do not scratch deeper for lines that you want to be darker. That is done by the acid.

Varnishing the back
The back and sides of the plate have to be protected from the acid. Use a special 'stop-out' varnish, and carefully paint the sides and back. Hard-ground (asphalt) can be used equally effectively.

Biting the plate
Lay two pieces of string across the bath so that two ends overhang at each side. Lower the plate onto the strings and submerge in the acid. The strings are there so that the plate can be lifted out by holding the ends. This way one avoids contact with the acid.

Lines of different thickness (blackness) are achieved by leaving the plate in the acid for a longer time so that more metal is bitten away giving a thicker, darker line.

One can control this in two ways. Let us assume there are to be three different tones of grey. Call the darkest tone C, the middle tone B, and the lightest tone A.

The first method Scratch the areas to be the darkest tone C first. Place the plate in the acid bath, and allow to bite for say 5 minutes. Take the plate out of the bath and carefully rinse off all acid. Scratch out the middle toned areas, B. Place the plate in the bath and allow to bite for 5 minutes. Take the plate out of the acid bath and rinse off. Scratch out those areas to be the lightest tone A. Immerse the plate in the acid for 5 minutes. Take out and rinse off. It will be seen that the areas A have been in the acid for 5 minutes, B for 10 minutes, and C for 15 minutes. Since length of time in the acid = darkness of tone, you have achieved your objective.

The second method Keeping to the letters used for the tones in the first method: All the lines/areas are scratched out at the same time. The plate is then placed in the acid bath for 5 minutes. Take it out and rinse off. Those areas to be the lightest tone A are painted over with stop-out: this prevents the acid biting into

Etching needles:
1 Point and burnisher; 2 Point;
3 Point in adjustable handle.

Drawing on the ground with white poster colour.

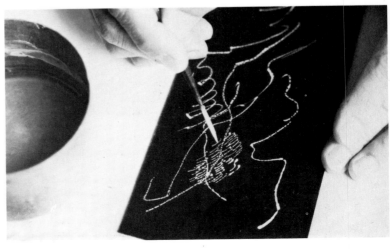

them any more. Immerse the plate in the acid for another 5 minutes. Take out and rinse off. Paint out those areas of middle tone B with stop-out. Place the plate in the acid again for a final 5 minutes. Take out of the acid bath and rinse off. Once again, those areas C have been exposed to the acid for 15 minutes, areas B for 10 minutes, and A for 5 minutes.

(The timing specified above is given only to explain the method; it does not refer to the amount of time required by the etching process.)

Acids for etching

Zinc plates are etched in nitric acid, 1 part acid to 6 parts water. (Gives off hydrogen bubbles.) Copper plates are etched in nitric acid, 1 part acid to 3 parts water. (Gives off bubbles of nitric oxide.)

Feathering

As the acid bites into the plate, bubbles of gas form along the lines. If the bubbles remain, the acid cannot bite there, so there will be uneven biting. To get rid of the bubbles, one can use a feather to brush along the lines. One can use other things, such as a brush, but there is a very satisfying 'feel' in the resilience of the feather along with the delicacy.

Taking the plate out of the acid bath

Tilt the liquid to one end and pick up the plate by two corners, and wash immediately. Dry with paper towels.

Removing the ground

This is done with the appropriate solvents: the ground is dissolved with turpentine, the stop-out with alcohol. The plate is now ready for inking and printing.

Lifting the print from one corner of the plate in a steady movement using finger pads to protect the paper.

Inking the plate

Warm the plate on a stove. Put a little ink on it, and with a hard roller, spread the ink over the plate, forcing it down into the lines or hollows.

Wiping off the ink

You only want ink in the hollows, so it must be wiped off the flat shiny surfaces that were protected by the ground. With a circular movement, wipe off the excess ink. It will probably be necessary to have a pile of rags handy (traditionally tarlatan). Take care that you do not wipe the ink out of the lines as well. Make sure that there is no ink on the edges of the plate, and that they are bevelled smooth before printing. If they are left sharp they will cut the paper and perhaps even the blankets.

Taking the print

Warm the inked and wiped plate on the stove. On the clean bed, lay the plate, face up. On the plate lay a piece of damp paper. Pull the blankets down one by one, without jogging the paper on the plate. Roll the bed through the press slowly and evenly without stopping. Lift off the blankets onto the roller. Peel off the paper starting at one corner.

Stretching the print

Lay the damp print onto a sheet of formica, or plywood. With brown sticky tape, stick the top edge of the paper to the formica. Next tape the bottom edge, stretching the paper flat as you do so, then the remaining two sides. When the prints are dry they will be flat, and can be cut out from the sticky tape 'frame' with a razor blade.

SOFT GROUND ETCHING

The ground is one which does not harden. Melt down some hard ground and add half as much again of Vaseline. Lay the ground as for hard ground etching. Almost anything which is pressed into this ground will lift it off the plate, revealing the zinc. One can either press materials, net, lace, feathers, etc. directly into the soft ground, or lay a thin piece of paper over the ground and press the objects through that. One can draw on top of the paper, the pressure from the point lifting the line away from the zinc onto the paper. Etch and print in the normal way.

AQUATINT

This is the technique to use for large areas of tone. The ground is sprinkled onto a plate and the plate warmed, so melting the ground. Work in a place free of draughts. In a 6-in. square of nylon stocking, put 6 tblsps of powdered resin, and tie up into a bag. Holding the bag over a perfectly clean plate, knock the side of the bag. As resin falls on the plate, move the bag around to get an even layer of resin dust on the plate. When about half the surface total is covered with resin, place the plate *very carefully* on the heater. As the plate heats the resin melts, and should look as though it were covered in dew-drops. Remove from the heat, and allow the dew-drops to solidify. If the resin powders in your hand when you rub it over the plate, it has not been heated enough.

An aquatint quality can be achieved in other ways. Lay on an ordinary hard ground. Place the plate face up on the printing press, and onto this surface lay a sheet of medium-coarse sandpaper, and roll through the press (with slightly less pressure than for a print). When you remove the sandpaper, you will see the surface pitted with the tiny holes left by the sandpaper. Move the sandpaper around and run through the press a few more times. If you use too little pressure in the press, the sandpaper grains will not reach the metal; if too much pressure is used the grains can actually go into the metal, and it will be impossible to have any white areas.

While the ground is still warm on the heater, sprinkle table salt over the whole plate. The salt will go through the ground down onto the plate. When cool, put the plate in water, which will dissolve the salt, and expose fine dots of metal all over the plate.

Heat the plate without any ground on it on a heater. Thoroughly coat some hessian or other coarse-textured surface, such as lace, or a string block (experiment), with hard ground. Lay it on the warm plate, and press down all over the hessian. The ground will be transferred to the plate, and you have a ready-made texture.

Biting the plate

A weaker solution is used for aquatint than for etching. If you use nitric acid, dilute it with water. Alternatively, use Dutch mordant and iron perchloride, which has a milder action than an acid. With stop-out varnish, paint in those areas to be left white. Place the plate in the bath for 1 minute to begin with. Take out, rinse and dry the plate. Paint out some other areas, and put back in the bath for another 1 minute. Take out, rinse and dry. Repeat until you have a range of four to six tones.

Keep a careful note of the times the plate was in the bath. There are so many variables in etching the plate: the thickness of the ground, the strength of the bath, the age of the acid in the bath (how many times it has been used before) and, with an aquatint ground, just how much ground there really is on the plate. In any of the etching techniques listed, it is really essential to do a test plate first to get the feel of the ground, the bath, and the technique itself.

All the above techniques are intaglio methods: i.e. the ink is rubbed into the etched areas (those areas lower than the surface of the plate) and the ink is rubbed off the other areas. The opposite technique is called relief printing: i.e. the ink is only rolled on to those parts left of the original surface. Any ink that gets into the hollows is carefully wiped out. Lino printing, wood cuts, wood engravings and zinc plate etching are all relief techniques.

RELIEF ETCHING

Draw on to a perfectly clean zinc plate with wax crayon or stop-out varnish. Varnish the back of the plate (as in *all* etching processes), and immerse the plate in the acid bath. Take out, rinse and dry. If you wish, draw again, and etch in the bath. Take out, rinse and dry. Remove the varnish and/or stop-out with turps.

There are two sorts of rollers, hard and soft. Hard rollers keep the ink to the surface of the plate, soft rollers deposit some ink in the hollows. Explore their various possibilities yourself.

Another technique you might move on to when you have experimented with the ones above is 'lift ground etching'. It is a complicated method but a very 'free' one to use. The main difference between this process and the others is that the brush strokes of stop-out in this method will print black instead of white.

INTAGLIO

Traditionally, this method is what etchers called 'drypoint'. A zinc or copper plate is scored with a steel tool: ridges of metal are raised either side of the line, in a burr. A similar effect is achieved when hardboard is scratched with the point of a compass. One can also scratch Perspex (Plexiglass) with the point of a compass.

To print the scratched surface by the intaglio process, the ink is rubbed into the hollows of the scratched lines, and carefully wiped from the rest of the surface. Moisten the printing paper with water to make it pliable. Cover the 'plate', whether zinc, Perspex, or hardboard, with the moist paper, and over the paper place a sheet of felt. Roll through an intaglio plate press under high pressure. (An intaglio press is essential for this method.) This forces the pliable paper into the hollows in the line, to take up some of the ink. One can take an intaglio print from a lino block with the right press.

To experiment and get the 'feel' of the technique, one can use a piece of cardboard, and scratch it with a needle. Rub in ink with a pad of cloth, making sure it is going into the hollows of the scratch, and print in an intaglio press.

Without an intaglio press, one could still try taking a print from one of the above materials by rolling the softened paper with a 'soft' roller.

FURTHER READING

COKER, P., *Etching Techniques* Batsford
DANIELS, H., *Printmaking* Hamlyn

Drypoint needles 1 and 2 Steel points, heavy and light. Note wrapping for improved grip, 3 Diamond point.

1   2   3

Fabric and Yarn

Fabric is produced by weaving from various raw materials such as cotton, wool, silk, flax, hemp, and jute. Yarn is the spun fibre which is ready for making into cloth, and can be of cotton (single- or multi-strand), linen (line or tow), wool (fluffy and elastic), worsted (smooth and strong), net silk (organzine or tram, both quite strong), or spun silk. The different weights and textures of fabrics can be used in harmony or striking contrast, and experiments combining fabric and yarn, and perhaps other materials and objects, can produce imaginative designs.

Linear mesh effects which can be achieved with hessian and burlap.

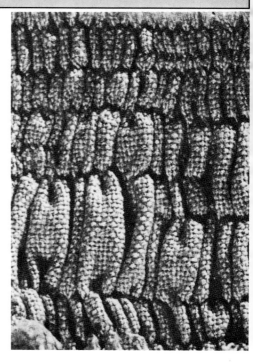

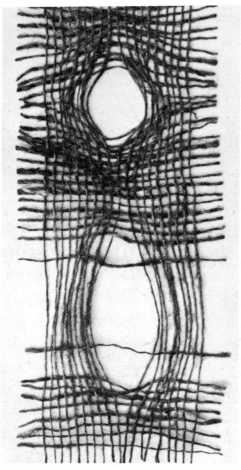

Experiments exploring the qualities of cloth.

FURTHER READING
CARTER, J., *Creative Play with Fabric and Thread* Batsford
HARTUNG, R., *Creative Textile Craft* Batsford

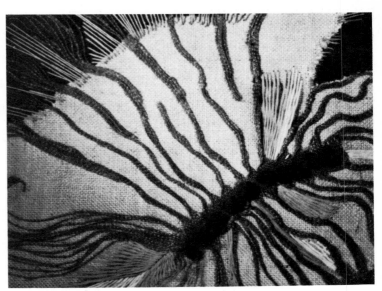

Fabric has been pulled apart and the threads glued down.

A variety of yarns have been experimented with in embroidery stitches very freely worked.

Cut-out and frayed pieces of fabric are interlaid with net.

Overlapped shapes behind holes cut into felt.

Net has the possibility of overlaid transparent colour which is similar to water colour washes, or tissue paper.

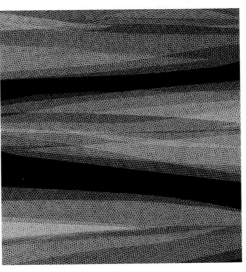

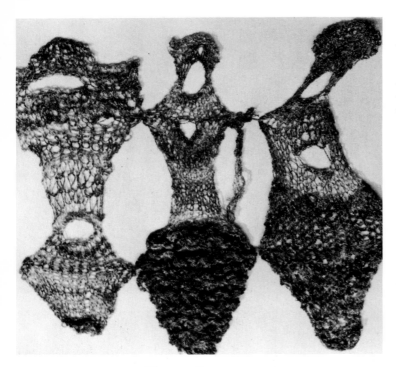

Free shapes made
by knitting with
various thicknesses
of yarn.
Knitting with large
wooden beads
threaded onto the
wool before knitting
is begun.

Feathers

Traditionally in England feathers were used to
make pictures of birds. They are usually shown
sitting on the branch of a tree in leaf. The
branch and leaves are painted in water colour
on a white or cream-coloured paper, and the
outline of a bird is drawn perched on the twig.
This is then filled in with feathers, starting
from the tail and working up to the head. A
small glass bead is used for the eye. At A la
Ronde in Exmouth, and at Arlington Court in
Devon there are many examples of exotic birds
done this way.

Examples of Chinese decorative tags,
using feathers or parts of feathers to make
butterflies.

Feathers can be obtained cheaply from
butchers selling game birds, and UHU,
Copydex, Marvin and Elmer's Glue-All are
all suitable glues. Besides birds, try making
robots, cars, butterflies, wedding cakes; the
possibilities are endless.

Findings

This is the name given to all the miscellaneous
links and attachments used in making jewellery.
Although they can be made in silver and stainless steel, most are made in a cheap anonymous
metal. The standard of design is very variable
and before buying, see as many catalogues as
you can and choose the shape most suitable for
your stones. This only really applies to the
choice of blanks for rings or bracelets or
pendants when the shape of the blank is seen
surrounding the stone. There is no fitting to be
done when these findings are used because the
stones (or tumble polished pebbles, or purchased cabochons) are glued to the blank with
an epoxy adhesive. Before applying the adhesive, both the stone and the surface onto
which the stone is to be glued must be rough-
ened with sandpaper to make a secure bond.

Jump rings, bolt rings, and oval and bar pins
are standard and more or less invisible. Jump
rings, which are available in more than one size,
are rings with a small gap in them and are used
for linking units in a necklace, or for attaching
to bell caps on pendants. A bolt ring is the little
fastener that is attached to each end of a
necklace. The outer ring is hollow and an
inner ring held by a spring closes the gap and

makes the necklace secure. Oval or bar pins are fastened at the back of brooches, depending on the shape of the front. Bell caps are glued onto pendants, and have a small loop attached to the top through which is looped a jump ring. Through this jump ring is threaded the leather thonging or chain. The design of bell caps is particularly variable, so see a variety before you choose. Ear wire and ear screws are available for attaching pendants for ear-rings. There are also copper blanks of all sorts used in enamelling. These range from pendants, to copper bowls and inset copper in lids of boxes, matchbox covers, etc.

Bell caps.

Jump rings. Bolt ring.

Ear wire with loop. Ear screw with loop.

Small oval pin. Bar pin.

Flower Making

PAPER FLOWERS

Equipment
scissors (surgical or dissecting are best); pliers or tin snips (for cutting the wire).

Materials
Crêpe paper and tissue paper (these both come in a wide range of colours, but of the two, crêpe paper is by far the easier to use); wire: reels of fine wire (almost as fine as fuse wire), tray wire (covered in cotton thread, white or green, millinery wire will substitute), fine (No 22) wire and medium (No 20) wire, 10 in. long, thick (No 18) wire, 14 in. long, extra thick wire (No 12–16), this can be galvanized wire which is available from hardware stores where it is sold in rolls by weight; PVA glue or white glue; floral tape, or gutta-percha; cotton wool; purchased stamens; bleach; candles (white); spray adhesive; 3B pencil.

METHOD
If making a lot of flowers, trace the pattern onto a piece of cardboard. Trace round this with the pencil onto the crêpe paper. Fold the paper so that you cut out five or six petals or leaves at the same time. Place the pattern on the paper with the grain (if you are using crêpe paper) of the paper running parallel with the centre of the petal or leaf. Cut out all the leaves and petals before you begin.

Leaves are a very important part of flower-making. The overall success of the flower will rest to a large extent on how well these have been observed and made, and how they are arranged on the stem. Make them in various sizes, small, medium, and large. Look at real leaves and make some drawings. Cut the leaves as carefully as possible; always cut them double: either use the same colour for both, or use a contrasting one for the underside. Spray the two pieces with a spray adhesive, and after laying a piece of wire down the centre of one of them, press the two parts of the leaf together. The wire makes it possible to arrange the angle of the leaves very precisely. Check to see how the leaves of the flower you are making actually grow on the real flower. When attaching the leaves to the main stem, allow a good 1½ in. of wire to be bound into the main stem. Always begin wrapping the stem at the calyx and bind in the leaves as you move down the stem.

Flowers Always begin by attaching the stamens to the main stem first. Use fuse wire for this, wrapping it several times around the stem wire to finish off. The flower centres themselves can be ready-made stamens of rough sisal, frayed out, and the threads painted black, or wire covered in crêpe paper, or small balls of cotton-wool covered in stretched crêpe paper wired with fuse (fine) wire at the base, and these can

A thick wire forms the stem, onto which the bundle of wrapped paper is wired with thin florist's wire. The other flower shows the finished stage, when the second colour has been wrapped around the flower head, and strips of crêpe paper wound very tightly around the wired part, hiding the wire and forming the calyx. The paper wrapping is continued all down the stem.

The wires are wrapped in gutta percha, or florist's tape, and the sprays are attached to the main stem at intervals.

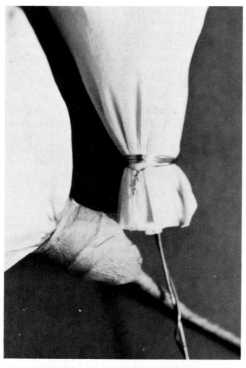

The finished flowers arranged in a vase.

be used singly, or in groups of three. Beads can be wired singly, the wire twisted very tightly immediately underneath the bead, singly or in groups. The wire can be bent roughly at the top into a lump and tightly wrapped with crêpe paper. Glue a sequin or beads to the tip, or dip in PVA and roll in poppy, coriander, or mustard seeds. Tissue or crêpe paper can be fringed and rolled tightly into a bunch and wired. For party decorations, use tiny Christmas tree baubles for the centres, or cellophane-wrapped sweets and candy.

Using reel wire, attach the petals one by one pulling the wire very tight as you do so. Again wind a few times round the stem to finish. Cover the base of the petals by wrapping another strip cut as a calyx around it. The wire this time will be attached to the stem wire only. Finally, wrap the wire with either gutta-percha or a strip of crêpe paper, starting from the calyx.

The flower petals themselves can also be used double, and glued with a spray adhesive. A subtle change of colour between each side of the petal looks attractive, or paint a very fine line of bleach along the edge of the petal. The hollowing of some petals (roses, for example) can be achieved by stretching gently as one presses with the thumbs. The cut edge can also be frilled by gently pulling all round the edge. A curled edge is made by rolling the edge around a knitting needle.

One can make paper assume the crinkled quality of a just-opened poppy petal by first rolling the paper round the handle of a wooden spoon, then pushing from both ends towards the centre, crushing it. Pull it off, smooth it out, and the paper is ready for use. Alternatively, fold some tissue paper in half and cut out some petals. Put five or six of them in a pile inside a handkerchief. Hold the base of them firmly down on the table with the heel of your palm, and with the other hand squeeze the handkerchief and very gently, pull, creasing the petal along its length.

Fruit can also be made very simply. For *blackberries*, wrap some wire with a ball of cotton-wool, the size of a blackberry. Cover with some purple crêpe paper pulled taught, and wire at the base of the ball with fine wire. Paint with dilute PVA and cover with coriander seed, or tapioca and paint. *Snowberries* can be made in a similar way from white crêpe paper, omitting the seeds. The berry is then dipped into hot candle wax until a thick layer of wax is built up. To make the berry very shiny, dip immediately in cold water. It is possible to omit the crêpe paper altogether, and dip the tightly screwed-up cotton wool, which has been wired onto the stem, directly into the hot wax.

Finishes

Waxing Use candle wax, melted in a double boiler. Make sure that there is enough wax in the saucepan to completely cover the flower, without bending the petals at all. Wax the flowers and leaves before they are wired together. Submerge the flower or leaf completely in the hot wax, but quickly lift it out, twizzling the flower as you do so. Shake off any drips of wax promptly. The leaves can be plunged into cold water to cool the wax rapidly, and this gives it a shiny translucent appearance. Do not put waxed flowers near a radiator or in the sun.

Lacquer or clear acrylic This can be sprayed onto the finished flowers, or try dipping them in thin lacquer.

Flowers from a circle of paper Cut out circles of tissue paper, make a cut in the centre of the circle, and curl over a pair of scissors. Glue the centre to some white thread-covered wire. Fold into four, creasing only the second fold. Glue the creased edges together and glue to a piece of wire.

Flowers from a crumpled folded strip Around a long rule wrap a length of tissue, wide enough to go around the rule several times, and leave an inch or so over. Push together, then pull out the rule, and roll up the crumpled strip, using the length of paper at the bottom. Insert a length of wire into the centre of the flower with some glue on the tip, and wire the flower to it firmly.

FURTHER READING

IVES, S., *Making Paper Flowers* Batsford

Flowers made by wrapping paper round a broom handle, and crushing it into a small bundle. When it is released and taken off the handle the creases made are permanent.

The edges of these petals were lightly touched with some domestic bleach, which, on crêpe paper, runs down in irregular streaks.

FABRIC FLOWERS

Materials

organdie, silk, velvet, voile, cotton; dyes (Dylon cold dye, thickened: Magic markers, felt-tip pens, coloured inks); stiffening (gum-arabic, spray starch); wire (15-amp fuse wire, 5-amp fuse wire, florist's wire); transparent glue (UHU); purchased stamens; paint brush; nail varnish, or PVA glue (white glue) or Elmer's Glue-All.

Equipment

scissors; bran cushion; curling tongs.

103

METHOD

The shapes of the petals and the construction of the flowers are the same as for paper flowers. The main difference is that with fabric one has a woven material and the petals are all cut with the centre line of the petal on the bias of the fabric. This is essential, because without this, it will be impossible to shape the petals.

Trace round the shape of the petals and leaves with a soft (3B) pencil, or tailor's chalk if the fabric is dark, on the fabric, making sure they are on the bias. Before cutting them out, paint round the line you have drawn with clear nail varnish or dilute PVA glue, in such a way that the nail varnish is on both sides of the line. When dry, cut out the shapes, which will not fray because of the nail varnish. To colour the petals, damp the white cloth, and apply either the inks, dye, or felt-tip pens, shading if you choose. When dry, stiffen the petals with spray starch or gum arabic.

To make the gum arabic, dissolve $\frac{1}{2}$ oz gum arabic crystals in $\frac{1}{4}$ pint water by placing them in a jar in a saucepan of water, and heat until the crystals have dissolved. Strain and keep in a screw-top jar. A solution of this gum, 5 tsps to $\frac{1}{4}$ pint water, is made and the petals are soaked in this, taken out, and laid flat to dry. Iron within 15 minutes of applying the solution with a medium hot iron. To shape the petals, press over a bran cushion with a warm iron.

To make a bran cushion, make a cotton cushion approximately 6 in. by 9 in. and fill with bran from a pet food store. If you have a pair of curling tongs, use these to curl the tips of the petals of roses, in particular. The wire stiffener used in between two layers to make a leaf can be attached when the two parts are fused together with a double-sided contact adhesive film (such as Bondina Wundaweb). This very fine cobweb-like substance disappears completely when the leaf is ironed.

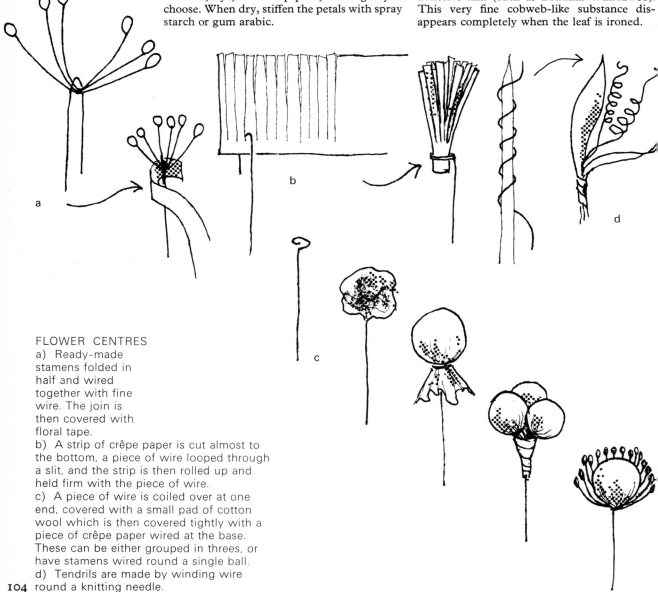

FLOWER CENTRES
a) Ready-made stamens folded in half and wired together with fine wire. The join is then covered with floral tape.
b) A strip of crêpe paper is cut almost to the bottom, a piece of wire looped through a slit, and the strip is then rolled up and held firm with the piece of wire.
c) A piece of wire is coiled over at one end, covered with a small pad of cotton wool which is then covered tightly with a piece of crêpe paper wired at the base. These can be either grouped in threes, or have stamens wired round a single ball.
d) Tendrils are made by winding wire round a knitting needle.

e) Petals are cut in two layers, and a strip of double-sided sticky tape is placed down the centre and on this is laid the wire.

f) The two pieces are pressed together and the top edge stretched by pulling between the thumbs. Two such petals wrapped around a completed centre, and wired.

g) The final petals are attached overlapping the previous joins in the petals, and after wiring, wrapped in floral tape.

h) Another method of curling the edges of a petal by rolling it around a stiletto or fine knitting needle.

i) To hollow out the centre of a petal, stretch gently between the thumbs. The arrow shows the direction of the 'grain' of the paper.

j) Leaves are made by folding the paper in half (the dotted line is the fold) drawing the edge shape and then cutting the shape out. Two layers are needed for each leaf, which are constructed in the same way as the petals.

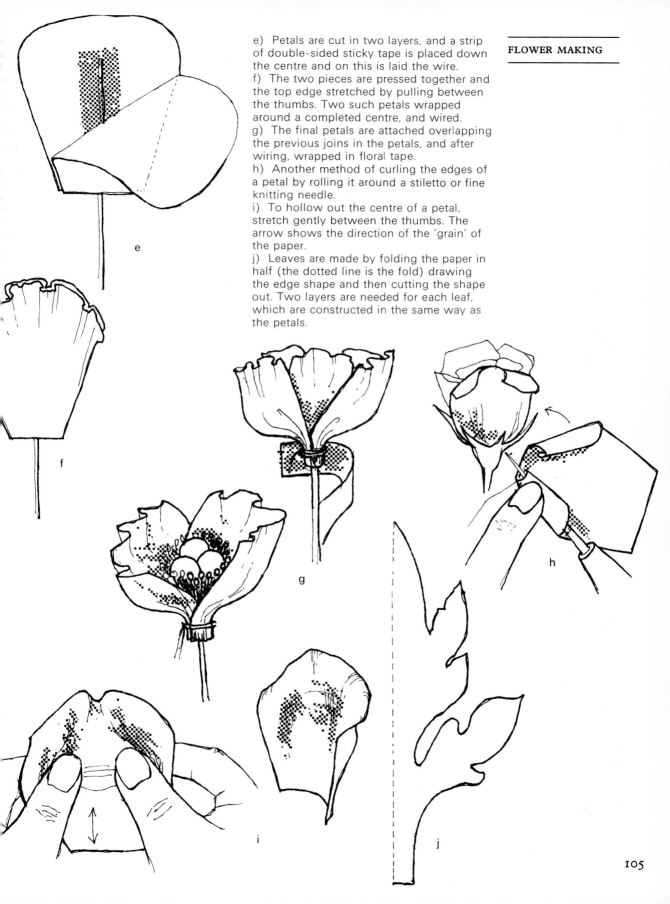

e

f

g

h

i

j

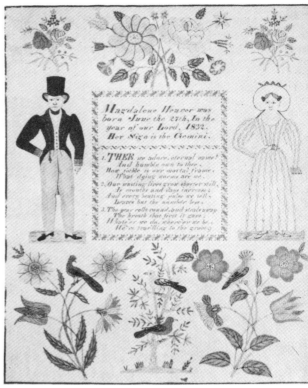

Four very old examples of fractur: two
birth certificates, a family register and a
baptismal certificate.

Fractur

Fractur is the name given to a combination of decorative calligraphy and watercolour painting which reached its distinctive American heights in the late 1700s and early 1800s. Brought to America (Pennsylvania in particular) by German immigrants, it was the art of *fractur-schriften*, meaning the art of writing in a particular German Gothic style based on the type face called *fractur*. The new settlers in America needed documents – birth certificates, marriage certificates, family registers, etc., and almost every group of eighteenth-century settlers in Pennsylvania had a schoolmaster or minister who could supply them with these documents, written and decorated in this very particular way. Gradually the calligraphic importance was replaced by emphasis on the decorative figures, animals and plants which bordered the certificates. Schoolmasters and clergymen for generations had specialized in these hand-made certificates, each one quite unique. By 1819 the vogue for fractur was so great that an instruction book was printed and it was taught in schools. The schools in the German communities of Pennsylvania taught Gothic lettering and illumination until the 1850s, when the English school system was established, coinciding with the introduction of printed certificates. The need was no longer there, and fractur work almost disappeared.

The choice of subject matter in the border was specific and symbolic, the meaning being important to the recipient. The position of the hands of a clock on a birth certificate indicated the time of birth of the baby, unicorns represented virginity, hearts, love and marriage, etc. 'House blessings' were another stock in trade of the itinerant fractur artists, as were valentines, book marks, and special presentation pictures. The early house blessings on sale in Britain in the nineteenth century were also written in a rather tormented Gothic script, e.g. 'God Bless This House', 'What Is A Home Without A Mother', etc. The earliest American fractur was done for nonconformist sects such as the Moravians, and it is intriguing to see just how much of the folk art of Middle Europe was kept alive in America. (See also Glass-painting.)

FURTHER READING
LIPMAN, *American Folk Decoration* Dover

French Knitting

Although 'knitting dollies' can be bought, French knitting used to be done on an empty wooden cotton reel (thread spool). Now that most reels are made of plastic, and impossible to put nails in, its demise is imminent, unless really cheap plastic dollies are produced, for this is essentially a children's craft.

The only equipment needed is an old cotton reel and four small nails. These are arranged evenly around the hole, and hammered in to within $\frac{1}{2}$ in. of the nail head. Nails without any heads are best. Make a single knot around one nail, about 6 in. from the end of the wool, which is poked down the hole in the cotton reel. Hold onto it by wrapping it around a finger on the left hand. Wind the wool around the remaining nails. Now the first row is started. Continue in the way you were winding, and lay the thread across the next nail (the one you put the knot on). With a blunt needle, or a small crochet hook, take the loop of the knot, slip it up and over the nail but leaving the thread you have just laid there in place. Continue going round and round, slipping one thread off at each nail as you go. To change colour, simply tie the next colour of wool onto the end of the previous one. Keep pulling at the tail of wool or knitting hanging out at the bottom of the cotton reel, to keep the tension tight. Otherwise, the stitches might all slip off the nails, and all the knitting will disappear down the hole, coming undone in the process.

A tube of knitting is produced, and though it cannot be done with less than three nails, the only restriction to the number of nails is the size of the hole. The striped tube can be very attractive, and the lengths can be made up into hats by coiling like a coiled pot, and sewing each coil to the next, or purses, belts or scarves.

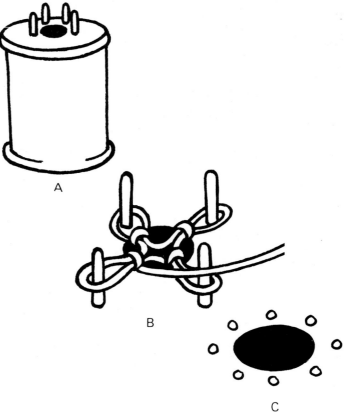

A

B

C

Glass

GLASS ETCHING

Acid etching on glass was made possible by the discovery in 1771 of hydrofluoric acid. If used absolutely pure, it will 'eat' away the surface of the glass, but leave it perfectly clear, so, in order to produce the pearled finish which is what we recognize as etched glass, an alkali is added to the acid to produce either sodium bifluoride, or ammonium bifluoride.

Begin by experimenting on a piece of flat glass, as opposed to an old jam jar, because it takes skill to keep the acid on a curved surface while it is actually etching the glass. The concept is yet another variation on stencilling. The clear glass is protected by a material while the glass being etched is left exposed. The simplest blocking-out material is a self-stick vinyl contact paper, such as Fablon, which can be cut with a craft knife, and the design peeled off. The backing is then peeled off, and the Fablon film is stuck onto the perfectly clean sheet of glass.

The parts of the glass which are etched are clearly visible in this lampshade, appearing pearly white.

Leave the film on for at least a couple of hours, if possible overnight, because it sticks even more firmly if left for a long time. If it is not really well stuck down, there is the risk that the acid will leak under the edge, and give a very ragged look to the design when the Fablon is peeled off. If working on a curved surface put a lump of Blu-Tack (Plasti-Tak) either side of the glass to stop it rolling about.

Apply the acid with a ball of cottonwool tied onto the end of a piece of dowelling or with cotton swabs. Leave it on for 5 to 10 minutes depending on the manufacturer's instructions but since there are so many variables, experience is the only real guide, which is why the need to experiment first is always stressed. Wash the acid off with warm water, peel off the Fablon, and it is finished.

Remember, although it is a weak solution, it is still acid, and could cause a burn. If you get any on your clothes, or in your eyes, splash with lots of water.

An etching transferred to glass, the background blacked out and the shapes of the people and the snakes backed with crushed coloured metal foil.

LEADED GLASS

Leaded glass is a jigsaw made of pieces of glass which, unlike the jigsaw of cardboard, are permanently held together after they have been fitted. The method of holding them together is, traditionally, with strips of lead which in section are like a capital letter H. The cross bar of the H follows the edges of the pieces of glass, which are hidden by the two projecting arms of the H. When all the pieces of glass have been cut, and the lead 'came' cut to fit each part, the whole is assembled, piece by piece, and when it is finished, the joints are all soldered together.

A variation on this method is the use of copper sheet, either self-adhesive strip or sheet copper cut into strips, to enclose each piece of glass. These wrapped pieces of glass are then fitted together and soldered.

The main difference between lead came and copper foil is that lead is soldered only at the joints, while copper foil is soldered along the whole length of the copper, no copper being visible at all on the finished product. Thus it has the advantage of being very strong for hanging glass objects, and because it is very simple to cut strips of different widths, pieces of glass of very different thicknesses can be used with ease in one piece of work. In lead came, the height is generally $\frac{3}{16}$ in. (the height of the inside of the cross bar of the H) although there are other sizes available. It becomes complicated if different thicknesses of glass are included in one design, or if one wants to include 'jewels'.

A mahogany-framed room divider of leaded glass, by Tom Rodriquez, San Rafael, California.

Leaded glass can be used for very large projects such as church windows, or for small three-dimensional projects such as lamp shades. First get to grips with the materials used, and master the techniques of cutting glass and soldering. Tidiness is important; the working surface must be frequently brushed free from the smallest glass splinters, which are a hazard to you, and make the accurate cutting of glass impossible.

The equipment and materials needed for leaded glass are flat sheet glass, lead cames or copper foil, glass-cutting equipment, lead working equipment, soldering tools and materials, tools used in actually carrying out the work.

Ordinary commercial clear glass was used to make this interesting solid geometrical shape, which is used as a terrarium.

A detail of the famous Tiffany 'dragonfly' lampshade, showing the use of rounded ovals (globs). The wings of the dragonfly are of filigree bronze applied onto the glass.

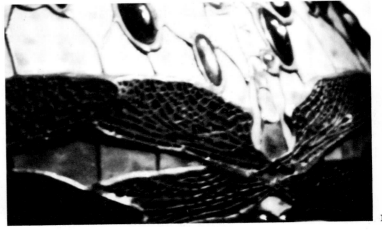

Glass cutter with interchangeable wheels. (Courtesy A. shaw and Son, London.)

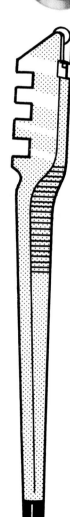

Types of glass

There are two main divisions: transparent glass (used in windows) which is seen only by transmitted light, and opalescent glass which both reflects and transmits light, and so is used in those projects where the glass is required to be seen 24 hours a day. Of the transparent glass, there is *pot glass*, which is coloured in the pot of molten glass, and so is a uniform colour throughout the sheet of glass, and *streaky*, which is glass with streaks of colour running through it. It is hand-mixed in the pot, so no two sheets of streaky will be the same. There is also the ordinary *clear commercial glass*. The pot and streaky glass are called 'antique', and are hand-made, though both hand-made and commercial glass can be made with a *textured surface*. Opalescent glass is made in both one colour and streaky.

Mirror glass is clear glass with a silver backing, and can be used as any other glass. *Flashed glass* is either white or clear glass with a coloured layer fused to it.

Bullions (or bull's eyes) are cut from the centre of a sheet of glass which has been spun into a large flat disc of glass. The outer edges of these discs were used for cutting window panes, and in old houses one can easily spot the swirl of the disc crossing through the pane. The nearer the centre of the disc of glass the pane is cut from, the more marked are the swirls, making the view through them quite distorted; in the centre of the disc, where the glass-blower's pipe (the pontil) was attached, is the bull's eye itself, the very centre of the bull's eye being where the pontil was broken off. These were the cheapest panes of all, since one could see nothing through them at all, hence their use in poor cottages; bullions are now specially sought after and are expensive extras. *Roundels* are commercially made bullions which are a uniform size and made in a disc-shape. *Jewels* are the coloured, faceted small pieces of glass seen in so many Victorian and Edwardian leaded glass door-windows. *Globs* are lumps of glass, partially melted in a kiln until they have formed smooth rounded shapes.

Materials which can be used in *copper foiled glass* are Philippine transparent shells, and sections of stones or polished pebbles.

Tools for glass cutting

Buy the best possible glass cutter you can afford. Without a first-class cutter, all your skill will be wasted. Diamond cutters are not suitable; one needs a wheel cutter, with interchangeable tungsten wheels. Shaws and Diamantor are two recommended makes. Keep it in a jar of oil when not using it, otherwise rust can form on the wheel, and this makes it impossible to cut with it. The oil also helps to keep the score-line open prior to cracking it open. Some cutters have a *ball end* to tap the score line from the underside and produce a crack which will run along the score line.

To cut circles there are special *circle cutters*, which can cut circles up to 24 in. diameter. *Glass pliers* (nippers) are used to break off pieces of glass after they have been scored and tapped. Those with a jaw width of $\frac{3}{4}$ in to 1 in. are the most suitable: the smaller width for sharp angles in the score line, the wider ones for breaking off long strips of glass. *Grozers* are flat nosed, soft pliers which are used to remove any uneven pieces of glass remaining after cutting, i.e. the shape is 'grozed'.

Panel showing 'antique' streaky glass.

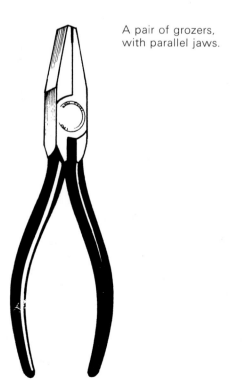

A pair of grozers, with parallel jaws.

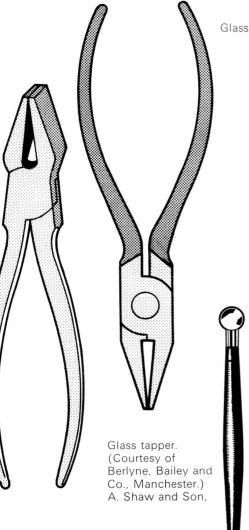

Glass tapper.
(Courtesy of
Berlyne, Bailey and
Co., Manchester.)
A. Shaw and Son,

By turning the top handle, a circle is
scribed on the glass.

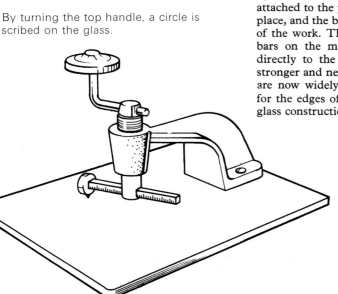

Lead cames

H-frame lead cames are made in 5-ft lengths,
and are either flat-section or round-section.
The widths of the came range from $\frac{3}{16}$ in.,
$\frac{1}{4}$ in., $\frac{5}{16}$ in., $\frac{3}{8}$ in., $\frac{7}{16}$ in., $\frac{1}{2}$ in., $\frac{5}{8}$ in., $\frac{3}{4}$ in. to $\frac{7}{8}$ in.,
and a selection of widths in a large project adds
a lot of life to a design. Whether one chooses
flat section or round section is really a matter
of personal choice, though round section is
usually used for the inside leading of a picture,
and in lamps. The main measurement used to
describe cames is the width of the face. The
width of the cross bar of the H, known as the
heart width, will always be supplied $\frac{1}{16}$ in. The
height of the heart is, unless otherwise specified, $\frac{3}{16}$ in. Before ordering the came, check on
the thickness of the glass you are using. Some
glass varies in thickness, along its edge,
especially hand-made glass, in which case
choose the size of came to accommodate the
thickest part of the glass. The most widely used
came width for both panels and lamps is $\frac{1}{4}$ in.
and $\frac{5}{16}$ in., but leading all of one size becomes
very monotonous.

There is a special lead came known as
reinforced steel core lead. These are used for
strengthening large windows every 2 ft, on
windows over 3 ft square. Note that the heart
width of these cames is larger than the standard
width, and if you are making a window to fit a
precise opening, this difference has to be
allowed for when measuring the design.
Another method of reinforcing larger projects
is by attaching *saddle bars* to the finished piece
of work at the back. Because these cylindrical
bars are made of steel they cannot be soldered
to the work, and are fastened to the glass panel
by means of copper wire ties. The rods are
attached to the piece before it is set in its final
place, and the bars must span the entire width
of the work. There are now some galvanized
bars on the market which can be soldered
directly to the window, which makes for a
stronger and neater product. U-section cames
are now widely available and these are used
for the edges of lamps or other free-standing
glass constructions.

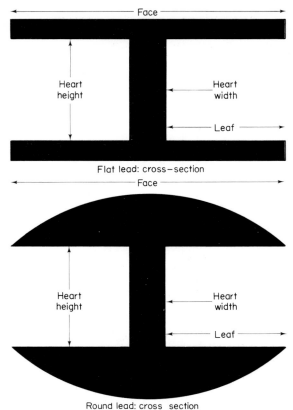

Flat lead: cross–section

Round lead: cross section

The two sections of lead came.

When you have completed your design, measure all the lines and work out how much came you will need, and in which widths. Lead came is sold by weight, and is expensive, so estimate as nearly as you can exactly how much you need, erring on the over-estimate. This is to avoid finding yourself a few inches short, and unable to complete a project without returning to your suppliers. Keep the came flat and straight when storing it.

Lead working tools

The lead cames have to be cut, and though there is no special came-cutter on the market yet, a putty knife or lino-cutting knife can be used. Lead knives must be kept sharp by regular honing. Use a rocking motion to cut through the came, gradually pressing down as you do so. Do not saw your way through. A *lathekin* also has to be improvised from a piece of wood such as a ruler, whittled down to a rounded end. It is used to open out the leaves of the came, just before it has the glass placed in it.

Three methods of making the outside joints in the came around a panel: (a) is a direct butt (b) both parts are mitred (c) the leaves of one side of the came are opened up a little to accommodate the adjoining section of came. The outside edge of panels which are to be fitted into a window, or other frame, is usually H-section came. This is to allow for any possible inaccuracies in the final measurements of the panel.

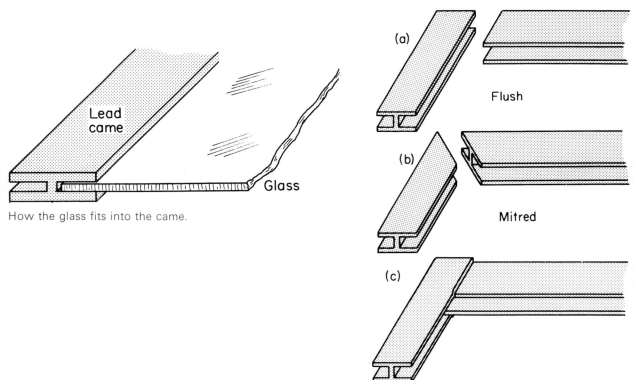

How the glass fits into the came.

(a) Flush

(b) Mitred

(c)

A *lead vice* is used to stretch the came before it is cut, to strengthen and straighten it. It, too, has to be improvised. Use a cleat, which can be bought at any yachting shop. Fasten one end of the came in this, and grip the other end very firmly with a pair of pliers. Give a slow, steady pull. A sudden jerk can make it snap. A *stopping knife*, another improvised tool, is used for making sure that the pieces of glass all fit snugly into the lead came. The end of the blade must be smooth and rounded, and an oyster knife can be turned into a stopping knife by holding the tip over a flame until it is red hot and then bending it with pliers.

Lathekin in use, opening up the channel in the came.

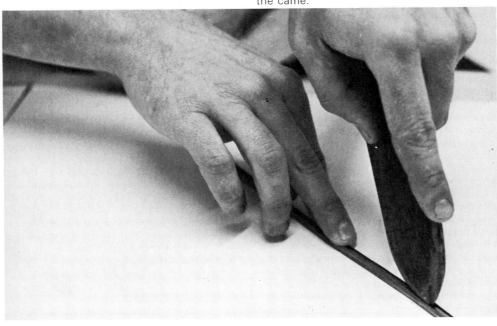

Cutting the lead came.

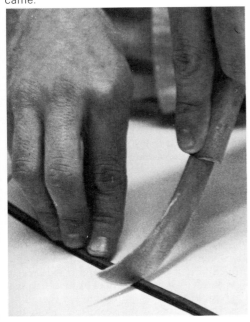

Two improvised lead cutters, below, a linoleum knife, above, a putty knife.

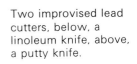

An oyster knife with its tip made into a stopping end.

A boat cleat, or lead stretcher.

Soldering equipment

Choose an electric soldering iron in the 60–125 watt range, with interchangeable bits. The Weller 60-watt iron is excellent for this work, because it has a temperature control unit, called a 'sensor', which keeps the temperature of the iron within certain defined limits. This is very important, because if the iron gets too hot, the solder melts too rapidly, and can run straight through to the underside of the work, and even melt the lead came itself. If on the other hand it does not get hot enough, the solder does not melt sufficiently and drags on the iron, leaving a rough textured surface. Soldering 'bits' can be left in the natural copper state (all bits are made of copper), or coated in nickel or iron, iron being the most long-lasting. The disadvantage of copper tips is that they corrode, and they *must* be tinned every time before use. Nickel and iron plated bits are kept clean the same way, simply wipe them with a wet cloth. Always place the soldering iron on its cradle inbetween soldering, because the hot tip will burn whatever it is put down on.

Solder is a metallic substance which has a lower melting point than the metal being joined. The solder fills up the gaps between the two pieces of metal by running into the gaps when hot, and then solidifying to make the joint permanent. The most appropriate solder for leaded glass is 60/40, i.e. 60/tin, 40/lead. Use the stick solder, called blow-pipe solder.

Flux, the mildest possible, made from tallow and oleic acid, is used on the cleaned lead came to prevent it oxidizing and to help the 'weeting' by the solder. It acts as a catalyst between the lead and the solder. It is available as either a liquid or a paste; use the paste, as the liquid flux tends to run off the joint. Use a brush to apply the flux paste, brushing it well into the joints.

The Weller electric soldering iron (100 watt) in its bench-holder (cradle). The tip is iron-plated and has a 'sensor' in it which controls the temperature within set limits.

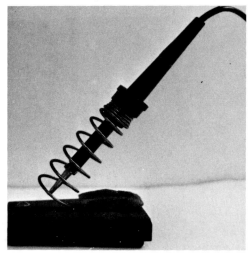

Tools

Nails are needed to hold the pieces of glass in place while the pieces and the came are being assembled. Horseshoe nails are the best for this; if you have to use round nails, cut a 1-in. piece of came between the glass and the nail.

Brushes Three will be needed: a stiff one for brushing the flux paste on (an old paint brush cut down); a wire brush (e.g. a suede brush or steel wool) for cleaning the lead came to remove the oxidization that forms on it, and which must be removed before soldering can be successful; and a brush for sweeping down the bench. A very weak pair of *sunglasses* is useful to protect your eyes from any particles of glass which might fly around.

Moulds are essential for free design in lampshades. For this use the copper foil technique, because it gives much more freedom of design than does the lead came. These can be improvized from polythene bowls found around the house, but if you want a special shape, this will have to be made out of wood or plaster of Paris.

Pattern shears are expensive, but specially constructed so that when you cut up your design into the various shapes, $\frac{1}{16}$ in. is automatically cut out as you do so. This is the space that will be taken up by the heart width of the cross bar of the came. One can construct a very effective cutter by fastening two razor blades on either side of a strip of wood $\frac{1}{16}$ in. thick.

How to cut the glass

Sweep the work top, and ensure that it is perfectly flat. Take a small scrap of glass to practise on, and hold the glass cutter exactly as shown in the photograph. Hold the glass steady with one hand, and beginning at the edge furthest away from you (about $\frac{1}{8}$ in. from the edge) draw the tool towards you in one continuous movement and run it off the edge. Go back to the beginning of the cut and run the tool off the edge in the opposite way. Keep the same pressure throughout the cut, otherwise the glass will not break along the score line. Never go over a score line for a second time. Practise cutting straight lines in the glass until you have mastered the technique.

To break the piece of glass, hold it firmly at each edge of the score line, and give a sharp snap downwards. It should break cleanly along the score line. Another method, if cutting straight lines, is to lay the score line exactly on the edge of the workbench, and, holding each part of the glass firmly, bend the glass down sharply, and it should snap along the scored line. If the piece of glass is too narrow to hold in your hand, use a pair of glass pliers. The same technique can be used over the edge of a ruler.

Cutting curves is more difficult. Make a series of curved score lines, starting with a slightly curved line, making it more and more curved as you move along the piece of glass. Using the ball-end of the glass cutter, tap the score line directly underneath the score line. Hold the

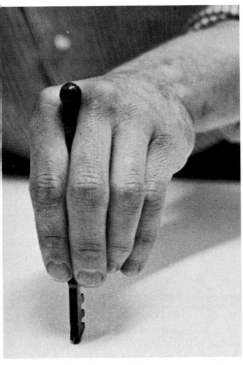

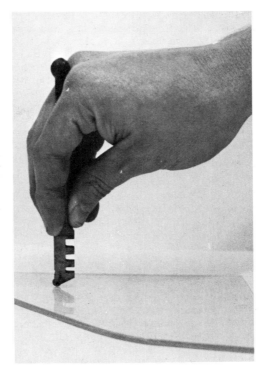

Front and side views of the correct way to hold a glass cutter, that is, absolutely vertically.

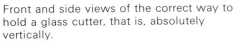

The score mark on the glass has been made more visible as a result of tapping with the ball end of the glass cutter.

Hold the glass very firmly near the score line at the edge of the glass, and snap sharply downwards. (For safety, the beginner should wear gloves for all glass cutting operations.)

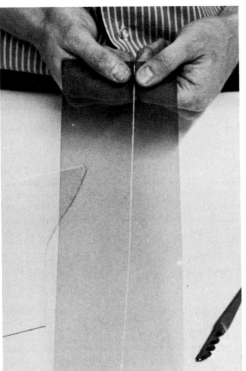

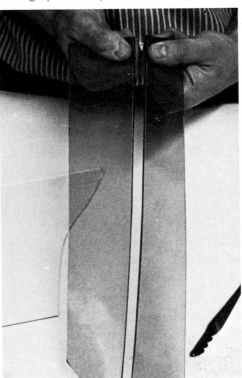

glass so that both sides of the score line are equally securely held while the tapping is being done. Do the tapping very gently. If the pieces do not separate while the tapping is being done, part them with the glass pliers.

The sequence of cuts for making
(a) a convex cut (b) a concave cut
(c) a semicircle.

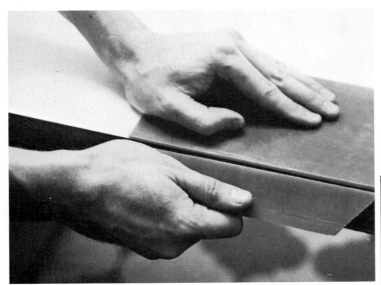

Another method of snapping the glass, which has been scored in a straight line, by resting the score line exactly along the edge of a work table, and pressing down.

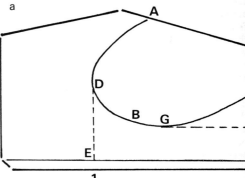

a

Glass pliers used to break off the curved piece of glass.

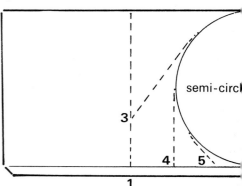

b

c

semi-circle

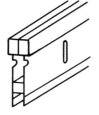

Two razor blades fastened together to cut out the exact width of the came 'heart' ($\frac{1}{16}$ in.).

Tapping leaves a rather jagged line to the edge of the glass. Nibble away at these pieces with the grozer.

For the sequence of cutting score lines for circles, concave and convex curves, see the diagrams. It is not possible to cut these shapes in one go: the glass would shatter.

Working a flat design

Make your first piece a simple flat design. Do not begin with a lampshade: they come later. Draw a simple design on a piece of paper the actual size you want it to be. Colour it with felt-tip pens or oil pastels. Draw in the actual thickness of the lead lines, and colour them in with a black felt-tip pen. These strong black lines are an integral part of leaded glass, and should be made a positive part of the design.

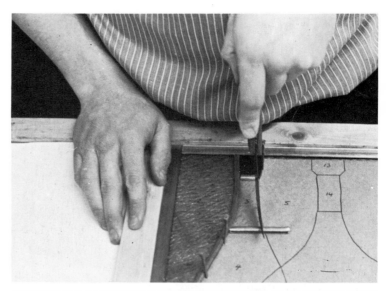

You will need two pieces of paper, one piece of manilla paper and two sheets of carbon paper the size of the drawing. Put the manilla paper at the bottom, the carbon paper ink-side down onto it, then thin drawing paper with the second sheet of carbon paper face down on that, and the finished drawing on the top. Go over all the lines very carefully with a ball-point pen, pressing quite hard so that the pressure goes right through to the manilla paper. The lines you draw will be the centre line of your leading. The top drawing is pinned up in front of you with each part numbered and coloured. The second copy is placed on your workboard and the panel will be assembled on it, each part of the glass jigsaw being placed on its matching shape. The manilla paper, which is sturdy, is carefully cut up into the pieces. These are placed onto the appropriate coloured glass and secured there with double-sided tape, so that it does not move a fraction of an inch while you are cutting. The cutting of the manilla is done with either the pattern shears or with the arrangement of two razor blades. Cut the pieces out, taking care to keep the line of the drawing running exactly down the centre between the blades. With the pattern piece securely attached to the glass, follow the edge exactly with the glass cutter. Groze all the irregular pieces of glass away until the edge is smooth. Continue until all the pieces have been cut.

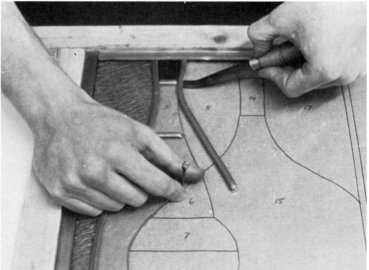

Cutting the lead came at an angle so that it will fit snugly against its adjoining came. Note the drawing underneath, with all the pieces numbered, and the two pieces of wooden battening, into which two pieces of came for the outside edge are placed and into which the pieces of glass are inserted.

The stopping knife is used to push the lead firmly against the glass.

The back of the lead knife is used to push the glass firmly between the lead came leaves and right up against the 'heart'.

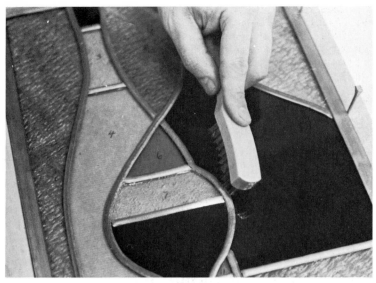

The pieces of glass and the came have all been fitted together. The remaining two sides of the battening have now been placed in position and are held there with farrier's nails, keeping the work completely immovable while the preparation for soldering and the soldering itself goes on. The wire brush is being used to remove the oxidized film on the lead at the joints.

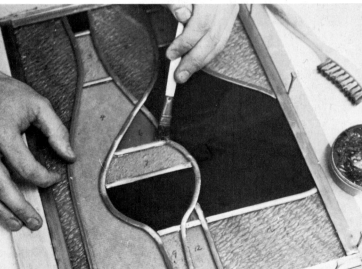

The flux paste being brushed on with a stiff bristle brush into the joints.

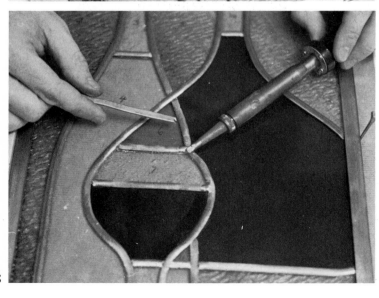

Solder the joint by holding the stick of solder directly over the joint, and bringing the soldering iron directly down on it.

Assembling the glass

Nail two strips of wood onto the work bench at right angles to each other. The first piece of glass is fitted into this corner and all the rest follow from it, but two lengths of H-section came are laid along the wooden battens first. The drawing is also in place before the first piece of glass is fitted into the came. You will, of course, have run your lathekin between the leaves of the lead came first. When you feel it fits snugly, keep it in place with a nail. Lay the next piece of came in place, pressing it home with a stopping knife, and cut it off at the angle of the line it intersects: this is important. The end of each piece of came must be cut so that it fits flush against the intersecting came. Place the next piece of glass in the preceding came, press home, hold in place with some nails, cut the next piece of came, and so on until the whole is completed. Finally, put on the remaining two outside lengths of came. The panel is now ready to be soldered.

How to solder

Clean all the joints with a wire brush to remove the oxidization, and immediately brush on the flux paste with its brush. Heat up the soldering iron, and holding the solder stick *on* the joint and not in the air above it, just touch the solder with the tip of the soldering bit so that only a small blob of solder is formed, which bonds the joint. Do not keep the iron on the spot, or you might melt the lead as well. Begin at the furthest point from you to prevent solder accidentally dropping on the glass. Work systematically through all the joints. Turn the panel over and solder all the joints on the other side in exactly the same way.

If it is an indoor panel, it is finished, apart from washing off the flux and excess solder, and going all over the lead leaves with the stopping knife, pressing the lead firmly onto the glass to make a really firm bond. If the window is to be used outside, every piece of lead will have to have putty forced between it and the glass. The putty used is more liquid (because it has more linseed oil in it) than the normal windowpane putty, and is brushed on with a stiff brush. Whiting is sprinkled onto the glass window to help the putty to dry quickly. Press the edges of the leaves down again onto the glass; this will force out some of the putty, which will have to be scraped off with a pointed wooden cocktail stick. Add some more whiting to the window, and scrub the glass clean with another brush.

COPPER FOIL TECHNIQUE

Any three-dimensional shape which can be put together flat on the work bench and bent into its final shape can be made with lead came. Otherwise, use copper foil. Copper foil can be bought in sheet form which you cut up into the width strip that you need for a given project, or in coils of self-adhesive copper strip which comes in various widths, the most useful being $\frac{3}{16}$ in., $\frac{1}{4}$ in., and $\frac{3}{8}$ in. The length is a standard 36 yd. It is possible to make your strip self-adhesive by spraying one side of the strip with a spray adhesive. 3Ms produce a range of excellent spray adhesives which, although initially seeming expensive, will prove to be a very economical buy in the long run, and are excellent adhesives. The tape is both easy and fast to use, and if you have a great many pieces of glass to wrap, it is worth the extra expense to save the time. A useful size of reel to buy is the $\frac{1}{4}$ in. width: if you need some narrower strips, it can be cut down in width.

In addition to pieces of glass, polished slices of rocks, pebbles and Philippine shell can be used; experiment with anything which is permanent and translucent.

Preparing the glass

Prepare the pieces of glass as for leading, but remember, *you do not have to allow for the width of the heart* when cutting your pattern pieces. Instead, cut them just a fraction smaller than the actual drawing, to allow for twice the thickness of the copper foil itself. Wash the pieces of glass in warm water and detergent to remove any oil which might still be on them from the glass cutter. Any trace of oil will prevent the foil from sticking to the glass.

Each piece of glass has to be wrapped all round its edge with the foil strip. Place the edge of the glass in the centre of the strip and fold the two sides around the glass. Continue rolling the glass shape along the foil strip, making sure that it is always in the centre of the strip, and folding the foil around the edge as you go. When you reach the point where you started, overlap it by $\frac{1}{4}$ in. or less and cut off the tape with a pair of scissors. Holding the piece in the air, squeeze the foil between your fingers all around the edge of the shape, and finally lay it down on the work bench and press it flat with a lathekin. The process of applying the foil strip is exactly the same as applying bias binding to the edge of a piece of cloth. The width of the foil must be the same on both sides of the glass shape for a really craftsman-like job.

Prepare all the pieces of glass in this way.

You do exactly the same thing if you are using sheet foil. Since it is sold in large rolls, cut up a piece into workable sized pieces, such as 6 in. by 12 in., and cut the strips from that. A copper sheet of 0·016 in. thickness is the advised thickness for copper foiling. If using sheet foil, the overlap on each piece of glass must be fluxed and soldered to hold it firmly on; it would fall out otherwise.

Assembling the glass for a flat piece of work

Lay the drawing onto the work table, and nail a strip of battening along two adjacent edges

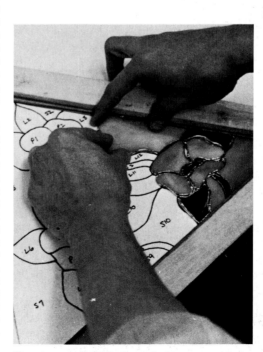

Wrapping copper foil around a cut piece of glass.

The copper-foiled pieces being assembled for a flat project.

(as for leading glass). Fold a strip of copper foil and lay it along the edge of the wooden battening. The pieces of foiled glass are laid into it as was the glass into lead came for leading glass. Fit all the pieces of foiled glass together, checking with the drawing underneath that you have got the pieces in the right place. If you have some small gaps between some pieces, they can be filled with solder; if the gaps are rather large, a folded piece of copper foil can be used to plug them. They will disappear when the soldering is applied, hiding the extra piece of copper foil. If, however, a gap is caused because some piece has been cut over size and throws all the other pieces out, then the remedy is to throw away that piece and cut another that fits properly.

Tacking
When all is in place, the pieces are 'tacked' together. This is done by putting a blob of solder at each point where the foil was overlapped on the glass shape. This will hold the whole thing together while you are doing the rest of the soldering proper.

Soldering
After tacking, the whole project is systematically soldered over every single join. No copper should be visible at all when you have finished. More solder is added until the line of solder is rounded uniformly. This process of building up the solder until it is rounded is called 'beading', and the craftsmanship of a piece of copper foiled glass is measured by the quality of the beading, which has to be done on both sides as for came leading. The width of the line made by the adjoining copper foil strips around the glass shapes is narrow, so you will have to change the bit in the soldering iron to one of $\frac{1}{4}$ in. size. The soldering on copper foil is continuous around every single piece of glass, not, as in lead came, only at the joints. This makes for a tidier finish to the copper foil, as well as a very strong structure. When both sides have been beaded, clean off all the flux and bits of solder with a soft brush and some liquid detergent. Dry with paper towels.

Finishing
The final stage is colouring the beading to give it an antique finish. This is done with a commercial blackener sold by gunsmiths and called 'gun blue'. Follow the instructions for application to the beading.

To finish the edge of a copper-foil project, as in the bottom edge of a lampshade, the copper is fluxed along the edge, and solder melted all the way along to give a smooth, even finish. Alternatively, you could use U-section lead came. There is no technical reason why you should not mix the two.

Although one has much greater freedom of construction with copper foiled glass, it is both slower and more expensive, because a great deal of solder is used making all the beading; both solder and lead came are sold by weight, and solder is the more expensive.

Three-dimensional work
Do not attempt a three-dimensional flowing shape unless you have a mould to work on: it simply is not possible. Paint your polythene bowl (plaster moulds will not need painting as they are white already) with white emulsion paint (house paint); draw out your design on it in pencil. Do not be too ambitious for your first project: one motif, which can be traced off and repeated two or three times round the lampshade will be fine. Remember that you have to actually draw it on the mould, and all the infilling pieces too. The glass is flat, and each piece has to be small enough to take this into account. Although you might be able to fit all the pieces of paper together, glass will not bend as the paper does, so do not cheat yourself in the designing stage.

Number every single shape drawn on the mould, and trace off the drawing onto a piece of paper, numbering the drawing as well. You will not be able to trace it off all at once. Because of the curves of the mould it will have to be done part by part, but since you have numbered every shape, you are not going to duplicate any

Attractive use of glass jewels in the flower centre. By 'Sirius', Swiss Village, Paris, France.

piece when it comes to cutting out the glass shapes.

The tracing paper is then laid onto a piece of manilla paper, with a piece of carbon paper ink-side down to the manilla paper between them, and the design is traced through. Cut the manilla paper into pieces, but again remember that this time you do not have to allow for the width of the heart, as in lead came. They should, though, be just a fraction smaller than the actual drawing because although there is no lead 'heart' to allow for, you still have to allow for twice the thickness of the copper foil itself. Decide on the colours of each part of the design before you begin cutting the glass. Check too on how the glass will actually look by holding it up to the light, either daylight or artificial. The colours must not be chosen in a vacuum: only certain colours are available in glass and these are the ones that you are going to have to design with.

Special lamp holders are obtainable for lampshades, both ceiling and table lamps in England, but special table-lamp bases are currently only available from America.

The design is drawn onto the lampshade mould.

When all the pieces are wrapped in foil, place them on the mould, beginning at the top, and holding them in place with pins. When working on a three dimensional project, tack each piece as it is assembled. When all has been tacked, solder and bead all the joins, first outside, then inside.

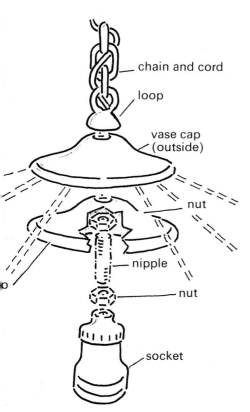

chain and cord

loop

vase cap
(outside)

nut

nipple

nut

socket

Electric fittings needed for a hanging lampshade.

This is an exciting craft with spectacular results, but do not attempt a project until you have gained some degree of expertise in cutting glass and soldering. Experiment substituting the epoxy 'leading' described in the section on stained glass-epoxy resin for lead came; it has a lot of potential.

FURTHER READING

DUNCAN, A., *The Technique of Leaded Glass* Batsford

'LEADED' GLASS USING EPOXY PUTTY

Epoxy putty method

A method of achieving an effect very similar to that of stained glass is to use an epoxy putty, stained with black, rolled into a thin sausage, and applied to a sheet of glass like the lines of lead in stained glass; the areas left between the epoxy are coloured with coloured stains. It can also be used to hold cut and shaped pieces of glass together as in traditional stained glass which would have used lead.

The simplest method of doing this is to draw out your design to the finished size, each line representing a line of epoxy putty. As with *cloisonné* enamelling, each area of colour must be bounded on all sides by a line of 'lead', so this must be taken into account when the design is made. Over the drawing lay the sheet of glass, which must be exactly the same size. The lines can be clearly seen through the glass and these are followed very carefully as the glass cutting tool is drawn carefully over the glass. Before starting this stage, make sure that you have had practice in cutting glass freehand, and in following lines on a piece of paper underneath it (see previous section).

When all the glass is cut, it is like a jigsaw that has been finished, but now, each piece has to be moved from its adjoining piece, and a length of rolled epoxy putty placed between them. The two pieces are then pushed back together again, squeezing the putty, so that a little is forced above and below the glass, while some remains between the two shapes. The finished piece of work will be larger than the drawing because of the spreading of the glass caused by the epoxy putty between each piece. It is for this reason that, for example, replacements to front door windows by this method are not recommended for a beginner, because the amount of expansion of the original design is so variable, and will be different for each design.

The putty must now be firmly pressed down onto the glass to ensure a good adhesion. To do this, either use a damp finger, or a roller which must also be dampened from time to time, or it will stick to the putty and lift it away from the glass. Leave it for 3 or 4 hours to harden off. Tidy the edges of the putty by rubbing with steel wool. The glass must be absolutely clean, so wipe with methylated spirits (denatured alcohol), surgical spirits or CTC. The glass can be painted with several materials: acrylic paint which dries very quickly; French enamels, which also dry very quickly; and the paints sold with the kits of epoxy putty, which take a lot longer, up to 6 hours, and it is recommended that no overpainting is done for 2 days.

With French enamels or acrylic paints the overpainting can be done as soon as the first coat is dry, within minutes.

Epoxy from a tube was used to draw black lines directly onto the shade. The black lines were treated as cloisonné and all shapes were enclosed and filled in with french enamels.

Putty laid on glass

To make a 'stained glass' panel without any cutting of shapes, lay the sheet of glass over the drawing as before, but this time apply the putty directly onto the glass, following the lines underneath. The glass still has to be scrupulously clean, so follow the instructions for cleaning above. How professional the finished panel will look will depend partly on how even the 'lead' lines are, which in turn depends on how evenly you rolled out the putty in the first place. It can be rolled either on a table top, as for the coils in coiled pottery, or by standing up and rolling the coils in your hand, allowing them to hang down as you roll. In either case, the end result should be a coil of about $\frac{1}{8}$ in. diameter and be as equal in diameter along its length as possible. Make sure that there are no gaps between the lines. Before the putty hardens, go over it with a dampened roller to flatten it until it is about $\frac{1}{4}$ in. wide.

The painting is done on the reverse side of the glass. Wait for the putty to harden off then turn the glass over and again clean thoroughly. Paint the spaces bounded by the lines, taking the colour just over the edge of the line (which is on the other side). This is to make it look neat on the right side. Do not paint right up to each adjoining colour. A gap must be left because the putty sticks much better directly to the glass. When the painting is finished and dry, roll out more putty and fill in the lines as before, trying to match them exactly to the lines on the other side. Leave to dry.

Ready-made plastic on acrylic and glass
An even simpler technique can be used to decorate acrylic and glass. The design is drawn in soft pencil, then these lines are followed by squeezing out a black ready-mixed plastic (like icing a cake). The black line stays raised up and becomes hard in half an hour. The areas are filled in by painting with French enamels. These dry rapidly, and another coat can soon be applied to intensify the colour, or overlay with another colour to make a new shade. The brushes must be washed in spirits before they begin to harden. They will be impossible to clean once they get really hard, and just have to be thrown away. These French enamels are perfectly fast to light, and are waterproof.

Resin on glass
Another method of applying colour to glass is with resin. Mix 225 grams of resin with 200 drops of catalyst (colour with the resin manufacturer's colour). Pour this over a sheet of horizontal glass. It will have jelled in about 4 hours and in this state it can be cut quite easily with a craft knife, and the unwanted shapes peeled off with the greatest of ease. Mix up some more resin and catalyst in either the same colour or a different one. If you use the same colour the intensity will be increased where it overlaps: if you use a different colour you will get a new colour where the two colours overlap. In 4 hours, it can again be cut and unwanted shapes peeled off. This can be done a third time if you choose. The most economical and efficient way of designing for overlaid resins is tissue paper.

Similar to the resin is the material used by shop window-dressers, a ready mixed liquid plastic paint called Krautol, which is painted on the inside of the window, and when dry can be cut and the unwanted pieces peeled off. It can also be painted over another colour without 'bleeding'. The range of colours is not very large, but is subtle.

PAINTING ON GLASS

Equipment
brushes (one very fine, one medium size); a sheet of glass; paints (acrylics, French enamels, oil or gouache); matt black paint (for the initial lining) and matt white (for the final backing); carbon tetrachloride (for cleaning).

Method
Draw a design, abstract or figurative, onto a piece of white paper which fits the piece of glass being used, using a fine felt-tip pen. Wash the glass carefully, dry it and lay it over the drawing. Clean the uppermost part of the glass with carbon tetrachloride, to make sure it is

absolutely grease free. Rest your hand on a scrap of paper or cloth to prevent fingerprints, and following the drawing underneath, paint a fine black line. Put in all the details. When it is dry, fill in the various parts with colour. Keep within the lines, because although you can go over them on the side you are painting, and apparently correct any slips of the hand, in fact when you turn the glass over, you will see that it still shows. Oil paints used to be used, but try acrylics: they dry fast, and have a huge range of colours. When all the areas have been completed, coat the whole of the painting with white paint. If it is not opaque, give it another coat (the paint should be a matt white) to give the greatest possible luminosity to the colours.

Temporary glass painting can be done on windows by mixing powder paint with thick Polycell (wallpaper paste), and painting directly onto the glass. This is fairly easy to wash off when required.

Painting on glass.

GLASS PICTURES

These were very popular in England between 1690 and 1790, enormously popular in Central Europe at the same time, and, on the lower half of American wall clocks, especially those made by the Ansonia Clock Co. in Connecticut, in America, too. The decline in popularity in all three areas was a result of the production of cheap colour prints.

A black or white engraving or mezzotint is placed ink-side down on a piece of clear glass coated with adhesive turpentine or Decal-it. The print is carefully pressed down all over the glass. The paper on which the engraving was made is moistened with water, and while it is still damp, the paper is rubbed off with a finger. This can be done leaving the black lines of the ink embedded in the adhesive. The line drawing is then filled in, with brilliant colours, from the back. Crushed foil can be applied on top of the painting, which adds a glitter to the colour when seen from the front.

FURTHER READING

CLARKE, H.G., *Story of old English Glass Pictures, 1690–1810* 1928

ROSE, J.A., *English Glass Pictures, or the art of painting mezzotint, 1690–1790* Paper 113, Circle of Glass Collectors

Glass Prints (Cliches-Verres)

These were a result of the invention of photography and the interest it aroused in the Barbizon painters, Corot, Millet, Daubigny, and T. Rousseau, in particular.

Paint a sheet of glass with opaque white paint, then make a drawing with an etching needle by scratching the lines into the paint, until the glass shows through. When the drawing is complete, lay the glass on a piece of light-sensitive paper, and pass light through these areas, thus reproducing the drawn lines in black on the white background. Several prints can be taken from one drawing in this way (see Photograms).

God's Eyes

These are known as ghost traps in Tibet where they are fastened to the roofs of houses. This very simple form of weaving across two sticks fastened in the form of a cross is found in many parts of the world. Nowadays they are made mostly in Mexico and South America, where they are given to children on their birthdays, the number of colours representing the number of years of the child.

Materials

Scraps of wool or thick embroidery thread: the wool can be of any thickness from 2-ply to rug wool. Any fibre may be used: wool, cotton, nylon, and other synthetics. Collect a range of yarn surface too: shiny and dull, bouclé, mohair, crêpe, chenille, etc. Rainbow wool gives interesting colour effects.

Two sticks are required; these can be: cocktail sticks (to make little god's eyes to hang on the Christmas tree); ice cream sticks; green plant-supporting sticks; thin dowelling; square section wood used in model making; half-round dowelling; even two branches of a tree. Also required: small screw eyes, and screw hooks; wooden beads with a large hole; glue (rapid drying).

METHOD

Mark the centre of both pieces of wood, apply a spot of glue to each of the sticks, then press them together at right angles. If not using wood with one flat side, cut flat notches where the arms intersect. Secure the end of the wool with glue, then bind the wool in a figure of eight knot to cover the centre. Begin winding round the four arms. When enough of that colour has been done, cut off the thread on one of the arms and glue it down. Start the new colour by gluing the end down, then continue winding until the wood no longer shows. If cocktail sticks have been used, fasten a bright glass or wooden bead on the tip of each point. If round dowelling has been used, screw eyes can be secured into the top, and when several have been done, they can all be connected. Alternatively, attach tassels to each end. More than one arm can be put across the upright.

God's eyes made from coloured wool.

Constructing and joining God's eyes.

Hair-pin Crochet

This was called Maltese lace in the nineteenth century, when it was very popular. The crocheting is done over a metal frame which looks like a huge hair-pin, the two ends of which are secured in a wooden bar. Loops of wool are wound around two parallel bars, and fastened together down the middle. One has to have a frame to work on, to keep the tension tight, and to make sure the loops on either side are the same length. The stitch in hair-pin crochet is made with an ordinary crochet hook between the two uprights, the wool being taken around the wire before each stitch, first on one side, then on the other.

Equipment

a crochet hook (the size will depend on the thickness of the wool or yarn used); a hair pin for crocheting on; wool of any thickness or type.

The frame has been turned three-and-a-half turns before working the centre.

Looping the thread.

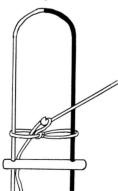

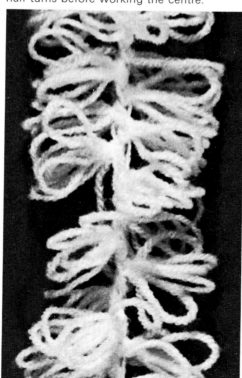

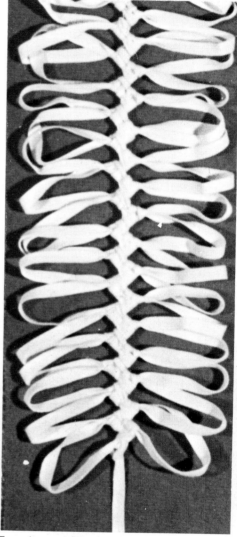

Experiment with different types of thread: mohair, Raffene, rainbow wool, string, polypropylene, etc.

FURTHER READING
BARKER, J., *Making Plaits and Braids* Batsford
KINMOND, J., *The Coats Book of Lacecrafts: Crochet, Tatting, Knitting* Batsford

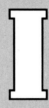

Ikat

Ikat weaving consists of tie-dyeing the yarn before weaving; it is a common method of weaving in, for example, Malaysia and Africa. One can tie-dye the warp and use a plain weft, and weave in such a way that the warp pre-dominates – or one can do the same with the weft. One can also do a double ikat with both the warp and weft tie-dyed. String the yarn to be dyed on a frame, then wrap it and dye it in successive dye baths. The pattern forms as the material is woven, and this gives a nicely blurred outline to the design.

A skein of white cotton dyed in various colours while still in the skein. One end of the skein is placed in one pan of dye, and the other end in a pan of different coloured dye. The white area left in the centre can either be left white, or put in another pan of dye later when the other two ends have been rinsed free of excess dye.

Inks

Ink can be bought either as a powder, to which one adds water, or ready-mixed. Indian and Chinese inks are usually waterproof, i.e. when dry, water can be spilt or deliberately put over the drawing as a wash, and there will be no 'bleeding' from the ink drawing. The ink powders listed in school catalogues are usually in a fairly limited range, but if too much powder to water is used, especially with the purple and green, when the ink dries there is a golden iridescence on the surface which is just like the elusive iridescence on a starling's breast. There is one make of powdered inks, however, which is available in a huge range of colours, and is inexpensive. Called Brusho, and sold by Ducketts, it can be made up into ink and used for pen and wash drawing; painting; screen printing when thickened with Polycell to give it body; painted onto cloth for stage clothes and puppet clothes; batik on cloth and on paper (as long as it is not washed).

Powdered inks are not so readily available in the United States. Both Higgins and Speed-ball produce a wide range of liquid inks for drawing and printing; wash inks for water-colour painting, waterproof drawing inks, fluorescent lettering inks, etc.

TOOLS FOR DRAWING IN INK
There are traditional pens with metal nibs in various shapes and widths. Experiment with bird feather quills, using both the shaft and the feather, bamboo with the end cut at an angle, a twig, a roll of paper, a straw, a hair grip, a piece of cardboard, or a twig with the end cut and a piece of felt put in the split. Also try brushes of all kinds, from a distemper brush to a cottonwool bud.

PAPER
Use cartridge (white drawing) paper, a good quality white paper. One can use newsprint but it tears easily, especially when wet. The ink also 'bleeds' on this paper; this is a quality which is very attractive when you want it and can control it. Experiment with scrap wrapping paper, or coloured paper. If you have none, make some. Brush some white paper with a strong solution of potassium permanganate (from any chemist or drug store). Alternatively, colour some paper with Brusho inks or strong tea. When the colouring agent is dry,

127

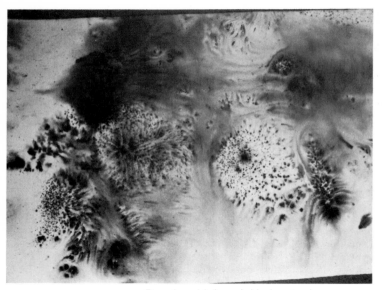

instead of drawing with black ink use a bleaching agent, and you will have a delicate white or ivory coloured drawing. On potassium permanganate use lemon juice. On dyed paper use an ordinary domestic bleach. As it dries, the line becomes white. Use a twig to draw with, or some other expendable tools, as both bleach and potassium permanganate rot the hairs of brushes.

TECHNIQUES USING INK

Wet the paper; let the excess run off, and draw into that with ink. Notice the change in colour of the inks or dyes, the 'feathering' at the edges if waterproof ink is used.

Try dropping, very sparingly, some powdered ink onto damp paper, and watch the explosions of the grains of powder as it dissolves in the water.

Draw in thick white gouache paint (or gum arabic) onto white paper. Allow to dry completely. Carefully paint over the whole piece of paper, white drawing included, a layer of black waterproof ink. *Leave to dry completely.* Immerse the whole sheet under a slowly running tap. Very gently, with a soft brush, rub the areas that had the white drawing on them,

Powdered ink sprinkled onto damp paper.

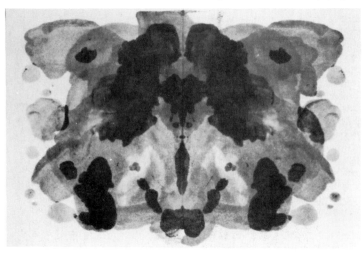

The blots shown here (left) are made by pouring a drop of ink on one half of the paper or in the centre, and while the ink is still wet folding the paper in half, pressing the ink as you do so. Try using several colours. You might find it interesting to read up the literature on the Rorschach Blot Test (which are blots just like these), to see what other people have seen in blots, and read his interpretations.

The 'drawing' around the edge of the dark shape happens automatically when black Indian ink is dropped on damp paper.

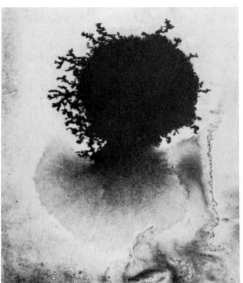

and the gouache will float off the paper, taking with it the black ink which was over that part, leaving a white drawing (the paper itself) in the black ground. This white drawing on a black ground has a quality that no other technique has.

Pour a small pool of ink onto the paper, and blow in all directions with a straw. Drop more than one blob of ink, in other colours. Blow them while they are both still wet, and watch the colours mixing. Wait until one colour has ried before starting the other colour.

On some fairly absorbent paper, drop some ink onto one half, then fold the other half over and gently press down, squeezing the ink round as you do so. Open out, wait until the ink has *completely* dried, and do the same again, using a different colour, and in a different place. Fold in half, and press. Try adding some line drawing with black or sepia coloured ink to the result. As well as a mapping pen try drawing with a twig, or any other tool suggested above.

Try both the above techniques on wet paper instead of dry.

Fill a bottle with ink and attach a fixative spray to the top. Use in conjunction with cut paper shapes (see section on Stencilling) or to build up layers of tone by the amount of ink sprayed on any one place.

In the technique called by the Surrealists 'decalcomania', ink (they used paint) is dropped onto paper, and another sheet of paper is laid on top. Putting one hand on top of the paper where you think the ink is, press upwards. Then separate the two pieces of paper. What can you see? This activity is the reason for using this technique, to explore your particular 'interior'. In doing this, you are following the illustrious footsteps of Leonardo da Vinci, who did this by looking at clouds, flickering flames, damp patches on walls. These fortuitous shapes suggested to him faces, landscapes, sea-scapes, etc. Exaggerate those aspects by drawing into them with black Indian ink and a mapping pen.

INK

APPLY TO	IN SOLUTION
Wet paper	Blown blots
Paper	Folded blots
Wood	Ink and candle wax
Celluloid	Ink and wax crayons
Cloth	Indian ink and gouache
Plaster	Splatter-work
Tissue paper	Bleach on ink
Stones	
Leather	*Draw with*
	Mapping pens
	Lettering pens
	Feathers – quill and feather end
	Sticks
	Twigs
	Card on edge
	Print with
	Shaped sticks
	Cardboard tube on edge
	Matchbox on edge
	Corks
	Junk

Inlay

This is a method of decorating a surface by inserting one contrasting material into another so that the finished surface is level. Inlay is used on furniture, jewellery, swords/armour, objets d'art. *Damascening* is the inlaying of gold wire on steel or iron. *Niello* is the inlaying of silver and gold with other metals. *Intarsia* is the inlaying of wood of one tone in wood of a contrasting tone.

There is a fundamental difference between inlay and marquetry. In inlay, the material from which the object is made is hollowed out in some way and the hollow filled with wood, ivory, metal, mother of pearl, etc. Marquetry is basically a jigsaw of various types of wood, all the same thickness and laid on the surface to be covered in such a way that none of the base shows. In other words, inlay is sunk into the original surface, while marquetry sits on top.

Gold inlay in tortoise-shell.

Japanning

The term was coined in the eighteenth century and applied to objects which had a very high polish on them, usually on a black background. The decoration was applied to tin, wood and papier mâché. They were in imitation of the prized lacquer work from Japan. Black japan is a mixture of natural resin varnish, molten asphalt, drying oils and turpentine. The natural resin is now replaced by synthetic resins, and after being sprayed onto the metal objects, e.g. bikes, it is baked in ovens at 250°–350 °F (120°–170 °C). Liquid enamels, as domestic japan is called, dry very fast, and to a much higher gloss than oil paint, but are not as durable.

Jewellery

Jewellery is a term applied to any detachable body decoration: rings, necklaces, earrings, crowns, tiaras, waist and toe decorations. The range of materials used in its manufacture covers the range of human ingenuity, from the teeth and bones of animals and fish, feathers, shells, wood, and glass, to sophisticated products made from metal and precious stones. (The making of simple jewellery from beads, paper, and polished pebbles is covered in the sections dealing with those materials.)

This is one craft that takes up very little space at home, and does not need an enormous outlay on tools or equipment, though those you do buy should be of the best quality, as in any craft. Plan something modest to begin with, so that you do not spend too much on silver or stones before you have mastered the techniques. No silver is wasted though, for it can all be melted down and used in another project. If using sawn-out shapes of silver, experiment using thin card at the design stage. Metal is available in many forms: rod, bar, sheet, wire, and tube. Experiment with each medium.

MATERIALS

Tools
   Planishing hammer (for forging); saw frame and selection of blades (for cutting sheet metal); files, a half round, a hand file, and selection of needle files; bezel mandrel (for making rings); curved burnisher (for setting stones in bezel); tweezers (for placing solder); rawhide mallet (for bending and hammering metal without leaving marks); ring clamp (to hold rings while filing); pliers (flat and round nosed pliers).
For soldering
   charcoal block; gas torch, propane, with various tips; solder, easy, medium and hard; flux; iron binding wire (27 SWG).
For buffing
   tripoli; rouge; buffing sticks.
For pickle
   sulphuric acid.
Far better than the traditional pickle is a proprietary pickling solution which can be used instead of sulphuric acid and is safe for use by children.

TECHNIQUES
Granulation
This is the fastening of granules of gold onto another piece of gold by heating both with a reducing flame which fuses the granules to the background. To make the granules, clip small pieces from gold or silver wire, or clip small pieces from sheet silver. Put a layer of powdered charcoal into a crucible. Onto this sprinkle some of the small pieces of gold/silver, cover with another layer of powdered charcoal, then another layer of gold pieces, then charcoal. The crucible is then heated in a kiln or with a torch until the metal has melted. When it does it forms itself into little spheres which keep their shape when cool. To fasten the granules to the background, pick them up with a sable brush dipped in gum solution. Place them on the base; the gum will hold them in place. With a reducing flame in your torch (a yellow flame which does not heat the metal too quickly) heat the granules and the base until they fuse. It is possible to stick them on with Araldite (DuPont Duco Cement, or Evergrip Contact Cement).
Fusing
Fusing is a method of joining metals together without using solder, only heat. Clean the metal base very carefully, and lay it on a heating frame on a charcoal block. Place both on a pumice pan. On the metal base arrange scraps of metal or lengths of wire. They can be random, or in an arranged plan. Liberally apply flux to the metals, and then heat with a torch until the metals melt and fuse together. Allow the piece to cool and then pickle.

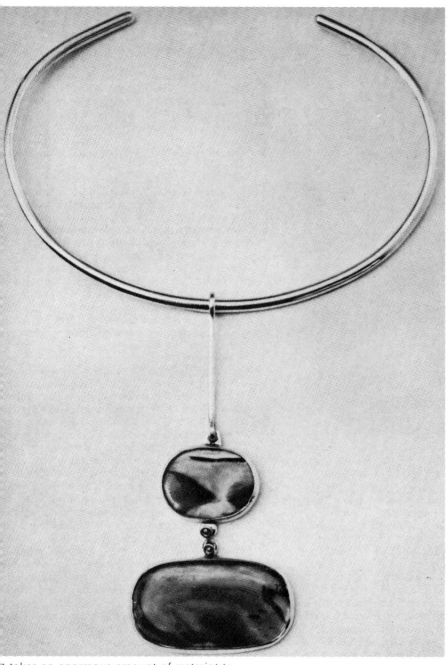

A domed moonstone fitted with a silver gilt bezel set between two rings of silver, attached to each other on the palm side, and opened to accommodate the stone.

t takes an enormous amount of restraint to implify all the elements in a design to xpress something as beautifully balanced s this pendant of silver and agates by athleen Grant. The stones themselves are he focal point; the silver mounting holding hem is scarcely seen, and note the tarkness of the collar and the bar holding he pendant. The only additions are those etween the two agates, and it is additions ke these, and suppression in the other arts of the design, that take an object rom being a competent piece of craft to a vork of art.

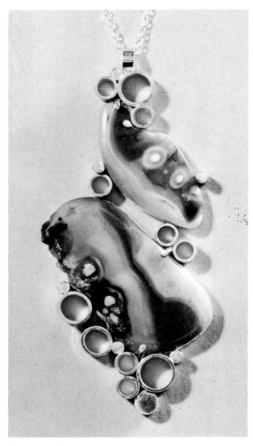

These polished agate sections were an irregular shape and had very positive markings in the stone. It was this aspect that was followed by designing additions to the stones made of sections of silver tubing of different diameter to 'echo' the rings of different sizes and colours in the stones.

Forging

Forging means altering the shape of a piece of metal by hammering. As metal is hammered it becomes hardened and eventually would crack if it was not annealed while being hammered. Annealing is heating the metal to a dark red colour, allowing it to cool until the colour is just disappearing, then plunging it in pickle. Forging is done with a flat face planishing hammer on a steel block. To make a bowl shape, begin by hammering in the centre, and spiralling round and round until the outside is reached. Then anneal it.

The drawplate

This is a plate of hardened steel with holes of various sizes in it which are tapered from one side to the other. The holes are square, round and half round, and triangular. It is used for reducing the diameter of a length of wire, so that one need only buy wire in a few gauges. To reduce the diameter, the wire is first rubbed all over with beeswax to make it slip through more easily. The drawplate is fixed firmly in a vice which is attached to a heavy bench. File one end of the wire to a point, and push it into the smallest hole it will fit into. Grip the small end firmly with draw tongs, and pull the wire through with one steady pull. If you stop and start again the wire will have kinks in it. Then pull the wire through the next smallest hole and so on until it is the right gauge. If it has to be reduced a lot it will have to be annealed.

Bezels

This is securing a stone by wrapping a length of metal around its base and pressing the top firmly all round to fit snugly against the stone. Because one presses the bezel onto the stone with a burnisher, it is important that the bezel metal is especially malleable, so special bezel wire is used. The length of wire is measured by wrapping paper around the base of the stone, marking the overlap. Cut the bezel wire exactly that length, and file the ends parallel. The wire must be deep enough to hold the stone securely, but not too deep, otherwise the wire can wrinkle when pushing it with the burnisher to make the close final fit.

Bend the wire into an oval with the ends meeting snugly, and solder with hard solder. Pickle and rinse. Using a mandrel, put the bezel collar on it and form until it makes a good fit. Take off the mandrel and check that the stone fits. If it is too small it can be stretched by returning it to the mandrel and hammering with a planishing hammer. If it is to be attached to a flat surface, rub over an emery cloth. If it is to fit onto a curved surface, it must be filed to fit the curve. Solder the bezel onto the base and fit in the stone. With a burnisher, apply pressure working in one place, and then the opposite side of the stone. Do this all round the stone.

Soldering

Soldering is the fixing together of pieces of metal with solder and heat. Solder comes in stick, wire, and sheet, and since solders melt at different temperatures, they should be labelled. Hard solder is used for the first solder on a job, medium solder for the second and soft or easy solder for the last.

Flux is always applied to solder and metal to help the solder flow more easily. Apply the flux with a sable brush. The surfaces must be absolutely clean when soldering. This is done with an old toothbrush dipped in diluted ammonia, and rinsed off under the tap. Hold the piece in place with a pair of tweezers, and heat with the torch for a few seconds only. If soldering the bezel of a ring bind it tight with iron binding wire (27 SWG). This can be used to hold any pieces in position while soldering; the solder does not stick to iron wire.

Place the piece to be soldered on the charcoal block (or sheet of asbestos) and position the small pieces of solder in position. Using the

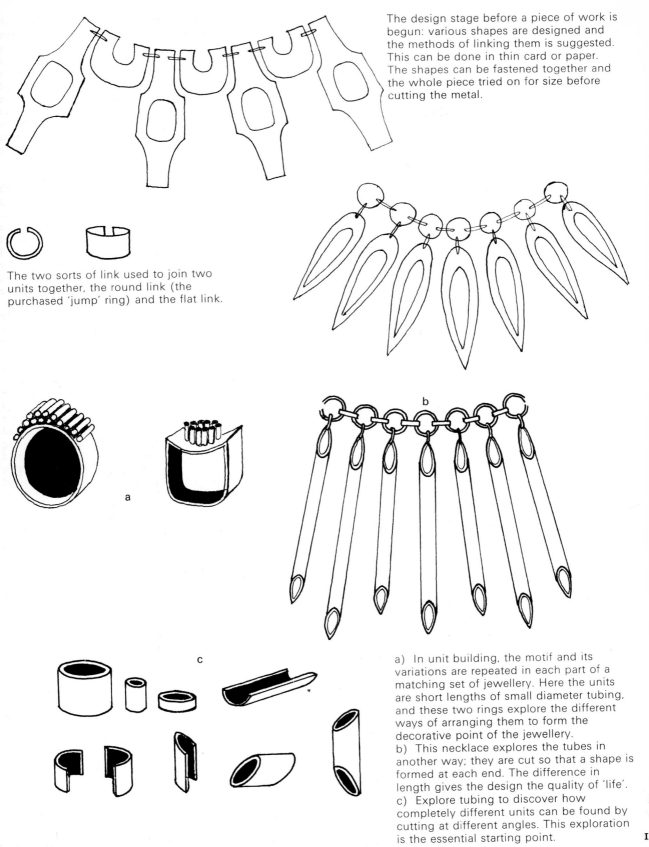

The design stage before a piece of work is begun: various shapes are designed and the methods of linking them is suggested. This can be done in thin card or paper. The shapes can be fastened together and the whole piece tried on for size before cutting the metal.

The two sorts of link used to join two units together, the round link (the purchased 'jump' ring) and the flat link.

a) In unit building, the motif and its variations are repeated in each part of a matching set of jewellery. Here the units are short lengths of small diameter tubing, and these two rings explore the different ways of arranging them to form the decorative point of the jewellery.
b) This necklace explores the tubes in another way; they are cut so that a shape is formed at each end. The difference in length gives the design the quality of 'life'.
c) Explore tubing to discover how completely different units can be found by cutting at different angles. This exploration is the essential starting point.

medium tip of the torch, play the flame over the piece, and when the solder is about to flow, bring the flame closer and concentrate the flame on it. The solder will have melted when the metal turns a bright red.

Sawing

A piercing saw and a selection of blades are needed for this. Blade sizes are 2, 3, 10, 20, 30, 40; 2 is coarse, and 40 fine. The teeth of the blade must point outwards and downwards towards the handle. To insert a blade, push the end furthest from the handle into a bench side. Fix the blade in the handle-end first and then the far end. When the saw is taken away from the bench and the tension is released the blade will be very taut. Hold the saw vertically against the metal and do not push the saw against the metal. Let the up and down movement do all the work. The cutting is only done with the down stroke.

Making a hole in the metal

Drill a hole with a hand drill. Undo the saw, and slip the blade through the hole and fasten the blade in.

Twisting wire

Fit a bent nail into the chuck of a hand drill and loop the folded end of a piece of wire over it. Fix the other two ends in a vice, then twist the hand drill to produce a perfectly twisted length of wire. To make links, wind wire around a knitting needle or dowelling very tightly, keeping the links close. Take the coil off the needle and saw along the length, so forming a collection of links. A wide variety of simple jewellery can be made by simply coiling the wire.

Pickling recipe

Glass container; 1 part sulphuric acid; 10 parts water. *Always add acid very slowly to the water, never, never the other way round.* Never put steel or iron tools in the pickle. After pickling, rinse in a solution of 2 cups hot water plus 2 tblsps baking powder (sodium bicarbonate).

Buffing

This is the final stage. Scratch marks are first removed with fine files and emery cloth. Then the three buffing powders are used: first tripoli on a buffing stick, then red rouge on a cloth, and if a very high polish is required, white rouge.

FURTHER READING

CRAWFORD, J., *Introducing Jewellery Making* Batsford

DAVIDSON, I., *Ideas for Jewellery* Batsford

EDWARDS, R., *The Technique of Jewellery* Batsford

GENTILLE, T., *Jewelry* Pan Books

MEYEROWITZ, *Jewellery & Sculpture Through the Ages* Studio Vista

SCARFE, H., *Cutting and Setting Stones* Batsford

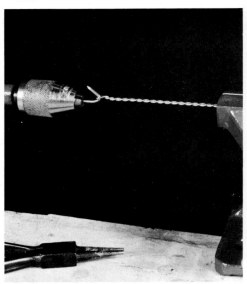

Two reels of wire and a hand drill with a bent piece of wire in the chuck is used in a quick method of making twisted wire. A piece of wire is folded in half and the loop is hooked over the wire in the chuck. The other end is securely held in the vice.

The long-lost technique of granulation. This example is a gold Minoan bead.

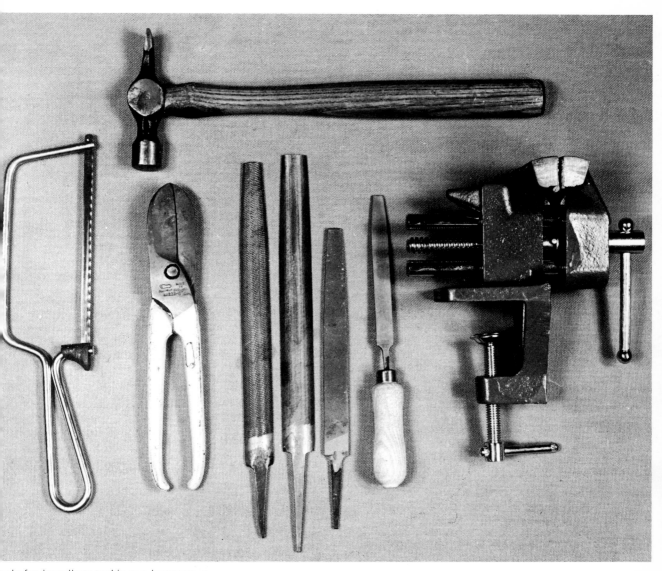

ools for jewellery making: a hammer, a
cksaw, a tinman's snips, four files, and a
all vice.

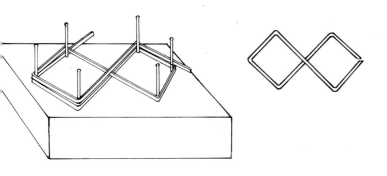

method of making many exact
pies of a 'unit' (known as a jig).

Coiling a piece of wire with a pair of
flat-nosed pliers.

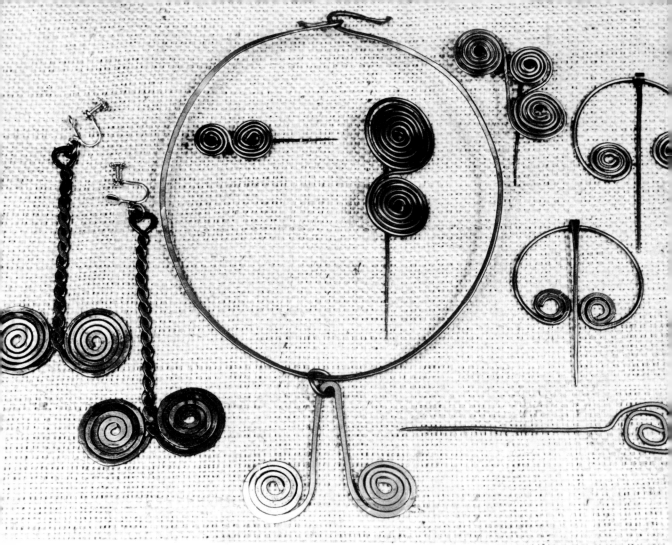

Various ways in which the coiling of a piece of wire can be used to make pieces of jewellery.

Junk Modelling

Waste materials, empty boxes, cartons, tins, scraps of wood, fabric, yarns, or string, are fastened together into three-dimensional models. The techniques involved are to be found in the sections on fastenings, paper, card, wire, etc., and the section on adhesives.

Junk or scrap materials are a perfectly valid material to use. It is the intentions behind their use, and the reasons for their choice that are often so questionable. Schwitters used old bus and tram tickets, and Picasso, Braque, and others, used scrap of all kinds. The whole Dada movement exploited them, but the use of scrap requires at the very least a high degree of visual humour.

FURTHER READING
CAPON, R., *Art from Scrap Materials* Batsford
HUTCHINGS, *What Shall I Do with This?* Mills and Boon
JACKSON, B., *Model Making in Schools* Batsford

The junk materials used in this imaginative structure include nuts, bolts, scrap metal, and a candle.

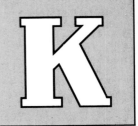

K

Kites

Although kite-making was Chinese in origin, it is the Japanese who really exploited the craft, and from whom the most beautiful and inventive kites now come. The famous Centipede kites, made from a series of disc kites connected together with string and sometimes reaching 60 ft in length and requiring six or more men to manoeuvre them, come from the island of Shikoku. From Nagoya come the kites which are beautifully decorated as either birds or insects, and from Bekkako come kites of very curious shapes.

Kites are comparatively simple to make: there is enormous scope in the decorations on the sail: the skill in flying them is one that can be practised and perfected, and for those with a scientific bent, the aerodynamics of the sail and the problems of design can be very challenging. A kite is made up of a sail, a frame to which the sail is attached, a bridle of thin string, a hand line (or tow line) which is the part of the kite the flier holds, and a reel (spool) onto which the line is wound.

The sail

This can be made from many kinds of material: crêpe paper, wrapping paper, thin drawing paper, architects' detail paper, newspaper, thin polythene sheeting, thin cloth such as muslin, or any fine, strong, cotton cloth. The fabric sail can be decorated by any of the methods described in the section on fabric printing: tie-dyeing, batik, screen printing, stick printing, fabric crayons. The paper sail can be decorated by drawing with wax crayons, washes of coloured inks or dyes, stick-on cut-out shapes from different coloured papers or thin aluminium foil. The decoration must be bold and strong to give pleasure at a great distance.

The frame

This is made from thin dowelling or cane. For large kites you will need bamboo canes which are strong and pliable, or balsa wood. The frame is the most important part of the kite to make well, because if the frame is not perfectly balanced the kite will not fly well, however well-made the sail.

For the simplest of kites, cut two sticks of about 26 in. and 22 in. long; the longer one is for the spine, running from top to bottom of the kite, the shorter one is for the spar. Mark the centre of each with a pencil, and check that it really is the centre by balancing the cane on

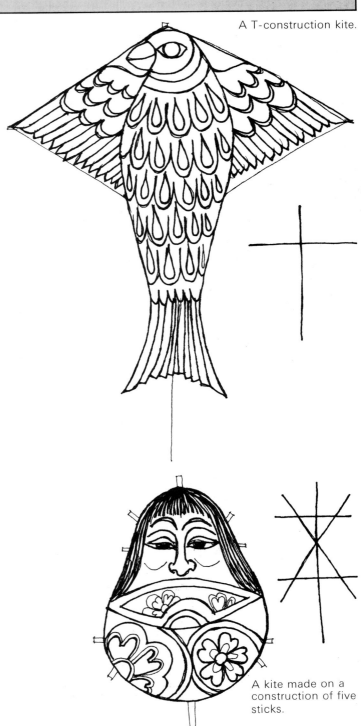

A kite made on a construction of five sticks.

a table knife or ruler. If it does not balance perfectly, move the knife or ruler a fraction until it does balance perfectly, and mark the final position. Do this to each cane, apply PVA (white) glue to the marks, place the canes at right angles to each other on the spots of glue, and bind firmly together with thin string.

Notch the ends of each cane; tie a length of string onto one and connect up the ends of the other canes; fasten off. Keep the string taut between the ends of the canes, but do not let them bend. The frame is always fastened to the underside of the sail (the 'wrong' side as far as the decoration is concerned). Cover the frame with PVA glue and lay it carefully onto the sail, after carefully positioning it, and leave to dry. Reinforce any weak parts at the ends of the frame or where the bridle is attached with small pieces of sticky tape.

Wrapping the fine string round to secure the two strips.

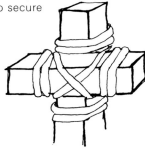

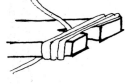

The ends of the cross-pieces have a notch cut in them to secure the string which forms the 'bridle'.

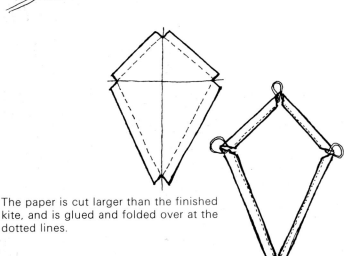

The paper is cut larger than the finished kite, and is glued and folded over at the dotted lines.

The bridle

This is made of strong linen thread for small kites (book-binding thread is ideal, as is buttonhole thread), or smooth fine parcel string for larger kites. The points at which the bridle is attached to the kite are always shown with the plans for kites, as it varies with each different shape. A kite which needs no bridle at all is the circular kite, made on a cross frame. The towing line is attached to the crossing of the two canes, and it flies very well.

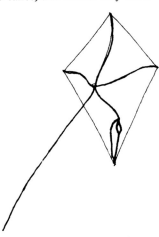

If thin fabric (muslin) is used for the kite, machine stitch a hem all round first. Thread string through this hem, and loop over the kite frame, pulling the thread taut and tying it tight.

For a simple cross frame, tie a length of string to each end of the spine cane, making it slack enough so that at the centre it is approximately 12 in. away from the cross piece, and has a curtain ring threaded onto it. Tie another length to each end of the spar piece, threading this too through the curtain ring. Move the ring around until all parts of the string are equally taut, and to this ring attach the towing line. To save the kite from damage in high winds, the lower part of the bridle can be cut and a strong rubber band tied in.

Securing the hand line to the bridle using a small piece of dowelling and a curtain ring.

The tail

This is usually about five times the length of the spine, and is made of small bundles of paper (crêpe, tissue, cellophane, etc.) tied together with clove hitches at 12 in. intervals. If the tail is too short, the kite will fly in a very erratic way; if it is too long, the kite will have difficulty in rising off the ground.

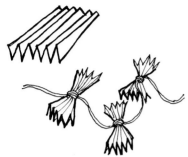

The tail of a kite is made from pleated or rolled paper, knotted together with clove hitches.

Reel

A reel is needed to wind the line of the kite in and out. It can be wound onto a 10 in. or so length of old broomstick, but a reel such as the one illustrated is far quicker to use. One holds the projecting pieces of dowelling, and the line is wound onto the two lengths of dowelling in the centre. Remember to tie the first piece of string onto the cross piece very securely, or you will let out the string and suddenly see your kite flying away from you for good.

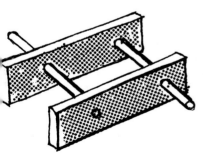

A simple hand-reel for winding in the flowing line, made from dowelling and two pieces of wood.

(Top) A Japanese traditional kite.
(Centre) Detail of head.
(Bottom) Detail of tail.

KITE FLYING

Do not fly kites near buildings, overhead wires, or busy roads. Find an open space like a park. In London, the place to fly kites is on Hampstead Heath or Parliament Hill Fields, on a Sunday, when all the aficionados are there. Choose a fine, dry day, with a light to medium breeze. To get the kite off the ground, stand with your back to the wind, and hold the kite in your hand as high as you can reach. As the breeze starts to lift the kite, slowly and steadily let out the tow line. If you let it out too quickly it will drop to the ground. To keep the kite rising, reel it in occasionally, giving it a short sharp tug as you do so. If the kite suddenly drops while it is in the air, reel in steadily until the wind catches it again. The most dangerous time for a kite is just before it lands, as you are winding it in. You must wind slowly and steadily; that way the kite will not behave erratically as it comes down, and you will avoid a crash landing.

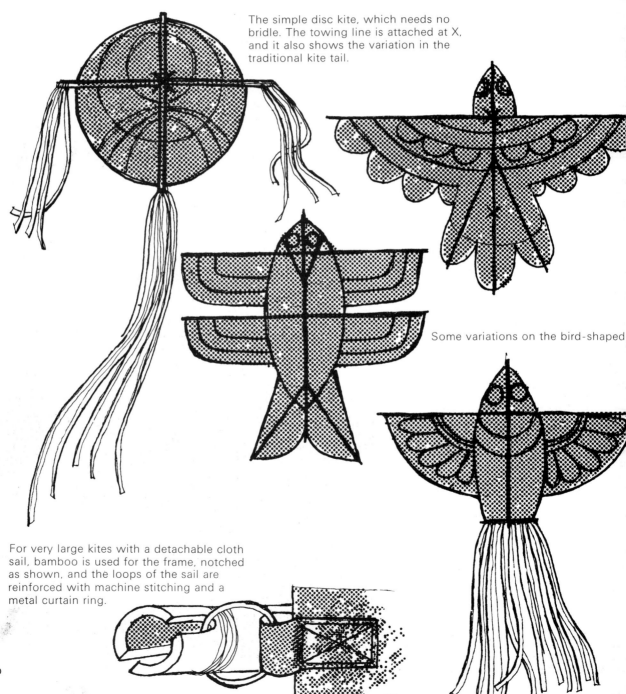

The simple disc kite, which needs no bridle. The towing line is attached at X, and it also shows the variation in the traditional kite tail.

Some variations on the bird-shaped

For very large kites with a detachable cloth sail, bamboo is used for the frame, notched as shown, and the loops of the sail are reinforced with machine stitching and a metal curtain ring.

Lacquer Work

Japan and China are the homes of this celebrated ware. Lacquer is a resin, the sap from a tree, the *Rhus vernicifera*. The tree is indigenous to China, and has been cultivated in Japan since the sixth century AD. The ten-year-old tree is tapped and the sap collected from June to September. A special quality lacquer called *seshime* is obtained by cutting off the smaller branches, and soaking them in water for ten days. The tree is killed in the process, but the larger pieces of wood are used in carpentry.

The sap has several peculiar qualities. White or greyish at first, it yellows and eventually becomes black. After having been stirred thoroughly until it is of a smooth even mix, it is strained through cloth to remove any extraneous bits. Excess moisture is evaporated in sunshine or over a slow fire, and then the lacquer stored in air-tight containers. Lacquer is a poison to which those who work with it soon become immune. Chinese lacquer has 55·84% of *urushiol* compared with an average of around 70% in Japanese lacquer, the difference being attributed to climatic differences affecting the tree. *Urushiol* is the name given to the particular constituent of lacquer.

Though occasionally applied to porcelain or brass, it is almost always applied to wood, although there are instances of carvings being made in solid lacquer. The wood used is extremely thin pine. The first coating on the wood is of rice paste and seshime, and covers over any cracks and joins. A thin coat of seshime lacquer is applied next; 20 or 30 coats of lacquer are applied and each one has to harden and be ground smooth. The last coat at this stage is very fine and has burnt clay added. This coat is left to harden (12 hours), and onto this is pasted, with either lacquer or rice paste, a hemp cloth in Japan, paper in China (c.f. the muslin in papier mâché). Many more coats of lacquer are applied with progressively longer periods of hardening. This is the preparation for the decoration, and takes 3 weeks.

Lacquer dries extremely hard but does not become brittle, and curiously its maximum hardness is obtained when it is damp, so between each coat, the article being lacquered is put in a moist/damp box. The object being lacquered is then decorated with gold dust, slivers of gold or silver inserted into the lacquer (*hirame*), or with relief decoration. Charcoal, lamp black, and white lead are added to the lacquer to make a paste with which one can model, camphor being added to make it more malleable.

The spread of Buddhism brought about an increased use of gold decoration on lacquer ware; the gold lacquer of the Ashikaga craftsmen was renowned. Domestic utensils were either black or red, and were to Japan what ceramics were to China. Precious metal and shell were inlaid on ceremonial ware.

The speciality of the Chinese lacquer craftsmen was their carved lacquer work. As the lacquer was built up, the layers were coloured differently, each colour being used for several thicknesses of lacquer. When the layering was complete, it was carved, but in such a way as to show only one colour at a time, and the constituent parts of the design would have quite discrete colours. It was a very exacting process, no allowance being possible for mistakes. The colours used include buff, brown, dark and light green, aubergine, and black. The famous red lacquer of China was made by adding cinnabar. Another famous Chinese lacquer style was called *Lac Burgautee*, which was shell (the *haliotis*, an iridescent blue/purple/

An antique example of Japanese lacquer ware. This is the lid of a box.

green) inlaid in black lacquer. They also applied jade, coral, ivory, soapstone, and porcelain.

Coromandel ware was usually made into screens, the lacquer being cut into, and then painted either in colours or gold. They were called coromandel because the French and English traders who did the importing into Europe had their headquarters on the Coromandel coast. The Dutch had theirs at Bantam in Java, and this technique is sometimes called *Bantam ware*. The porcelain and lacquer work imported by the East India companies began in the eighteenth century to be copied by European craftsmen. The oriental resins could not be equalled, but it was found that the resin from the juniper tree, known as sandarac, was the best for lacquer work in Europe.

Laminates

These are materials bonded together with an adhesive or fused with heat. The materials bonded can be identical, as in the case of plywood, or two dissimilar materials can be used, e.g. wood and sheet plastic, or plastic and paper. It is used when a strong material is required and where the basic material is weak, or where it is more economical to use an expensive material only on the surface, or for protection. There are special machines available now which can laminate plastic to glass, metal, wood, and textiles; the plastic can be either on one side or on both.

An easy method of laminating paper is to use a laminating film which is heat-sensitive. Drawings can be sealed by applying heat from a domestic iron set at the lowest temperature. Put a piece of paper between the iron and the plastic when applying the heat. You can either apply the seal to one side, or fold the plastic in half and slip the paper between the two halves. The actual sealing takes place as the plastic cools down, and as it cools, rub the area that has been ironed with a pad of cloth to make sure that there are no air bubbles and that there is a really good seal. The heat needs to be applied for a very short time, 10 to 15 seconds is plenty. It is a very useful protection for card games designed in school or a very personal set of playing cards.

Another method of laminating is with dry mounting-tissue, a very thin paper with a waxy surface which is laid between two layers of paper to bond them together. It is very useful for fragile papers like tissue. Fotoflat, manufactured by Seal Co, is one such laminating tissue, and this too can be sealed with a domestic iron set at a low temperature.

A diluted PVA glue can be used for laminating tissue paper, and embedding grasses, etc., and clear candle wax can also be used to fuse tissue paper together.

Newspaper and a cellulose wallpaper paste are excellent for laminating. If whole sheets of newspaper are laminated, six sheets at a time they can be cut up while wet and moulded into shapes which will be quite rigid when dry, and unbreakable (see the sections on Papier mâché and Tissue paper).

Leathercraft

TYPES OF LEATHER

Animal skins are stripped of hair or wool, and treated to become either grain leather or suede leather. Grain leather is the smooth outside of the skin, suede the soft velvety underside.

Sheep skin provides fine quality leathers for jackets, suits, skirts, and dresses. South African sheep are the source of the smooth gloving leather known as cape. An extra soft leather known as nappa comes from sheep, lamb, goat, and kid. Cow hide provides the soft 'calf' leather used for coats and handbags. The skin can also be split; the resulting double-sided suede of the lower half of the split has a longer pile and is used by the shoe trade.

Goat provides a very soft, supple skin. Pig skin has a very distinctive pattern, resulting from the hair follicles. It is the very hard-wearing leather used for luggage and saddlery. Horse leather is used for shoe soles, and is very thick and stiff. Watersnake and python skins are bred on special farms; although these were originally used for shoes and handbags these can now be 'soft-dressed' so that they are pliable enough for clothes.

Grain leather can be surface treated in many different ways.

Antiqued The surface is randomly sprayed to produce irregular shading.

Embossed Patterning as a result of stamping into the damp leather with metal dies.

Gold and silver The leather is coated with gold or aluminium in leaf or foil.

Patent A waterproof, very shiny film produced with lacquers and varnishes.

Pearlized The leather is coloured with a pearl-like lustre.

Sole (shoe) leather Leather compressed in the tannery, first while damp, then again when dry.

Morocco Goatskin leather grained by hand after a special machine glazing. The natural grain is raised and emphasized by working while still wet with a cork-covered graining tool.

Cutting leather

Animal skins have variations in colour and texture, and occasional blemishes, and are thinner at the edges, so plan the cutting carefully. Leather does not have a warp and weft as fabric does, so fit the parts of the pattern together in the most economical way.

For soft leather and suede, a good pair of dressmaking scissors is sufficient. For thicker, stiff leathers, a Stanley knife, Exacto or similar craft knife is needed, but it must be really sharp or the leather will be ragged and frayed. After cutting, the edges are skived or bevelled if the pieces are to be laced, stitched or riveted. This is done on the wrong side. Skiving is done to the ends of each piece of thonging when they are being joined so that they form a continuous thong of even thickness.

Preparing leather

For thonging and hand stitching, holes must be made in the leather first. A revolving punch gives a choice of six different sized holes. Alternatively use a thonging chisel which can be 3, 4, 6, or 8-prong, the width of the prong varying from $\frac{3}{32}$ in. to $\frac{1}{8}$ in. There are also round prong chisels, 2, 5, or 6-prong. To use, the chisel is placed on the right side of the leather, and the handle is hit with a mallet. To keep the slits in a straight line, mark a line along the edge of the leather with the outside tine of a domestic fork. Make the mark with the outside tine, keeping the next one to the edge of the piece of leather. To keep the spaces regular between one chisel cut and the next, always place the first prong in the last hole made by the previous cut.

Holes for hand stitching with thread can be made with an awl. To get the spacing right between the holes, run along the line of stitching with a special spacing wheel, which has little spikes on it arranged at intervals of either five, six, or seven holes per inch. To make the hole with an awl, place the point in the indentation made by the spacing wheel, and tap the handle sharply with a mallet.

A *fid*, which has a triangular blade, is used to enlarge the hole. An *eyelet tool* is used for making holes to be laced. The tool is similar to a punch, and after making a hole the eyelet is fixed on with a firm squeeze of the eyelet tool. Eyelets are available in many colours and in brass, but they are limited in size, so if you wish to make a larger hole and have it protected with a metal rim (like the holes shoelaces are threaded through) use *grommets* (sail eyelets). These are available in a range of sizes, but the most useful domestic size can be bought at a good haberdashery department. After having punched an appropriately sized hole, the two parts of the grommet are hammered together.

Needles

Curved needles (glovers' or harness needles) have a very sharp triangular point. Lacing needles are flat, straight and have gripping teeth where the 'eye' of a needle normally is. Where a normal needle has the thread going through it at right angles, the thonging needle has the thong laid in the sprung slit at the end and in line with the needle.

Thread

Saddler's thread is thick, suitable for use on heavy duty articles like large bags and briefcases. Bookbinder's thread is very strong and comes in several different thicknesses. Carpet yarn is strong and available in several colours. Buttonhole thread (silk) is suitable for very fine leathers, for gloves and small articles.

MACHINE SEWING LEATHER

Cutting out the leather

Do not pin the paper pattern to the leather. Fix it on with double-sided adhesive tape. On some suede there is a 'nap' (pile); in this case make sure that it is running in the same direction on each part of the garment. Lay the pattern on the right side of the leather to avoid any blemishes on the skins. Draw round the paper pattern with chalk, marking darts, buttonholes, etc. Remove the pattern and cut out with a really sharp pair of scissors. Staple the pieces together ready for stitching.

Sewing the leather

Use a pure silk or a synthetic sewing thread, because they have an elasticity that will match that of the skin. Use a No. 11 sewing machine needle for fine suedes, a No. 14 for kid and fine cape, and a No. 16 for heavier leather. Lengthen the machine stitch to 8 to 10 stitches per inch, and reduce the pressure of the machine foot. Lay a piece of tissue over the feed teeth and beneath the leather to be stitched, and stitch this as well. It is easily torn off when the line of stitching is done, and it prevents the teeth marking the leather. It also helps the whole piece to move more easily through the machine. Stitch *slowly* and take care not to pull and stretch the leather. If joining leather to cloth, place the cloth on top.

Seams

Plain seams and darts Open out, and stick with Copydex (leather cement). Pound gently with a rubber mallet to flatten the seam. If sewing suede, this might result in the pile on the right side getting flattened, so rub it up with a scrap of suede.

Curved seams If the allowance is on the outside, clip it to allow the leather to open out and lie flat. If on the inside, cut out V-shaped notches to reduce the bulk.

Corners On collars, trim to slightly less than $\frac{1}{4}$ in. and snip off corners completely.

Hems Either trim level and leave, or turn up and glue flat, not less than 1 in., not more than 2 in.

DECORATING LEATHER

All leather can be painted or dyed. Acrylic paints retain their elasticity when the article is in use, come in a complete range of colours, and can be opaque or translucent. French enamel paints must be applied to leather which has been treated and is white. Felt-tip pens work well on suede. Poker work is very good on leather and is permanent. Also try stencilling and tie-dyeing. For large areas of dyeing use Dylon cold water dye. A large range of metal decorations can be bought and applied by means of metal lugs directly to the leather of handbags, for example.

Leather can also be inlaid or onlaid, or decorated by weaving, thonging, or tooling. Tooling is done by stamping into damp leather with a metal stamp. Run a damp sponge over the leather on the grain side, then the underside; as the original colour reappears, make the impression.

Folding leather

If the leather is thick, fold it by cutting out a shallow groove on the wrong side of the leather. To make a concertina fold, in addition to gouging out a groove, damp the leather and pound the outside of the fold.

ARTICLES TO MAKE

Clothes: skirts, coats, jackets, waistcoats, hats, sandals, gloves. Accessories: necklaces, bags, purses, belts, watch-straps, key ring fobs, spectacle cases. Toys, loose book covers, book marks, cushion covers; soft sculpture, collages.

Large holes are used for the lacing together of this belt. These cannot be rimmed with the eyelet tool. The size of eyelet rims one buys in the shop is the maximum size one can make with one piece of metal. For the larger sizes one has to use a rim made in two pieces, and these are called grommets. A different tool is used for this, and hand pressure is not enough. Grommets have to be hammered together.

The patterns made on this piece of leather were made with tools which have to be purchased specially for leather work. The tip with the stamp on it is held on the damp leather and hammered in with a leather mallet.

An experimental piece by a student to make a naturalistic image.

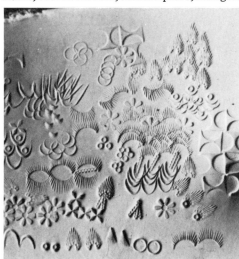

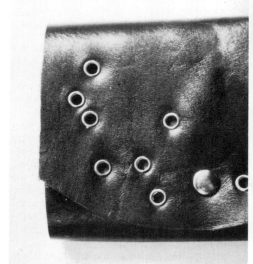

This purse has been decorated with eyelet holes.

The eyelets have to have a hole punched first. Some eyelet tools are combination punches and eyeletters; if you only have the eyelet tool (they are very inexpensive) the hole will have to be made with a rotary punch. It is important that a hole is actually removed from the leather. Making a hole with an awl will not do.

Grommets can be made in very many sizes, and are used for such things as the holes through which the ropes go in sails on boats. The 'tools' used for attaching grommets are a metal cup (the metal ring on the bottom left) and the length of solid metal with a projection at one end. The grommet is also made in two parts. The larger part fits into the metal cup part of the tool and the hole in the leather is fitted over this. The smaller second part of the grommet is placed into the hole, and the metal rod fitted into this.

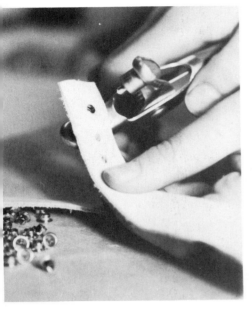

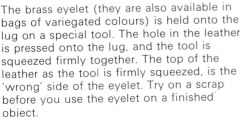

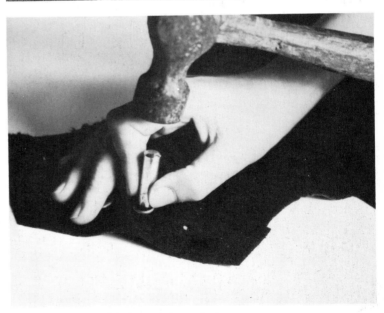

The brass eyelet (they are also available in bags of variegated colours) is held onto the lug on a special tool. The hole in the leather is pressed onto the lug, and the tool is squeezed firmly together. The top of the leather as the tool is firmly squeezed, is the 'wrong' side of the eyelet. Try on a scrap before you use the eyelet on a finished object.

Hold the rod absolutely upright and give a very sharp blow with a hammer.

The four parts needed to attach poppers. Each half of the popper is made of two parts. These are very useful in many areas: they are simple to use, and cheap.

A piece of leather inlaid with other leather. The design was drawn onto a piece of tracing paper, then transferred to the dark top leather by placing a piece of yellow dressmaking carbon between the drawing and the leather, and going over the lines with a biro. The shapes were cut out with a sharp knife.

This finely cut pattern used glove leather, which is thin enough to take intricate cuts. It was glued onto a fabric clutch bag.

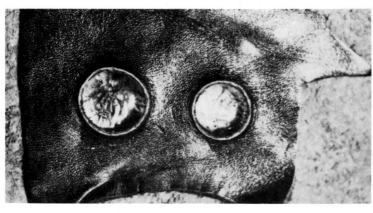

An experimental inlay, using glass cabochons glued to the leather with an epoxy glue. They were backed with aluminium foil to make the glass glitter.

French enamel was painted onto white leather before the two pieces were stitched together.

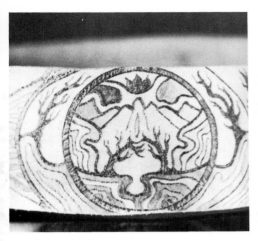

Pokerwork is a very exciting method of decoration on leather. One can vary the thickness of the line by the length of time one holds the heated tip of the pokerwork tool in one place, or by the amount of pressure used when making the line. This example has a combination of pokerwork and paint.

Greenland decoration using leather thonging in contrasting colours to make a pattern. This is more difficult to do than it looks.

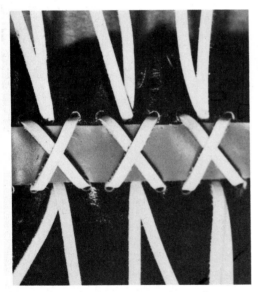

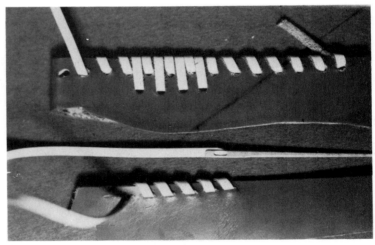

Experiments with cutting and weaving strips of contrasting leather.

Above Holes are punched first, through both pieces at the same time. By altering the arrangements of holes, different patterns can be made in the thonging.

Below The special thonging needle threaded with the thonging. Instead of holes in this example slits have been made with a special tool.

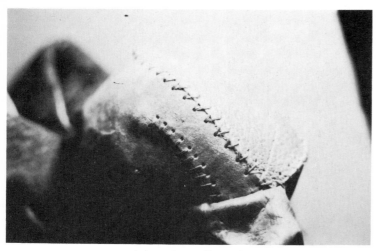

A free three-dimensional shape sewn together with linen thread. The holes were punched by the smallest of the rotary punch cutters.

An attachment for fastening handles. The two rings are attached to each other by a strong metal bar. This bar is fastened to the flap of a handbag, at the top, and is hidden on the inside by the handbag lining.

A few examples from the huge range of purchased handles which are available.

Metal supports attached to the handbag, to which the handle in turn is attached.

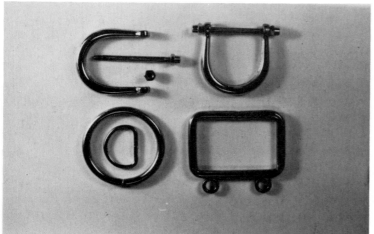

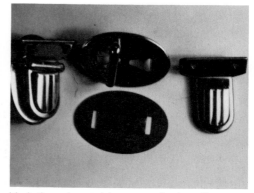

Varieties of metal fasteners for handbags.

LEATHER

FASTEN WITH	DECORATED BY
Poppers (snaps)	*Painting*
	Acrylics
Thonging	French enamels
	Deka leather dyes
Purchased fasteners	Leather shoe dyes
Saddle stitching	*Poker work*
	Plain
Machine stitching	Coloured
	Tooling
	Embossing
	Appliqué
	Suede
	String
	Fur
	Brass rings
	Other leathers
	Sisal
	Nails
	Metal
	Findings
	Inlay

FURTHER READING
ROSEAMAN, I.P., *Leatherwork* Dryads
STOHLMAN, A., *Figure Carving*, available from
    Hobbyhorse
WILLCOX & MANNING, *Leather* Pitman

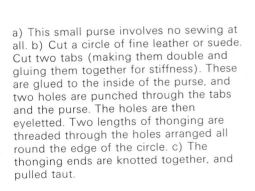

a) This small purse involves no sewing at all. b) Cut a circle of fine leather or suede. Cut two tabs (making them double and gluing them together for stiffness). These are glued to the inside of the purse, and two holes are punched through the tabs and the purse. The holes are then eyeletted. Two lengths of thonging are threaded through the holes arranged all round the edge of the circle. c) The thonging ends are knotted together, and pulled taut.

Lino-cutting

Lino-cutting is half-way between woodcuts and wood engraving. One can use it either for fine line 'drawing' or to produce large areas of tone/shape. To make a print with a lot of fine line cuttings, rub it all over with wet and dry sandpaper (finest grade) first. This is to roughen the surface slightly, so that when you are cutting the tool does not skid. Because of the grit inherent in the material, lino cutting tools soon lose their edge, so keep a wet stone handy to sharpen them. The process of printing lino blocks is exactly the same as that for printing wood cuts (q.v.).

Lino-cutting is cheaper and considerably easier to work than wood, which for centuries had been used for book illustration and printing wallpaper. It is still used in India for producing lengths of fabric (by hand). As an 'art' form, the Japanese artists Hokusai and Utamaro used wood as their medium, the prints being made in many colours. Traditionally the Japanese woodcuts were printed with water inks which were mixed with rice paste. Apart from the English Herbal illustrators, who were anonymous, the best known English artist in this field is Thomas Bewick, whose one-colour wood engravings of animals and birds are superb.

MATERIALS

Linoleum blocks
Linoleum off-cuts are often cheaply available from stores that sell floor covering. Linoleum should be kept flat, not rolled up – otherwise it will crack. If it is difficult to cut, try warming it by a radiator or by holding it under hot water for a few minutes. If one is going to print fabric with a lino block, it is advisable to glue the lino onto a block of wood the same size. Ready-made linoleum blocks, with or without wood backing, are available from art stores.

Paper
The softer the paper the better, if one has no press. There are some lovely soft Japanese papers, but they are very expensive. Try tissue, or disposable paper sheets.

Inks
There are two types of ink: oil-based and water-based. Water-based inks are pleasant to use and have the great advantage of being easily cleaned off all equipment as they wash off with water only. The disadvantage is that they take a long time to dry out thoroughly, especially if they contain glycerine. The addition of glycerine, however, is essential if you have neither proper water-based paint nor oil-based paint and have to use instead powder paint or poster colour: without the addition of glycerine, these will dry much too fast.

Oil-based inks, although more complicated to use, have a lovely range of rich, glowing colours, and are touch-dry in hours. But they have to be cleaned with turpentine substitute and can be messy, so be sure to wear overalls and be organized.

Equipment
A metal straight edge and a Stanley knife are used for cutting the lino into blocks. Gouges cut the design on the lino. They can be bought with cutters permanently fixed in the handle (expensive for large numbers of students), or one can buy handles into which different shaped 'nibs' can be fitted. These are either V-shaped, which give differing thickness of line, or U-shaped, used for cutting out areas quickly. Wood engraving tools (which are of very good quality) can also be used for cutting lino. A lino cutter extractor extracts the nib from the handle when it has been firmly pushed in during the course of cutting. Also required are rubber covered rollers, 2 in., 4 in., and 6 in. wide; flocking mordant (in tubes) and flocking powder (by the pound) for use in fabric printing; glass slabs; a palette knife, thin and flexible, for mixing the printing ink on the slab; a tablespoon for rubbing the paper to take the print; and turpentine substitute for cleaning the blocks, slab, and rollers.

METHOD

Cutting the lino
Hold the lino firmly behind the hand doing the cutting (keep a supply of Band Aid or bandage in case of cuts!). Use a scrap of lino to get the 'feel' of cutting lino. Use the different nibs to discover the different sorts of line they make. Practise cutting lines and cutting away large areas. Always cut with the point of the tool directed away from your other hand.

Flocking the lino block
This is required only when the lino blocks are being used for fabric printing. Clean the block to ensure that it is grease free. Squeeze a line of flocking paste onto a glass slab and roll up as for taking a print. With the roller well inked, roll it across the surface of the lino cut as if you were going to make a print. Shake some flocking powder over the wet surface of the block and put it aside for 24 hours. Tap the side of the block and tip the excess powder onto a piece of paper. This can be stored and used again. If a large amount of printing is to be done, this process will have to be repeated, with another wait of 24 hours, but one coating should be enough.

Printing in colour
Lino prints and wood cuts can be printed in colour in a variety of ways. One can either colour the paper, or colour the block itself. The paper can be coloured free-hand with washes of ink or dye; free brush and ink drawing can be done before printing; or try making a collage of various slightly-textured papers, and print on that.

One can ink up the block using various

colours on different parts of the block; or, like Munch, one could cut up the block into several pieces, ink each piece separately, fit them together again and take a print.

The elimination process involves a technique similar to that when doing a batik in several colours. Cut out a small part that you want to be white in the final print. Take off five or six prints (use the burnishing method or a press) in, let us say, yellow. Clean off the lino block (with water or turpentine, depending on the ink). Cut more out of the lino and print again, say in red. Print on the prints that are in yellow. Now on the prints are: white – those parts cut out before the first printing; yellow from the first print; red from the second print. Wash the blocks clean and cut out even more lino. Finally print again in black. Now we have three colours and white, plus some other colours that are a result of 'overprinting', i.e. mixing. In this case, the red and yellow should give an orange, depending on how transparent the inks are.

Colour prints using a block for each colour
Note the following: a block is required for each colour; each block must be the same size; trace a copy of the master drawing onto each block. Sort out which parts of the picture are to be which colour and cut out all those parts that are not to be printed in that colour; for example, having decided which parts of the picture are to be red, cut out all the rest. Then move on to the next colour and cut away all those parts not in that colour. Only one colour can be printed at a time; wait until each print is dry before going on to the next colour.

LINO PRINTING, ETCHED
Remarkably fine detail can be achieved using this method. Clean the lino with methylated spirits (denatured alcohol). Paint the design on with molten wax. If some white poster paint is added to the wax it makes it a little easier to see what you are doing. Using a plastic brush, paint a mixture of caustic soda (lye) and water onto the lino. Leave it overnight so that the caustic really bites into the lino, and the next day scrape off the wax, and remove the soda, with a scrubbing brush under a hot tap. It is possible to delete the wax stage and just use the caustic soda. The lino is now ready for printing.

FURTHER READING
DANIELS, H., *Printmaking* Hamlyn
ELAM, J., *Introducing Lino Cutting* Batsford
GORTABY, N., *Printmaking with a Spoon*
  Reinhold

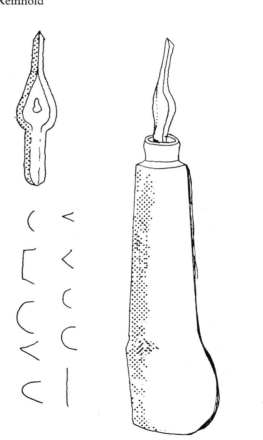

(Above left) Gouging nib and the various cutting shapes obtainable from different nibs. (Centre) Pen nib gouger. (Right) Gouging tool.

Linocut by Picasso.

(Top) These patterns were produced by making different types of cuts with different tools: rocking the tool at a steep angle, turning U-shaped tools round to form a circle, rotating the lino round while cutting, etc.

(Right) The simplest method of obtaining a second colour is to use a paper mask. Roll light coloured ink onto an uncut lino block and place the shaped paper mask on top; this will allow only part of the inked block to print. Roll darker ink onto the cut lino block, and print over the first image.

Print with white ink on black paper (above) and black ink on white paper (below) to achieve negative and positive images.

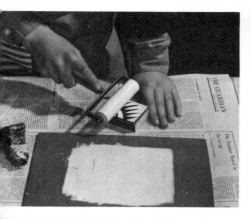

(Top left) Spread flocking mordant onto a glass slab, then roll it onto the lino block.
(Top right) Sprinkle flocking powder over the surface.
(Left) Spread the powder until the white mordant is completely covered.

Lithography

As Senefelder discovered it, it was practised on stone, hence the name – lithos = stone, graphos = drawing. As stones are very heavy to move around, and grinding them down is a specialist's job, the material most used now is a zinc or aluminium 'plate'.

Since it is impossible to practise this craft without an enormously expensive printing press, only the briefest outline of the technique is given here.

Before beginning work, the plate must be counter-etched. To do this, place the zinc, aluminium plate in an enamel (photographer's) tray. With a clean soft brush, brush a saturated solution of powdered alum and water over the plate, leaving it for only 2 minutes. Remove the plate, and rinse under a running tap. Draw or paint on the plate with anything containing grease: children's crayons, soap, lipstick, lithographic crayons, 'rubbing ink', anything which you can rub with a finger or smudge, draw or paint with, on the plate. Thinned asphalt and turpentine will make a *tusche* with which one can paint or splatter on the plate. A tusche can also be made from ground lithographic crayons mixed with turpentine. (Liquid Tusche is available from L.L. Weans Co Inc, New York.)

When a print has been taken, make notes on it explaining how a given effect was achieved, it will be an invaluable mine of information later.

Etching the plate

The etch is not the same as the one used to etch a stone. The mixture is made from: 3 oz gum, $1\frac{1}{2}$ oz saturated solution of bichromate of potassium, $\frac{1}{8}$ oz phosphoric acid. Clean off the drawing on the plate with turpentine; it is now ready for inking and printing. Use damp paper with which to make your prints, experiment with different types of paper until you find one that suits you.

FURTHER READING

WOODS, G., *Introducing Lithography* Batsford

(Top) A line tracing of a photograph was attached to a zinc plate with lithographic carbon paper in between. Ruled lines were drawn with a ballpoint pen, and extra pressure was applied to obtain the darker areas.

(Bottom) A portrait drawing was made with litho-chalk directly onto the plate. Litho-chalk cannot be erased, so the main lines can first be mapped out with blackboard chalk. Corrections can be made during the processing of the plate.

Macramé

However complicated macramé looks when finished, it is based largely on two knots: a blanket stitch, called a half-hitch, and the flat knot which needs a minimum of four threads to make it.

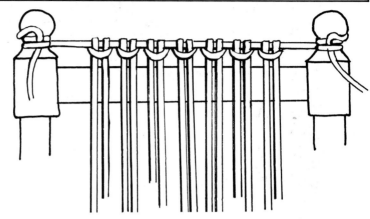

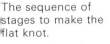
How to hold the cords when making the flat knot.

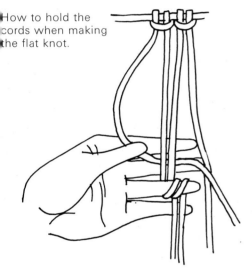

The threads in macramé can be held taut by a padded macramé board, or a drawing board with the heading cord fastened by drawing pins, or one can tie the thread to the knobs on the back of a chair. Attaching the cords is known as 'setting on' and this is done with a long length of cord folded in half.

Making the loop.

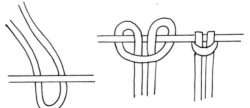

The sequence of stages to make the flat knot.

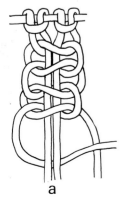

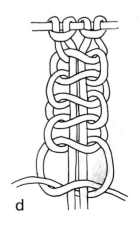

a   b   c   d   155

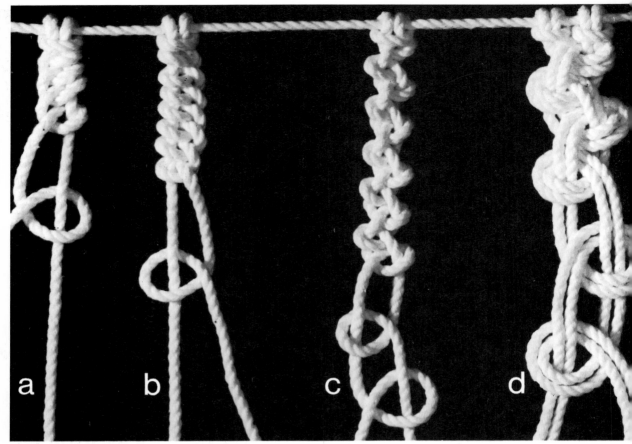

Blanket stitch or half-stitch is worked on a
single thread which hangs straight down,
a) with the left-hand thread, and b) with
the right-hand thread. When a length has
been worked on it, it can be twisted round
the straight cord into a spiral. In c) and d)
the half-hitches are made alternately with
both cords, c) with single threads, and
d) with double threads.

How to shape an armhole when working
from the top by increasing.

Increasing into chains and flat knots.

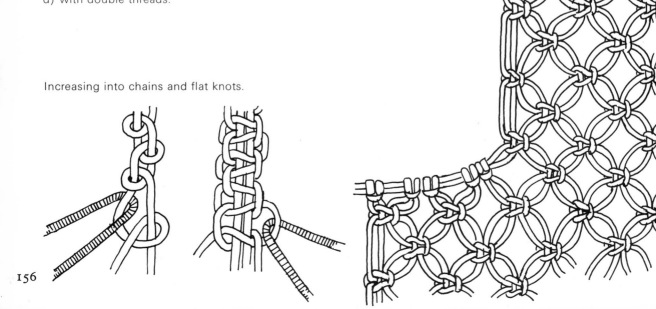

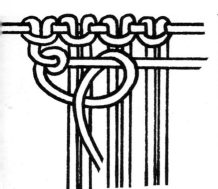

The foundation leader, on which the knotting is done, is always laid on top of all the cords. Usually it is one of the knotting lengths, and with each cord, two half-hitch knots are worked over it. For horizontal cording, the foundation thread is either the left-hand thread or the right-hand thread, and must always be kept taut.

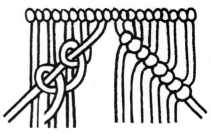

Any of the knotting lengths can become the leader.

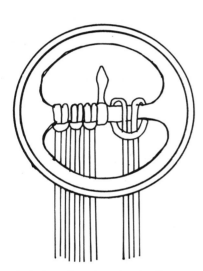

Threads being directly set onto the crossbar in a belt.

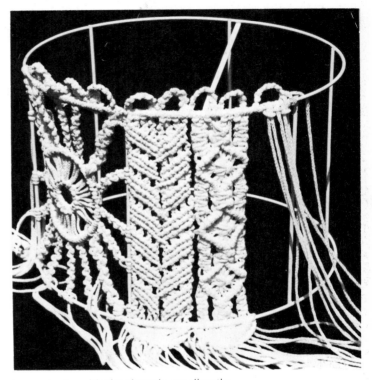

Lampshade with the threads set directly onto the painted frame.

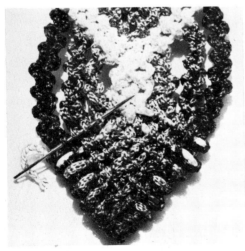

Sewing in the ends of the cords when one has reached the end of the belt.

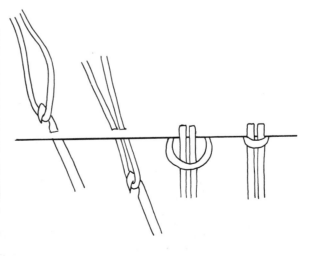

To attach the cords directly to a fabric, use a crochet hook to make the knot.

157

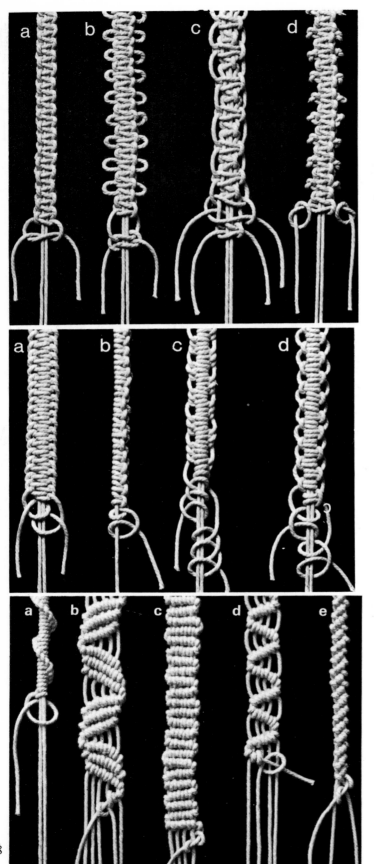

(Top) (a) Solomon's bar (b) Picots formed by completing the flat knot down the centre core then pushing it up tightly (c) Solomon's bar using 6 threads (d) Between alternate flat knots an overhand knot is worked to form a side knot.

(Centre) (a) Single genoese bar (b) Single tatted bar (c) treble genoese bar (d) tatted bar.

(Bottom) (a) corkscrew bar (b) braid using the left and right hand cords alternately as the leader (c) braid using left hand leader held horizontally (d) braid using left hand leader (e) braid using left hand thread as leader for each row.

(Right)
This macramé wallhanging has been worked as a sampler. Using 21 strands of white seine twine, mounted double to give 42 working strands, with extra strands introduced at intervals for the horizontal rows, it includes different types of sennits, knot buttons and patterns. The first row includes a berry knot, the second flat knot buttons, the third a Chinese crown knot, and the fifth a Josephine knot.

FURTHER READING
SCHMID-BURLESON, B., *The Technique of Macramé* Batsford
SHORT, E., *Introducing Macramé* Batsford

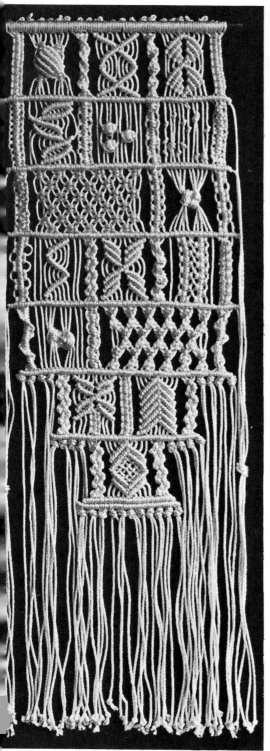

Lampshade with deep macramé fringe and with single chains emphasising the struts.

Josephine knot.

Japanese knot.

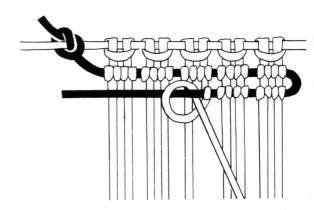

Horizontal and vertical cording in Cavandoli work, which forms a densely knotted fabric.

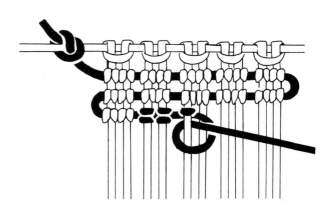

Shoulder bag in Cavandoli work using rug wool, and with a braided shoulder strap attached.

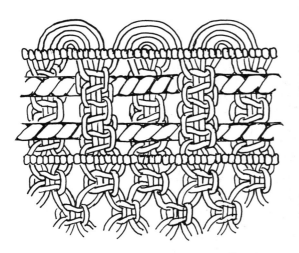

When making an open work bag using flat knots, a drawstring can be threaded through Solomon's bars at the top of the bag.

Experiment when you have learned the various stitches. Try using various colours, arranged randomly and arranged in an order.

160

Plaiting can be used to make a firm edge for an otherwise flimsy article.

Decorative edges can be made by forming picots with flat knots and cording, or scallops of chains.

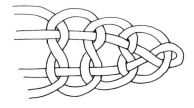

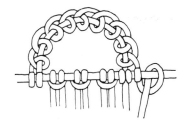

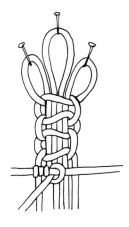

Marbling

Materials

trough (developing trough or roasting tin lined with aluminium foil); carragheen moss (a seaweed); ox-gall; alum; special marbling colours, or artists' oil colours, or waterproof inks; turpentine substitute or paraffin (kerosene); marbling comb; water; plain paper. Marbling can be used to make end papers, book covers, small boxes, collages, wallpaper, découpage, and mounts for pictures and greetings cards. There are two methods of marbling: the controlled and the uncontrolled method.

UNCONTROLLED METHOD

Use waterproof inks, or oil colours, thinned with turpentine. These are laid on the surface of the water with a brush. If the ink is dropped on it will just fall to the bottom. How far the colour spreads will depend on how long the brush is left touching the water. Use a separate brush for each colour. When there is enough colour on the water, stir gently with a pencil tip to mingle the colours a little, but the colours are perpetually moving on the water, so there is no point in trying to make any deliberate shapes. Holding a sheet of paper that will just fit into the trough in both hands, gently lower one edge of the paper onto the surface of the water, and let the whole sheet roll onto the water. Almost at once, lift the paper off the water with the same 'rolling' motion, and hang up to dry.

CONTROLLED METHOD

Instead of water, which keeps the inks permanently moving, this method uses a 'size': carragheen moss. When the colour is dropped onto this clear jelly-like surface, it will spread, but once it has reached its maximum spread (about 5 in.), the colour remains static, and can be moved around into various patterns with a comb. The pattern you see on the surface of the jelly is the one that will be picked up on the paper.

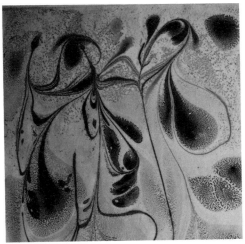

The very fine lines in this picture were made by drawing the colour out from the central blobs with an awl.

A detail from a piece of 'feathering'. Stripes of colour were laid on the jelly, and a home-made comb with four needles was drawn across the stripes at right angles.

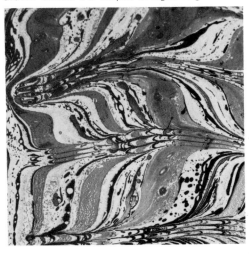

This type of pattern is caused by the addition of ox-gall to the surface after the colour has been applied.

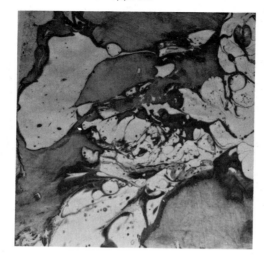

Some colours have very particular qualities when applied to carragheen moss. This is especially true of Prussian blue. The granulation happens most on the colour applied at the beginning. Less and less spreading happens with subsequent application, but at no time do the areas actually merge: there is always this curious fine white line which remains to separate the shapes.

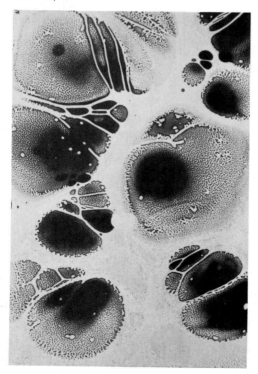

MATERIALS REQUIRED

To prepare the *carragheen moss*, boil a quart of water, and add 1 oz moss. Boil for 5 minutes, stirring continuously. Remove from the heat, and add another pint of cold water. Leave to stand for 24 hours. If it is to be kept for more than a day, add moss size preservative, 1 oz to 3 pints of size. Do not keep it for more than 6 days. When you are ready to begin marbling, strain the size through a piece of cotton or muslin into the trough. Do not squeeze the bag, it will make the size cloudy.

Veining liquid is made by adding 2 oz spirits of soap to 1 pint water, and shaking well. This will keep in a screw-topped bottle. *Alum water* is made by boiling 1 oz of alum in 1 pint of water until the alum is dissolved. This too can be kept in a capped bottle. Ox-gall must be bought ready prepared. Ox-gall water is made by mixing 12 drops of ox-gall with 6 tblsps water. Marbling colours are thinned with five or six drops of ox-gall to ¾ of the ounce bottle. The colours form sediments in the bottles, so shake well before pouring out.

Have one *brush* for each colour. Use *newspapers* for skimming the top of the 'jelly' to remove any skin that might have formed on it. This is done by laying the newspaper on the surface, and gently peeling it off. Have ready a pile of *paper* cut to the size of the trough on which you will do the marbling, and a *sponge* to damp (not wet) the paper with the alum water immediately before laying it on the 'jelly'; the alum absorbs the colours well, lifting the colours off the 'jelly'.

TURKISH, or STONE MARBLING

The jelly must be thinner for this than for the combed patterns. A blob of colour should spread about 7 in. for this method. The colours are dropped one on top of the other and have to be mixed with a different amount of ox-gall for each colour.

USING OIL COLOURS

Oil colours in tubes can also be used. They are thinned with turpentine substitute or paraffin (kerosene) (do not use both at the same time). Use about 2 in. of colour to a tsp of paraffin. If it drops to the bottom when the colour is splashed on it is too thick. If it spreads out too far, and there is hardly any colour left, add some more colour from the tube and stir well. When there is enough colour on the surface, you can start drawing a nail or a pencil point through the colours. The paper does not need to be sponged with alum water for oil colour. One can often take two prints from one colour sprinkling, though the second print will be paler than the first. Rinse off the excess colour and paste, and hang up to dry. All marbled papers can be ironed flat when they are dry.

USING BANANA-OIL-BASED COLOUR

This technique has many advantages over traditional marbling. It dries immediately, and can be applied to a wide range of materials: candles, egg-shells, wood, plastic, glass, leather, fabric, and metal. The pattern cannot be controlled, only the colour combinations. The colours are floated on top of a container of water. The object is immersed in the water so that it passes through the surface oil and is completely submerged. It is then taken out quickly, and as it breaks the surface oil, a layer of swirling decoration is deposited on the surface of the object as it is lifted out.

Colour-dip

Colour-dip marbling colours are deposited on the article as it passes down through the layer in the water. If the surface is not cleared while the article is submerged, when the article is lifted through the water, another layer (that remaining on the surface) will be deposited as well. This can be very attractive, if you want this type of effect.

'Free' marbling, done on water instead of jelly. The different effects are the result of the particular combinations of colours, and the manufacturer of the paints.

(Right)
This was made on a home-made jelly, using domestic gelatine. The result is always much softer than on carragheen moss and although the colours do move, they can be controlled.

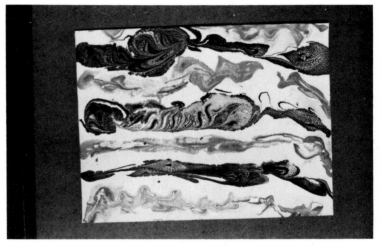

(Below)
The colour in this example was applied with a pipe cleaner. Pipe cleaners are pliable enough to be bent into many shapes and the cotton on them holds enough paint to apply to the jelly. (I am indebted to Jessica Butcher for this technique.)

These were made by dipping in the Colour-dip twice. The decoration was done on white card.

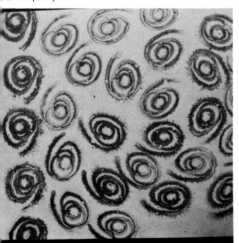

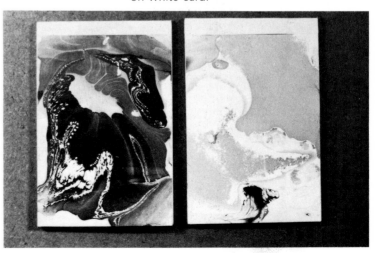

163

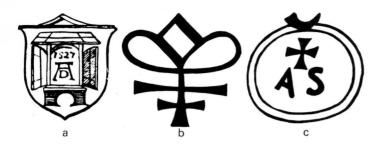

a   b   c

Marks

Marks have always been used by manufacturers, particularly printers, goldsmiths and
silversmiths and potters, and by artists. They
have also been used as personal embellish-
ments and signs of rank and status, or as means
of identification and ownership, such as cattle
brands. Another type of special distinguishing
mark is the mon. This is the name given to a
Japanese family crest, designed within a circle.
It is used on all that belongs to the family, and
on all except marriage, mourning, or hara-kiri
clothes. Woven or embroidered, it is placed at
the back of the neck, on each breast, and each
sleeve.

PRINTERS' MARKS

In the mid-fifteenth century printers and publishers were one and the same. In 1457 the
first printer's sign appeared, and in 1476 the
first decorated title page. Thomas Bewick
designed and cut thousands of wooden engravings for printers who might use many different
marks. Today a publisher retains a single distinguishing mark, known as a logotype.

d

e   f   g

A sample of marks used by artists and
monarchs: a) Dürer, b) Michelangelo,
c) the violin maker, Stradivarius,
d) Cellini, the Italian sculptor, e) Cardinal
Richelieu, f) Martin Luther, g) Cesare
Borgia, h) Henry VIII, i) Marie-Antoinette,
j) a hieroglyphic mark of Cleopatra II,
k) a cuneiform mark of Xerxes, l) a fluid,
abstract mark used by the great Hokusai.

h   i

k

l

j

164

A small sample of the enormous field of
Mon designs.

Marks of the potteries: a) Caughley,
b) Stafford, c) Bow, d) Sèvres,
e) Nymphenburg, f) Capo di Monte,
g) Worcester

b

c

d

e

f

g

The symbols of alchemy are particularly inventive. These represent: caustic lime, lime, urine, powder, iron filings, bismuth, fumes, egg-shells, to compose, vitriol, cinnabar and burned alum.

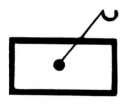

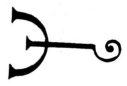

Marquetry

HISTORICAL

Wood for marquetry has to be in thin slices called veneers, so it was not until a process was found for cutting logs into thin ⅛ in. slices that the craft could develop. This came about in the sixteenth century when, in 1562, the wooden bow fret-saw was invented. Marquetry, like its predecessor intarsia (inlay), spread from Italy to France, Germany, and Holland in the sixteenth and seventeenth centuries, where it was used in the main on furniture. Doors and drawers were the favoured places to apply decoration, which was usually floral, or arabesque.

The marqueter to Louis XIV, André Boulle, developed a technique using thin tortoiseshell and brass or copper. A cunning method, it cuts the design out of both tortoiseshell and brass at the same time, resulting in two finished surfaces. In one the brass pieces are set into the tortoiseshell 'network', and in the other the tortoiseshell pieces are set into the brass 'network', one being called Boulle, and the other Counter Boulle. The furniture decorated in this way was made in matched pairs.

In England, Adam and Sheraton used marquetry, but not as it had been used in France. In 1780 the invention of the marquetry cutter's donkey enabled marquetry to be produced in a limited mass production, since up to ten pieces of veneer could be cut at the same time. Marquetry continued to be used in small quantities throughout the nineteenth century, and hardly an upright piano made before 1930 escaped being decorated with a little marquetry.

Tunbridge ware is a curious English offshoot into wood mosaic. It was made in and around Tunbridge Wells from the end of the seventeenth century to its full flowering at the time of the Great Exhibition of 1851. It was made on the same principle as seaside rock. Long strips of veneer were glued together into a solid block. The block was sliced up, like a loaf of bread, and each slice would have the same pattern on it. The cross-section of each strip was a square, and hundreds were used to make the smallest objects. One of the examples at the Great Exhibition was a table, which was made of 129,500 pieces of 33 different woods! All sorts of domestic objects were made in this ware: tea caddies, workboxes, pencil cases, writing cases, tables, games boxes. There is a museum devoted to this ware at Tunbridge Wells.

VENEERS

The patterning on the wood is called the 'grain'. The exact figuring of a piece of veneer depends ultimately upon the way the wood is sliced up, a change of angle producing a completely different figuring.

Straight grain is found in the main part of the wood where the fibres of the wood run parallel to its length.

'The Dovedale Eagle' by N. Douglas.

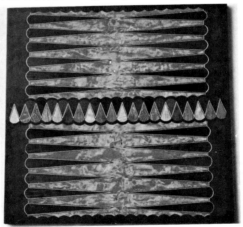

The contrast of woodgrain was important in the design of this backgammon board, to sharply define the areas required for the game.

Irregular grain is found where the tree divides to form branches, or where there is a knot or blemish caused by disease or insect attack.

Interlocking grain is found in tropical timbers where fibres in successive growth periods grow spirally in opposite directions.

Wavy grain is where the direction of the fibres undulates. Found in sycamore, maple, and African mahogany, known as fiddle-back as it was often chosen for the back of violins.

Burr veneer is cut from knobbly lumps growing naturally on the outside of some trees.

Curl or crotch veneer is cut from the junction of a branch and the main trunk of the tree. It has an ostrich feather type patterning.

Butt veneers are cut from the very base of the tree where the roots begin to spread out.

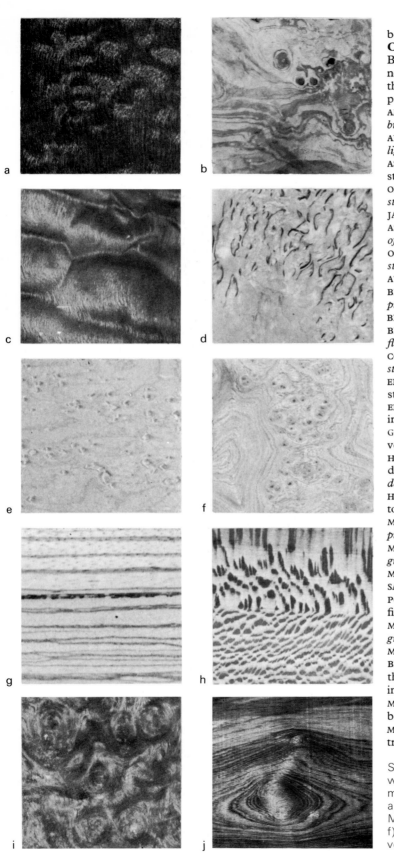

These last three are expensive veneers because of their scarcity and fragility.

Colour and quality

Because we are dealing with a natural material, no really accurate description can be given, but the following is a guide to colour, and some particular qualities.

AMBOYNA BURR close figured, brittle, *reddish brown*

ANTIARIS interlocking grain, very soft to cut, *light yellow*

ASH crown cut, wavy figuring, quarter cut, striped figuring, *off-white*

OLIVE ASH as above but with *light brown staining*

JAPANESE ASH wild grain, *straw coloured*

ASH BURR burr figuring in small patches, *off-white*

OLIVE ASH BURR very wild figuring, *light brown staining*

AVOIDIRE oblique quilted figuring, *pale yellow*

BIRCH, CANADIAN close grain, no figuring, *light pinky yellow*

BIRCH, SWEDISH as above, lighter in colour

BIRCH MASUR has groups of *dark markings, flecks*

COUBARIL *pink, dark brown/black irregular striped figuring*

ELM wavy figuring if crown cut, quarter cut striped, *pinkish brown*

ELM BURR porous, groups of knots, wild swirling between knots, *pinkish brown*

GREEN CYPRESS BURR *green*, best available in veneer

HAREWOOD chemically treated woods, figuring depends on original wood, *silver grey, blue grey, dark slate grey*

HORSE CHESTNUT almost no figuring, soft, easy to cut, *white*

MACASSAR EBONY hard, brittle, difficult to cut, *pinkish brown with black stripes*

MAGNOLIA soft, close texture, easy to cut, *light green, greenish brown*

MAHOGANY various *shades of reddish brown*

SAPELE MAHOGANY close regular stripe

POMMELE MAHOGANY a freak sapele, blistered figuring

MANSONIA very straight grain, easy to cut, *dark greyish brown*

MAPLE straight grained, *pinkish*

BIRD'S EYE MAPLE many tiny marks scattered throughout the grain, the result of insect infestation

MAPLE BURR soft, easy to cut, swirled figuring between knots, *pinkish brown*

MOVINGUE brittle, interlocked wavy grain, tricky to cut, *bright yellow*

Some of the very distinctively patterned woods which are of great importance in marquetry:
a) Pommele b) Olive Ash Burr c) Quilted Maple d) Masur Birch e) Bird's Eye Maple f) Elm Burr g) Zebrano h) Plane i) Burr veneer (maidu) j) Rosewood.

AK *light beige/brown*

USTRALIAN SILKY OAK like lace wood, well marked, *pinkish brown*

ADAUK brittle, open grained, little figuring, *carlet*

LANE TREE (LACEWOOD) well patterned (see llustration), *pinkish-orange brown*

URPLEHEART straight graining, little figuring, *urple violet*

OSA PEROBA sometimes has freak figuring, *almon pink*

RAZILIAN ROSEWOOD striped, or wild figuring, *eddish brown with black*

NDIAN OR BOMBAY ROSEWOOD *purplish stripes n brown background*

(rosewoods are all brittle, very difficult to cut)

YCAMORE plain, or faintly striped or fiddle-acked, *white*

EAK straight grained, with darker stripes, *rown*

HUYA BURR groups of very small almost *black nots, mid brown*

VALNUT, ENGLISH *mid-brown deep brown figur-ng*

VALNUT, AMERICAN darker with *greyish black arkings*

VALNUT, CHARBONNIER *very dark, real black in laces*

ENGE *dark brown* with very fine *close black tripes*

EBRANO coarse open grain, *brown stripes on uff*

How to alter the
hape of a knife
lade to make it
xactly right for
harquetry cutting.

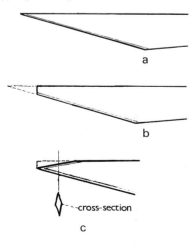

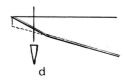

TOOLS

The main ones are a knife, a sharpening stone, a cutting board, carbon paper, tracing paper, sticky tape, glue.

Knives

Almost all the cutting is done with the tip of the knife, so the most useful shape is one which tapers to a fine point. The blade should be as thin as possible without snapping easily. Pen-knives are really too thick. The best sort are ones with interchangeable blades. There are lots of these knives on the market, called craft knives, but a surgical knife (a handle with interchangeable blades) is sharper, though fragile. A number 4 handle with a size 23 blade (curved) for heavy cutting, and for cutting against a straight edge: and number 3 handle with a size 11 blade for all other cutting will be adequate. Having chosen your knife, it must be kept sharp. A few strokes of the blade on a small oilstone every 15 minutes or so will be enough to keep it sharp normally. When the point breaks, resharpen, do not throw it away. The resharpened blade is more efficient. The new diamond-shaped cross section slides easily through the veneer.

Cutting board

This should be of a soft wood ($\frac{3}{8}$ to $\frac{1}{2}$ in. plywood), so as not to blunt the knife too easily.

Carbon paper

Black carbon paper is used for transferring the design to the veneer. Do not use the blue carbon paper, it is indelible. Yellow (dress-maker's) carbon paper is useful when working on dark woods. For marking through, an old biro will do, but it makes a rather thick line. The rounded end of a toothpick is better.

Gummed paper

This holds the various parts of the design as they are cut. Blu-Tack (Plasti-Tak) is quicker.

Glue

Cold glues such as Cascamite one-shot, Resin W, or Evostik are suitable, as long as there is some sort of press in which to hold the veneers while they are setting. They have the advantage of enabling you to move the pieces around until they are correctly positioned. Impact glues such as Evostick Impact (Elmer's Contact Cement) need no press, but the pieces must be placed in the right position first time. Once the piece is set down, it cannot be moved.

Presses

The larger the picture the more essential a press is, either the old-fashioned type of centre-screwed letter press, or a home-made one from two pieces of blockboard and G clamps (C clamps).

a) Six G-clamps, two sheets of blockboard, and six wooden slats are used to make a simple press.

b) The home-made press assembled.

CUTTING THE PICTURE

The 'window' method

The line drawing, on tracing paper, is hinged with a length of brown sticky paper at the top of a sheet of waste veneer. (One that is light in colour and easy to cut, sycamore, or horse chestnut.) Stick brown sticky tape along the edges of the waste veneer on the back to prevent it splitting. Slip a sheet of black carbon paper under the tracing, and with a fine hard point, trace the line drawing through the tracing paper and onto the waste veneer. Remove the carbon paper, and turn back the tracing paper.

Using the point of the knife, make a series of short, pricking cuts, following the line as exactly as possible. Do not try to make long cuts. Do not try to cut right through the veneer at one go. You will probably have to go over the line several times before the piece is loose and you can take it out. When it is loose, lift it out.

You now have a hole in the waste veneer, the 'window'. Behind this 'window' you can slip various pieces of veneer, until you are satisfied with the colour, grain, and figuring. When you have decided on the piece of veneer, temporarily fix it on the back of the window with some Sellotape (Scotch tape).

With the point of the knife, carefully following the edge of the window, make short pricking cuts as you did to remove the window. Once you have marked the shape, the piece can be taken from behind the window, and worked in the open. Finish the cutting. The cut piece is then fitted into the window (as if you were putting in a piece of a jigsaw puzzle) and with small pieces of brown sticky tape, fasten it at the back to the waste veneer. The next piece is then cut and so on, until the whole picture is completed.

The base board

Never use solid wood: it is too prone to warp; use either plywood, or blockboard. Cut the base board exactly to size, making sure the corners are at right angles. Roughen the edges with a hacksaw blade to provide a 'key' for the glue.

Gluing the marquetry to the base board

The face of the marquetry is now covered with strips of brown sticky tape. When this has dried, the small holding pieces used on the back can be wetted and removed. Do not use too much water. A sponge dipped in water and wiped over the pieces is the safest method. Leave the picture to dry.

Apply the glue to the blockboard and to the back of the marquetry. The marquetry piece is on the table glue-side uppermost, and the base board is laid carefully down on it. Turn the base board over, cover with a sheet of polythene and several layers of newspaper, and place in the press. Do not use too much pressure; all that is needed is to get rid of any excess glue. Too much pressure can deform the veneer, and cause splitting later. When the panel is taken from the press, any veneer extending over the edges is sandpapered flush with the edges.

PARQUETRY

This is the term for geometrical marquetry. It is often found on eighteenth-century furniture; it is quick to do, and can be very effective. It is essential to make a special jig for this work, the two strips of wood must have absolutely true edges, and be set at an angle of exactly 60 degrees. Arrange strips of two contrasting colours in alternating rows, staggering them as you do so. Tape them together with sticky tape. The fabricated sheet is then placed on one edge and parallel strips cut. The resulting strips are then re-arranged to produce various geometric patterns.

The 'window' method. Cutting the first window in the waste veneer.

Removing the small holding pieces of brown sticky paper from the back with a sponge and very little water.

Brown sticky paper is glued to the front to hold the pieces together.

Gluing the blockboard to the back of the piece of marquetry.

The Llangattock table, made by Jean François Oeben. (Courtesy of Christies.)

The jig, steel rule, etc. for making geometric marquetry (parquetry).

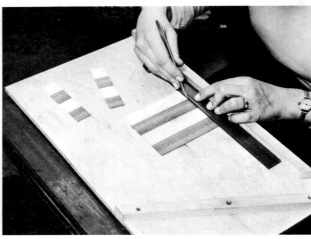

Cutting the taped stripes at right-angles.

Cutting the parallel strips.

Arranging the pieces in a checker-board pattern.

Taping the strips together, with brown sticky tape.

Cutting the stripes diagonally.

Some possible arrangements of diagonally-cut strips.

Chest of drawers decorated with parquetry.

MARQUETRY SOCIETY

Chairman: J.D. Savage, 141 Conway Rd, London, N14.
Hon. Sec.: Mrs G.M. Walker, 113 Kingsway, Petts Wood, Kent.

FURTHER READING

CAMPKIN, M., *Introducing Marquetry* Batsford

HAMILTON JACKSON, F., *Intarsia & Marquetry* (1903)

KITSON, K., *Marquetry & Veneers* Foyles Handbooks

LINCOLN, W., *Wood Technology* Art Veneers Co. Ltd

PENNY, C., *The Fascination of Marquetry*

PINTO, E.H., *The Craftsman in Wood*

Table commissioned by Liberty's one-off department from Peter Niczewski, 1975.

Metal Mesh Embroidery

This technique opens up two-dimensional embroidery, by virtue of the fact that one is no longer bound by a rectangular edge to the picture. The metal can be cut to any shape you choose, and because of the rigidity of the metal mesh there is almost no limit to the objects which can be appliquéd or held on to it. There is no distortion, and no problem with fabrics or threads shrinking as in the traditional embroidery panel.

An endless list of objects, from metal rings, large polystyrene packing blocks, and children's wooden cube beads, to toy cars, can be attached to the mesh or chicken wire. Curved stitching is an obvious technique to use on this base, but if you use it, remember to work the background shape first before doing the curved stitching. It is very difficult to fill in the shape left by curved stitching once it has been done.

Use folded clear tape all round the edges to prevent the edges of the mesh catching on the thread all the time, and a blunt (tapestry) needle. This way a child can use this technique. The skills involved in using a needle and thread are very easily mastered when the base is rigid.

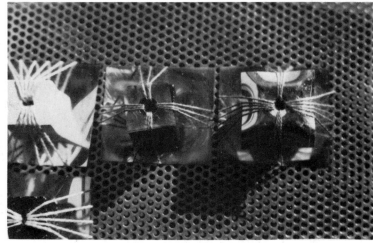

The rigidity of metal mesh and its capacity for holding large objects to its surface without buckling was explored in this example. Various methods of securing the wooden cubes were tried, including the use of stiff Melimex. The curves formed by bending the Melimex with the threads added a very interesting new dimension to work with.

If the background of curved stitching is to be filled in, this should be done first. This particular example also uses a sheet of coloured acrylic with circles cut out of it, which is held in with superimposed stitching. (For curved stitching technique see Pin and Thread section.)

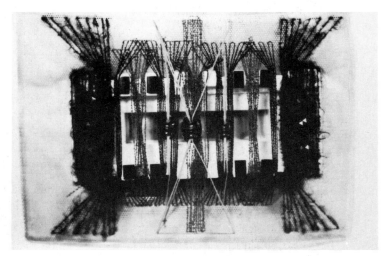

This followed the experiments of the above illustration using a large polystyrene block (Styrofoam) used in packing.

Mizuhiki

Mizuhiki is a traditional Japanese artform. Bundles of wire which have been tightly covered in gold or silver paper are interwoven into symmetrical shapes of breathtaking delicacy.

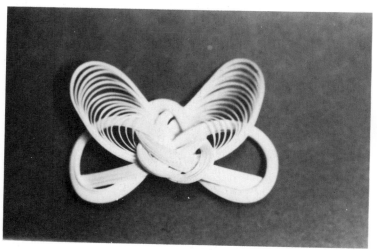

A commercial hair decoration made of bundles of split bamboo, using the mizuhiki technique.

Monoprints

The first artist who is known to have used this technique is Castiglione in 1635, in Rome. There are many examples of his work in the Royal Library at Windsor Castle. Blake also used the monoprint technique, but it was Degas who really explored its possibilities. He produced hundreds, from 1 in. by 1 in. to 24 in. by 17 in. Gaugin, Pissarro, and Corot all made monoprints, and in this century, Klée, Picasso, Rouault, and Matisse all used it, but Ernst as always experimented with it more freely than the others.

METHOD

Draw with a brush onto a piece of plate glass using block printing ink. Lay a sheet of paper onto the glass over the ink drawing. Press all over with the palm of your hand. Carefully peel off the paper. There will now be a print of the drawing on the paper.

FURTHER READING

PALMER, F., *Monoprint Techniques* Batsford
RASMUSEN, *Print-making with Monotype* Chilton Co., 1960

To make a monoprint by inking up the glass plate itself, gently lay a sheet of paper over a glass plate which has been inked up evenly, and draw into this paper with a cocktail stick or fingernail.

Peel off the paper carefully, and the lines appear as 'soft' lines on the paper. The grey areas at the edge in the illustration are made by rubbing the back of the paper with a finger. A neat border can be made round monotypes if a 'window' is cut out of a piece of paper and placed on the inked slab before the paper is laid on and the drawing made.

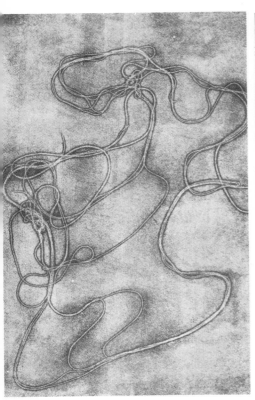

For this thread monoprint the glass plate is inked-up, threads are laid at random on it, and a print is taken. The thread is then removed from the inked plate, and another print is taken from the slab. The mark of the thread is left on the slab, and it is this that makes the line. The print is grey because most of the ink was taken up by the first print (the thread would have appeared as white on the first print). The darker outlines around the line are typical of this method.

Glass filament mosaic by Tom Fairs.

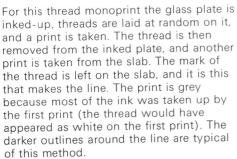

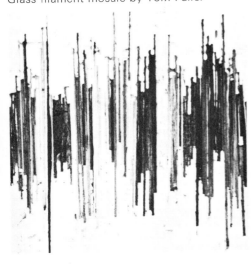

Paper shapes can be laid on an inked slab, and when a print is taken, the paper acts as a stencil, leaving its shape in white on the paper.

Mosaics

Mosaic is the technique of applying small pieces of material closely together to decorate an object or surface, and was developed by the Sumerians, Greeks, and Romans. The high peak of mosaic art was reached in the eleventh and twelfth centuries by the Byzantines; but even the glory of the Byzantine mosaics pales before the exuberance of the mosaics of the Aztec civilization. Obsidian, quartz, garnet, beryl, malachite, marcasite, jadeite, shell, gold, mother of pearl were the materials used in their mosaics, but the favourite was turquoise. Rather than applied to architecture, the Aztecs used it on religious ceremonial objects, clothes, masks, shields, collars, medallions, knife handles, ear plugs, mirrors, and skulls. The materials were stuck with vegetable gum onto wood, leather, pottery, shell, stone, and possibly paper.

MATERIALS
Smalti
These are opaque glass cubes, square or rectangular.
Tesserae
These are thin square pieces of opaque glass or stained glass. They are expensive, but have a

huge colour range; the finest quality comes from Venice. The cheapest are the earth colours, burnt umber, terracotta, yellow ochre; gold and silver colours are the most expensive. The earliest tesserae were $\frac{1}{4}$ in. by $\frac{1}{4}$ in., but now they are usually $\frac{1}{2}$ in. by $\frac{3}{4}$ in., and uneven, which is what gives the glittering quality so typical of mosaics. Smaller tesserae, made from long threads of glass cut up into small pieces, are known as *filato*.

Much cheaper are the commercial tesserae bought either loose by the pound, or stuck onto 1 ft sheets of paper. These are $\frac{3}{4}$-in. square. The colour range is small, but they can easily be cut by tile cutters into smaller squares, strips or triangles. Home-made tesserae can be easily made if one has access to a kiln. They can be dull or glossy (depending on the glazes used) and can be any thickness, shape or colour.

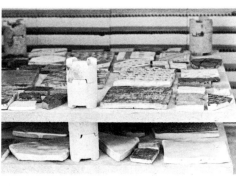

a) Stacking the kiln. The tall circular discs are the supports for the next shelf.
b) The tesserae in the kiln.
c) Marbles ready for firing.

Commercial ceramics

These are bought in tile form either glazed or encaustic. A glazed tile has the colour in the glaze which is only on the surface of the tile; this has the advantage of a large colour range. The encaustic tile has the colouring matter added to the clay before it is fired, and the colour therefore goes right through the tile. All the early Roman tiles were encaustic.

Stained glass

This can be bought as offcuts or as sheets. The hardest glass is that which has the colour 'flashed' on, i.e. it is on one side only, and that should only be cut on the unflashed side. Colourless glass can have colour backed to it; coloured glass (as used for stained glass) is used on a white base so that the colour shines through.

Slab glass

Imported from France, 8 in. by 12 in. by 1 in. thick, it has a wide range of colours but is expensive. It is used in concrete where the concrete itself plays a very important part in the design. Slab glass mosaics are usually designed over a light box.

Bottle glass

Break up empty bottles by putting them inside some very thick brown paper bags, or under several layers of sacking, and smashing them with a hammer.

Pebbles, stones

These can be collected from most beaches. (See the section on Pebbles.)

Shells

Most varieties of shells can be used for mosaics except the tellins and razor shells which are much too fragile. The tough shells such as limpet, whelk, mussel, top, cockle, scallop, venus winkle, cowrie, wentletrap, and saddle oyster are fine. Most of these will have to have their hollow side filled in with a fine cement such as Nic-o-Bond Thickbed, and then glued onto a wooden base with Unibond, Evostik or Bostik (DuPont Duco Cement, Contact Cement).

Seeds, beans, bark

These include such things as runner beans, lentils, wheat, peppercorn, hollyhock, cow parsley, bark, and driftwood.

Other materials

Wood offcuts sawn up, metal bottle tops, etc.

METHOD

In the traditional method the tesserae are set into wet mortar. Today, one uses a flexible adhesive and glues directly onto a plywood or hardboard surface. If the mosaic is to hang against a wall the backing board must be waterproofed, and the hangers (heavy duty ones) fixed on before the mosaic is laid. One possibility is to lay out your chosen design, and then very carefully pour over it a casting resin. These are highly durable and absolutely impervious, and one can experiment by adding stainers to them.

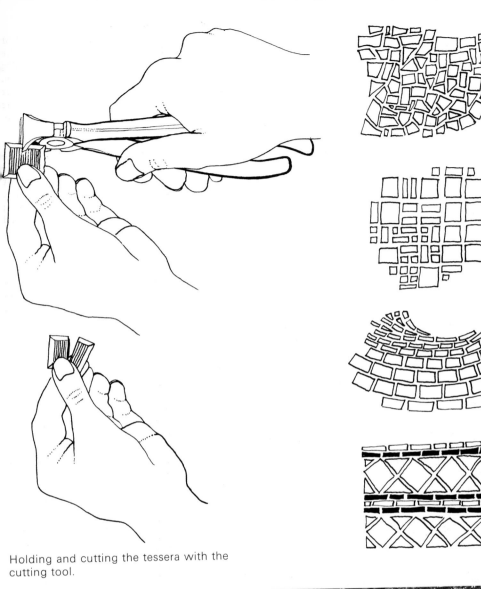

Different methods of arranging the tesserae.
a) Irregular shapes fitted closely together.
b) Rectangular shapes of different sizes to fill the area.
c) Tesserae cut up into small pieces to 'follow the form'.
d) Tesserae arranged in a very formal way to make an organized, repeating pattern.

a

b

c

d

Holding and cutting the tessera with the cutting tool.

Large tiles made up of many sections. This method is used in the large mosaics put up on prestigious new buildings.

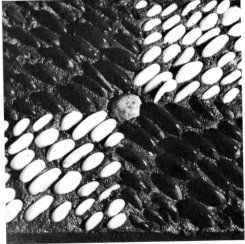

The pavement tile uses pebbles arranged in formal pattern blocks, and often consists of sea-worn ovoid pebbles.

Another very simple method of making a mosaic is to nail a frame onto a plywood base. The frame is to contain the plastic cement. Fill the framed base with a layer of Nic-o-Bond trowelled to a depth of 1 in. Onto this lay the stones, pebbles, ceramics, or whatever you have chosen, and when the arrangement satisfies, press them down into the plastic cement. The cement can be coloured with Cementone (a powder added to cement as used in the building trade), which comes in a few colours. Nic-o-Bond is fairly slow drying, about 2 to 4 hours, but when making a mosaic picture, it is advisable to leave it 3 or 4 days to really dry out.

A third method is to use plasticine. For this, roll out the plasticine until it is the same size as the final picture, and of a more or less even thickness. A tracing of the design of the final size is laid over the plasticine. Roll a tailor's wheel along the lines of the tracing paper when you have finished. The design will be impressed into the plasticine in a series of dotted lines from the tailor's wheel. Set onto the plasticine the pieces of tesserae, cut to shape where needed. When the picture has been completed, take a rolling pin and roll gently all over the picture, pressing the tesserae down into the plasticine – but no more than $\frac{1}{3}$ in.

Alternatively, one can place a piece of wood over the whole picture, and gently hammer all over. This is to ensure that the surface is even. Roll a strip of plasticine and place all round the mosaic to make a little wall to hold the glue. Clean sacking (burlap) is now placed over the mosaic. Mix a syrupy mixture of gum arabic and with a stiff paint brush, brush the glue all over the sacking. It must be water soluble because at a later stage this sacking has to be soaked off. Leave until the glue has quite hardened, preferably overnight. Place a board over the entire mosaic, and turn it upside down onto a table. The board is now on the bottom, the sacking on that, the tesserae glued to that, and right on the top is the plasticine. Starting from one end, carefully roll back the plasticine. Any tesserae that have not stuck to the sacking can be glued back onto it.

A prepared frame is placed around the mosaic. A piece of expanded metal, $\frac{1}{2}$ in. smaller all round than the frame, is cut and put on one side. Mix 1 part lime and 8 parts sand with 2 parts cement. Add water slowly until the mixture is of a thick syrupy consistency. Pour over the mosaic to a depth of $\frac{1}{4}$ in. and press into all the cracks between the tesserae. Leave to dry for an hour. Now place the expanded metal on this mortar grout. A different mortar is now mixed to fill up the frame: 1 part cement with $2\frac{1}{2}$ parts sand. Mix to a stiff consistency, and trowel on evenly. Tamp down until the water begins to rise.

If the mosaic is to be permanently fixed to the wall, it is left uneven so as to form a 'key' to attach it to the wall. If it is to be hung on the wall, the surface is finished off level. Leave it to dry for 4 or 5 days. When dry, take off the frame, turn it over, and strip off the sacking. If the sacking sticks, sponge it with a damp sponge. Any tesserae that have pulled off, stick back with Evostik (Duco Cement). Finally sponge the surface with warm water to remove all traces of the glue.

For laying patios use the following foundation mortar: 4 parts sharp sand, 4 parts gravel ($\frac{1}{2}$ in.), 1 part portland cement. Lay to a depth of $\frac{1}{2}$ in.

MAKING TESSERAE

Cutting tesserae
Although tesserae, smalti, ceramics, and tiles can be cut with ordinary nippers, mosaic cutters are far better. They are adjustable to different thicknesses, and produce clean, accurate cuts. Hold the tessera in the left hand; with the right hand hold the tool far up the handle and close the cutters over just $\frac{1}{16}$ in. of the edge of the tessera. With a sharp nip, it will cut cleanly in two. If the tessera is placed right inside the jaws of the cutters, it is much more likely to shatter.

Glass cutting
Lay the glass on a perfectly level surface, on a cloth. Lay a steel rule on the glass and run the cutter along the edge of the rule. Do not stop in the middle of a cut. It must be a smooth, continuous movement. Do not saw the glass, or apply too much pressure. Score the glass into squares. Turn the glass over and gently tap across the line with the ball end of the cutter. Glass is always tapped on the reverse side of the cuts.

When using glass tesserae, either lay the pieces onto a ground that is prepared with white Polyfilla, or white paint, or back the pieces of glass with aluminium foil. A sheet of glass can itself be used as the base for a mosaic, and the pieces of coloured glass can be stuck onto the glass base with Bostik, Araldite, or Tensol (Duco Cement). Several layers of glass can be used and one can overlay pieces of glass of different sizes, and experiment with overlapping colour.

Putty for glass mosaics
Mix 3 parts whiting, 1 part Sirapite (or plaster of Paris), lamp black powder (to mix to a dark grey black), linseed oil (to mix to a dryish paste), turpentine (to make to a putty consistency). This 'putty' is worked into the cracks between the glass tesserae when making translucent glass mosaics.

Making clay tesserae
Onto a square of sacking or polythene lay a ball of clay. Roll it out between two strips of wood so that it is of an even thickness ($\frac{1}{8}$ in. to $\frac{1}{4}$ in.). Cut the clay up into regular sized pieces and impress into the soft clay either man-made objects, such as screw heads, keys, cogs, etc., or natural objects such as dried grasses, leaves,

fingers, shells, etc. Draw in wax crayons onto the almost dry clay before glazing.

From this stage one can proceed in two ways. Allow the clay tesserae to dry out completely (takes about a week), fire them in a kiln to 1650 °F (900 °C) (biscuit firing). When cold, apply glaze to the porous surface, then re-fire them at 2010 °F (1100 °C). Alternatively dry the clay until it is just 'leather hard' (this takes a few hours), apply the glaze and fire just once at 1910° to 2010 °F (1050° to 1100 °C). This method produces less intense colours than the first.

Slip is a mixture of sieved clay diluted with water until it is like thin cream. It can be coloured by the addition of oxides, or a white slip can be used as a good reflective base for other coloured glazes. Glaze is the glass-like coating applied to the clay to protect it, and make it impervious to water. Glazes are bought ready for mixing, with full instructions for use. During the firing process, the clay and glaze expand and contract, the final size of the clay object having noticeably shrunk. Normally, suppliers of pottery materials supply the glazes appropriate to the type of clay supplied, because the clay and the glaze applied to it must expand and contract at the same rate. If in any doubt about the glaze, add up to 30% of the clay being glazed to the glaze being applied.

First, coat the underside of the clay slab with melted candle wax. This is to make sure that the slab does not stick to the kiln when it is being fired. Melt the paraffin wax (candles melted down or lumps of candle wax) in a large *enamel* or *metal* baking tin. It should be large enough to take the sheet of clay which has been rolled out. Lift the slab of clay out, and when the wax has hardened (a matter of moments) the slab can be dipped into a large receptacle of slip or glaze. Make sure that there are no greasy fingerprints on the side that is being glazed. The grease will react to the glaze or slip in the same way as the candle wax is designed to, i.e. it will reject it. Allow a short while for the glaze/slip to dry before either cutting it up completely into separate pieces, or just score into the shape you want, and leave the breaking up into pieces until after the slab has been fired, either by tapping gently on the back with a tack hammer, or using a tile nipper on the edge of the scored line. Scoring a line is marking it with a knife only on the surface, not going even half-way through the thickness of the clay.

It is obviously quicker to load a kiln up with several slabs of clay than with a quantity of little tesserae, but in making them individually you can experiment with different shaped pieces.

Firing

The kiln shelves must be coated with flint or kiln wash before the tesserae are stacked, even if you have waxed the bottoms of the slabs. Firing is expensive, so always load the kiln fully before starting a firing.

Glass can also be melted down in the kiln. Stained glass, bottle glass, and marbles can all be used. When they have been melted down, all the edges are rounded and they can be used like pebbles, using them as they come from the kiln. Marbles can be set in a clay trough. Bottle and stained glass can be broken up into the sizes required, and laid directly on the kiln shelves, or if large pieces are required, use terracotta flowerpot saucers. But in either case, the kiln shelf and the flowerpot saucer must be coated with kiln wash or the melting glass will fuse to it. Melting points for glass are as follows: at 1270° to 1314 °F (690° to 730 °C) the glass begins to bend at the edges, and from 1314° to 1350 °F (730° to 750 °C) the edges of the glass are completely rounded. Melted glass is a very useful addition to any sort of mosaic.

The pattern units of this table top design were arranged face down on squares of tracing paper. With the edges of the paper being used as handles, the units were lifted into position. Adhesive was applied to the surface, and the table board was pressed on top. When the adhesive had dried, the table was turned the right way up, and the tracing paper was peeled off the mosaic's surface.
(Below)

Methods of laying the tesserae

This will depend firstly on the material being used for the mosaic, whether seeds, smalti, bark, or random shaped tesserae, and secondly upon the kind of design, whether a repeating all over pattern, a figure set in a plain background, or an abstract arrangement of shapes, textures, lines (Filato) or colours. In a repeating pattern they can be placed in a regular way, but utilize a wide variety of sizes, if not shapes. (To bore in art, as in anything else, is unforgivable.) If the subject is a figure they can follow the main directions of the lines of the figure. If the picture is an abstract arrangement they can either be haphazard, or directly related to the shapes in the picture, but either way must follow a recognizable theme.

FURTHER READING

HUTTON, H., *Mosaic Making Techniques* Batsford

STRIBLING, *Mosaic Techniques* George Allen & Unwin

MOSAICS

TRADITIONAL	HOME-MADE	FOUND
Smalti	*Clay*	Bottle glass
Tesserae	Glazed	Pebbles
Filato	Impressed	Stones
Millefiore	Encaustic	Shells
Commercial ceramics	Slip	Seeds
Stained glass	Melted:	Bark
Slab glass	Bottle-glass	Scrap metal
	Marbles	
	Scraps of wood (natural or man-made, sawn into regular units)	

Façade in Mexican mosaics of stone, ceramics and coloured glass by José Chauvez Morado.

Nails, Pins and Screws

NAILS

BOX NAIL round flat head (smaller diameter than common nail)

CLOUT NAIL large-headed nail for fixing thick materials, e.g. felt to wood

CHAIR NAIL usually brass finish, has decorative large domed head for edging upholstery, especially leather

COMMON NAIL round flat head, strong nail for heavy work

HARDBOARD PIN developed for use with hardboard with a special head for sinking down into the hardboard

FINISHING NAIL small deep head (lost head or brad head) round or oval, countersunk and therefore less visible than flathead nails

FRENCH NAIL for rough work only, large head

LOST HEAD NAIL for fine work, the head is punched down below the surface of the wood

MASONRY PIN for fixing direct into masonry, made of hardened steel; can snap suddenly if hit incorrectly

PICTURE SPRIG for holding glass to picture frames; has no head

PANEL PIN very small pin for lightweight work, often used with glue

TACK very short, very sharp, very large head, used in upholstery for fixing fabrics to wood

WIRE NAIL, OVAL thin nail, oval to reduce likelihood of wood splitting; can be bought in round section too

WROUGHT NAIL fairly soft metal (iron) which can be turned over for a better grip

PINS

STAPLE legs can be the same length or one longer; used for fixing wire to wood

INSULATED STAPLE for attaching flex to woodwork

SADDLE TACK wiring is laid in the opened-out tack, which is then buckled close

CORRUGATED FASTENER for butt jointing quickly and simply

SCREW NAIL very strong grip

NEEDLE POINT a fine pin for invisibly fixing mouldings; the head is snapped off flush

DOWEL NAIL has a point at both ends, used in hidden joints

JOINERS BRAD small flat carpentry nail

1 round, flat head

2 round, lost head

3 box

4 oval brad head

5 oval lost head

6 lath

7 panel pins

8 clout

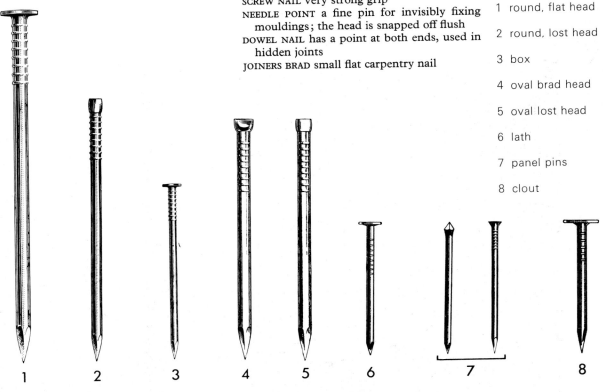

1   2   3   4   5   6   7   8   183

SCREWS

There are three types of heads to screws: a *slit*; a *cross* (Phillips); or *Posidriv* (a cross plus another grooved cross).

COUNTERSUNK WOOD SCREW top of the screw lies flush with the surface of the wood

ROUND HEAD SCREW whole of head remains above level of surface

POSIDRIV HEAD, COUNTERSUNK has grooves in the top in the shape of a cross, special design to stop slipping, and has to be used with appropriate Posidriv screwdriver.

All the above have special cups or washers to improve the appearance or spread the strain.

COACH SCREW extra large screw with a square head so it can be tightened even more with a spanner (wrench)

SELF-TAPPING SCREW for sheet metal, cuts its thread as it is screwed in

DOWEL SCREW each end has a screw thread on it, for invisible fixing

SCREW EYE put in by hand, the head is a complete ring, used for threading wire or string through

Metal sculpture of steel, brass, and bronze rods, by Dusan Dzamonja.

Op Art

Op (optical illusion) art relies on confusing the brain with particular ambiguous arrangements of shapes. They consist of an equal proportion of black and white, however they may be distributed. We are designed physiologically to make 'sense' of what we see, and we do this by finding the structure of any arrangement. If there are two identical structures, one white and one black, the eye moves rapidly from one to the other trying to find the dominant one, and this rapid eye movement causes the dazzle typical of op art. Vasarely began working on op art between 1931 and 1938, and continued after 1951, but in England, Bridget Riley is the most well known practitioner.

Equal portions of complementary colours (red and green, orange and blue, etc.) may be used instead of black and white.

Exactly the same procedure of cutting out concentric circles could have been used in this example, but instead of altering the stripes at a fixed 90° change each time, they are moved progressively a little more off the horizontal.

Most op art images are worked out carefully to some predetermined plan, and all the edges of the shapes must be very sharp for the visual disturbance to work. The original paper could have been painted in black and white stripes of equal widths. Concentric circles with an equal distance between each circle could then have been cut out. By rotating the outermost ring until the stripes were at right angles to the background, keeping the next ring parallel to the background and so on until the centre was reached, one could achieve the effect in this picture.

This time great care has been taken to see that the black stripes of one circle correspond exactly to the white stripes of the previous circle and so on, producing the checkerboard pattern. Most intriguing is the effect of changing the colour of the border around the design. By shifting the emphasis of the shapes, one can see black shapes on a white ground, or vice versa.

185

'Super novae' by Victor Vasarely. The structure of this picture is symmetrical vertically. Notice the grey spots which appear at the intersection of the white lines. These are called 'after-images'.

FURTHER READING

LANCASTER, J., *Introducing Op Art* Batsford

Origami

This is a technique of paper folding invented by the Japanese. There are two main rules to observe: the first is that the paper must always be square, the second is that nothing can be added to the shape, or pieces cut away from the square shape. Traditionally the paper used was white, but most origami paper which one buys in packs now is white on one side and coloured on the other. It does have one advantage being bi-coloured in that it is easier to follow the instructions for folding.

Traditionally the shapes are made into figures, animals, and birds. It is a very exact craft, and all the folds must be made as accurately as possible, because any inaccuracy in an early fold becomes exaggerated with the succeeding folds. The crease of the fold must be 'sharp', so rub the fold with a bone folder or the back of your thumb nail. When reading the instructions to make an origami, make sure that you understand the symbols before you start. There is no uniformity of symbols so check what a given author means by his particular symbols before you begin. Very simple folding is all that is needed to make a variety of paper party hats, masks, boats, decorations, and mobiles.

FURTHER READING

HARBIN, R., *Secrets of Origami* Octopus

1

2

3

4

5

6

7

This hat can be made from newspaper. The change in tone in the final drawing shows how the hat will look if origami paper coloured on one side only is used. These hats are very simple to make, and can have decorations added to turn them into party hats.

Paints

Great improvements have been made in the manufacture of paints for school use, for the amateur, and for the professional.

Powder colours

They are the cheapest of all, and are available in a wide range of colours. They can be mixed with water, or made into finger paint with a *non-fungicide* wallpaper paste. A dilute PVA (white) glue can be mixed with it, and when dry, is waterproof and shiny. If the powder colour is used with PVA, remember to wash the brushes out very thoroughly, or they will dry hard and be useless.

When choosing colours, it is important to buy three blues, cerulean, Prussian and ultramarine (or cobalt), and two yellows, a warm and a cooler one. Firms have different names for their colours; a cold yellow is generally listed as lemon yellow, a warm one as yellow. It is vital to have these colours, because it is only when one has a range of blues that one can make a range of greens or lilacs. Viridian is another colour which cannot be mixed, and which makes an exciting addition to one's colour choice. These plus a warm orange-red and a cooler red and plenty of white and black will provide a stimulating area of colour exploration and mixing.

Poster colours

These are powder colours mixed to a paste and ready to use from the pot.

Designer's gouache

Designer's gouache colours are very finely ground colours, with a high pigment content, and are manufactured in colours not available in poster colours.

Designer's acrylic gouache

These are completely waterproof when dry, and are flexible. They can be used on film, plastic and acetate as well as paper, and can be diluted and used through an airbrush.

Acrylic polymer colours

These are artist's quality pigments bound with an acrylic resin, available in different consistencies: Rowney Cryla is thick and buttery, and is used when a thick textured surface is wanted, and Cryla Flow Formula is of a softer consistency, and has been designed for flat textureless painting. It can be used diluted in a spray gun. When a completely uniform colour is required, a water tension breaker can be added. The finished surface of the colour can be matt or gloss, depending on the medium (diluting liquid) you choose. The colours dry quickly (this can be slowed down by using a retarder) and the brushes must be washed clean while the paint is still wet: this can be done in water. If the colour has hardened on the brush it can be softened with methylated spirits (denatured alcohol). Cryla colour can be painted on a very wide range of surfaces, paper, board, canvas, fabric, glass, plastic, hardboard, etc. Weber Acrylic Colors and Grumbacher's Hyplar Acrylic Polymer Color (USA) are quick-drying and water-resistent and available in a wide range of colours and packages.

PVA colours

PVA colours are powders ready mixed with dilute PVA, and can be used straight from the tube or diluted further with water. The addition of PVA gives a tough flexible waterproof film to the colour, which can be used thickly or in thin glazes of colour and, like the Cryla colours, can be used on glass, plastic, wood, cardboard, canvas, etc.

Redicolour

Redicolour, made by Rowney, is a ready mixed colour in a PVA base, with a high pigment content giving more brilliancy than the normal powder colour, and regardless of how thickly it is applied it does not crack, and is completely flexible. It is ideal for painting models which have been constructed from a wide range of materials because it will adhere to polystyrene, glass, plastic, acetate, perspex, paper, etc. It can also be used for printing onto fabrics (string prints, cork, potato, etc.), and for drama work; when papier mâché masks and puppets are painted with it they are strengthened considerably.

PVA medium

This is a creamy white treacly liquid which is used as an all purpose glue for heavy materials and diluted with water for paper collage, especially in tissue paper collage where no bleeding of the colour is wanted. It can also be used to make PVA paint by adding it to powder colour, or to artist's powder colour. To do this mix the powder colour with a little water first and then add the PVA medium. Remember that the brushes must be washed out in water.

FURTHER READING

GITTINGS, F., *Polymer Painting Manual* Studio Vista

Paper

SIZES OF PAPER

Paper sizes in Britain are being altered to comply with the adoption of the ISO paper sizes. The basic series is the A series. A0 is the basic size, A0 halved becomes A1, A1 halved becomes A2, and so on. The B and C sizes are larger. The basis of the ISO system is that the ratio between the long and short size remains unchanged when halved along the long side; the ratio is $1:\sqrt{2}(1\cdot414)$. Domestic notepaper and envelopes are also available in these sizes now.

Table of ISO sizes

	mm	in.
A0 =	841 by 1189	= $33\frac{1}{8}$ by $46\frac{3}{4}$
A1 =	594 by 841	= $23\frac{3}{8}$ by $33\frac{1}{8}$
A2 =	420 by 594	= $16\frac{1}{2}$ by $23\frac{3}{8}$
A3 =	297 by 420	= $11\frac{3}{4}$ by $16\frac{1}{2}$
A4 =	210 by 297	= $8\frac{1}{4}$ by $11\frac{3}{4}$
A5 =	148 by 210	= $5\frac{7}{8}$ by $8\frac{1}{4}$
C0 =	972 by 1374	
B0 =	1000 by 1412	

Paper is sold in three ways. Firstly by *quantity*: 24 sheets = 1 quire; 480 sheets = 1 ream. Secondly, by *weight*: so that a ream of paper which weighs 120 lb will be twice as *thick* as a ream of paper of the same size weighing 60 lb.

Thirdly by *size*: folio is a whole sheet folded in half; quarto (4to) is folio folded in half again; octavo (8to) is quarto folded in half. Folio, quarto, and octavo do not of themselves indicate any particular size. Of the old sizes: double crown (D/C) = 30 in. by 20 in.; crown = 15 in. by 20 in.; royal (roy) = 25 in. by 20 in.

TYPES OF PAPER

Brightly coloured papers

Surface paper This has colour on the surface, on one side only. Available in matt and shiny surfaces, the matt surfaces are easily marked by sweaty fingers, although it is used for origami and cut paper work.

Gloss paper Usually gummed, comes in small squares, also in packets of ready-cut shapes, stars, circles, triangles, crescents, etc. Can be used for collage and structured pattern work.

Ostwald paper These papers are in colours selected from the range of colours used in the Ostwald colour theory.

Metal foil paper One side is white paper, the other side is covered with a very shiny metallic surface. Colours blue, red, green, silver, gold. Easily stuck because of the paper side; used in collage, puppets, dolls, mobiles, and festive decorations.

Metallized plastic foil Aluminium metallized PVC sheeting with a coloured lacquer coating on each side; in blue, red, green, silver, gold. Very expensive, difficult to glue.

Crêpe paper Basically a stretchy paper, absorbent. Huge range of colours both bright and subtle. Not suitable for sticking. Used for paper flowers, dolls, puppets, decorations, etc.

Tissue paper Huge range of colours, from very bright to subtle (for uses see section on Tissue paper).

Fluorescent paper Very bright: available in yellow, red, pink, green, orange. Useful in very small pieces. Marks very easily. Used for collage, etc.

Colart paper rolls Very bright, in yellow, pink, orange. Can be useful for printing on.

Construction paper Vivid colours. Useful for collage, paper sculpture, cut and fold, etc.

Subtly coloured and white papers

Ingres paper Very large range of coloured papers, for drawing on in any medium. Interesting surface to draw on, rather expensive.

Japanese rice paper (mulberry) Expensive, usually imitation sold. Good for printing on.

Brushwork paper Thin, off-white paper, used for painting, drawing (ink, charcoal, chalk, etc., not pencil), printing, collage. Cheap.

Poster paper Available in the sheet and the roll. Colour range includes bright and subtle colours. Matt surface: used for collage, torn paper, cut paper.

Bank paper Available in small (typewriter-size) sheets: varies from very flimsy to quite tough, and good for paper cutting with more than one fold, and for early origami. Small children can cut this when folded quite easily. Cheap.

Sugar paper Available in rolls and sheets, in a range of subtle colours. Thick paper useful for painting, drawing (in charcoal, oil pastels, felt-tip). Has an interesting rough surface.

Pastel paper Very subtle colours: greys, browns, blues, greens. Excellent for printing on, drawing on with ink with a brush, making rubbings on. Thin/medium weight.

Kitchen paper Off-white. Thin, cheap, but useful for practice printing, experimenting cut and fold, drawing implements.

Cartridge paper (drawing paper) White, very good for drawing on in any medium. Excellent for very fine detail. Can be painted on with acrylics, gouache.

Coloured cartridge (known as art cover paper) Qualities as above, available in a range of soft colours.

Brown wrapping paper (kraft, string) Very strong, good base for collage, frieze: one side rough, other smooth.

Card and boards

Card Weights given in microns: 2 sheet = 200 microns; 3 sheet = 230 microns; 4 sheet = 280 microns; 6 sheet = 380 microns; 12 sheet = 750 microns. The cheapest will usually be the 2 sheet – the most expensive the 10 or 12 sheet.

Cardboard Available in 10, 16, 24, 32 oz weight (strawboard) and 9, 13, 24 oz (greyboard). Used for bookbinding, book crafts, model making.

Millboard, paste board Smooth finish, some coloured, useful for mounting.

Pulp boards White, available in many thicknesses. Also colours. Suitable for paper sculpture, models, etc. Also used for shadow puppets, paper, fabric collage, string collage, seed collage (also use cardboard). As base for wax engravings.

SUMMARY OF PAPER TYPES

CARD	COLOURED PAPERS	WHITE PAPERS
Cardboard	*(Bright)*	Brushwork
Strawboard	Tissue	Newsprint
Greyboard	Fluorescent	Kitchen paper
Millboard	Colart	Cartridge
Paste board	Construction	Sugar
Pulp board	Ostwald	Bank
Bristol board	Metal foil	Dover mill
Ticket board	Metallized	White poster
Clifton board	plastic foil	Antique laid
Cover paper	Crêpe	Bond
	Surface	Bank
(USA)	Gloss	T.H.
Newsboard	Cellophane	Saunders
(chipboard)		Ingres
Binder's	*(Subtle)*	Japanese
board	Tissue	papers in
Tag board	Ingres	variety
Darby	Mulberry	White tissue
illustration	Pastel	White crêpe
board	Cartridge	
	Sugar	
	Japanese papers	

EXPERIMENTING WITH PAPER

Constructions for play made by lacing corrugated card.

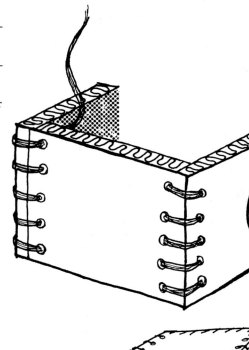

Experiments using strips of paper stapled
together.

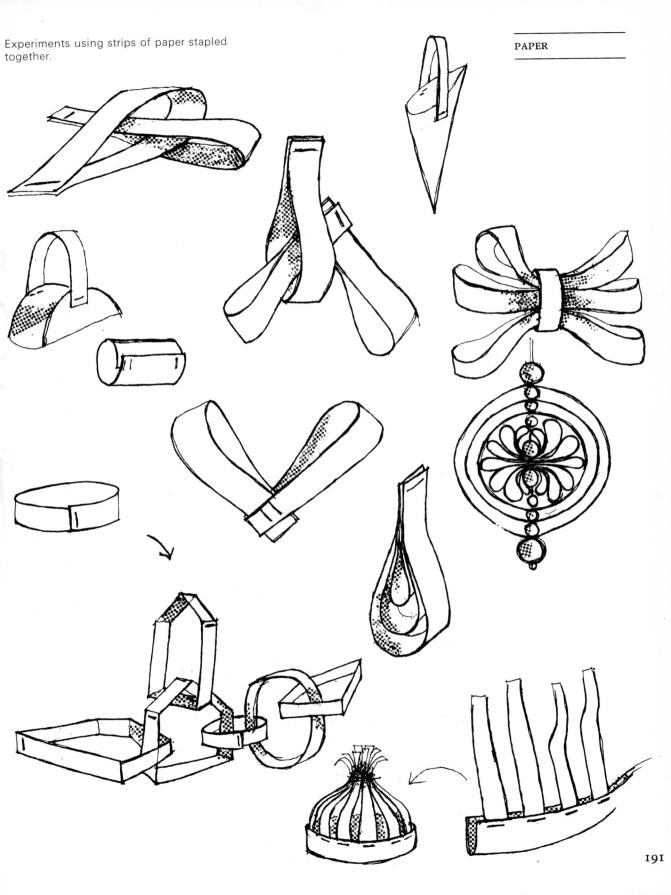

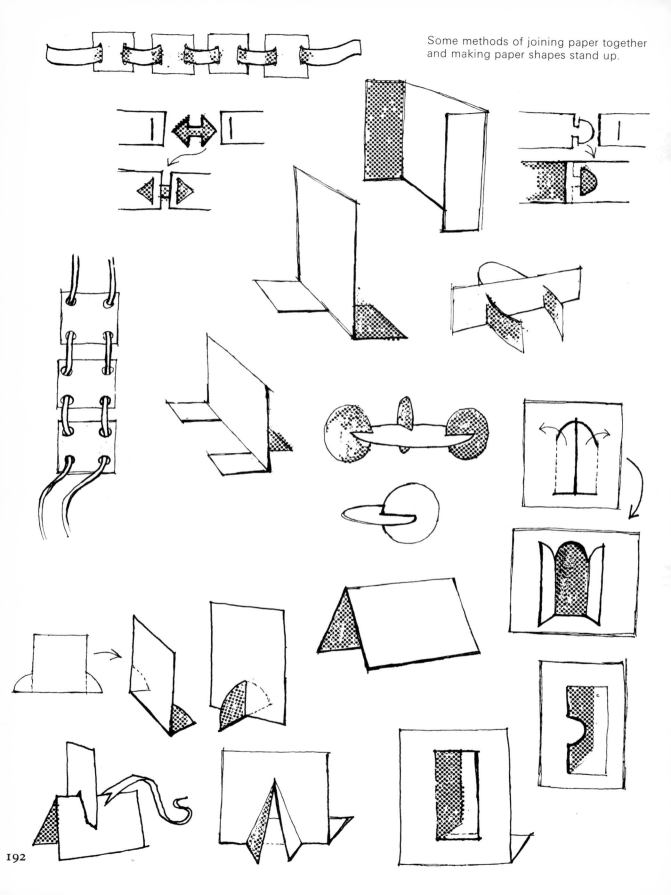

Some methods of joining paper together and making paper shapes stand up.

192

Some more methods of linking paper, or it
could be felt or leather.

This is a traditional straw-work motif which can be made in a paper strip. Do not turn the star over as you make it. The star grows as the paper is wrapped round the corners, but three layers at each corner will probably be enough. Tuck the last end under the previous strip at the back.

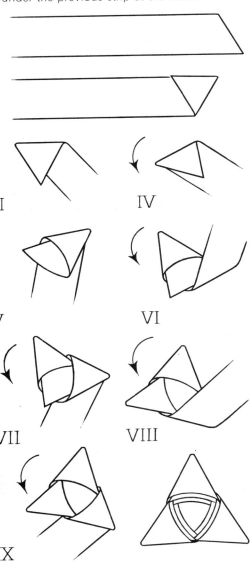

I

IV

V

VI

VII

VIII

IX

Paper Cutting

Paper cutting can be divided into two categories. The first can be classified as folded symmetrical cuts (e.g. Polish paper cuts) and open asymmetrical cuts (e.g. Chinese paper cuts). The second can be classified as silhouettes: in the pure silhouette the attention is concentrated on the outside edge of the cut, the inside of the cut being left quite intact; in the 'paper doyley' type of cut, the main decoration is produced from the complicated cutting on the inside. Of course, cuts frequently cross these main categories. It might seem a little pedantic to divide them up in this way, but in the long run, it is easier to see what areas are still unexplored if you are clear about what aspects of paper cutting you have tackled so far.

Amelia Blackburn used several techniques together. The cut paper picture on page 206 uses paper-pricking to decorate the body of the bird and the tree trunks; the snake is painted with water colour; the ground has a collage of paper cut leaves; and finally there are two butterflies which have been cut separately, coloured, and glued onto the ground. Her work was very popular in Victorian England, and there was a time when paper cuts were called Amelias. Another type of picture making, also called Amelias (because again they were thought to have been invented by her), were fashion prints of the early part of the nineteenth century, in which the clothes were actually made of tiny scraps of fabric and braids, and glued onto the illustration, leaving just the faces, hands, and background in the original paper.

In the 1830s and 1850s there was a craze for buying small prints of popular actors and actresses in famous roles, or some royal figure, with clothes ornamented with scraps of cloth, feathers, tiny sequins, small scraps of lace, coloured metal foil, etc. Although these were sometimes applied to the front of the paper, more generally the part to be decorated was cut out from the print and applied to the back, and backed with paper. Coloured paper cutting was practised by Mrs Delaney (1700–1788). Boxes and boxes of her remarkable flower pictures are in the Print Room of the British Museum. They are remarkable not only for the quality of the cutting but also for the observation of the plants depicted, for they are really superb botanical illustrations.

Although early paper cutting in Britain and Europe was in white and mounted on a dark background, it soon changed to black on white, except in Poland where it became coloured. Black is not often used in contemporary Chinese paper cuts, but red, maroon, and dark blue are often used; the really covetable ones are those cut in a paper as fine as tissue and brightly coloured. These are generally of theatrical figures, fish, flowers or dragons. The one illustrated is about 3 in. high, and the

FURTHER READING
ASK, G. & H., *Simple Paper Craft* Batsford
OGAWA, H., *The Art of Papercraft* Batsford

cutting inside incredibly fine. Apparently they are cut 60–70 at a time, the layers fastened together and attached to a board. They are dyed before being removed, the dye being applied to the top layer and allowed to seep through. In addition to scissors the Chinese also use specially made stamps to do the internal cutting.

The paper cuts themselves are used purely as household decorations in Poland, but in Mexico they are used at funeral ceremonies, as they were in China. They are also used in the home as good luck charms to ward off the evil eye.

A Polish paper cut, using several colours superimposed on each other. They are also symmetrical along a vertical fold.

Materials

These are of the simplest:

Paper

Tissue, typewriting paper, origami paper, but not thick paper like sugar paper if you want to do folded cuts. The colour can be black or white, if you want to do silhouettes, or any colour you choose.

Scissors

The sharpest possible, and short. Pointed ones, such as dissecting scissors, are the best for really fine work. For really intricate internal cutting, some sort of craft knife will be needed, e.g. Exacto knife.

Adhesive

If possible, use a spray adhesive, spray onto the background and simply press the cut paper onto it. Alternatively use a wheat or wallpaper paste, such as Polycell. A PVA (white) glue is too tacky for manipulating a paper cut.

METHOD

When doing free cuts on fine paper like tissue, staple it between two sheets of typing paper. Draw the design on that and cut out the shapes, with a craft knife (Exacto), on a piece of formica or similar. It is possible to staple eight or nine sheets of tissue together and cut at the same time (this is useful when making Christmas cards). Laying a thin piece of paper between two thicker pieces is a useful tip when cutting thin paper in a guillotine (paper-cutter). Always cut the most difficult parts from the centre working outwards. It is much easier to do tricky cutting in a whole stiff sheet of paper than from a floppy cut one.

If using scissors for silhouettes, cut off the large unwanted areas first. Right-hand bends or acute changes in direction are better cut with the handles of the scissors underneath the paper. Left-hand changes of direction are better if cut with the handles of the scissors on the top. Try filling in areas that have been cut out with coloured tissue paper or any other coloured paper. Experiment with mounting on folded and dyed paper, or any of those listed in the section on materials.

FURTHER READING

ROTTGER, E., *Creative Paper Craft* Batsford
STODDART, B., *Paper Cutting* Batsford

A totally free Chinese paper cut, showing much use of cutting away areas in the inside of the design. Compare this sort of cutting with silhouettes.

This modern Chinese paper cut is tiny, no more than 2 in. × 3 in., so the fantastic skill that has been used is even more amazing. These paper cuts are coloured, but, unlike the Polish cuts, are stained in various areas: there is no applied paper.

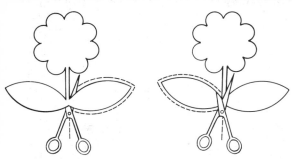

Paper can be cut and treated like leaded glass, the shapes being filled in with coloured tissue paper.

Note the method of holding the pair of scissors, depending on whether one is cutting from the left or the right.

Paper, Cut and Spread

This approach to design involves taking one sheet of paper, and without taking any parts away, creating a design by cutting the paper and either spreading the parts until a gap of the size you choose appears, or rearranging the cut-out shapes to form mirror-images of the cut-out spaces.

This is a Victorian theatrical print of an actress in a famous rôle. Various parts were cut out from the paper, and filled in with pieces of fabric, lace, and small bits of metal foil and sequins.

This design was created by cutting the paper and spreading the parts until gaps of different sizes appeared.

(Left)
An automatic method of producing a negative—positive image. In each case, the shape cut out of the original piece of paper is placed at the point where the scissors entered the paper and glued down on the white background to produce a mirror image, called the negative. Whether it is the negative or positive depends on how you see it.

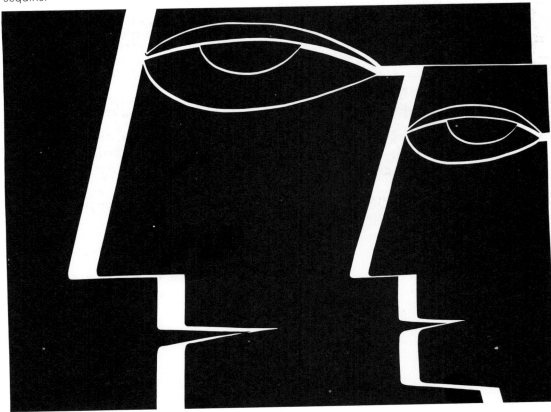

The technique of cut and spread was used to indicate the shoulders, hands, and breasts in this creative rubbing. Strips of paper were glued onto the basic shape to form relief detail, then a sheet of paper was laid over the top and a rubbing was taken.

Paper, Fold and Dye

MATERIALS

Dye

coloured ink (powdered and drawing); food colouring; cold/hot water dyes.

Fastenings

clothes pegs (clothes pins); paper clips (all types); rubber bands; string/thread.

Dyeing bowls

jam jars; saucepans; any glass, plastic, enamel, stainless steel container.

Papers

These can be divided into three categories: fragile, medium strong, tough. Fragile papers are the very absorbent ones, such as paper napkins, paper towels, paper tissues, crêpe paper. Crêpe paper is best edge dyed. Because of its construction, it does not hold the patterns made by the folds when it is wet with dye. For the other papers, fold them but do not tie. Use pegs (plastic or wooden) or any sort of paper clip. Because these papers are very absorbent, only dip them in dye for 5 seconds.

Tissue paper is in a category on its own. It is not as absorbent as the above papers, but neither is it strong enough to come into the category of medium strong papers. When wet it is fragile, but it takes quite complicated folding very well. The tissue paper used by shops for wrapping bread, glass, china, etc., is fine. If it is rather crumpled iron it before folding with a warm iron.

Medium papers include cartridge (drawing), lining paper, envelopes. Quite the best paper is cartridge paper. It is strong enough to withstand the most intricate folding, and takes the dye very well. For a softer result, try soaking the paper in warm water for 5 minutes before putting it in the dye. These papers can be bound with string, or gripped with spring paper clips. Depending on the absorbency of the paper, it needs to be dyed for between $\frac{1}{2}$ and 1 hour. An interesting paper to try is the foil and paper wrapping of biscuit (cookie) packets. Keep the foil and paper together, and fold and dye in the normal way: the foil backing gives great luminosity to the colours.

Hard papers include brown wrapping paper, Kraft paper, and greaseproof paper. Although these are far from ideal, if you have to use them, they can be made more absorbent by soaking in warm water first (when folded, but not tied) or by dyeing in hot dye (ink). If the paper to be dyed is not white, use a strong dark colour; patterns will not show up very much if light-coloured dyes are used.

DYEING

Make the dye very strong. It can be kept in screw-topped jars almost indefinitely. If the colour is too strong when you come to use it, it can be diluted with water. Remember that the colour will be considerably lighter when the paper is dry.

Brusho powdered dyes are splendid for tie-dyed paper. They come in a large range of colours, and are inexpensive. Used hot they are very penetrating, and paper dyed in it needs only half the time allowed for cold dye. If pegs are used to hold the folds, choose a bowl large enough to take the pegs and the paper. When dyeing at home, pretty paper napkins can be made using food colouring as a dye, applying it with an eye dropper. The use of an eye dropper is an advantage when small areas of different colours are needed on large samples.

Although the paper can be of any shape, it is easier to begin with if it is either rectangular or circular. Fold the rectangular shape into strips concertina-wise, and fold the resulting strip until it is a square. If you start with a circle, fold it in half and then in half again as many times as is possible. There are two ways of dipping the paper: either while the paper is dry, or when it has been wetted in water after it has been folded. The first method produces a hard edge to the coloured area, whereas wetting the paper before dyeing produces a softer blurred coloured area.

Immerse the folded paper in water, and with the heel of your hand squeeze out the excess water. Pinching the paper very firmly between the thumb and forefinger, dip each corner into the dye, or each edge, or any combination you choose. The reason for pinching the paper so firmly is to prevent the dye from flooding the whole sheet of paper, leaving no pattern at all. Keep some spare kitchen paper handy so that any excess dye can be squeezed out of the corners.

Try dipping the corner *very briefly* in bleach after dipping a corner in the dye. Also try dipping first in a pale colour and then in a darker colour. The second dye will creep up the first one, but do not leave it too long in the dye or it will completely obliterate the first colour. One can also dry the paper, refold in a new way, and dip in dye again. Although large samples, or those using medium strong paper, need to be dyed for $\frac{1}{2}$ hour, and completely immersed during that time, absorbent papers can have the dye poured over them using a spoon, making sure the sample is on a saucer or something similar first.

The paper was folded in half down the centre, and the subsequent folds are seen by the straight dark lines.

This was also folded in half to start with and folding each half separately, the folds were made fan-wise starting from the centre.

Dyeing with felt-tip pens

Fold the paper as for fold and dye, dip it in water, and squeeze out the excess water. The water aids the spread of the water-based ink. Draw a design on the top layer; open the folded paper up until you reach the layers where the ink has not penetrated so completely. Go over the lines carefully, and repeat until all the layers are coloured. Wet tissue paper is extremely fragile, so only open the paper as far as is absolutely necessary.

Finishing the sample

When the dyeing is complete, the sample is removed, and allowed to drain. (Do this over a jam-jar. The surplus dye will be caught in the jar, and can be used another time.) When dry, undo the string or remove the pegs/paper clips.

Unfold, and iron flat. If ironing the sample directly, always use the iron sideways on, never the point first, because it easily gets caught in an unevenness in the paper and tears it, especially if the paper is still damp. If the paper is wet, or even damp, it can stick to the iron, and that tears it too. Always wipe the iron carefully after ironing dyed paper. Any surplus dye on the iron can be deposited on the next thing ironed.

Dip-dyed tissue must be protected, either with spray lacquer, or a clear contact paper (fablon), or paint a dilute PVA (white) glue all over. Paste the glue to the paper and not to the tissue itself. Lay the tissue on top, carefully, and rub down with a pad of crumpled paper over a layer of transparent polythene. This way you can see what you are doing, and PVA will not stick to polythene. If the paper is to be used for book covers, there is a product made for strengthening maps which is cotton fabric with one side coated with glue. This is ironed onto the paper, or even better onto Vilene, or disposable paper sheets.

Use wheat or wallpaper paste (Polycell) for collage. Very absorbent paper requires a dilute PVA glue. If the pieces are very fragile, photographic mounting tissue can be used (but is expensive). This is placed between the backing paper and the collage pieces; a hot iron rubbed over the collage pieces will fuse them to the backing. A spray adhesive is the easiest to use, and the most efficient.

The irregular pattern is the result of the thickness of the paper when it is folded. The outside of the folded paper inevitably is dyed more thoroughly than the paper on the inside of the fold.

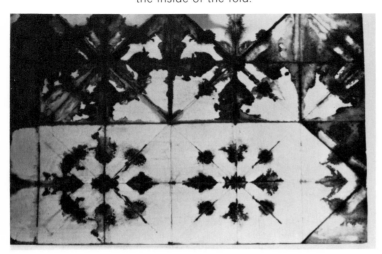

Methods of creasing, folding, and tying the paper, prior to dyeing.

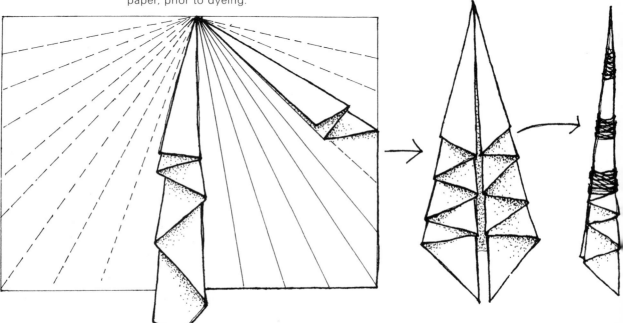

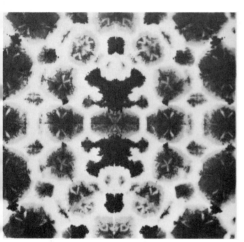

This is made on the fold and dip method, using either the thinnest Vilene, which absorbs inks particularly well, or the paper used to make disposable paper sheets. It is tough but at the same time absorbent. It does not have any crease lines as does the folded paper which was dyed.

A variety of different folds and different arrangements of pinching the paper with spring metal paperclips of different sizes.

Here paper napkins were used. The softness of this paper leaves no lines at all, only soft shapes. Do not leave a very absorbent paper in the ink or dye for very long. It takes only seconds for the paper to absorb enough dye to make these patterns.

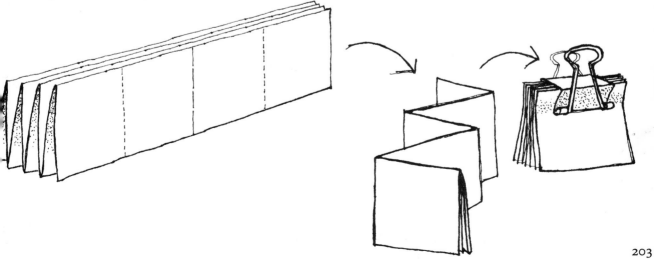

Paper Making

As with so many inventions, this one too is Chinese. First produced by Ts'ai Lun AD 105, paper remained a hand-made product for almost 1700 years. The manufacture of beautiful papers is now an exclusively Japanese activity. They perfected the craft of making papier mâché, and raised the products made in this material (small boxes and dolls) to works of art. And, of course, Japan is the home of origami. Commercial paper is made from wood pulp or rag, but for hand-made paper almost any vegetable fibre can be used. Different plants give different characteristics to the papers made from them.

MAKING THE PULP

Some suitable plants are nettle, cow parsley, coarse grasses, and the leaves of broad leaved plants like iris, montbretia, and gladiolus. Experiment. Large quantities are needed to make even a small quantity of paper, so collect a large bagful. Ideally, leave them to rot in a heap on the floor of a cellar or a garden shed, or in a large bucket of water. This is to break down the fibres. To save time, chop up the plants into ½-in. lengths and put them into a saucepan. Fill up with water and add 2 dessert-spoons caustic soda (lye) to every 2 pints of water. *Wear rubber gloves* because caustic soda is damaging. Simmer the mixture until soft and pulpy. Strain through a sieve, and rinse. What is left is the fibrous tissue. Put the sieve in a

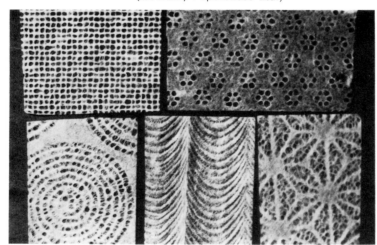

Japanese hand-made papers; torn pieces of coloured paper have been embedded in the one above, and string in the one below. (Courtesy Paperchase Ltd.)

Japanese hand-made decorative papers.

Paper made from rush and iris leaves.

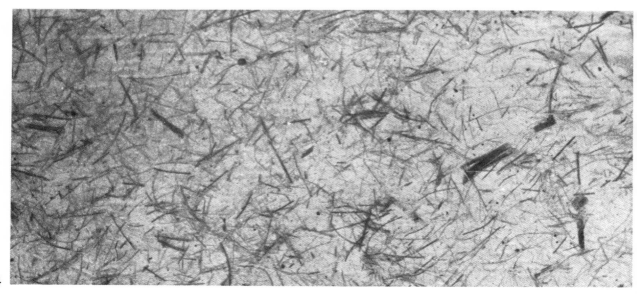

bowl of warm water and stir the contents by hand. The smaller fibres are rinsed away, and you are left with the longest fibres. If you want a white paper, add a cupful of bleach to the bowl into which you have put the fibres. For natural coloured paper, do not add bleach. The paper will be stronger without bleach. Leave overnight, or longer. Wash again to remove the bleach.

For rag paper, collect only cotton rag, and keep white and coloured cottons separate. Cut them up into 1-in. squares. Boil for 7 hours using the same solution of caustic soda as for the leaves. Drain, wash thoroughly, and tip in a pile in an enamel bowl. Pound with a pestle and mortar. When there are no lumps left, the beating is finished. Some interesting papers are made if a few pieces of grass or cloth are left in the pulp at this stage. One can also use any old discarded paper, by tearing it up into 3 in. or 4 in. squares, adding water and reducing it to a pulp in the blender attachment of a food mixer.

THE MOULD

Traditionally, this is a wooden frame as used in screen printing, but instead of organdie, there is a sheet of woven wire. However, organdie works very well with pulp from the blender.

The mould frame should be made of a wood which will not warp with the continual wetting and drying. Straight-grained mahogany is suitable. The nails used should be rustproof, as rust or iron will stain the paper pulp.

A removable deckle may be used with the frame. This is a raised edge for holding the pulp and ensuring an even distribution of it as it is poured over the wire mesh. The attractive, rough, uncut edge so characteristic of hand-made paper is called a deckle edge.

THE VAT

This can be a large square polythene bowl, large enough to take the mould, with 2 in. or 3 in. at the sides to have room for one's fingers. You will also need several pieces of felt ready beside the bowl. It is easiest to work with the pulp warm, so fill up the vat to within 3 in. or 4 in. of the top with warm water. Add two jugfuls of pulp and stir briskly. If it is too fluid add some more pulp. Dip the mould into the vat 3 in. below the surface, and keeping the movement as smooth as possible, give a shake front to back, and then side to side. This is to 'felt' the fibres. Lift out of the vat, but still keeping the mould over the vat, tilt to one corner to drain off the surplus water. The thickness of the pulp should be at least $\frac{1}{16}$ in., though this only comes with practice.

Now lay one piece of felt down on the table. Tip the mould upside down onto the felt; press the whole surface down, thus transferring the wet pulp onto the felt. Lay a sheet of felt on top of the pulp, dip the mould into the vat and lift out another layer of pulp, turn upside down onto the felt, and so on. Keep the liquid in the vat well stirred up, and after every four dips, add another four cupfuls of pulp.

There will now be a pile on the table of layers of felt, pulp, felt, pulp, felt, pulp, ending with some felt. With a wooden board (a drawing board, or a pastry board) at the bottom of the pile and another at the top, put them all in a press to squeeze out the excess water. Loosen the press and remove the pile. If there is no press available, stand on the pile and trample round it to squeeze out the excess water. Wet sheets are very fragile! So take great care. Lay out some clean sheets of newsprint on a layer of newspapers, and *carefully* lay the newly made paper on the clean newsprint to dry.

Before the sheets are bone dry, place overnight between boards and under a weight. If the paper is too thick or too thin, this can be adjusted next time. Paper made from plants is now suitable for printing or painting: paper made from rags is absorbent and needs sizing. One can either size the paper as a separate operation, or one can add the size to the vat, if one has some way of keeping the paper warm in the vat. One can also spray the dry sheet of paper with laundry starch/silicone and iron gently.

TO MAKE THE SIZE

Use powdered skin glue: cover and leave overnight to soak. Add boiling water and stir. To prevent the growth of mould, add one-tenth the weight of powdered glue of chrome alum. Do not attempt to size the sheets for at least 3 weeks – they might disintegrate! Pour some warm size into a shallow dish. Put a piece of glass in the dish, and immerse a sheet of paper onto the glass. Continue until there are several sheets. Lift the glass and all the sheets of paper out of the dish of size. Remove the glass and put a piece of wood at the top and bottom of the pile. Give a quick nip in the press – separate out the sheets and lay them to dry. If the size is too strong, they will not separate, they will just stick together, and you will have made papier mâché!

EXPERIMENTAL PAPERS

Try adding a few pieces of coloured rag to the white rag vat. It will give little flecks of colours in the final paper. Lay one piece of paper on the felt (as it comes out of the vat) and lay (couch) another layer of paper on top immediately without a piece of felt between them. They will fuse together, and if you have two vats of pulp in use at the same time, one white and the other coloured, you will have a piece of paper with one side white and the other side coloured.

This method can be used for sealing in all sorts of objects: e.g. lengths of threads, skeleton leaves, pressed flowers, petals, which should be first wetted. If you wish to write on the paper, iron both sides carefully.

Paper Pricking

The most famous exponent of this technique was Amelia Blackburn (c.1830s). She used a combination of paper-cutting of quite unbelievable delicacy with pin-pricking to achieve a three-dimensional effect, and the whole composition was coloured. Sometimes an engraving or print would be used as the basis, and all the clothes, draperies, etc., would be carefully pricked with a variety of needles which were securely fixed in short handles, from very fine ones to very thick ones. A variety of sized holes was needed for really interesting work. When a print was used as the base, the head and hands and feet were usually left untouched, and because the paper has been so disturbed by the pricking, one is not really aware of the fact that originally there was a complete print. Examples are to be seen at the British Museum and in the Radio Times Hulton Picture Library.

A good quality writing paper will make an excellent ground, and instead of a selection of needles, one medium thick one will do, as long as it has a sharp point. For small holes push the needle in only a little way: for larger holes push in further. It is best to work with a thin sheet of plastic foam or felt under the paper, and clip the paper and foam to a drawing or pastry board. The best effect is achieved when the paper is held up to the light, and black paper lit by artificial light is the most dramatic.

Paper Sculpture

Equipment

scissors: a pair with long blades, for long smooth cuts, a pair with short blades for smaller work, and a very short-bladed pair for intricate cutting; knives: Exacto, or a dissecting knife; a blunt penknife for scoring the paper (i.e. marking it but not actually cutting it; a piece of thick cardboard or formica on which to do the cutting; a metal rule for cutting straight lines against; a compass, for drawing circles; a pencil and eraser; a knitting needle for circling paper strips on; paper clips; stapler; double-sided adhesive tape; UHU or similar transparent glue, quick drying.

As its name implies, this technique is concerned with transforming a flat two-dimensional piece of paper into a three-dimensional form. It also includes a half-way stage called 'relief', where the surface of the paper is no longer flat, but the piece of paper as a whole is. There are four basic methods of making this transformation: curling; cutting and folding, curling or bending; scoring and bending; inserting other pieces of paper.

METHOD

All paper has a 'grain', that is, the fibres lie more or less parallel in one direction, and it is in this direction that paper most easily bends, and tears. If you damp a piece of paper it will curl along its grain as it dries. Take two pieces of paper, and try curling them in different directions: one way will be easier, and that is the direction to curl in order to make all constructions requiring curled shapes. To curl paper, press it firmly onto a table with a metal rule (or wooden) and with the other hand, pull it firmly against the edge of the rule as you do so.

FURTHER READING

BORCHARD, G., *Paper Sculpture* Batsford

Narrow strips can be curled by passing the strip between your thumb and the edge of a ruler or a closed pair of scissors, pulling the paper down along the side as you go.

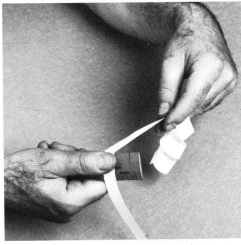

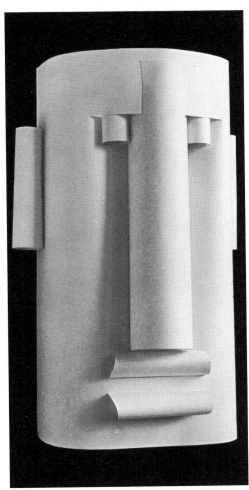

An arrangement of tubes (some are inserted into slits) to make a head.

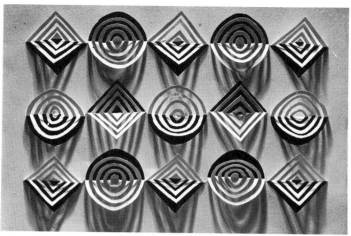

Cast shadows are very important in these relief examples. All these examples are made by cutting the shapes with a very sharp knife. Similar treatment can be done by folding the paper and cutting with a pair of scissors. After the cuts are made, the strips are folded over.

Strips cut in the edge of a piece of paper, curled and with one end pulled out to form a conical tree.

Pleating like this can be done only if the lines are all neatly scored first.

The score lines for V-pleating.

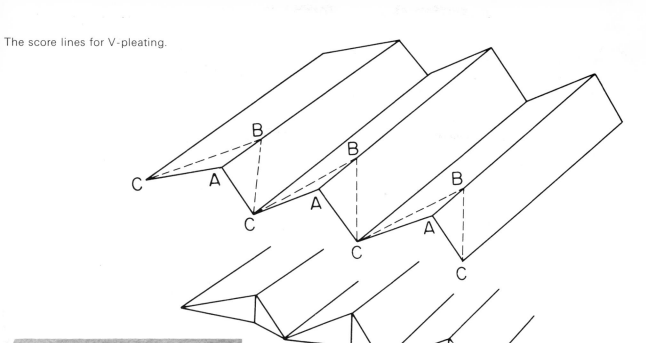

Cones are made by cutting a slit from the outside into the centre. Slide one edge over the other until you get the steepness you want. Do any scoring and folding before gluing the sides of the overlap together.

Discs divided into various areas by curved scored lines.

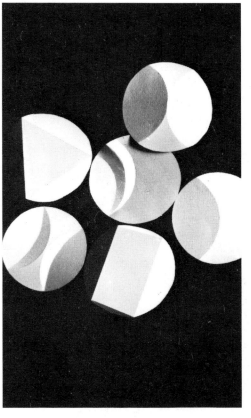

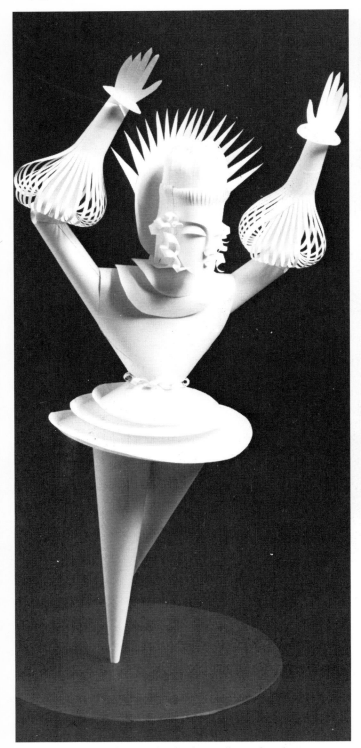

This relief picture uses bending, straight and curved scored pleats, strip curling, and fringing.

A completely three-dimensional paper sculpture, which has been constructed on a piece of dowelling nailed to the base. The dowelling runs through one leg and up to the head.

PAPER COSTUME

After exploring some of the particular qualities of paper, and some of the techniques of paper sculpture, use your knowledge to make paper costumes for children's fancy dress and school plays.

Join units of paper by gluing or stapling, or link them by threading string through punched holes, or by passing arrow-headed tabs of paper through cut slits. The costume can be decorated by paint spraying.

FURTHER READING

HOYES, J., *Making Paper Costumes* Batsford

VES, S., *Childrens' Costumes in Paper and Card* Batsford

These paper gloves are based on a study of armour. Cartridge paper was carefully measured, cut and folded, then linked together.

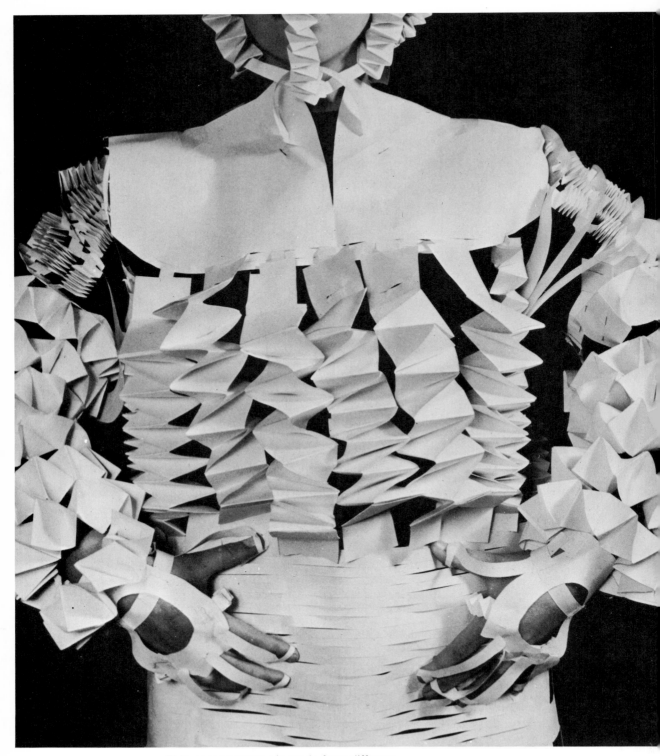

This paper costume is made from different
sizes of a plait known to children as
Chinese Stairs, or a two-plait.

Papier Mâché

Once again, this craft first began in China. Chinese soldiers wore helmets made of it; children played with toys made from it. The craft spread to Japan, Burma, India, Persia, and wherever it was practised, the greatest care was taken in its decoration, however humble the objective of the article. These countries are still producing articles of papier mâché and the standard of both design and decoration is still high.

Interest in the craft in Europe developed in the early eighteenth century and the range of articles made included snuff boxes, spectacle cases, small writing desks, trinket boxes, work boxes, trays, chairs, sofas, and bedsteads. Coach panels, sedan chairs, and even houses were made from it!

In Birmingham, Henry Clay perfected a technique of laminating layers of paper with glue, and treating them with oil and varnish during the drying process. They were dried between sheets of metal in order to control the thickness and flatness, and they were heat dried. It was a very complicated process, but it resulted in a product which, when it had been japanned, was fantastically durable, and could be moulded into shapes not possible with wood. Traditionally, the articles were always black, with the decoration in gilt, mother of pearl and coloured painted decorations of flowers and leaves.

In Mexico, at festival time, Christmas and Easter, papier mâché really comes into its own. Huge figures, skeletons and devils are made of papier mâché, the larger ones filled with fireworks and exploded or burnt on Easter Saturday. At Christmas, pinatas, animals or birds are made and filled with sweets, then broken in order to get the sweets out.

Papier mâché can be made in the form of pulp or of layers of paper glued together, and can be used for covering existing objects, for free modelling, and for moulding.

Materials

old newspapers or dehydrated pulp; wheat or wallpaper paste such as Polycell or Glutas, Metylan Art Paste (USA), dilute PVA (50/50); wire, soft iron, galvanized wire, or chicken wire, for armature.

COVERING AN EXISTING OBJECT

This is the simplest method to start with. One needs some article which is structurally sound, but for one reason or another no longer gives pleasure. Suitable articles are boxes of all sizes, both tin and wooden; trays of all shapes and sizes, tin or wooden; mirror frames; lampshade bases; vases. Remember that the article will remain inside the coating of papier mâché.

The object must be clean, and without grease. Old newspaper (for a fine texture), absorbent household kitchen paper, paper tissues or sugar paper (for a more marked texture) can be used, or dehydrated pulp (Arnold, UK; Celluclay or Shreddi-mix, USA). The paper can be torn up into strips or squares, or cut into triangles. If the finished effect is to be smooth, then the edges of the paper must be torn. If, however, there is to be no further decoration to the article once the paper has been applied, then a most attractive texture can be achieved by cutting the edges of the paper and making the triangles more or less the same size, and arranging them in a regular pattern over the shape. Either dip the strips of paper into a bowl of adhesive and pull the paper between two fingers to get rid of excess paste, or paint the glue directly onto the squares with a brush.

The paper is then neatly applied to the article. If covering a tray, start at the outside and work in circles towards the centre, or vice versa. With a rectangular shape, start along one edge, and work in rows. Overlap each square a little as it is glued down. One layer of newspaper is quite sufficient if one is working on a tin object, or wood or glass. If one is working over a card box such as a paper tissue box, two or three layers will be needed to give it enough rigidity to withstand handling when finished. For an object that will be used a great deal, white glues are by far the best. Allow the object to dry overnight.

The paper must then be sealed. Dilute white PVA glue can be painted all over to seal the surface, but since it dries transparent, unless the newsprint is the final finish that you want, it is better to paint it with a household latex paint used for painting walls. There are gessos which one can use but domestic household wall paint is much cheaper.

Methods of decoration

High relief: made from layers of paper glued together, cut, moulded into shapes, and glued on when dry. Low relief: from string, lace, seeds, dried leaves, paper doylies, stones, tassels, mother of pearl, buttons, matchsticks, feathers, twigs, etc. Flat decoration: straight painting; fabric; magazine photographs.

MAKING A PULP

The simplest method is to soak torn up pieces of newspaper in a bucket of warm water. Have at least ten to fifteen newspapers ready to tear up if you want to use a bucket in which to mix the paper pulp. In the classroom at least three newspapers will be needed per pupil if they are going to do some modelling with it. Do not cut it up; it takes a very long time to disintegrate if you do. Torn paper is already on its way to loosening up the fibres: the warm water will do the rest quite quickly (it is a good idea to leave it soaking overnight). Mash it up with a stick, take out handfuls of the pulp, squeeze out as much of the water as possible, and leave in lumps on the table. Do not tip the sludge at the bottom of the bucket down the sink (or it will block it).

When the paper has been reduced to a pulp, it is squeezed out and put on a worktop. Still more water is squeezed out into a bowl.

Another word of caution. After handling the newsprint one's hands turn a deep shade of grey. Finish preparing the pulp before you wash it off. It comes off easily, but if you wash when you are still in the middle of making the pulp, you wash off the natural oils in your skin, and then when you get the newsprint ink *into* your skin, it really goes in, and *is* difficult to wash at that stage.

Break the damp pulp up into crumbs, and either sprinkle dry paste onto it or add some dilute white glue and squeeze thoroughly through the crumbs. At this point it becomes slippery with the glue or paste. It is now ready for use. If one needs some very fine papier mâché, the papier mâché and the glue can be put into an electric blender. Make sure there is enough liquid in the machine and do it in small quantities. It only takes a moment to make a small quantity in the blender. Very fine detail can be worked with this type of papier mâché.

GLUING LAYERS OF PAPER TOGETHER

These can be either moulded around a former (bottle, pencil, knitting needle) to make beads, bangles, napkin rings, and candle holders, or freely modelled into a three-dimensional shape to make flowers, hats, and stage jewellery.

USING A MOULD

To cover an existing article, such as a basin, protect it with plastic 'cling wrap'. This makes it very easy to take the papier mâché mould off the article when it is dry. Vaseline can be used as an alternative but it is messy to use. Choose a shape without any undercutting. (If the papier mâché comes off the mould easily, then there was no undercutting: if you cannot get it off the mould, then there is undercutting.) If the papier mâché tears when you take it off the mould, it is a simple matter to patch it by gluing some more strips of newspaper across the tear.

Tear strips of newspaper up and dip them into a bowl of Polycell paste, running the strip between two fingers to get rid of excess paste, then lay the strips over the mould. Cover the entire mould, then cover again with another layer, the strips this time running at 45 degrees from the first, the third layer at 45 degrees from that, and so on until four or five layers have been stuck on. If the article needs to be quite strong cover it in a layer of muslin which has been dipped in a mixture of white PVA glue and plaster of Paris.

Make sure that the paper is well pressed down and that there are no air bubbles. If one is making a small tray, at least nine layers of paper should be pasted on, more if the article is large. Take care not to overlap the edge of the mould. If you do, you will not be able to get the mould out. Before the paper is dry, trim the edges with a pair of scissors. When the papier mâché is quite dry it can be taken off the mould. Tidy the edges by overlapping pieces of paper around the edges going from one side to the other. Combinations of articles can be used to make a mould, e.g. a bowl and a plate can be used to make a hat.

Using a mould which is undercut

Cover the article with aluminium foil or plastic wrap. Then cover with strips of newspaper as described above. Cover the article if large with both vertical and horizontal strips. Paste on four or five layers. When the papier mâché is dry, cut it in half down one side across the bottom and up the other side. Use a Stanley knife or some other sharp craft knife. The paper shell then will come off the mould easily. The two halves are now taped together with masking tape, and covered with another two or three layers of paper strips. When it is quite dry, seal the paper, and decorate in your chosen method.

PAPIER MÂCHÉ OVER AN ARMATURE

An armature is an underlying structure made of wire; pipe cleaners; rolled up newspaper; pieces of wood; chicken wire; cardboard boxes; stryoform balls; plastic cups; bottles. An armature is used when the desired object is so large that it would require too much papier mâché if it were made of that alone. It is also used to give support to slender shapes when drying to prevent them sagging, and when dry to prevent them snapping off. The pieces of sculpture made may be decorated in a variety of ways, and dolls can be dressed with scraps of fabric.

THINGS TO MAKE IN PAPIER MÂCHÉ

Maracas, small figures and animals, toys, dolls' houses, beads, bangles, necklaces, trays, boxes, vases, lampstands, waste paper baskets, masks, puppets, carnival animal heads, stage props, Christmas decorations, coat hangers, chess pieces.

A simple way of making a puppet head is to cover a light bulb with layers of papier mâché. When hard, cut open the shape to remove the light bulb, then glue the halves together again and continue adding layers, then model the features. Since this involves glass, it is not a technique for young children.

FURTHER READING

LORRIMAR, B., *Creative Papier Mâché* Studio Vista

MEILACH, D.M., *Papier Mâché Artistry* George Allen & Unwin

CAPON, R., *Papier Mâché* Batsford

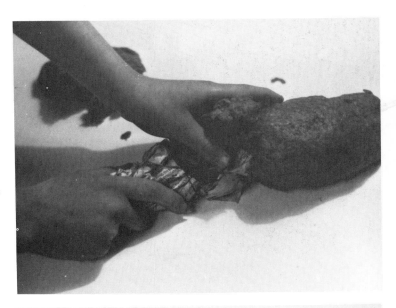

A tightly crushed newspaper held together with plastic bands helps the supply of papier mâché to go further and can act as an armature if some wire is used in the middle of the newspaper bundle.

A crocodile made with a crushed paper core. It has been put on a cake rack to help it dry more quickly.

Small items like these little people can be made from solid lumps of pulp.

Solid pulp is splendid for making toy food. Observe real food properly to make it really convincing.

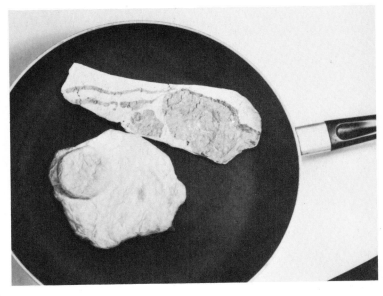

This bee was made using a polythene bottle as a base: this saves on papier mâché, as well as enabling one to work large, fairly quickly. The wings were made from old nylon stockings, stretched over a wire shape.

Lots of possible shapes were cut out of black paper. They were made in newspaper first, the shapes cut from folded paper. They were opened out flat on the black paper and traced round before being cut out.

Paper beads can be made by cutting long triangular strips of newspaper and rolling them, after pasting, round a knitting needle.

This ornate theatrical pendant was made with laminated paper. The decorations are various sequins glued on.

A pile of beads made this way.

These petals were cut from six sheets of newspaper pasted together (laminated). The shapes were cut out while the paper was still wet, and the shapes moulded. Once dry, these shapes are permanent.

The flower when painted.

Laminated paper can be moulded into many shapes not possible in other materials (except metal, where one would need a great deal of expertise in fixing the shape). When dry it is extremely tough.

The shape of this bottle has not been altered in any way: only several layers of newspaper strips put round it. It was then painted in acrylic paints.

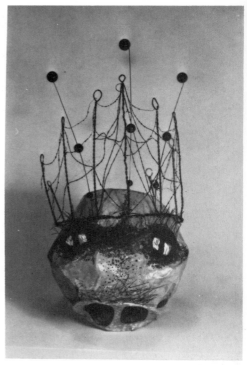

This bottle had several additions made to it. The bottle was covered in several layers of newspapers, then the eyelids and nose were attached. The eyelids were a semicircle of laminated paper, the curved edge of which was slit all the way round. When the lid was bent into a curve, the slits opened up and it was these which were glued and fastened onto the face. A hat was also made from laminated paper, and after the whole head and hat was painted, the feathers were added.

Chicken wire was used as the base for this mask, and net, wire, and large beads were added.

Papier mâché can be used to take a cast of an object (in this case, a pottery chicken). To prevent the paper strips sticking to the surface, it was covered in aluminium foil. Over this the strips of paper were pasted. Eight or nine layers are needed if the result is not to collapse when pressure is applied later.

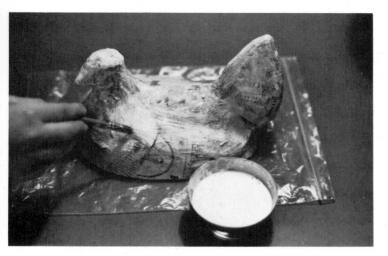

The excess round the bottom of the mould has to be trimmed off before the cast can be removed.

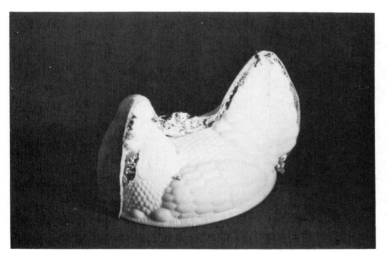

Since the cast would not come off because of the shape of the chicken, a line was drawn down the centre, and the cast was carefully cut apart. Then the foil was removed, and the two parts were glued together again inside and outside with strips of newspaper.

This particular cast was decorated with sequins and gold doyley pieces.

PAPIER MÂCHÉ

TECHNIQUES	METHODS OF DECORATION	SOME THINGS TO MAKE

Covering an existing object
Modelling on a wire
    armature
Modelling on a chicken
    wire armature
Using a mould
Gluing layers together
Making the pulp
	High relief
	    Modelling (with glued
	    layers of paper)
	
	Low relief
	    String
	    Lace
	    Seeds
	    Matchsticks
	    Ferns
	    Fur
	    Feathers
	    Wire
	    Wool
	    Hessian
	    Mother of pearl
	
	Flat decoration
	    Painting
	    Fabric
	    Photographs
	    Newspapers
	    Illustrations
		Beads
		Puppet heads
		Masks
		Small animals
		Figures on polythene
		    bottles
		Tumbler doll
		Tray
		Chairs
		Shelves
		Bangles
		Flowers
		Mirrors
		Tops of screwtop jars
		Buildings
		Figures (tiny to life size)

SUMMARY OF PAPER CRAFTS

DECORATED	FLAT (2D)	3D

Fold and dye
Tie and dye
Marbling
Printing
Stencilling
Batik
Splatter/airbrush
Drawing
Wax crayon
	Chinese and Polish
	    paper cutting
	Frottage
	Paper weaving
	Cut and spread
	Paper pricking
	Tissue paper
	    (collage)
	    (embedding)
	    (colouring)
	Tissue paper twisting
	Découpage
	Paper plaiting
	Creative rubbing
	Book making
	Silhouettes
	Pantins
	Shadow puppets
	Dressed paper dolls
	Books
	Kites
		Origami
		Cut and bend
		Paper sculpture
		Paper filigree (quilling)
		Paper flowers
		Corrugated paper
		Paper laminating
		Paper beads
		Mobiles
		Rolled paper dolls
		Papier mâché
		Kites

Pebble Polishing

Collecting pebbles can have a twofold pleasure: shape and texture for the hand, and colour and pattern for the eye. Sea-worn pebbles are a source of great satisfaction to handle; many cultures accept the soothing effect of stones, and indulge in it with their 'worry stones'. Semi-precious stones are to be found on most beaches of Britain and North America, such as citrine, agate (banded and moss), carnelian, serpentine, amber, jet, jasper, cairngorm, and the very beautiful Blue John (fluorspar) from Derbyshire.

Precious and semi-precious stones are extremely hard and are very difficult to cut, requiring highly specialized equipment, and a knowledge of crystallography. However, manufacturers now produce inexpensive tumbling machines, which take off the rough outside of the pebble, grinding it away to reveal the full beauty of the stone. These can be made directly into jewellery with the wide range of 'findings' on the market – the blanks onto which the polished stones can be stuck to make bracelets, cuff-links, rings, pendants, etc. They are made in stainless steel and silver, but the quality of the design of these blanks is very variable, and one needs to see many catalogues to choose some really sympathetic designs, sympathetic that is to the innate qualities of a polished naturally-shaped stone.

There is a range of stones that cannot be tumbled for they are either too hard or too soft. Quartz-veined sandstones, for example, are too soft. Flints are too hard to tumble, but as a result of their initial geological formation appear in a great variety of irregular shapes which might suggest an animal or bird, which with a little painting can be made into an amusing adult toy, or which give the aesthetic pleasure of a Henry Moore or a Barbara Hepworth. The acceptance of naturally weathered stones as a valid and valuable object of beauty is not a Western concept, but in Japan they are just that. Large stones are an essential element in the traditional Japanese garden, and there are certain stones which are considered very beautiful whose whereabouts have been recorded for centuries, and these change hands for thousands of pounds.

The knapping (splitting) of flints is a craft common to the areas where flints occur and they are frequently used to surface the exterior of buildings in Britain. There are some beautiful churches in Ipswich which are decorated on the outside with a combination of knapped flint and stone. Small mosaics could be made from the smaller pieces of broken flints set in plaster. Ovoid pebbles have been used for centuries to make a good surface for light traffic. Many modern buildings have the ground around them set with ovoids to contrast with and give relief to the monotony of the man-made paving slabs.

PEBBLE COLOUR CHART

REDS	YELLOWS
Serpentine	Carnelian
Carnelian	Sandstone
Jasper	Citrine
Sandstone	Smokey quartz
Red slate	Serpentine

BLACKS	BLUES
Jet	Blue shale
Chert	Slate
Basalt	Dolerite
Furnace slag	

GREEN	BROWNS
Schist	Jasper
Serpentine	Dolerite
Jasper	Chert
Greenstone	

WHITE	GREYS
Opaque quartz	Flint
Flint	Schist
	Granite
PINKS	Chert (A chocolate coloured stone found only on the beaches at Felixstowe.)
Sandstone	
Rose quartz	

PURPLES	
Slate	
Sandstone	
Jasper	
Amethystine	

POLISHING BY HAND

Although it is possible to polish the curved surfaces of a pebble by hand, it is far easier to polish them in a small commercial pebble polisher. Hand polishing is best used for the flat surfaces of stones which have been machine cut. These sections are available in shops selling stones and polishing equipment.

Materials

silicon carbide grits, 220, 320, and 500; tin oxide or cerium oxide (for polishing); sheet of plate glass (on which the grinding is done); two pieces of suede each stuck on a piece of plywood (for the final grinding, and polishing).

The polishing is done on a sheet of plate glass, and is done in four stages, the first three grinding the surface as smooth as possible, the last being the polishing proper.

METHOD

On the plate glass, sprinkle a teaspoon of 220 grade grit, and moisten with a little water to make a paste. Press the flat surface of the stone into that, and move over the glass in a circular movement. Continue until there is a noticeable difference in the surface being polished. Check this from time to time by washing off under a tap. When satisfied of a change, wash all the grit off the glass and the stone, removing all traces of grit from each. Next sprinkle some

320 grade grit onto the glass, and enough water to make a paste, and continue as before. Again wash the glass and stone very thoroughly before the next stage. Most of the work involved in producing a really smooth surface is done in these two stages, so if in doubt, carry on for another half hour. (The best time to do this is while watching TV or listening to music.)

The third stage is done on a piece of suede glued onto a piece of plywood, not on the plate glass; 500 grit is sprinkled onto the suede and water is very sparingly sprinkled on the grit. If one used glass at this stage, the stone would skid around on the surface. The suede holds the particles firmly. Polish with the same circular movements as before. (Keep the suede in a polythene bag so that no other grits come in contact with it. It can be used over and over again.) Rinse off the stone when the surface is beginning to have a dull shine.

The polishing proper is also done on a piece of suede glued to plywood. Mix some tin oxide or cerium oxide to a paste with water in a small dish. Dampen the suede slightly, and put on it a little of the paste. Rub the stone on the suede very quickly now, but not pressing too hard, just lightly skimming the surface. Rub until the stone becomes warm and dries up the paste. Apply more polishing paste, and continue until the stone has a glorious sheen.

TUMBLE POLISHING

Tumbling produces irregularly shaped stones called baroques. One cannot control the shape of a stone in the tumbler. The process is very simple, requiring no expertise – only attention to detail. The pebbles are put into a barrel/drum which is revolved on two rollers for 7 days and nights continuously at each stage. The barrel/drum is filled two-thirds full of pebbles, the grit is added and it is then filled with water, and the lid tightly fastened on. It must be two-thirds full; if it is less there is too much room for the pebbles to fall around in and possibly crack or chip; if it is more, there is not enough room for them to roll around in and very little grinding takes place. Fill the barrel with stones of a similar size, with a few smaller ones to fill in the hollows of the larger ones, so that the hollows too get ground. Tumbling machines can be made at home, but small commercial ones are readily available, and are not expensive.

There are four tumbling phases plus an extra one for final rinsing. Phase 1 uses 80 grit; phase 2, 220 grit; phase 3, 400 grit. Tin oxide (or cerium oxide) is used in phase 4, the polishing phase. For the rinsing stage add half a cup of powdered detergent to the water (half that for each of the small double barrels).

The proportions of grit required will be given with the tumbling machine when you buy it. If you make your own tumbler, allow $\frac{3}{4}$ lb plus to 3 kg stones of 80 grit; $\frac{1}{2}$ lb plus to

These pebbles have been polished and wrapped in copper foil to make this lampshade. (Courtesy Joni Meyer, Manhattan, New York.)

3 kg stones of 220 grit; and $\frac{1}{2}$ lb to 3 kg of stones of 400 grit. You will also need 6 oz of tin oxide, and one cup detergent. If you allow extra time on stage 1, stage 2 can be omitted: 80 grit will eventually break down to 220 grit if left tumbling in the barrel long enough, so that one can move from 80 grit to 400.

The exact length of time taken is difficult to give exactly. For water-worn pebbles, 7 days of continuous running day and night should be enough at *each* of the first three stages. To prevent chipping at the polishing stage, add pieces of suede, or felt or polystyrene granules to the pebbles. The stones and the barrel must be very thoroughly washed in between the stages, and if some baking soda is added to the water when using the 80, 220, and 400 grit, it will eliminate the formation of gas during tumbling. Take out any cracked, broken or chipped stones at each stage. They are not worth bothering with, however special they might have been, and they run the risk of damaging the other stones.

The sludge that forms in the barrel after a session of tumbling must never be thrown down a drain: it will block it. Keep the tumbler as far away from the family as possible when it is in use. After a few days of continuous tumbling, the noise can become very irritating. A thick pad of felt under the machine will help reduce the noise.

The polished stones can have findings attached, and they can be made up into necklaces, key rings, bracelets, or try some three-dimensional constructions made with polished stones. Araldite is used for gluing the findings to the pebbles. To keep the stones steady while the Araldite sets, press them into a bed of damp sand, or plasticine, to prevent them tipping over. Another method of attaching a finding is to drill a hole on the top with a hand drill while holding the stone in a vice. Alternatively, cut a V-shaped groove in the top with a hacksaw, and with an Epoxy glue attach a jump ring to the base of the groove.

Cutting stones

It is possible to cut the stones into cabochons (domed, rounded stones with a flat base, either oval or circular in section). They are widely available at gemstone shops, or they can be made at home. To do this one needs to construct special diamond saws for cutting and grind stones for polishing. Details for constructing these are given in H. Scarfe's book, *Collecting and Polishing Stones* (Batsford).

FURTHER READING

ALLEN, J., *Guide to Craft Suppliers* Studio Vista

SCARFE, H., *Collecting and Polishing Stones* Batsford

SCARFE, H., *The Lapidary Manual* Batsford

Pebble Painting

Materials

smooth well worn sandstone or similar pebbles; brushes, one fine, 00, 0 or 1, and one medium, 4, 5 or 6; poster or gouache paint; felt-tip pens, ball-point pens; nail varnish; spray acrylic varnish, or dilute PVA (white) glue; mapping pen or Rotring, and Indian ink.

METHOD

Choose smooth, evenly worn sandstone pebbles; these can be found on almost every beach around the British Isles. Sometimes they have quartz veining running through them which appears on the surface as white lines, and these are often perfect in themselves with no additional decoration. Sandstone has an absorbent surface, and if the stones are intended to be handled, they should have some protection from grease. This can be done by spraying with acrylic coating, or by painting the stone with a dilute PVA (white) glue (one-third water, two-thirds PVA). Although this is white when painted on, it dries completely transparently. When painting with PVA, work on a sheet of polythene: PVA does not stick to it, so if any PVA trickles down, you can still remove the pebble easily from it.

Wash the stones you have collected, and once they are quite dry you can begin work on them. Gouache paints are the best, and are relatively cheap. Any acrylic or polymer-based paints are also suitable, but do not use oil paints or enamels. These take a long time to dry; one

has to wait for one colour to dry before adding another colour, and they are a trouble to store safely while drying.

The one expensive item that is well worth buying is a good brush. Choose a water colour brush which when wet will form a fine point; the larger sizes 4–6 for the large areas, and the small ones 00, 0 or 1 for the fine details. If when you have finished the pebble, you still feel that the pattern is not distinct enough, try outlining the edges between one colour and the next with a fine black line, made with either a mapping pen and Indian ink, or with a special draughtsman's pen which also uses Indian ink (Rotring).

As far as the colours of paint go, a lot can be done with only a bottle of black and a bottle of white. Striking Op art designs or Art Deco style designs can be done with just these two. If you want other colours, two yellows, a lemon yellow, and an orange yellow: two blues, a cerulean or Prussian, and an ultramarine: and two reds, a blue red (magenta) and a pure bright red, plus a black and white, will give you a very wide range of colours when mixed. I have listed two sorts of yellow, blue, and red, because certain pinks can come only from magenta, and particular lilacs and purples can come only from particular reds and blues. Since most of the stones will be dark, when using white, or any pale colour, you will probably need to apply two coats of colour, and in each case it is best to use white as the undercoat.

Sometimes the shape of a pebble will suggest something to you at once. This drawing of an owl was made in pencil, and painted in poster colour, and an acrylic sealer was used when the paint was dry.

Draw the design on the pebble with a soft 3B pencil, and fill in the areas with paint. If you choose an abstract design you will probably not need any reference material, but if you choose to do a fish or a bird, or any other natural form, do get some photographs to supplement your memory. If you do not have a supply of paints, cover all the pebbles with white emulsion (house) paint, and when this is dry make the patterns with felt-tip pens, ball-point pens, or nail varnish.

Experiment with different 'styles' of painting. Here the technique used has been to try and imply form, to give the illusion of real ribbon on the pebble.

Photograms

Materials

Paper If you have no access to a dark-room, use photocopying paper, Rapido-print by Agfa-Gevaert FCS1 grade 2, FCN 1 grade 3, FCH 1 grade 4, single weight, glossy; or Kodak projection paper P145; or Kodak contact paper C145. If you do have a dark-room, use Kodak P84 photographic paper.

Developer Either a powder or a concentrated liquid, diluted as per manufacturer's instructions.

Fixative Available as a concentrated solution, diluted as per manufacturer's instructions.

Red light A red light bulb or a flashlight covered with red cellophane will emit a 'safe' light for working in a dark-room. Not necessary if working in partially darkened conditions with photocopying paper.

Equipment

three photographer's plastic trays approximately 15 in. by 18 in.; a light source, the height of which you can control; running water; two plastic photographic tongs; a piece of glass, a little larger than the printing paper.

BASIC METHOD

The principle of making photograms is really that which lies behind getting a suntan, the areas which are exposed to strong sunlight change colour. If a key is laid on a sheet of light-sensitive photographic paper which is then exposed to light, when the key is lifted off, its image will still be white and the exposed paper will have turned grey. Then, just as a suntan will disappear out of the sun, so the image of the key will disappear, for as the white image of the key is exposed to the light, it too will turn grey.

To make the image permanent, the paper is placed in a tray of 'developing' fluid. The stage at which the image appears happens in the developing fluid when you are actually making a photogram, the exposed parts of the paper turning a very dark grey to a rich black. The paper is all white when it goes into the developing tray. When the exposed parts of the paper are black, it is taken out with the plastic tongs, rinsed, and placed in the bath (tray) of 'fixer', which, as the name suggests, fixes it, or makes it permanent. If the background is grey, it has not been left long enough in the light (the first stage). If the image itself is also beginning to turn black and disappear, then it has been exposed to the light for too long.

Photographic papers vary enormously in the speed with which they are affected by light. 'Proper' photographic paper can only be used in a dark-room, with a red light as the illumination for moving around the room. The instructions given here will be for making photograms in an ordinary living room/class-room/kitchen, with only partial darkening of the room. The method is the same wherever it is done, only the materials are different. Photocopying paper is very much 'slower' than proper photographic paper, taking 2 to 3 minutes in a partially darkened room. The paper itself, however, *must* be kept in the black wrapping paper in which it is sold, and only one sheet taken out at a time, and that only when you are ready to put it under the light. If it is left unwrapped and exposed to the light, it will turn grey and be quite useless.

The source of light must be a clear electric light bulb, not a frosted one. A frosted glass bulb will give a fuzzy edge to the image. Use a 100-watt bulb and have it hanging about 5 ft to 6 ft away from the paper. A table or chair will be needed on which to place the paper. If the surface is not flat, put the paper on an old bread board or drawing board, first protecting it with polythene sheeting. To keep the paper flat, lay a sheet of glass over it, but make sure the edges are not sharp. If they are, rub them down with a piece of emery cloth.

If you are working at night, do not use fluorescent lighting to see your way around. Use an ordinary bulb, and work as far away as possible from this source of light when making the photogram, and developing and fixing.

The three polythene trays are for holding the developer, clean water for rinsing, and for the fixer. The two pairs of plastic tongs are for holding the paper while it is being slid into the developer, and the fixing solution. Keep one pair for putting into the developer, taking it out, and putting it into the rinsing water; the other for putting in and taking out of the 'fixer'. About 1 litre of liquid is needed in each tray. Both the Kodak Universal developer and the Kodak fixing solution are diluted by seven parts of water to one part of chemical. If using other brands, check the proportions with their instructions.

To find out how 'fast' the paper is, it is necessary to do a test piece. Cut one of the pieces of paper in half for this. The test is done using a strip of card. A postcard, or a piece cut from the side of a cereal packet will be fine: the important thing is that it is opaque. You will also need a watch with a second hand, because the timing is done in seconds.

Cover the piece of photocopying paper with the postcard, leaving one-quarter exposed. Switch on the light for 30 seconds. Switch off the light, move the card down so that one-half of the paper is now exposed (i.e. the original quarter and another quarter). Switch on for 15 seconds. Switch off, and move the card down a further quarter, so that there are now three-quarters exposed. Switch on for 20 seconds. Switch off. Take the card off completely, exposing the whole piece of paper for a further 30 seconds. The first part of the strip has now been exposed for a total of 95 seconds, the second quarter for a total of 65 seconds, the third quarter for a total of 50 seconds, and the last for 30 seconds.

Now to develop the paper. Immerse the paper completely in the tray of developer, and leave it there until the most exposed part is a really deep rich black. This will normally happen after 1 to 3 minutes. Rinse the paper in the dish of clear water, and, shaking off the surplus water, slide the paper into the tray of 'fixer'. Leave it there for about 5 minutes, rocking the tray occasionally. Take it out, and rinse under running water, leaving it there for 2 hours if possible. When you inspect the trial exposure, you will probably find that leaving the paper exposed for 90 seconds is about the right length of time, with the light source 6 ft away.

The relative position of the equipment.

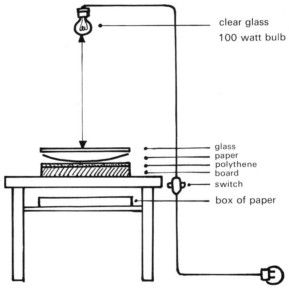

clear glass
100 watt bulb

glass
paper
polythene
board
switch

box of paper

The arrangement of the trays in sequence. Note the plastic tongs for removing from one dish to the other.

DEVELOPER   WATER   FIXER

It is very important that having made your test strip, you write on the back the type of paper, distance of light from the paper, wattage of the bulb, and the number of seconds of each exposure. A change in any one of these will make a difference to your results, but if you make careful notes, you will know exactly what to do next time.

Experiment with all sorts of objects and materials to make an image: paper, lace, string, glass, ferns, feathers. Sprinkle sand or salt directly onto the glass, and either leave it as it falls, or draw into it with a finger. If you use plant forms, ones which have been pressed first will give the most distinct prints. Work directly onto the glass with ink, poster paints: use the glass to do a monoprint on, but instead of taking a print with paper, place it over the light sensitive paper, expose to light and develop in the usual way. Splash or draw with the 'fixer' directly onto the paper, expose and develop in the usual way.

SOLARIZATION
The only restriction to this technique is that it can only be used with transparent/translucent objects, but the results are very subtle and decorative.
First method
Expose for 90 seconds and develop until the deepest black occurs. Leaving the photogram *in the dish of developer*, place the tray on the glass under the light. Switch off the light as soon as fine details begin to appear. Continue developing the paper until you are pleased with the picture, and then rinse and fix as usual.
Second method
As before, but instead of giving it a second exposure with the paper still in the developing tray, take it out, rinse, and pat dry before putting it back under the light.

MOVING THE OBJECT BETWEEN EXPOSURES
This is an intriguing technique to use with objects made of glass. Using one or more drinking glasses, lay them on the glass sheet, expose to light for 15 seconds, switch off, move the glass to another position, switch on and expose for another 15 seconds. Develop and print as usual.

USING MORE THAN ONE LIGHT SOURCE
Try using four light sources at the same level as the glass (the lights placed at 12, 3, 6, and 9 o'clock positions of a clock face). Each light will cast a shadow, which when developed will produce a pattern rather like that in a kaleidoscope. Any number of light sources could be used: experiment.

PARAGLYPHS
First make a photogram on translucent light-sensitive paper, develop and fix. Using this, lay it over a second piece of translucent light-sensitive paper, develop and fix in the normal way. You now have two photograms, one with the image in black on a white background (the positive), the other has a white image on a black background (the negative). Now, lay one on top of the other, so that they match exactly, and then slide one a little to one side, so that they are out of 'register'.

Tape them together at the edges so that they cannot move; photo mounts (Blick) are easier to use: they are double-sided and can be slipped between the two sheets at each corner. Lay this sandwich on a sheet of normal light-sensitive paper, put the glass sheet on top, and expose to the light for a much longer time than normal – somewhere between 3 and 5 minutes. The light source must be nearer too, about 2 ft away.

Prints can be taken using the fixer as 'ink'. Soak a piece of felt or thick cloth in the fixer. Press your hand onto the cloth, and then press your hand onto the light-sensitive paper. *Do not do this with children*. Children should be taught to treat all chemicals with great respect and not to dip their fingers into them. The paper is then developed and fixed as usual. Lino cuts can be wiped with fixer, pressed onto light-sensitive paper, and then processed.

USING SLIDES AND A PROJECTOR
Make up some 35-mm slides and project onto the wall, marking the corners of the projected image on the wall. Obviously the projector is going to be nearer the wall than usual because the projected image must be nearly the same size as the piece of paper on which the photogram will be printed. Switch off the projector, place the printing paper on the space marked on the wall, and switch on the projector. If you use this technique, it is important to do a separate test piece to see how long to expose the paper, because the strength of the light source has been changed. Develop and fix as usual.

MAKING PICTURES AND POSTERS
Pictures, posters, and illustrations for books can all be made using photograms. Use tracing paper as the base onto which the illustration is arranged. Lines can be made using thin wire, cotton, wool, or string. Areas of tone can be achieved with papers of different opacities, textures with salt, rice, coarse sand, etc. If lettering is wanted, use Letraset, Chartpak, or the loose plastic letters made by Morol, or the lettering text can be drawn directly onto the tracing paper. Remember that if a positive is to be made from the photogram, and you incorporate lettering in the picture, then the lettering will have to be reversed.

Lay the picture on tracing paper over a piece of light-sensitive paper. Place a sheet of glass on top to prevent things moving out of place on the paper; expose and print in the normal way. Try making a picture directly onto the glass. As always, experiment.

Photogram of honesty seeds.

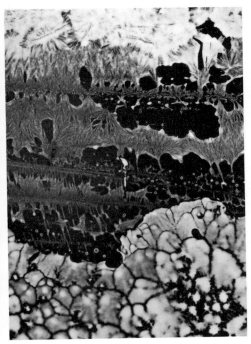

Photogram made by fixer crystals which have formed on the glass.

FABRIC PRINTING USING LIGHT-SENSITIVE CLOTH

Here the same principle is used for printing on cloth that has been made light-sensitive.

The sensitizer

Distilled water: 4 tablespoons. Potassium ferricyanide (PF) $\frac{1}{3}$ oz, or 2 slightly domed tsps of the powder. Ferric ammonium citrate (FAC) brown, $\frac{1}{2}$ oz, or 2 heaped tsps of the powder.

METHOD

Crush the powders separately, and add half the distilled water to each. Stir well with a glass or wooden rod. Mix the two solutions together and store in a light-proof jar. Label and date it. Keep it in a cupboard. The colour the cloth will turn on exposure to light is blue if the cloth was white to start with. If the cloth was pink, the exposed areas will become lilac/mauve. If the cloth was yellow, it will become green.

Wash the cloth to be used and dry it. Stir up the mixture in the jar, and dip in the fabric. Squeeze out the excess into the jar. Spread the cloth out to dry on a whole newspaper in a dark cupboard. Keeping as much in the dark as you

can, pin the fabric onto a board; this is to get rid of creases. To make a clear print, the stencil should be heavy. Make an arrangement of scissors, or keys, or coins. Take the board with the cloth and keys (or whatever) and put it in strong sunlight or strong daylight for 15 to 20 minutes. Lift a key to see if the image is clear enough; if not leave it in the sunlight for a little longer. When the fabric is a dark blue, wash it in plain water until no trace of yellow remains in the water. This is important. Any yellow left will turn the white images a pale blue.

Cut a shape or shapes out of sheets of gummed paper. Stick these on a piece of cloth which has been dipped in the liquid; the gum will stick to the cloth which is what you want it to do at this stage. Take it out into the sunlight, and when it has turned dark blue, wash off. (The gummed paper will come off when you are doing the rinsing.) Try spraying the liquid onto the cloth which has the shape glued on. Do this with a spray for fixative. Proceed as above.

FURTHER READING

BRUANDET, P., *Introducing Photograms* Batsford

Solarization: method 2.

Solarization: method 1.

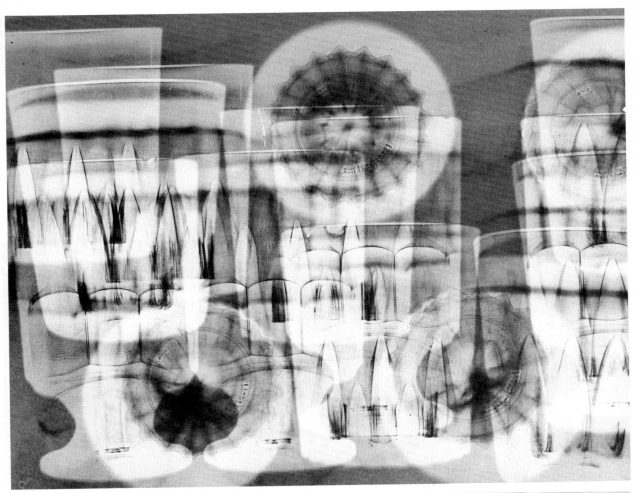

Moving the object between exposures.

Using more than one light source.

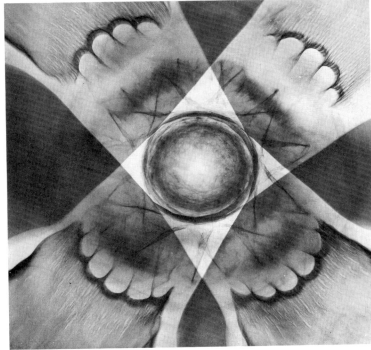

Positive photogram.

Negative photogram.

Exposing the paraglyph to the light.

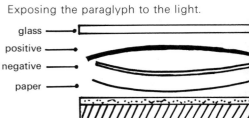

glass ●━━━━━
positive ●━━━━━
negative ●━━━━━
paper ●━━━━━

The finished paraglyph.

Pin and Thread

Materials

A base For pins one needs a base soft enough for them to be pushed into, either by hand or with a push pin (not a hammer). One can use a cork tile, as long as it is one of the fine grain type, or building boards. Building boards can be either lightweight insulating boards (softboards) sold by builder's merchants (lumber yards) in large sheets, under a variety of trade names, or medium boards, which are also a soft board, but firmer. For nails, the surface needs to be much firmer, e.g. plywood, chipboard, blockboard.

Pins Dressmaking pins, map pins, or spherical headed (glass) pins.

Nails Panel pins, brass nails, small-headed nails, or large-headed nails. Small children can use drawing pins and thin rubber bands in a variety of sizes and colours.

Threads Reels (spools) of sewing thread, wire, wool, nylon.

METHOD

With a compass, draw a circle roughly 6 in. diameter on a piece of paper. On this circle mark out the minutes of a clock. Take a ruler, and draw a line from 12 o'clock to 9 o'clock. Then draw another line from 59 minutes to 44 minutes. Then another from 58 minutes to 43 minutes, and so on all the way round the clock. You will notice that on the inside of the circle the straight lines have formed a curve. This is the particular quality of pin and thread work.

Now draw two right angles, about 6 in. long, and mark out dots along the bottom lines at $\frac{1}{8}$-in. intervals, and on the two upright arms, mark out dots on one of them at $\frac{1}{8}$-in. intervals, and on the other at $\frac{1}{4}$-in. (Since it is essential that one has the same number of dots on each arm, the arm with the dots at $\frac{1}{4}$-in. intervals will have to be double in length, i.e. 12 in.) Starting at the extreme right of the horizontal arm, join the last dot to the first dot on the upright arm. The next line is the second upright dot to the second from the extreme right and so on until all the dots have been connected.

Proceed in exactly the same way with the other one. Look at them and notice the change in the curve as a result of changing the distance between the dots. Experiment in this way, and work out various ideas which come to you. When you have understood *why* the pins are in a certain position, then is the time to try it out with pins and thread. Use a full reel of thread, and leaving it on the reel, tie onto a pin with a slip knot. Unlike the patterns you made with a ruler, the lines cannot be discrete when using thread, because to get to the pin to make the second line you take the thread with you, so making a second line. That is why there sometimes seems to be a discrepancy between your pencil drawings and the same thing done in pin and thread.

Keep the thread as tight as you can when winding round the pins, but not so tight that the pins pull over. When the last pin is reached, do another slip knot, put a spot of glue (UHU) on it, and when it is dry cut the thread. Push all the pins down so that only the heads are showing. This secures the thread.

With one pattern pushed down, try, on the same board, doing a different pattern over the first one. Experiment with many-colour pictures. Paint the background before you begin: cover it in felt, hessian, satin, or a piece of batik. The pin and thread kits one sees in the shops are not the last word, but the first. The last word is with you. Experiment with 3D over a wire armature. In a wooden box, try a drilled plywood construction.

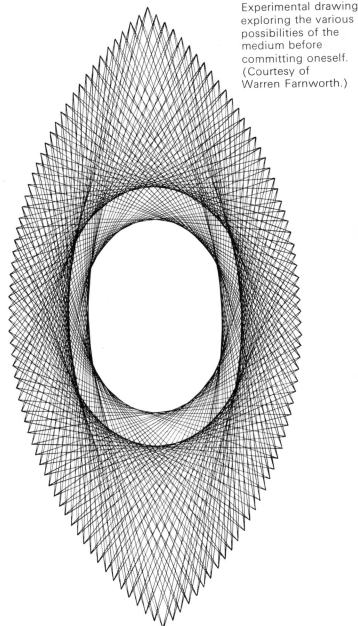

Experimental drawing exploring the various possibilities of the medium before committing oneself. (Courtesy of Warren Farnworth.)

231

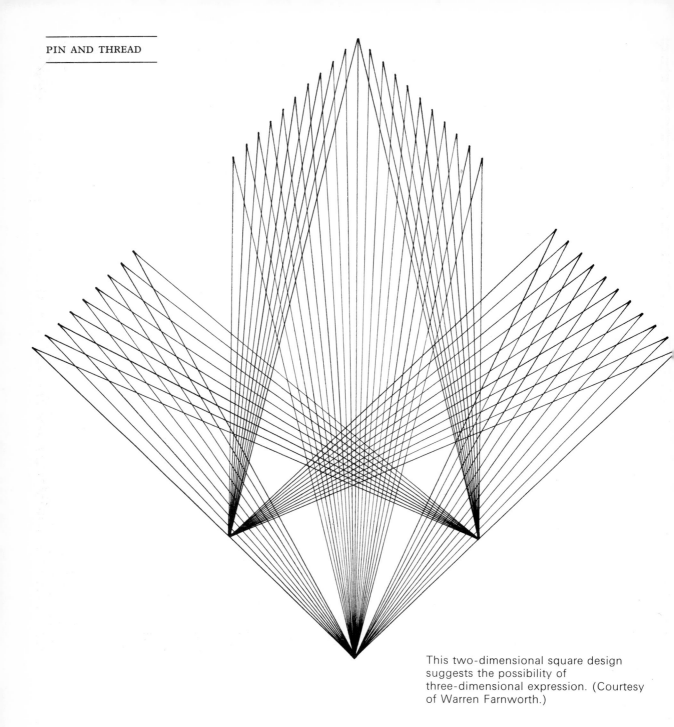

This two-dimensional square design suggests the possibility of three-dimensional expression. (Courtesy of Warren Farnworth.)

The threads in this picture are all taken to
the edge of the frame. (*String Composition*
by Sue Fuller, 1964, Tate Gallery, London.)

Notice the completely different effect when one sees the image as white on a black background as compared to the previous examples which have been black on a white background. (Courtesy of Warren Farnworth.)

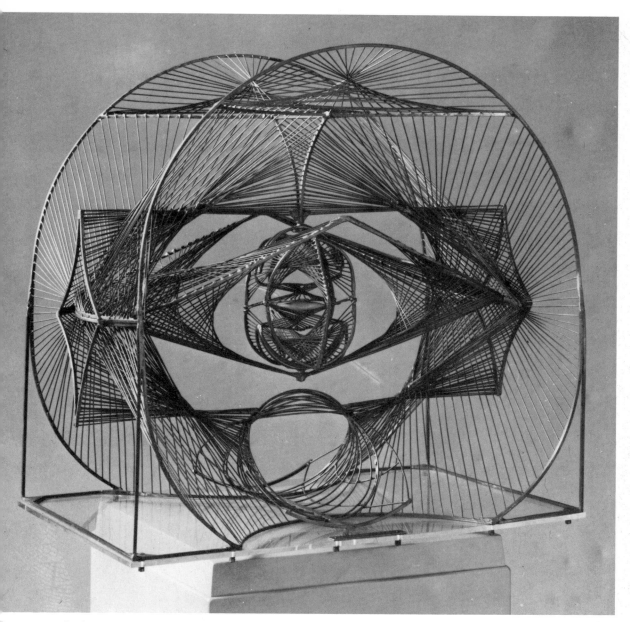

he concept is the same but wire is used in
is example and the construction is in
ree dimensions.
Maquette of a Monument symbolising the
beration of the Spirit, 1952, bronze, by
ntoine Pevsner, Tate Gallery, London.)

URTHER READING

RNWORTH, W., *Pin and Thread Craft* Batsford
RNWORTH, W., *Techniques and Designs in Pin
  and Thread Craft* Batsford

Plaiting and Braiding

A plait is formed by interlacing three or more lengths of yarn resulting in a decorative strip which is extremely strong. It can be simple enough for any child to work, or quite intricate, using various combinations and patterns with a large number of yarns. Most plaits can be made with a minimum of equipment – all that is needed is a method of securing the ends of the yarn so that they are held taut. Several methods of completing and securing the finished braid can be used: a hidden thread can be sewn through and across each end of the plait, or the ends can be hooked back into the reverse side.

A three-plait, using one thick and two thin threads.

Varieties of threads are used in each plait, but all have one thread pulled tighter than the others when the plait is finished.

FURTHER READING

BARKER, J., *Making Plaits and Braids*   Batsford

camel made from plaited rough twine:
he legs are firmly bound for rigidity.

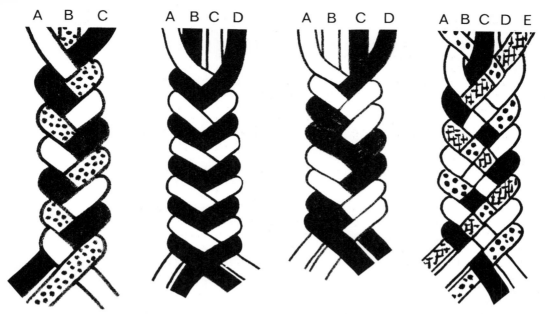

A B C D E F G

Working patterns for flat braids: three-plait,
four-plait, four-plait variation,
'odd-numbered' plait, and seven-plait.

A collage made of plaits, braids and some
knitting. (Pauline Oddy.)

Plaster of Paris

Plaster of Paris was introduced into England in the mid-thirteenth century, by Henry III, who was very impressed by the quality of French plaster work. Plaster is made from gypsum, and Paris was built on a large area of gypsum deposits. Deposits of gypsum are found all over the world. It was used in Egypt in the mortar used on the walls of tombs, and alabaster, which is the purest form of gypsum, is so-called from the Egyptian town of Alabastron. In England the Guild of Plaisterers was granted its Charter in 1501, and by the sixteenth and seventeenth centuries plasterwork on the ceilings of important houses and the pargetting on the houses of wealthy merchants had reached a high standard of design and technical expertise. Pargetting is a peculiarly English high relief modelling on the outside of timber houses, and can be seen on a lot of houses in St Albans and Ipswich.

A very high-quality plaster is dental plaster, which takes the finest details of casts. Various things can be added to plaster to change its qualities. It can be coloured: this is best done when the plaster model is finished. It takes an enormous amount of dry colour to make any difference to the white of plaster. It can have textures added to it in the form of sand, or sawdust, but in proportion of no more than a third, or it will weaken the plaster too much.

When plaster has been added to water there is a comparatively short time before it 'goes off' (hardens). If you need it to go off even sooner, use hot water instead of cold, or add some alum to the water. (This also results in a much harder plaster.) To slow it down, add more water than you would normally; by scarcely mixing the water and plaster after adding the plaster; or by adding five tsps vinegar to the water. Plaster must always be kept dry; if it is left in a damp atmosphere or standing on a damp floor it will be unusable in no time.

Always add plaster to water, never the other way round. Half fill a bowl (plastic for preference, it is easy to clean out when you have finished) with water. Use 1 part water to 2–3 parts plaster. Sprinkle dry plaster onto the surface, and continue until the level of the plaster reaches the surface of the water. Leave for 2 minutes, then plunge your hand into the liquid, and without making any bubbles, move your hand around mixing the plaster well. Do not dally over this; the plaster is hardening from the moment it goes into the water. While it is still very thin, use it for pouring into moulds. As it sets it becomes thicker, and when it reaches the stage of thick cream it is ready for using with scrim/muslin on armatures. Casts and moulds become very warm while they are setting; this is quite normal. As soon as it becomes crumbly it is useless. It cannot be rewetted, the change is irreversible (unlike clay) and it has to be thrown away. Always throw it away *in a rubbish bin*, never in a sink. Do not try and wash bowls out in the sink, because the plaster will set in the drains.

One of the most spectacular attributes of plaster is its ability to record the finest of details. To make a cast roll out some plasticine or, preferably, clay, into some sort of regular shape, and press an object into it. Before the plaster can be poured onto the impressions, a 'wall' must be attached to the base. Cut a strip of clay (or plasticine) and firmly press it to the base at the side, and where the two edges meet. If you want to hang the cast when it is set, push a hair pin into the wall. Do this before you pour in the plaster; once the plaster is in, you will forget which side is the top! When making large casts of over 12 in. diameter, add a layer of scrim/muslin to the plaster to strengthen it. When the plaster has cooled, pull off the retaining wall. Turn the plaster onto your palm, and pull the clay off the plaster. Any clay left sticking can be washed off the next day.

Sculpture which is very slender will need some support to make it rigid. This is called the armature, and is normally made of wire twisted to form a 'skeleton', or welded metal for large sculpture. Twigs, polystyrene, wood, and chicken wire are all quite suitable. Armatures can be either free standing, or nailed onto a block of wood. Plaster can be applied to the armature either by hand (or spatula) or muslin/scrim can be dipped in plaster and wrapped around the armature, and the model built up that way. Commercially prepared scrim is available which only needs to be dipped in water, and is usable immediately. A sand/plaster mix can be used for carving; the tool used to carve can be anything from a penknife to files and saws. A cast sheet of plaster $\frac{1}{2}$ in to 1 in. thick can be incised (engraved, scratched) and either left as it is, or used as a block for printing, or the grooves can be filled with coloured wax.

Pariscraft and Dick Blick's Plastercraft Sculpture Rolls are two types of pre-shrunk plaster-impregnated cotton gauze available in the USA. Dyes, transparent water colours, oils, acrylics and enamels can be painted directly onto Pariscraft models, but poster paints and tempera require sizing before use. Liquitex Modeling Paste, a marble 'putty', is also available in the USA to form three-dimensional models which can be carved and sanded.

FURTHER READING

COWLEY, D., *Working with Clay and Plaster* Batsford

FARNSWORTH, W., *Creative Work with Plaster* Batsford

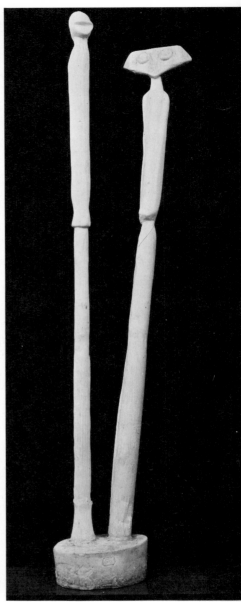

When making slender models in plaster, you will need an armature for support. Wire was used in this example by Giacometti.

This example by Max Ernst also used wire. Notice the very different surface treatment.

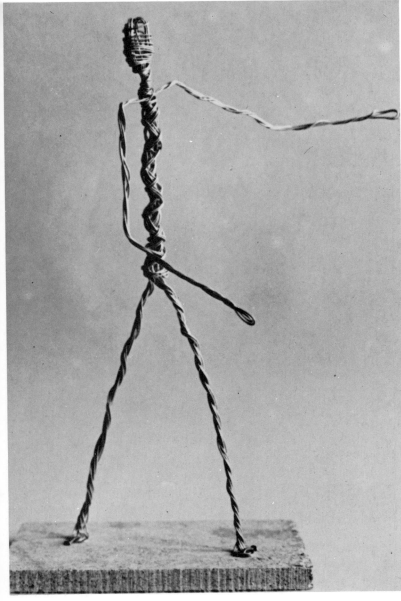

The wire armature is a sort of pin figure, but it must be nailed onto a piece of wood to keep it upright. If the armature does not fall over when in the wire state, then it need not be nailed down.

A sand and plaster mix.

Pieces of card can be used as an armature as in this example.

The armature can be built up with muslin or scrim dipped in plaster of Paris and wrapped around it (or with Pariscraft or Sculpture Rolls). It has a very distinctive, easily recognized quality.

Plastic Tubing

Plastic tubing is freely available, and not expensive. By applying heat, one can produce various shapes and structures.

Experiments with plastic tubing.

Experiment with plastic strip.

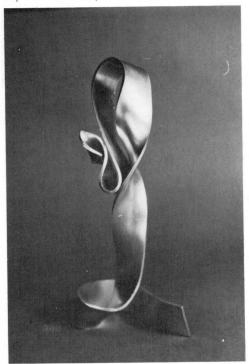

Pokerwork

Pokerwork (woodburning pen work) can be used on a wide variety of materials: leather, wood, or it can be used on acrylic lampshades, for example, where it does not leave a coloured line, but results in an opaque white line drawing on translucent white. It can be used to draw on polystyrene sheet (Styrofoam), for making printing blocks, or for engraving a material prior to taking a cast. The electric pokerwork tool (woodburning pen) has three different tips which can be set in, each producing a different type of line. A more expensive tool produces an extremely fine line by means of a red-hot wire tip. The craft was widely practised in Eastern Europe, and still is in Russia.

This stylized dragon head was used to fill a circle. Tone (shading) was applied to the eyes, nose and mouth (see pyrography).

The fine tip of the pokerwork tool was used to produce dots to create a linear design on this box lid.

A traditional piece of Russian pokerwork. Pokerwork is used extensively to decorate small toys, such as this house, as well as tableware. Constructed from blocks of wood of different proportions, the constant decorative themes are the turned finials (at the top of the building) and the pokerwork. Shaped tool ends are used to make the regular patterns.

One of the tips makes a circle, and this was used to make the outside of the halo. Most of the decoration was made by using dots to make lines, except for the hair, where continuous lines were drawn.

A detail to show just how 'lively' the medium can be. See how different the weights of line are in the veiling at the back of the hair and the hair itself. The very dark spots were made by simply holding the tip in the same place for a longer time.

Polyfilla (DIY plaster)

This material has so many possibilities in craft work: string can be dipped in it, arranged on three-dimensional shapes such as bowls, or balloons, and when the string is dry and hard, the filigree string can be safely lifted off. Gauze can be dipped in it for making small models. It can be used to make roller prints. As in pokerwork or any other method of making a fixed width line, the alternatives are a continuous line, dots, or a line made up of dots.

Polyfilla was mixed to a thin paste and put into an icing tool (the sort used for cake decoration), and then the design was piped out. The shapes will be flooded with either coloured candlewax or coloured resin, using the raised line like the metal cloisons in enamelling.

Polystyrene (Expanded)

This is a thermoplastic, softening when heated, and hardening on cooling. Although it can be cut and sawed, conventional tools can cause the material to break up and crumble. A hot wire (battery operated) tool is the most efficient and satisfying way of cutting it. There are also heated carving tools available, with interchangeable shaped wire heads. For very fine work, you can use a needle set in a cork heated in a candle flame. This method of heating tools (using metal knitting needles) is very good for younger children.

Expanded polystyrene (Styrofoam) lends itself to printing. Experiments in cutting and building three-dimensional shapes by gluing are a useful preliminary to acquiring expertise in cutting: experiment carving into solid blocks of polystyrene with the heated carving tool. The most successful method of gluing is to use a PVA glue (Marvin, or Tretobond). Wooden tooth picks are invaluable for pinning pieces together while they are being glued.

Heat can be applied in various ways: hot candle wax (coloured) can be painted on as can hot coloured wax crayons, which have been heated in jar lids over the flame of a candle. The flame of the candle can also be applied directly, but be sure the tiles are the self-extinguishing ones. The shapes of holes made

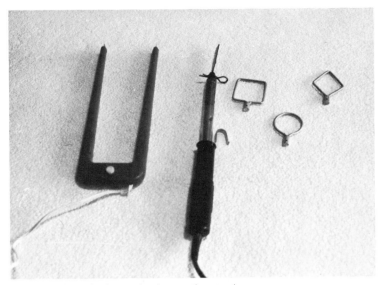

On the left is the heated wire cutting tool, and on the right is the carving tool with its various tips.

The material takes paint well, and in this example, is used in conjunction with a carved edge.

Some experimental pieces using the carving tools.

this way are quite distinctive, and can be achieved by no other method. Nail varnish, varnish, brush cleaners, and some glues can dissolve polystyrene, and produce some interesting effects. The surface also takes paint well.

Polystyrene has enormous 'grip' on threads pushed into it. Wool is held very firmly, but try ribbons, old nylon tights, string, etc. Lengths of wool can be pushed in at each end with a screwdriver, and will not come out. Polystyrene has been used in architectural sculpture. It is extremely light, is very quickly carved, and consequently it is becoming more and more popular for large scale casting.

Holes made in several tiles of polystyrene, and set one behind the other with a gap between each. The holes can be made in several ways.

Polystyrene has enormous 'grip' on materials such as wool when pushed into it.

A detail from a large mural, showing just how fine a detail one can get with this material.

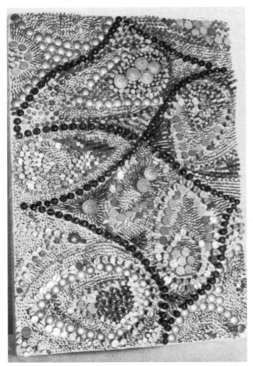

Pins of all sorts can be pushed into polystyrene as in this collage.

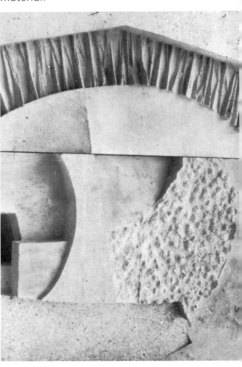

In the United States, Styrofoam is sold in various shapes: balls, eggs, cones, flat discs, blocks, sheets, etc. A clear plastic glue, Styrofoam Adhesive, has been especially designed for use on all foam plastics, and Styrofoam Spray Paint is also available (from J.L. Hammett Co, New York).

FURTHER READING

BARNSLEY, A., *Introducing Expanded Polystyrene* Batsford

Large cement mural cast *in situ* using a polystyrene mould.

EXPANDED POLYSTYRENE

CUT WITH	APPLY TO IT
Heated wire tool Heated needle (held in cork) Heated carving tool Saw	Drawing pins, pins plus beads Wool (pressed into surface) Paint Fibreglass plus resin Hot coloured wax crayon Hot coloured candle wax
MAKE HOLES WITH	
Nail varnish Varnish Paint stripper (not to be used by children)	USE IT FOR
	Carving Constructions (glued, pinned with tooth-picks, cocktail sticks, etc.) Casting (cement) Sculpture plus fibreglass skin Painting on

Poonah Work (Theorem Painting)

This is the name given to painting or stencilling on velvet, also known as Theorem Painting in the United States, where it was a craze which achieved the status of folk art. It was done on white cotton velvet, with 'theorems'. These are stencils cut out of 'horn' paper, i.e. cartridge (heavy white drawing) paper coated with linseed oil, and brushed with turpentine or varnish. The subject matter was baskets of fruit or flowers. They were painted in many bright colours, and each colour had its own stencil which had to be placed exactly in position to coincide with the others, as a multi-block lino or screen print is. The brush used was a short stiff stencil brush, the paint of a creamy consistency, and applied with a downward circular movement. Reeves fabric dyes in pots, or E.J. Arnold Polyprint could be used. The detail work was done with a fine sable and Indian ink.

There is a large collection of theorems at the Smithsonian Institute in New York, and in the New York Historical Society's collection there are some fine paintings on velvet done with theorems. Poonah was the name of a short stiff brush used for painting through the hole in a stencil.

'Fruit on a Platter', early nineteenth-century poonah work. (Courtesy of Holger Cahill Collection.)

Design and stencils for a theorem painting by Lucy McFarland Sherman, c.1850. (Courtesy of the Julia Munson Sherman Collection.)

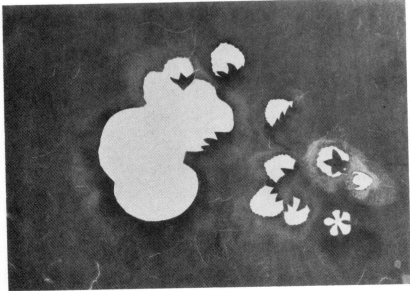

Pottery

CLAY

To keep clay in a fit state for use, it should be rolled into a compact block, wrapped in a damp piece of hessian (burlap, or rag) and finally wrapped in a sheet of polythene (plastic).

Unfired clay can be re-used quite satisfactorily. Sort it out into different colours, and break up the pieces of hardened clay with a mallet, or rolling pin. Put both broken pieces and powder into a bucket and cover with water. Leave for 2 or 3 days for the clay to become saturated. Into a clean second bucket, sieve the wet clay from the bottom of the first bucket. To do this place two pieces of wooden battening across the bucket, and rest the sieve across them. A stiff brush will help the clay through the mesh.

Leave another day to settle, and cup off any water from the top of the clay. Take the wet clay out of the bucket and squeeze into arches to speed the drying process. Wedge up the clay (knead it) and then form into large balls, or rolls for storage, which must be in a lidded container. A plastic dust-bin (garbage can) is ideal. Put some pieces of wood in the bottom and cover with some hessian. Onto this lay all the balls of clay, and lay another piece of damp hessian on the top. Cover securely with the lid. The clay bin must always be kept covered.

Types of clay

Kaolin is a natural clay, mainly consisting of alumina and silica. It makes the best white body, and withstands high temperatures.

Porcelain is also white, and requires the highest temperature firing – up to 2642 °F (1450 °C). When very thin it is translucent. Not very pliable, it is not for beginners. It is prepared from kaolin, feldspar flint, and ball clay.

Ball clay is similar to kaolin, fires almost white, but is more plastic (malleable) than kaolin.

Fireclay is also like kaolin, but has more iron in it, which gives it its distinctive yellow colour when fired. Used for the lining of kilns, etc.

Stoneware has the particular quality that it can hold water when fired without being glazed. It is made from several clays plus alumina and silica.

Earthenware is a low-fired natural clay, which turns buff or red after firing. It is very porous and used to be used to make flower pots.

Glaze

Glaze is applied in a liquid form onto pots, which, when fired, forms a layer of glass on the clay which is both decorative and practical, since it waterproofs the clay. There are glazes for clays which have to be fired at high temperatures and low-firing glazes for clays which are fired at low temperatures. Bisque or biscuit firing is the first firing of a pot. This hardens it and makes it strong enough to handle while glazes are applied.

The bottom of a pot must be kept unglazed otherwise it will stick to the shelf in the kiln while it is fired. The simplest method to ensure that the glaze does not stick to the base is to paint the bottom with molten candle wax. If this is done, the pot can be dipped into a bucket of glaze. Any unglazed areas can be painted in with a brush. To glaze the inside of a pot pour some glaze in until it is about one-third full, swill it round and tip out the remaining glaze. To glaze the outside, pour glaze over the pot holding it over a pan, and twirling it round as you do so. The thickness of glaze applied is important; it must be quite thin. A method of ensuring a thin even layer is to spray the glaze on.

Saltglazing is a special method of glazing stoneware which involves throwing common table salt onto pots in the kiln. Once a kiln has been used for salt glazing it cannot really be used for any other sort of glaze, for the interior of the kiln itself becomes coated with the volatile glaze.

Firing

Firing the kiln must be done slowly, both the heating up and the cooling down. Stack the kiln very carefully, so that no pieces are touching, and because it is costly to fire a kiln, it should be stacked as full as possible. The kiln is heated up for the first couple of hours with the kiln door open to let the moisture escape. Firing for earthenware takes 8 hours, stoneware 10. Heat the kiln very slowly: if the heat rises rapidly, the pots are likely to explode. Wait until the kiln temperature is down to 302 °F (150 °C) before opening the door.

Temperature is measured by cones which are made to melt at specific temperatures. They are set at an angle in front of the peephole in the kiln door, and must be watched to see what temperature the kiln has reached. As soon as the final cone has melted and keeled over, the kiln is switched off. Orton cones are all numbered and each number relates to the specific melting point of that cone.

Earthenware body is fired to 2012 °F (1100 °C), stoneware body to 2372 °F (1300 °C), bone china body to 2192 °F (1200 °C), and porcelain body up to 2642 °F (1450 °C).

TECHNIQUES
Wedging

Clay must be wedged to thoroughly mix the clay and remove air bubbles. Place a ball of clay on a steady surface (if the surface is porous it will dry the clay too much), and press with the heel of the hand. Keep turning and pressing the clay until it is of even consistency and quite malleable. Cut the wedged clay in half with a wire to check that all the air has been pressed out – if not, the air will expand in firing and shatter the pot. Slap the pieces hard together (to avoid trapping air), and continue wedging until the clay is ready for working.

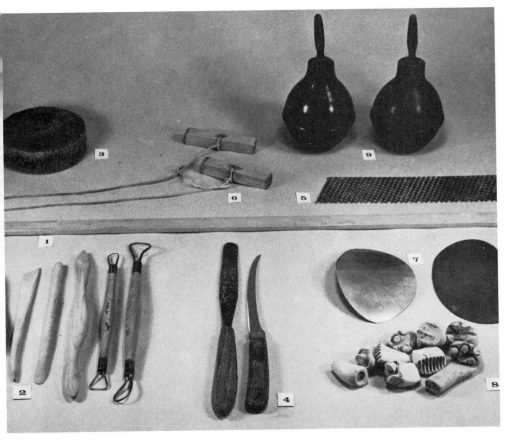

1) Straight edge: metal ones are best in the long run: hardwood is satisfactory but eventually tends to warp.

2) Modelling tools are commonly made of boxwood; they are variously shaped and some carry wire loops.

3) Sponges: it is best to have several sizes, the larger for mopping and wiping up, the smaller ones for shaping pottery.

4) Knives: domestic knives are generally satisfactory although an artist's palette knife may be found more suitable for fine work.

5) Planer files ('Surform' two-way tools): these are very useful for finishing work.

6) Wedging wire: similar to a cheese-cutter, this can be made by tying appropriately strong nylon filament, metal wire or string around, or through holes drilled in two wooden handles.

7) Kidneys (finishing rubbers): variously sized and curved rubber or metal tools for shaping the inside of curved forms.

8) Stamps: these are used to produce a texture on clay surfaces and can be made of virtually any robust material.

9) Slip trailers: these will need to be obtained from pottery suppliers.

Cutting the wedged clay.

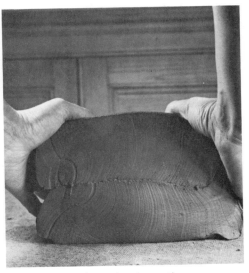

Slapping the pieces hard together.

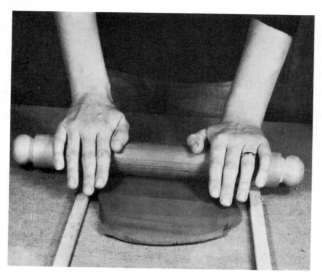

Rolling out

To ensure that a flat slab of clay is of even thickness, lay two pieces of wood of even thickness (keep a stock of wood of various thicknesses) on either side of the clay. Roll the clay out with a rolling pin until the rolling pin reaches the level of the wood and rests on it. The rolled-out clay cannot be thinner or thicker than the pieces of wood.

Rolling the clay evenly to a measured thickness.

Cut and pinched pots

Shapes can be cut from thinly rolled-out clay and pinched together to form a single shape.

Seven circles were cut from very thin clay and pinched together. The pots were glazed in white, and the edges were sponged with red iron oxide.

Cut and overlapped pots

Cut a circle from some clay which has been rolled to a little less than $\frac{1}{4}$ in. Mark a circle in the centre of the clay, and from this cut radiating lines with a knife to the edge of the circle. Lift up one 'petal' at a time, overlapping them just enough to fasten them together. The weakest part of this type of construction is at the base where there is almost no overlap. Close up all the joints on the inside with a modelling tool.

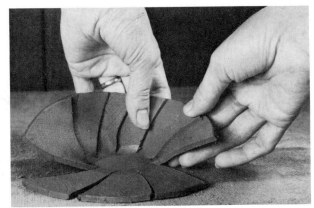

Cutting and overlapping the 'petals'.

The finished pots.

Another method of making a pot by cutting and slicing is to cut as shown in the photograph, then remove the pieces instead of overlapping them.

The sections are joined edge to edge.

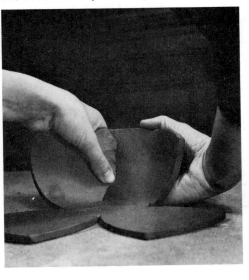

This was made in more than one piece and 'glued' together after firing.

Slab building

This uses rectangular pieces fitted together with slip (or wrapped round a core). To make a slab pot, one will need to make a special 'glue', to fasten the shapes together. The mixture is a thick slip made with clay diluted with a 50/50 mixture of water and vinegar.

To make a curved shape roll the slab of clay round a cardboard tube.

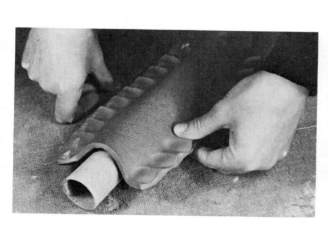

Two pieces of clay are used to make this pot, pressed round a cardboard tube. The slip to seal the edges is a 50/50 mixture of vinegar and water plus clay.

The finished pots, made by pinching the seams together.

a) The edges to be sealed together are cut in a series of small V cuts after the slip has been painted on the edge.

d) Excess clay is scraped away with a modelling tool on the inside. Add the second and third joints in the same way.

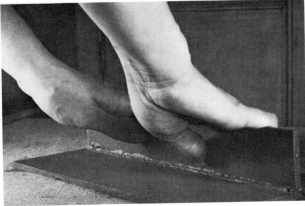

b) Brush on a little more slip again, and press the two sides together. *The shapes are allowed to dry out until they are stiff enough to handle without bending before any attempt is made to fasten them together.*

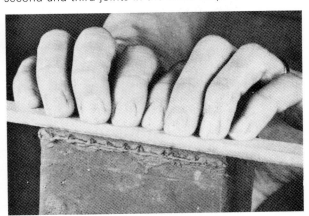

e) Clean the insides of all joints. Stand the shape on some clay and cut the base and lute to the body of the pot.

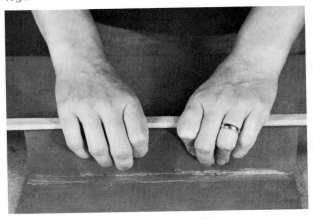

c) Equal pressure is applied along the whole join by a strip of wood.

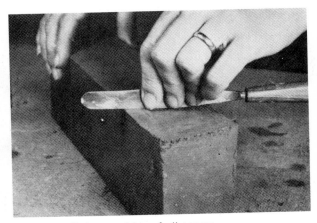

f) Clean off the outsides of all seams. Dry the pots out slowly. Any separation that might happen at the seams can be repaired with the same thick vinegar and water slip.

Slab pots moulded on a core

The core on which the pot is moulded can be a cylinder or of any cross-section as long as the angles are not too sharp. The sides must be parallel, otherwise it will not be possible to withdraw the core. Whatever the core, cover it in thin polythene. This will make it much easier to remove the clay. Unless you plan some very deep decoration on the pot, $\frac{1}{4}$ in. will be thick enough for the clay. Roll out the slab having decided on how tall the pot is to be. A steel straight edge and right-angle are needed.

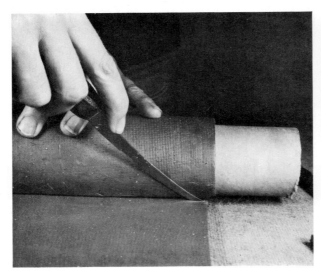

Cut two parallel lines (these will be the top and bottom of the pot, and a third at rightangles to these. Lay the core (in this case, a thick cardboard tube) along this edge, and roll the clay around it.

Wrap the core in polythene, and roll the clay round again, beginning in the centre, squeeze the edges gently together, then smooth out the joint with a finger.

Stand the cylinder on a piece of the original rolled-out clay, cut round the base, and lute. Any decoration to the surface is done now, or any handles added. Take out the core and the polythene.

Sling moulded dish

A piece of coarse openweave cloth is tied securely to the four corners of the legs of an upturned stool or chair. A curved shape is cut from rolled-out clay about ¼ in. thick. The inside is firmly stroked with a rubber kidney until the clay takes the shape of the cloth. The clay is allowed to stiffen, then removed from the cloth.

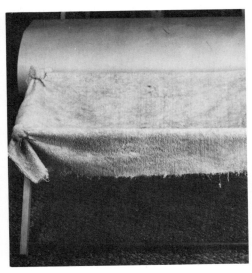

Tie the cloth to the legs of an upturned stool or chair.

Stroke the inside out of the rolled-out clay with a rubber kidney.

The finished dish when decorated.

Plaster-mould dish
Ease rolled-out clay into a mould made from plaster of Paris and trim the edges. Dishes made in plaster moulds dry out very quickly because plaster is a very porous material.

The rolled-out clay is eased into the mould, and is pressed into the mould gently with a sponge.
The edge is trimmed off level with the edge of the mould.

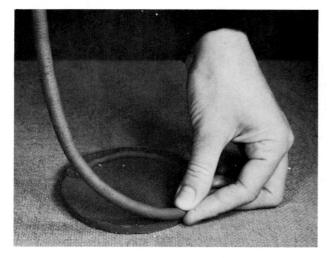

Coiled pots
Long sausages of clay are made by rolling out a ball of clay with both hands. The coils should be as even along their length as possible. The pot is then built up by putting one layer of coils onto another, then smoothing the surface over.

One can either start coiling in a spiral (flat) to make the base or one can use this method which has a rolled-out circle of clay for the base. The coiling in this case begins on the base.

Continue coiling, joining the coils together on the inside as shown in the photo. One can control the angle at which the pot curves after a little practice.

By holding the outside of the pot with one hand one can use the rubber kidney to help control the shape.

The outside of the pot can either be smoothed when finished or textured.

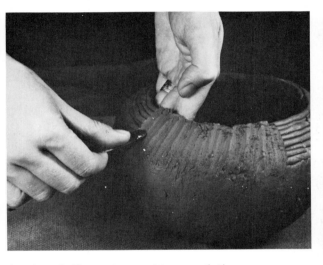

A palette knife can be used to smooth the surface and join the coils together.

This coiled pot was beaten flat at the top half to make the four flat 'faces'. The shapes were then hollowed with a rubber kidney to exaggerate the flattening by hollowing the faces still more. These four faces were then glazed with a thick white glaze. The rest of this lovely pot was left unglazed.

At the neck of the pot, use thinner coils.

259

Thrown pots

The technique of throwing pots on a potter's wheel requires a good deal of practice and skill to be successful. An electric or treadle turntable, roating at a speed of between 50 and 130 rpm, is used to produce many different shapes: plates, bowls, rounded pots and cylinders. A ball of clay is placed on the wheel, and centred by the downward and inward pressure of the hands, then opened from the centre with the thumbs. The walls are thinned and then shaped by being squeezed outwards evenly. When hard (but not dry) strips of clay are pared away with a tool as the pot is turned. The top can be trimmed with a wire, and decoration can be added as the pot rotates. For full details on the technique read *Pottery: The Technique of Throwing* by John Colbeck (Batsford).

Thumb pots (Pinch pots)

A ball of clay is held in one hand while the thumb of the other hand presses into the ball from the centre. While the ball is being rotated, the thumb continues squeezing and shaping the clay from the inside to the required shape.

The clay is opened out by pressing with the thumb from the centre.

Continue squeezing and shaping from the inside.

DECORATION OF POTS

Pots can be impressed, while they are still soft, with all sorts of objects: keys, wood, toothpaste tops, etc., or one can make plaster of Paris stamps. These can be made by pouring plaster into a plastic or paper cup, and when dry, carving a design into the bottom with a knife.

Sprigging

Is the name given to clay shapes appliquéd onto an object. It can either be in the same colour as the pot, or in a contrasting colour.

Waxing

Hot candle wax can also be used to decorate pots. (See section on Batik.) When the glaze is applied to the pot, the wax repels the glaze, so the decoration painted on the pot appears as the colour of the clay. Another technique using wax is to paint hot wax over the whole pot, and into the wax scratch a design. Glaze the whole pot, and the glaze will only adhere to the pot where the wax has been scratched off, resulting in an essentially linear design. This is called Sgrafitto, and can also be done by scratching through a layer of glaze before it has dried.

Staining

This method of colouring the pot produces a natural, unglazed look. Apply the stain either with a brush or a piece of polythene foam. The stain is made by mixing 2 tblsps of any oxide with 2 tblsps glaze, and half a cup of water. Mix until even, and apply with brush or sponge.

and the pot allowed to dry out thoroughly. A kiln is then heated to about 900 °C, and using long-handled tongs, the pot is placed in the kiln. Do not leave the kiln from now on, because as soon as the glaze becomes shiny (you can watch its progress through the peephole in the door of the kiln), the pot must be removed from the kiln using the long-handled tongs, and plunged either into water or the sawdust container. The kiln must not be left while the glaze is being melted, because there is no way of telling exactly how long it will take to melt; it might be as long as an hour, or as little as a few minutes. If the pot is plunged into water, the result is a shiny glaze: if into sawdust, the glaze is less harsh.

Slip trailing

Slip is very liquid clay, and the trailing is done by allowing the liquid (slip) to trickle out of a small hole in a polythene container. Some trailers have a rubber bulb which can be squeezed to control the flow. The size of the hole in the nozzle decides how thick the line is drawn. The technique needed to do slip trailing is the same as that needed to use the tjanting; the same elements of line and dot, and the same need for fluid, speedy movements.

The nozzle is held just above the surface of the clay: do not let it drag on the surface. It can be trailed on a 'plastic' clay base, or onto a wet ground (of slip). When done into slip, it sinks

Decoration was made by staining.

Slip trailing, on a dish by Thomas Toft.

Raku

This is the name given to a Japanese technique in pottery, named after the tea master Sen-no-Riku. It is a very dramatic process, involving plunging red-hot pots into cold water, or into a loose-built brick container which has been filled with wood chips, sawdust, or leaves. The pot must be made from high-firing clay, and bisque fired. The pot is then glazed with frit, lead or borax-based low-temperature glazes,

in and becomes part of the slip: onto the 'plastic' surface, it stands up like icing on a cake. The slip-trailed decoration of Thomas Toft is of this latter kind.

261

Feathering

This is a variation on slip trailing, done by trailing parallel lines and then with a brush or needle, lines are drawn across the trailed lines resulting in the patterning known as feathering. It is a type of decoration more often seen in baker's shops on small iced pastry cakes.

Feathering (made in slip). Note the similarity to one sort of marbling and to the decoration in icing on some pastry slices.

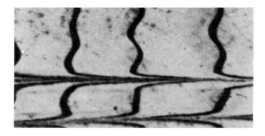

Agate ware. Instead of being a surface decoration this goes right through the clay like a marbled cake. The cat is Staffordshire, about 1745. (Courtesy Victoria and Albert Museum.)

Marbling

A decoration applied to the surface of the clay. The clay is covered with a thicker layer of slip than usual, and a darker slip trickled or trailed over it. The pot is then tilted and tapped and shaken to make the colours swirl around. As this is done some slip is poured off the plate, so ending up with the usual thickness of slip. If you start off with the normal thickness of slip, this technique cannot work.

Agate ware

Although it looks like marbling at first glance it is made in a different way. Clays of two different colours are mixed partially together. Most work in this style is made in moulds, using slabs cut from the lump of mixed clays. It can produce some very attractive slab pots. Keep the mixed clay wrapped in polythene for a few days before using, if possible, so that the clays really meld.

Marbling, in thicker than usual slip.

An antique Persian tile with freehand painted decoration.

Relief and impressed decoration in plaster is seen in this wall from one of the buildings in the Peoples Park of Culture in Moscow.

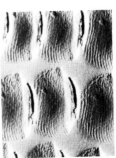

EGYPTIAN PASTE JEWELLERY

This is a process similar to that used in ancient Egypt. The main advantage is that the paste requires only one firing for matt and shiny beads. It can either be bought ready-made, from commercial suppliers, or the ingredients can be bought from them and you can mix them yourself. The peculiarity of the paste is that the glaze and the clay are mixed and made up into beads together. Two recipes (discovered by Jolyon Hofsted) are given, one for matt, one for shiny beads. The shiny beads must be strung on nichrome wire while they are being fired. The matt beads can be placed in a bowl to fire, they do not stick together. The ingredients are mixed to a paste with water until they reach a clay-like consistency. Fire at Orton cone 06–04.

Matt paste
Lead frit, 20 g; silica, 75 g; copper carbonate, 2 g; sodium, 2 g; bentonite, 20 g.

Shiny paste
Oxford spar, 800 g; china clay, 500 g; flint, 400 g; fine white sand, 160 g; soda ash, 120 g; sodium bicarbonate, 120 g; ball clay, 100 g; whiting, 100 g.

Colouring matter (both matt and shiny)
Black: 3 parts manganese dioxide; blue: 1 to 3 parts cobalt carbonate; brown: 3 parts red iron oxide; green: 3 parts chrome; turquoise: 3 parts black copper oxide.

SELF-HARDENING CLAY

Self-hardening clays are rather expensive, but widely available from hobby shops, and if you have no kiln in which to fire 'proper' clay, it does give you a taste of some clay techniques, such as building with slabs, rolling and coiling, and decorating the damp surface by pressing into it objects such as keys, pencils, etc., to make an impressed pattern. Some can be fired in a kiln, so that if you can at some time gain access to one the objects can be made permanent, but in the main this is not the case. They dry in 24 to 48 hours, by which time they are really hard, but they will not hold water. Each manufacturer produces his own varnish to be used on the dry 'clay', and they can be painted on with a very wide variety of paints, from poster colour to gouache and acrylics.

Some of the self-hardening clays available are DAS (UK), Marblex, Mexican Pottery Clay, and Amaco Modeling Dough (USA).

FURTHER READING

BILLINGTON/COLBECK, *The Technique of Pottery* Batsford

BIRKS, T., *The Potter's Companion* Batsford

COLBECK, J., *Pottery: The Technique of Throwing* Batsford

COWLEY, D., *Moulded and Slip Cast Pottery and Ceramics* Batsford

FARNWORTH, W., *Clay in the Primary School* Batsford

HARTUNG, R., *Clay* Batsford

JOLLY, T., *Introducing Handbuilt Pottery* Batsford

MILLS, J., *Head and Figure Modelling* Batsford

Impressed decoration can be made with a finger, a pencil, a modelling tool, a stick, or a hollow tube. All sorts of things can be used to impress soft clay. See the experiments used in plasticine for plasticine printing, and it is also possible to use plaster stamps specially designed to impress decoration. (See the section on casting for plaster stamps.)

FLAT (ROLLED)	THREE-DIMENSIONAL	SURFACES ALTERED BY BEING
Tiles	Coiled	Impressed
Mosaics	Slab	Glazed
Mobiles	Pinch/thumb	Burnished
	Thrown	Appliquéd
	Mould (sling, plaster)	Cut through
	Combination	Stained
	Coil and slab	Slip trailed
		Enamelled
		Sgraffito
		Painted with hot candle wax

Pressing Flowers and Leaves

Leaves are a splendid source of material for pressing. What they lack in colour they make up for in their variety of shape, size, and texture. Autumn leaves keep their colours quite well; and unlike flowers, they press better when they are wet. First wash off the grime and dirt under a tap, then wipe them dry with absorbent kitchen paper, before putting them between sheets of absorbent tissue in an old directory. (This is cheaper than using blotting paper, but should only be used for pressing leaves and grasses; flowers must be pressed between blotting paper for the best results.)

An advantage for the beginner in choosing leaves is that they are not as fragile as flowers. Glue does not show through a dried leaf as it can through a dried petal, and there is no dismantling of the leaf as there has to be with so many flowers before they can be successfully pressed. In addition to leaves and flowers, press a variety of stems, ferns, grasses and seed cases. (Also see section on Drying flowers.)

PRESSING

Equipment

a large old book with absorbent paper pages (an old telephone directory works very well); leaves, seeds or grasses; blotting paper (if pressing flowers); absorbent kitchen paper (if pressing leaves, grasses, etc.); a brick or other heavy weight.

METHOD

Place the leaves on a piece of blotting paper the same size as the page in the book in which they are going to be pressed. Do not overlap the leaves or petals and make sure that they are quite flat. Do not waste time pressing damaged lcaves. When there is no more room, fold over another sheet of blotting paper over the leaves/petals, and slip the sandwich between the pages at the bottom of the book.

Make a tag of paper onto which you have written the name of the plant between those two pages, and leave it sticking out of the bottom of the page in which you have put the plant. This will prevent unnecessary flipping through the book to find out what is in it, and the possibility of damaging them.

When the next lot of leaves are ready, place them five or six pages away and so on towards the top of the book. When you have finished pressing for the day, put the book away in a safe place (on the floor somewhere) and put a brick or other heavy weight on the book. Wait four weeks before taking a look at the leaves; this is most important. When you feel that you have sufficient variety of shape and colour, it is time to make an arrangement.

MAKING THE PICTURE

Materials

a piece of mounting card (from an art stationers shop), or stiff cardboard, or hardboard; a piece of glass the same size as the background; transparent glue (UHU or Elmer's Glue-All); hardboard, and mounting clips (for framing); an assortment of leaves.

METHOD

The mounting card will be the background to the picture. If you prefer, cover it with a piece of fabric such as velvet, or cotton velvet; the texture of velvet contrasts beautifully with that of leaves. The hardboard must be used as a background when one uses dried but not pressed flowers. There are several species of flowers which dry quite naturally in the air; Helichrisum, in particular, has a very wide range of colours from white, palest pink, cream, orange, mahogany, deep red. These flowers when dried are about $\frac{1}{4}$ in. high, so one has to make a special frame, such as those needed for shell pictures. (For instructions on how to make a shadow box frame, see the section on Shell pictures.)

When the picture is finished and all the pieces glued down, clean the piece of glass carefully so that there are no smears on the

Some of the wide variety of leaf shapes to look for when choosing leaves to collect for pressing. The wider the variety of shape to work with, the more satisfying will you find making the final arrangement.

side that is going to be placed down onto the leaves. Drill some holes in a piece of hardboard which is the same size as the glass, and placing the hardboard behind the picture and the glass on top, fasten together with metal mounting clips.

The conventional arrangements in either a 'C' scroll or a fan work well, and constitute a good starting point for a beginner. By using Blu-Tack (Plasti-Tak), one can rearrange the leaves until one is satisfied, because the Blu-Tack can be taken off quite easily without making a mark. Start gluing at the outside of the arrangement, taking the Blu-Tack off each leaf as you come to it. Work towards the centre, overlapping the leaves of the outer layer by just a fraction. On the stems of grasses, pull the stem along a part of the brush used for gluing that has a little glue on it, so that the merest trace of glue is deposited along the whole length of the stem. Press it gently along its length on the background. For the leaves, a small dab of glue in two or three places is all that is needed. Never put too much glue on.

THINGS TO MAKE

Greeting card or invitation card
Fold a piece of stiff paper or thin card in half. Size will depend upon the size of the leaf or leaves: allow ½ in. or so all round the leaf. With a tiny blob of glue on the main rib of the leaf, place it on the card. Cut a piece of transparent contact paper (Fablon). Peel off the backing paper and lay it sticky side down on the leaf, placing it so that it covers the paper exactly. Press all over so that no air bubbles show.

Calendars
Cover a stiff piece of card with a wash of ink, or stick some coloured paper over it (not patterned paper, as this would detract from the subtlety of the leaves). Make an arrangement of leaves on the paper, holding them in place with the smallest blob of a transparent glue (UHU), and then protect the whole thing with a layer of Fablon. Glue a ribbon at the back from which the calendar can be hung, and from the bottom hang a small bought calendar. For a more permanent picture, set the leaves in resin.

Bookmark
Use an unfolded piece of card, and make the size approximately 6 in. or 7 in. by 2 in. Choose the smaller leaves for this narrow width, and proceed as above.

CLASSIFICATION OF LEAVES BY SHAPE (TREES)

Oval/pointed	Palmate lobed
Hornbeam	Plane
Beech	Sycamore
Apple	Maple
Buckthorn	Currant
Escallonia	Vine
Fuchsia	

Quince	**Needle**
Cherry	Fir
Lilac	Spruce
	Larch
Ace of spades	Pine
Black Poplar	Juniper
Birch	Yew
Lime	Cypress
Poplar	Tamarisk
Elliptical	**Pinnate**
Privet	Ash
Buddleia	Ailanthus
	Rose
Rounded	Rowan
Aspen	False Acacia
Alder	Elder
Hazel	
Cotoneaster	**Palmate**
Amelanchier	Horse Chestnut
	Tree Lupin
Jagged	
Oak	**Long and narrow**
Hawthorn	Yew
	Willow
Straight lines	Bog Myrtle
Broom	

A CLASSIFICATION OF FLOWERS INTO NUMBER OF PETALS, STRUCTURE OF FLOWER HEADS, GROUPING ALONG THE STEM

Two petals
Enchanter's Nightshade, Goldilocks Buttercup
Three petals
Frogbit, Mossy Stonecrop, Tiarella
Four petals
Clematis (some), Poppy, Pearlwort, Celandine
Bedstraw, Cranberry, Blue Woodruff
Willowherb
Five petals
White Campion, Cinquefoil, Rose, Strawberry, Cranesbill, Cowslip
Pink, Ragged Robin, Mallow
Bogbean, Toadflax, Tomato, Lady's Mantle, Gypsophila
Buttercup, Silverweed, Mullein, Pimpernel, Forget-me-not, Bryony, Borage, Corncockle
Vervain, Bugloss (overlapping)
Love-in-a-mist, Saxifrage, Pearlwort, Rose of Sharon, Hellebore, Gentian Cranesbill
Violet, Pansy
Bell and cup-shaped flowers
Oxalis, Hellebore, Harebell, Sorrel, Heather
Lily of the Valley, Solomon's Seal, Cassiope
Spurge, Deadly Nightshade, Bluebell, Grape
Hyacinth, Foxglove, Bellflower, Gentian,
Snowdrop, Fritillary, Welsh Onion,
Bindweed, Tobacco Plant
Lipped flowers
(1) Wood Sage, Germander
(2) Honeysuckle, Vervain, Skullcap,
Balsam, Toadflax, Orchid, Antirrhinum

Miscellaneous
Cyclamen, Columbine, Daffodil, Martagon Lily, Monkshood, Iris, Gladiolus, Arum Lily
Globular heads
Chive, Leek, Clover, Scabious, Astrantia
Dandelion-like flowers
Salsify, Goatsbeard, Sow-thistle, Tansy
Daisy-like flowers
Aster, Michaelmas Daisy, Yarrow, Flea-bane, Knapweed, Hawkweed
Flat heads of small flowers
Umbellifers
Leafless and one-sided spikes
Dock, Plantain, Lily of the Valley, Vetch, Montbretia

FLOWER LEAF SHAPES

Round
Capucine (nasturtium)
Trefoil
Wood Sorrel, Oxalis, Clover, Medick, Broom, Laburnum
Triangular
Poplar, Ivy
Linear/grass-like
Grass-vetchling, Montbretia, Daffodil, Snowdrop
Heart-shaped
Campanula, Honesty, Bryony, Nettle, Cyclamen, Violet, Celandine
Arrow-shaped
Arum, Skullcap, Bindweed (Convolvulus)
Well-lobed
Hawksbeard, Dandelion, Oak
Palmate
Lupin, Hellebore, Monkshood, Larkspur
With tendrils
Pea, Vine, Vetch
Pinnate
Chamomile, Silverweed, Corn Parsley, Vetch, False Acacia
Very fine pinnate
Carraway, Coriander, Fennel, Chervil, Love-in-a-Mist, Pasque Flower

FURTHER READING

EALLER, S., *Wild Flowers for the Garden* Batsford

Printing

Although printing seems to embrace an enormous number of techniques, there are basically only three: screen printing, printing with a roller, and repeat printing with units held in the hand. In the home and in the classroom, organization is the key to clean prints, accurate registration, and an uncluttered working area.

A clothes line strung tautly across one end of the room with bulldog clips previously threaded on will hold the wet prints while they dry. Use plenty of sheets of newspaper over the working surfaces, so that the layers of newspaper can be discarded as they become too messy to work on. (For screen techniques see the section on screen printing.)

PRINTING WITH A ROLLER

When making prints with a roller (brayer), the surface can be irregular, gouged out, or raised up. The raised surface can be made by gluing objects or string onto paper or card; an irregular surface can be provided by a textured fabric such as hessian or lace. A gouged-out surface can be achieved by cutting lines into lino, polystyrene (Styrofoam) or wood; etching into perspex (plexiglass) or zinc; or pressing a repeated design into plasticine or balsa wood.

Registration of prints
This must be very accurate when making a print of several colours, either from one block (the elimination process) or from several blocks. A special registration board must be made for really accurate registration. This can be used over and over again, and should last for years. A piece of blockboard, thick plywood, or hardboard (20 in. by 14 in.) forms the base. The blockboard must be absolutely square (each corner must be a right angle).

Along two adjacent edges, securely glue two strips of battening, checking that the angle between them is exactly 90°. Draw a line indelibly between the battening marking the 45° angle. The strips of battening are permanent, and the printing paper is always fitted into that corner. The other right angle which has to be marked on the board is variable, depending upon the size of the block being printed, and the size of the paper. This is marked with gum strip (gummed tape) (parallel to the battening) and the 45° angle of the gum strip must be the same line (the one you have indelibly marked on the board) as the one for the battening. Ink up the block, and place it face up in the gum strip corner. All blocks used to make one print must be placed in the same gum strip corner.

Damp the paper for printing, and place it in the corner formed by the battening. Gently lower the rest of the sheet of paper onto the inked block. Either burnish with a spoon back or use a clean roller, to take a print. Lift off the paper and hang up to dry.

On the outside of the white shape (the printing board) are two strips of battening at right angles. The other L-shape on the board is made with brown sticky paper.

The inked printing block is set in the corner made by the brown paper, and the printing paper is fitted into the corner made by the outer wooden battening.

Balsa wood is a fairly soft wood into which it is easy to hammer indentations. Here, various cup hooks, screws, washers, etc. were pressed into balsa.

Not a lino cut, but lines cut in a block of plaster of Paris.

(Right)
This hardboard print has been made by scratching lines with a compass point. As the line is scratched (as opposed to being cut out), hardboard has been forced up either side of the scratch. The result is that ink does not lodge on the side of the raised up line, so printing white. It is therefore a cross between an intaglio print and a relief print, since both the line that was scratched has been filled with ink, and the surface.

The cowboy was drawn directly into the balsa wood with a hard pencil.

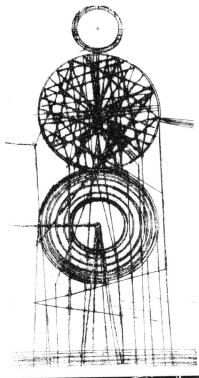

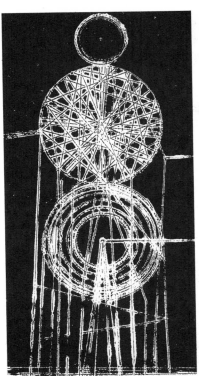

Prints made by scratching into perspex (plexiglass) with a compass point. On the left is an intaglio print (ink is rubbed into the scratched lines, and all the ink on the surface is carefully wiped off). On the right is the same piece of perspex, but this time it has been printed as a relief print (the reverse of the intaglio process) — there is no ink in the lines, only on the surface; when printed, the lines appear white on a black background.

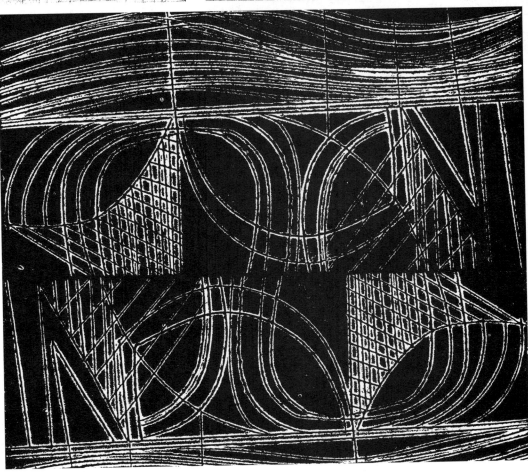

A collage was made from corrugated
card, string, lace, and some crushed
paper, inked, and printed.

Random (accidental) prints made by
crumpling a piece of paper and
inking it while it was crumpled.

Paper is glued onto a piece of card,
inked up, and a print taken from it. Notice
the difference in quality between the hard,
cut edges and the soft edges of the torn
shapes.

Plasticine is probably the best material to
use to teach children the concept of roller
printing. The material is easy to mark and
ink up, and simple to take prints from. The
examples are prints of toy cars pressed
into the plasticine.

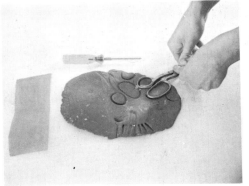

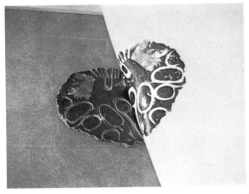

Roll out the plasticine as flat as possible.

Press into the surface any object you choose, or draw into it with a stick or blunt pencil, etc.

With an inked roller, roll over the surface of the plasticine.

Lay a piece of paper over the inked plasticine. Press all over with your hand, or gently with a clean roller. Peel off the paper.

A print made from expanded polystyrene (Styrofoam). The pattern was made by melting part of the polystyrene with a long metal knitting needle heated in the flame of a candle.

The block being inked up. To the left of the printer is the glass slab on which the printing ink is spread and rolled until there is an even layer over the surface. This ensures an even layer on the roller and hence an evenly inked block.

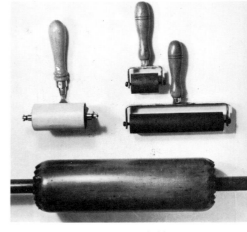

Rollers (brayers) used in inking up.

The second roller (i.e. the clean roller) in use, being rolled firmly up and down the print to get an even distribution of the ink.

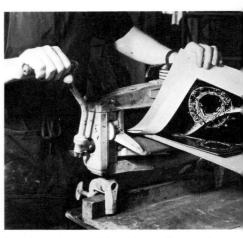

An old wringer with rubber rollers makes a very useful printing press. They often have a large screw on the top which adjusts the distance between the rollers. A piece of hardboard is used as a bed on which the block is laid, face up. The printing paper is laid on top of this, and a sheet of card (to protect the paper) is laid on top of that. The sandwich is rolled through together. It is a great help if two people are available, one to turn the handle, and the other to feed the sandwich through. Hold it very firmly until it is actually being gripped by the rollers. This is the stage at which smudging can occur unless care is taken.

On the left is an inking slab on which are tubes and cans of various sorts of inks used in printing. To the right are the wide bladed knives used to mix the ink to a good rolling consistency.

Offset printing

Offset printing involves picking up an inked image onto a scrupulously clean roller, then transferring this image by rolling (offsetting) onto another surface. A piece of patterned glass is here inked up with the inking roller.

Roll the roller over a clean piece of paper, and the inked image will be transferred from the roller to the paper. It has been offset.

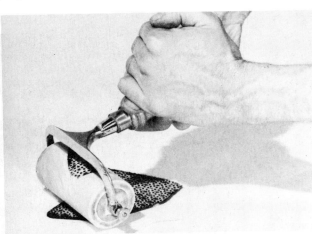

By rolling the clean roller over the glass (once only), the image will be transferred to the surface of the roller.

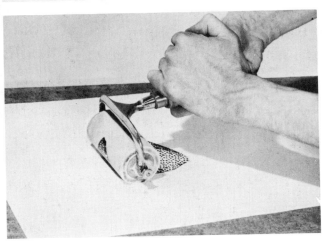

Once the image is on the roller, it can be transferred to curved surfaces, or around angles, or onto fabric. The limitation of this technique is the circumference of the roller used. The height of the image to be offset can be no more than the circumference of the roller, otherwise there will be overprinting on the roller.

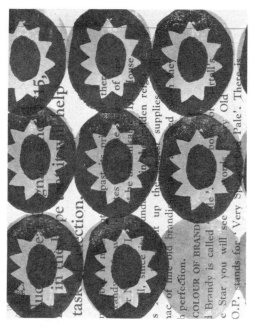

REPEAT PRINTING

This process entails pressing a relief stamp onto paper or fabric in a repeated series to form an overall pattern. The stamp must be inked between each impression, so that each print has the same amount of ink.

Finger prints

Finger printing is probably the first experience one has in a printing technique. Poster paint mixed thickly can be used, and children can be encouraged to explore the different prints made by palms, fingers, fingertips, and to look at the shapes to see what they suggest. A supply of detergent is needed to cleanse the hands after this activity.

Potato prints

Simple printing of this kind is ideal for children, and can be practised with any medium that is absorbent, and can be carved: a potato cut in half, a cork, or a wooden cotton reel (thread spool).

There is a rhythm to the even printing of any block. Press the potato onto an inked plastic pad between each printing, and press down hard each time. Position the potato before you press it on the paper, otherwise you can get an irregular printing. A thin sheet of plastic foam makes an efficient pad to hold the printing ink. Ordinary writing ink can be used for practice.

Preliminary prints are best made on old newspaper to see the effect of colour mixing, and how the units of the design fit together. A simple way to ensure that two prints will fit exactly over each other is to use the two halves of the same potato or cork.

Making the potato print using a cork stamp.

Using a lino cutting tool to cut a potato.
Some finely detailed prints can be cut this
way.

To print a small piece evenly, fold the cloth
in four, and iron the creases lightly. Fit the
very first print in the corner of one quarter
at the centre of the cloth. Continue
printing, using the crease as the line to
follow. Begin the second row immediately
underneath the first print, just touching the
centre crease.

The recurring motif in fabric printing is
known as the 'unit' (or the 'module'). Here,
the 'unit' is the little detached shape on
the right.

In this regular arrangement, the unit is a
triangle.

Mitring the corner when printing

Mark an angle of 45° at each corner. Do this with tailor's chalk (blue or white) or with a soft (3B) pencil. One could also mark the angle by folding and ironing the crease. Print the opposite side. This is important because the ink is wet, and if you continued printing in a clockwise method, the ink would smudge. At each corner, the paper must be laid along the 45° line when the printing is done. Always remember to use the paper to cover the other half of the corner.

Stages of mitring.

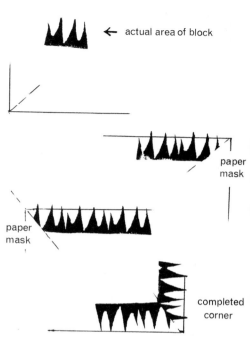

← actual area of block

paper mask

paper mask

completed corner

Fold a piece of newspaper and hold the folded edge along the 45 degree mark on the cloth. Print along the border, beginning in the centre and when you arrive at the corner, print as you have been doing, but this time part of the print will be on the paper. Remove the paper.

The finished cloth showing how the mitring looks when it is well done.

Card on edge printing

A piece of stiff card is dipped in a pad of cloth soaked in ordinary ink, and by pressing the edge on a piece of paper, a line is made. By repeating the process, one can 'draw' very fine illustrations.

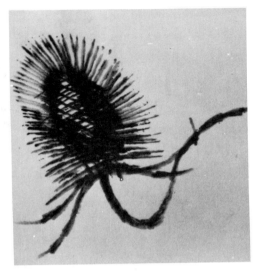

A drawing of a teazle produced by 'card on edge' printing.

FURTHER READING

ASH, B. & DYSON, A., *Introducing Dyeing and Printing* Batsford

CAPON, R., *Introducing Abstract Printmaking* Batsford

GOOCH, P., *Ideas for Fabric Printing and Dyeing* Batsford

HEIN, G., *Fabric Printing* Batsford

KAMPMANN, L., *Picture Printing* Batsford

O'CONNOR, J., *Introducing Relief Printing* Batsford

PALMER, F., *Monoprint Techniques* Batsford

PALMER, F., *Introducing Pattern: Its Development and Application* Batsford

SCOTT, G., *Transfer Printing onto Man-made Fibres* Batsford

TURNER, S., *Screen Printing Techniques* Batsford

PRINTING TECHNIQUES

INKING THE SURFACE WITH A ROLLER

INKED SIDE 'UP' WHEN PRINTING

Lino prints
Monoprints (negative and positive)
Etching
Engraving
Wood cuts/wood engraving
Trailed glue block
Offset printing
Pulled thread/string prints
Print through monotypes
Plasticine prints
Hardboard prints
Polyfilla (DIY plaster) prints
Plaster of Paris prints
Torn and cut paper prints
Plywood prints
Perspex (plexiglass) prints
Balsa wood prints
Polystyrene (Styrofoam) prints
Chipboard prints
Cardboard (silhouette) prints
Textured surface prints
(Printed on paper)

Miscellaneous: Roller prints
              Splatter prints
(Printed on paper, or cloth, for theatrical purposes)

INKING THE SURFACE WITH A PAD

INKED SIDE 'DOWN' WHEN PRINTING

Potato prints (etc.)
Cork prints
Stick prints
String prints
Pipe cleaner prints
Durafoam prints
Card on edge prints
Small lino prints
Collage blocks (small)
(Printed on cloth and paper)

PRINTING PROCESSES

INTAGLIO PROCESS	RELIEF PROCESS	STENCIL PROCESS

Etching
Engraving
Aquatint
Scratched-card
Perspex (plexiglass)
Hardboard
Celluloid collage
	Plaster of Paris
	Wood cut
	Wood engraving
	Lino printing
	Polystyrene (Styrofoam)
	Balsa wood prints
	Plasticine prints
	String prints
	Glued surface prints
	Polyfilla prints
	Collage prints:
	  plywood, cloth, card,
	  papers, natural objects
		Paper
		Wax
		Proprietary stencils
		Gum, green filler, rubber
		  solution
		Transfer lettering
		  (Letraset etc)
		Tusche
		Photographic screens
		Pick up of natural objects
		Duplicating stencils
		Gum strip

PRINTING BLOCKS INKED WITH A ROLLER

INCISING THE SURFACE			RAISING THE SURFACE	
CUTTING	PRESSING INTO	SCRATCHING	STICKING	PAINTING ON

Linoleum
Wood
Polystyrene
  (Styrofoam)
	Balsa wood
	Plasticine
		Zinc
		Copper
		Hardboard
		Perspex
		  (plexiglass)
		Card
		Chipboard
			Paper, tissue,
			  corrugated, etc.
			Card
			Cloth, hessian,
			  lace, canvas,
			  etc.
			String, wool,
			  thread, etc.
			Plywood
			Celluloid
			
			Naturally occurring surfaces which can be inked up directly (prints for collage)
				Impact glue
				Polyfilla (DIY
				  plaster)
				Plaster of Paris
				Inks/turpentine
				  (monoprints)

OFFSET PRINTING	ROLLER PRINTS	MONOTYPES	MAN MADE	NATURAL

Leaves
Textured glass
Crumpled paper
String, etc.
	Image making
	  direct with a
	  roller
	Roller printed
	  frottage
		Drawn with
		  brush on clean
		  glass
		Drawn into inked
		  glass
		Print through
		  plus paper
		  mask plus
		  fern/feather, etc.
		Thread monotype
		Pulled thread
		Negative
		  monotype
		Multiplate
		  monotype
			Corrugated
			  paper
			Crumpled paper
			Lace
			Hessian
			Nets
			Opened packets,
			  etc.
				Leaves
				Feathers
				Ferns
				Grasses, etc.

Puppets

THE MAIN CLASSIFICATIONS OF PUPPETS

1. Finger puppets – small domestic puppets worked either in a room setting or on a stage.
2. Glove puppets – most direct for the performer, and often used in psychotherapy, especially for children.
3. Jack-in-the-box – a glove-type puppet set inside a box.
4. Stick puppets – fixed dolls on sticks.
5. Rod puppets – these are the normal method of working shadow puppets. They can also be used in combination with glove puppets, worked from below, in front of the stage.
6. Pantins, or jumping jacks – simple jointed figures worked by pulling a string.
7. Shadow puppets – unreal, magical, possibly the oldest type.
8. Marionettes – the most complicated to make and work, with strings attached to the limbs of the figure.
9. Victorian children's toy theatre puppets – worked on slides and moved along the stage by wires.

FINGER PUPPETS

These are the simplest form of glove puppets, and are simply made out of the finger of an old woollen or leather glove, or from a cone made of paper, felt or leather. Eyes, ears, whiskers, or beards are sewn on the fingertip end.

GLOVE PUPPETS

These are made from two pieces of fabric sewn together at the sides to form the body and arms. The head is attached to the top opening, and may be of fabric (slightly stuffed) with embroidered features, or of papier mâché, clay or plaster, with painted features. The hand fills the body of the puppet, and the fingers are pushed into the head and arms to control their movement.

JACK-IN-THE-BOX

The jack-in-the-box is constructed as a glove puppet, but the lower edge of the body fabric is attached to the inside of a box, drum, or cone. A stick is put into the body of the puppet and attached inside to the head, and the other end extends below the bottom of the drum/box when the puppet is fully extended. When the stick is pulled down, down comes the head, the felt body collapses and the whole puppet is hidden in the depth of the box, to pop out suddenly when the stick is pushed up. When designing one of these puppets, concentrate all your attention on the head and making that the interesting part visually. Stuff the head firmly, and if you use a wooden spoon for the stick, putting the spoon end in the head, you will find it very easy to make the head turn from side to side.

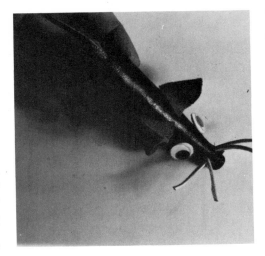

A finger puppet made in leather.

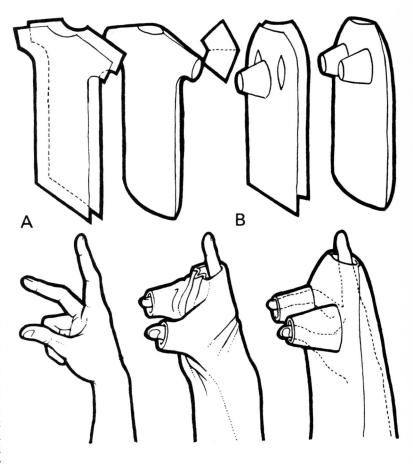

Two methods of making the fabric body for a glove puppet.

279

A jack-in-the-box puppet.

Fixed doll on a stick puppet. This is the traditional character Pretty Polly (Punch's girlfriend) from the early Punch and Judy plays. Later Pretty Polly was dropped from the story, but Judy's anger and violence as the deceived wife remain, unexplained.

STICK PUPPETS

A wooden spoon is useful as a base for one of these, the spoon part being used as the face and the features painted or glued directly onto it. The body, head, and arms can either be carved out of wood, with hinged arms, or modelled from paper mâché using the stick as the main armature with wire. This sort of puppet one can make as shapely, and dress as realistically and lavishly, as one chooses.

The earliest Punch and Judy shows used stick puppets.

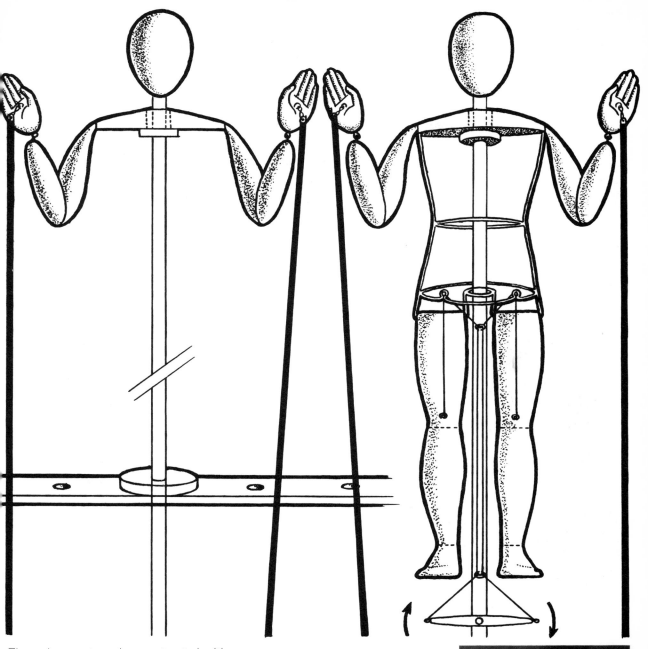

The rod puppet can be constructed with a central pole to be covered with fabric, or with a body and legs.

ROD PUPPETS

The rod puppet can be made with a papier mâché and plaster head, hands, and shoes, glued directly into a cotton body. The body can be screen printed with an ornate multi-coloured print, and if comparatively little differentiation is made between the heads, the characters can be established by the printing on the fabric. The fingers can be tightly curled so as to form a hole into which the rods can be placed, and a hollow in the base of the neck will hold the supporting rod.

A modern Japanese rod puppet.

281

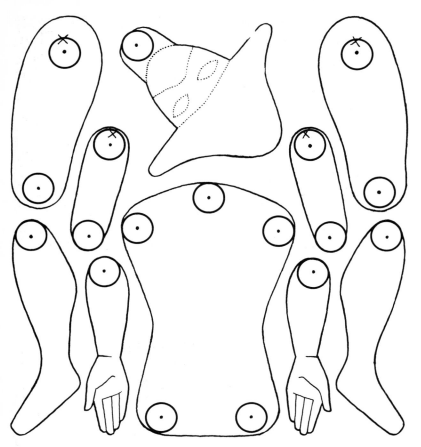

The individual parts
of a pantin.

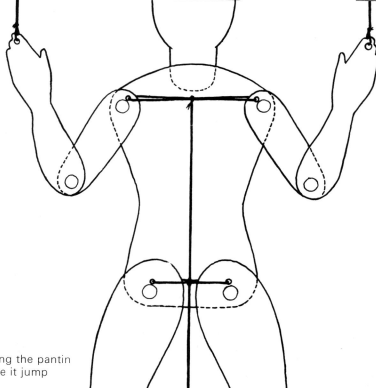

Stringing the pantin
to make it jump
about.

An original *Pellerin* pantin.

A simple pantin without strings.

PANTINS OR JUMPING JACKS

The craze for these swept through France in 1746, and was only crushed when a ban was put on them by the police. They are made of card or thin wood, and the jointed figures are moved by pulling a string at the back which jerks the limbs. Favourite popular figures were ballerinas, peasant girls, Harlequin and Columbine. The ones made from card can be decorated with acrylic paints, or collages of metal foil, sequins, fabric, etc.

Make a trial one in stiff scrap paper. The joints work on overlapping circles, so these must be incorporated in the design before it is cut. Make the holes in card with a needle, with a leather punch (smallest hole) in cardboard, and with a drill in plywood. The joints of the card and cardboard pantins can be fastened together with either split brass paper fasteners, or linen thread. The plywood will need cotton pins with metal washers between the moving parts.

String the pantin by fastening the shoulder to the shoulder, and the thigh to the thigh. These two strings are then connected vertically beginning at the shoulder. Leave a long length of string hanging down below the body. When this is pulled the arms and legs swing out, smoothly or jerkily according to how it is pulled.

Traditional pantin decoration: Harlequin.

SHADOW PUPPETS

A delightful account of the invention of shadow puppets is given in the tale of the Emperor Wu-Tu (121 BC) of the Han Dynasty. Distraught at the death of his favourite concubine, he commanded the court magician to summon her spirit to return to him. The magician satisfied the Emperor by producing at the far end of a darkened room a shadow on a screen which resembled the concubine. Shadow plays were given by Punch and Judy showmen in the 1830s, who stretched calico across the punch booth proscenium at night, and gave shadow puppet shows known as Galanty Shows. In Turkey, shadow puppets provided slapstick comedy, revolving around a bald-headed 'baddy' called Karagoz (Black Eye) whose attempts at hiding his baldness under various huge hats and turbans are constantly foiled.

In Western Europe puppets were of an opaque material, whereas in China, Turkey, and Greece, they were made of animal skins treated until it was translucent and then stained with colour. Javanese puppets are also made of skin but treated until they are only semi-transparent. They are remarkable and quite unique (see photo). The figures are very highly stylized, with few moving parts, only the elbows and wrists move. The heads are very distorted, and the arms enormously long; the hands reach

Shadow puppets showing the points of attachment for the rods. Note the similarity in construction between these and pantins.

Traditional Javanese shadow puppet. (Courtesy of the British Museum.)

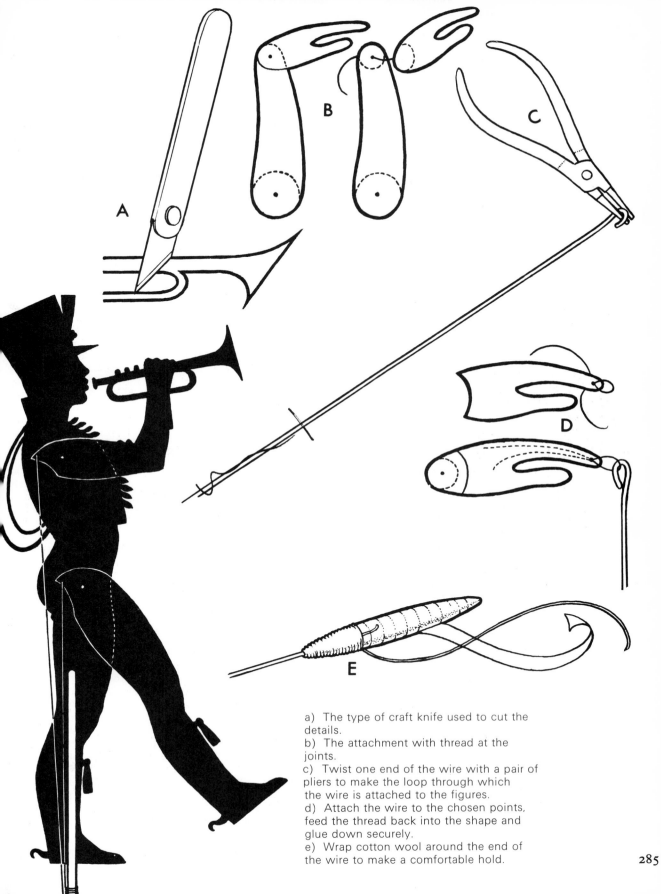

a) The type of craft knife used to cut the details.

b) The attachment with thread at the joints.

c) Twist one end of the wire with a pair of pliers to make the loop through which the wire is attached to the figures.

d) Attach the wire to the chosen points, feed the thread back into the shape and glue down securely.

e) Wrap cotton wool around the end of the wire to make a comfortable hold.

285

almost to the feet, and are very thin. All details of the puppet are symbolic: the angle of the head to the shoulders (indicating character traits), the various styles of headdress, and the type of decoration on the headdress, the colours used to decorate them and the positions of those colours.

Materials and equipment

card, thin plywood, sheet zinc or tin, or sheet acetate to make the puppets; paper clips (split brass), string, wire, or thread to fix the joints together; umbrella ribs, bicycle spokes, or wire for the rods which move the puppets; sewing needle, scissors, craft knife, and hacksaw.

Designing shadow puppets

The outline is the only clue to the character of the puppet. Decide which part of the puppet is needed to move in the story, and you may well find that for a cockerel, let us say, only the head and neck and body need be jointed, and a great deal of movement can be made with only one rod attached to the head. A lot of incidental movement can be created with jointed limbs left to move freely as the puppet is moved. As for the scenery, experiment with natural plants, twigs, ferns, sprays of leaves, grasses, etc. Experiment too with different tones by using organdie, various types of paper, net, scrim, perforated zinc, wire netting (in various sized mesh) feathers and cellophane.

Museums with collections of Javanese and other shadow puppets in England are the British Museum, Victoria and Albert, Horniman in London; the City Museum in Liverpool; the Pitt Rivers Museum in Oxford, and the University Museum of Archaeology and Ethnology at Cambridge. In America, in the Field Museum of Natural History, Chicago, there is a huge collection of nearly 1000 Chinese shadow puppets.

SHADOW PUPPET CARTOON FILMS

Lotte Reiniger made the first shadow puppet films in 1919 in Germany; in 1926 she made *The Adventures of Prince Achmet* on five reels, the first full-length animated film in the history of the cinema. Film strips of some of her fairy tales are available from the Educational Supply Assoc. Ltd, 181 High Holborn, London WC1, and are called Common Ground Film Strips.

The films are made as cartoons with the camera fixed above the table (glass-topped in this case) on which the puppets are arranged. A photograph is taken of the arrangements, the puppets are moved a fraction, another photograph is taken, the puppets moved and so on. Originally her puppets were of thin sheet lead, but later lead was only used for steadying the puppet, the main part being constructed of card. The joints are made of fine wire, and many many pieces are cut and jointed to make one puppet to allow the maximum possible sinuous movement.

MARIONETTES

Most marionettes are somewhere between $1\frac{1}{2}$ ft to 3 ft tall. Use $\frac{1}{2}$-in. dowelling for the arms, $\frac{3}{4}$-in. dowelling for the legs, and 2-in. diameter for the body; or carve it, simply, out of $2\frac{1}{2}$-in. square hardwood. Papier mâché could be used for hands and head, but if you use it, make sure that you incorporate a loop in the wire armature at the bottom of the neck and the ends of the wrists. Leave uncovered with papier mâché so that the wire loop can be attached to a screw hook to make the joint.

Cloth or nylon stockings can also be used to make the head and body, and feet and hands can be made of felt. Use a thick nylon stocking for the head and body. Stuff the heel for a head and cut off the rest of the foot. Tie the stuffing in tightly with thin string to form the neck. A piece of dowelling is inserted next to make the shoulders and a base for fixing the screw eyes for stringing. Stuff the body and make two rows of stitching to make a hinge at the waist. Slip a lead weight as used in weighting curtains in the lower half of the body when stuffing. This will make the marionette hang straight. Legs and arms can be made from stockings by rolling them into a sausage length and tying firmly in the centre and at each end. The top tying is hidden in the inside of the bottom half of the body when it is sewn up, and the other ends are hidden in the felt feet. The ends of the arms are hidden similarly in their hands and at the shoulders.

Making marionette joints

For the neck attach the base of the head to the hollow in the chest by a screw eye in each, closed with pliers when in place.

For the shoulder use a string joint; for the elbow a string or leather joint; for the wrist a wire and screw joint; for the hip a screw eye and wire, or leather and wire joint; for the knee a closed hinge or leather joint; and for the ankle a hinge or leather joint. Which joint you use depends on the movement you need to make with that particular joint.

String joint This makes the most flexible joint. Drill a hole through the projecting tongues and thread string loosely through. Knot on the outside of the joint, cut the ends close to the knot, and dab PVA (white) glue on the knot to prevent it coming undone. Be prepared to renew string joints from time to time.

Leather joints These are useful if only a backward and forward movement is required, e.g. knee, elbow, and ankle. The leather must be supple yet strong. Chamois is fine for small puppets, or an old leather glove for larger puppets. The saw cut should be the same thickness as the leather to be used for the joint. Run PVA (white) glue into the slit before inserting the leather. Fix the leather with a picture-framing pin nailed in each side of the joint. Trim off surplus with a razor blade.

Two carved wooden marionettes, showing the points at which the strings are attached.

Control bars

The mechanism for manipulating a marionette (moving the strings) is called a crutch, perch, or control bar. They are either horizontal or vertical; the horizontal is most widely used in the United States, and the vertical in Europe.

The horizontal bar is always used for four-legged animals, and is the better one for head movements. It is made from plywood, with thin dowelling used for the back and shoulder attachments. The vertical bar is better for walking movements, and one broom handle will supply enough wood for several control bars. The loops through which the strings run are screw eyes.

Each part of the control bar operates a different part of the body.

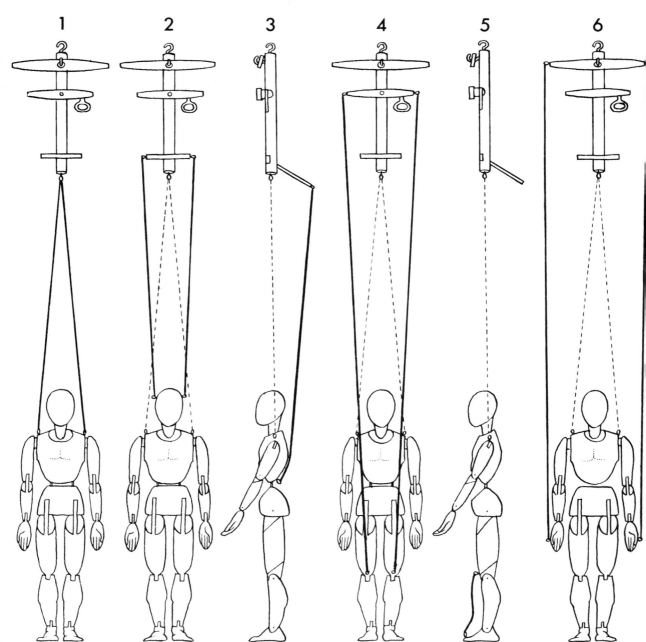

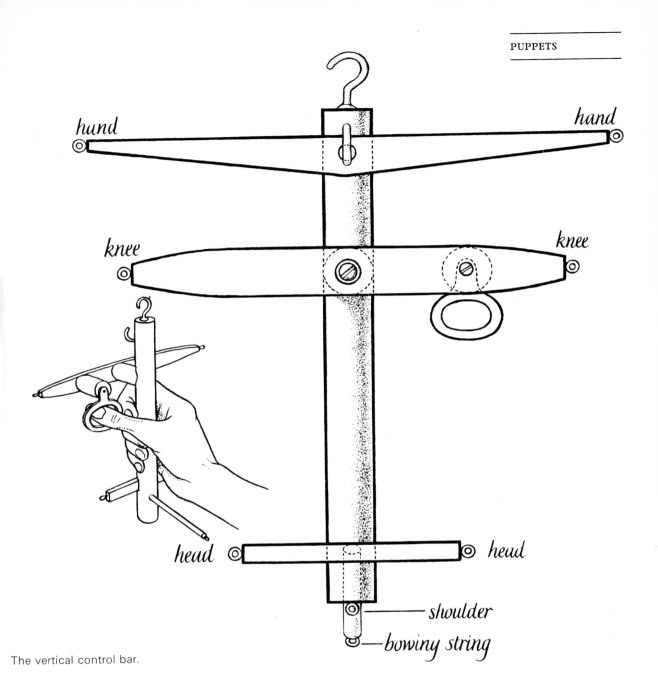

hand

hand

knee

knee

head

head

shoulder

bowing string

The vertical control bar.

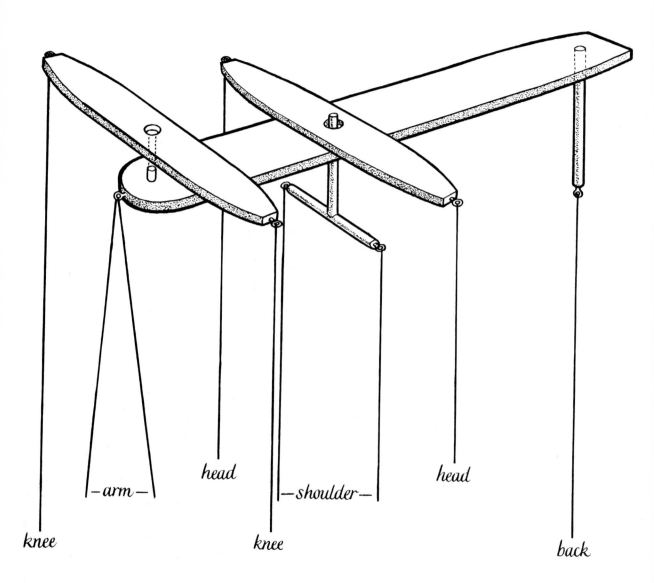

knee

—arm—

head

knee

—shoulder—

head

back

The horizontal control bar.

Attaching the head (papier mâché or wood)
to a carved wooden body.

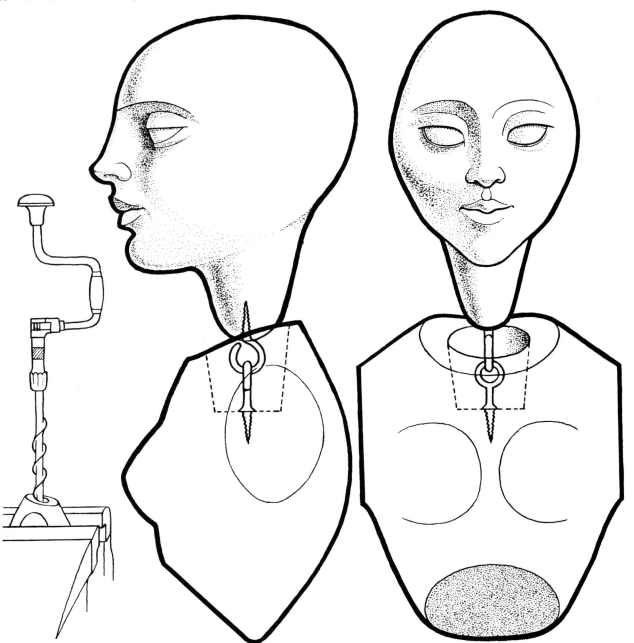

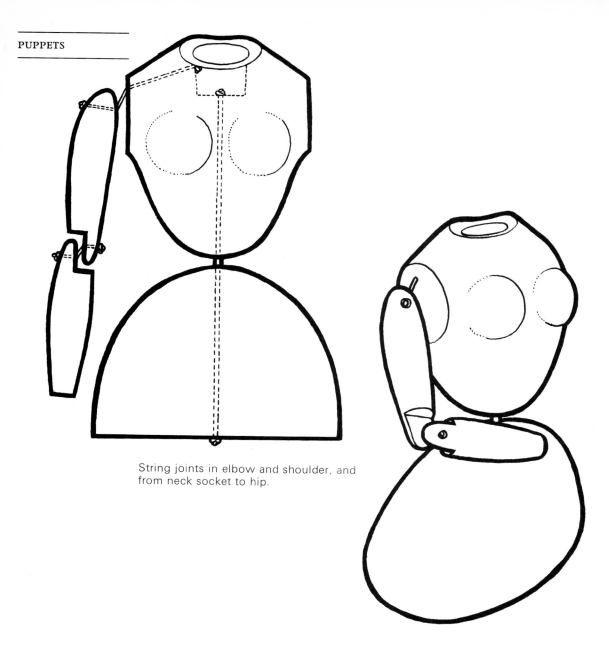

String joints in elbow and shoulder, and from neck socket to hip.

The embedded loop used for a head made of material other than wood.

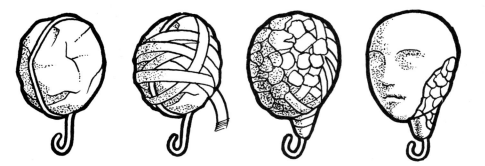

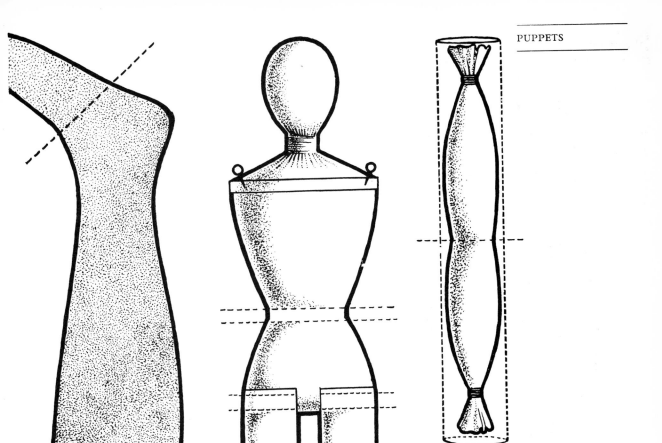

Using a nylon stocking to make the head, body, arms, and legs. Note the importance of the wood strip across the shoulders to secure the screw eyes for the attachments.

Wire and leather used in a hip joint, and leather used as a shoulder joint.

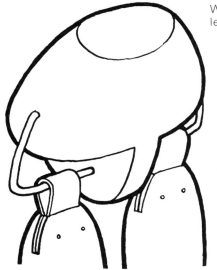

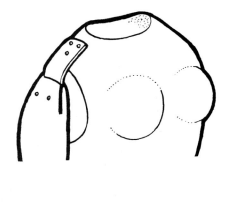

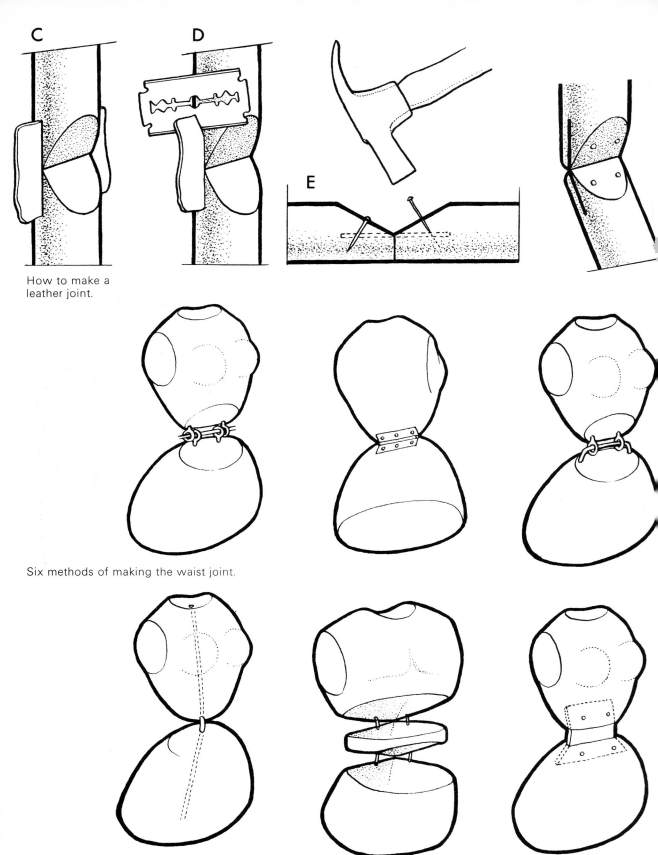

How to make a
leather joint.

Six methods of making the waist joint.

Six methods of making the hip joints.

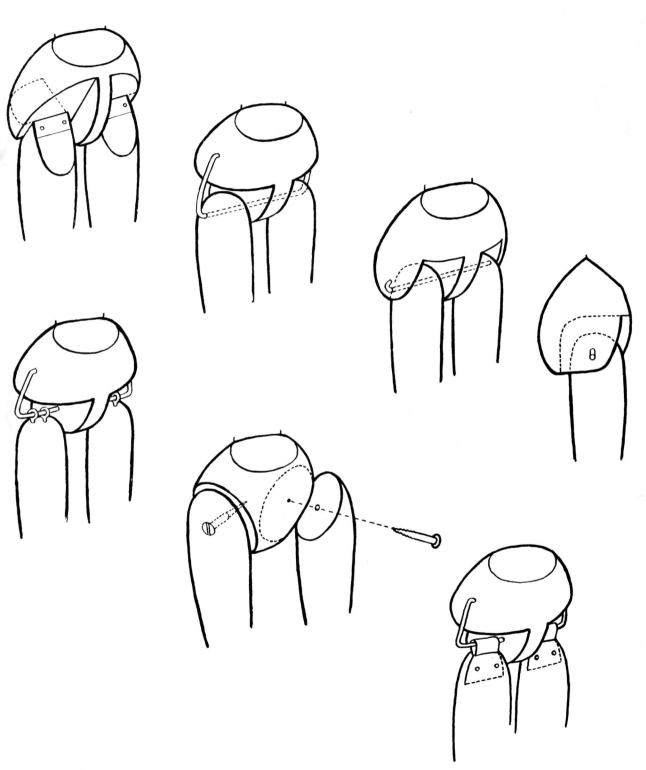

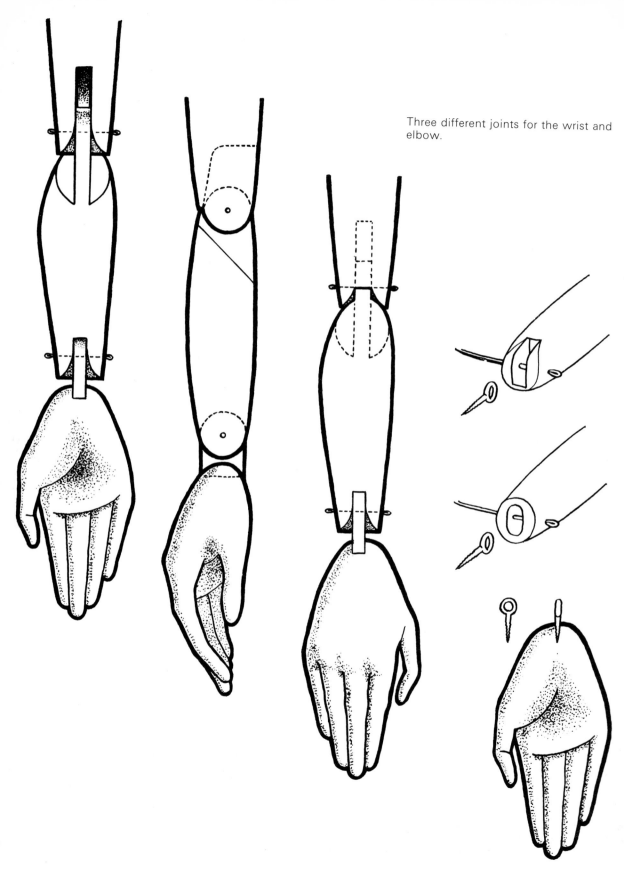

Three different joints for the wrist and elbow.

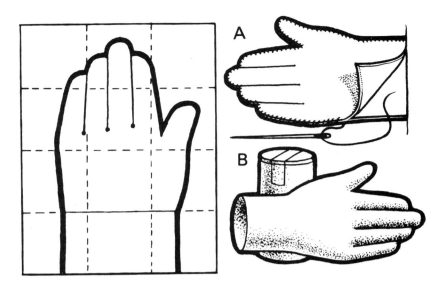

Making felt hands.

Attaching the wire to the piece of cork or dowelling.

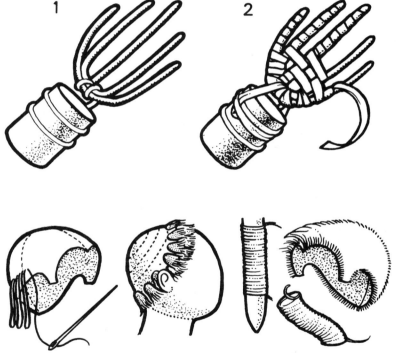

Attaching hair to the felt 'cap' before it is glued onto the head.

TECHNIQUES IN PUPPET MAKING

Applying the hair to a puppet head

Hair can either be carved at the same time as the head is being carved, or modelled directly with papier mâché, then painted, or it can be made from wool, fur, doll's hair, or real hair, and glued directly onto the head; alternatively a 'cap' of felt can be made to fit the head, and the hair or wool sewn onto this, the whole thing finally being glued onto the head. Whether you are sewing the hair onto a 'cap' or gluing it on directly, start at the outside edge (nearest the face) and work towards the crown of the head in concentric circles. Glue or sew the hair on in small tufts, overlapping each row and setting each tuft like the tiles on a roof.

297

To make curly hair, smear Vaseline over a large knitting needle. Wind wool (not overlapping the strands) along the length of the needle, and paint the wool with dilute PVA or thin gum. When it is dry, slide it off the needle. The glue will help the wool to keep its stiffness and curl.

Two ways of making hands

Felt These are suitable for glove or rod puppets, the main disadvantage being that the fingers must always be closed. Remember to allow almost the length of the palm for the length of the wrist, so that there is enough length when the hands are inserted into the sleeves. The hands should be one-seventh of the total height of the puppet. Oversew the edges, and if the hands are small, it will be best to leave them at that, just working three lines of running stitching to indicate the fingers. If the hands are large and the overstitching is firm, the hands can be turned inside out. If you have difficulty turning the thumb inside out, use a knitting needle which will also be useful to push the stuffing into the thumb. Stuff the whole hand with cotton wool or kapok, and then stitch in the lines to indicate fingers. Next make a small card tube to fit snugly into the wrist, closing the wrist end with a disc of card. Glue the tube to the inside of the hand, and the hand to the sleeve of the puppet.

Papier mâché (or Mod-Roc) These are made on a simple wire armature. Cut three lengths of wire. The lengths will depend on the size of the puppet. Two lengths are bent into a U-shape, one U forms the thumb and little finger, the other U-shape forms the index and ring finger. The third piece is twice the length of the other pieces, and is used for the middle finger and binding the other two pieces together. Place this piece of wire across the two U-shapes, making it longer than the other fingers, wrap the remaining length around the base of the U-shapes, to secure them all together, and the remainder of the wire is wrapped around a cork or roll of corrugated cardboard, or small length of dowelling.

Build up a thickness around the wire with bandage or strips of rag. Bend the fingers into position now. The hands are very expressive of character, so it is worth spending time to arrange the fingers in the most suitable way. Either cover with mod-roc (plaster of Paris impregnated gauze) which is dipped in water and wrapped round the hands (it dries rock hard) or dip the hand in wheat or wallpaper paste (Polycell), and then wrap with a strip of newspaper dipped in paste.

CONSTRUCTION OF PUPPET THEATRES

Take into account whether it is to be permanent, portable, temporary; what size of puppets are going to be used; how many people will be involved in working the puppets; which sort of puppets are to be used, glove, rod, marionette, etc. Theatres may be worked from below (glove, rod, shadow puppets); from above (marionettes), or from the side (Victorian children's theatre).

Glove puppet theatre

In the glove puppet theatre illustrated, notice the canvas sling where the puppets are put when their part is finished. The stretch plastic covered wire extends round each side and the front of the booth, and is used for hanging the puppets. The shelf is where the props are put. The track for the curtains is hidden behind the proscenium front. The playboard projects at the front; traditionally, fringe is attached all round this. Below this, reaching to the ground, is cloth. The other three sides are completely covered in cloth, the top too. The framework of the booth is made of four pieces of 1 inch by 1 inch wood for uprights, and cross-pieces of 1 inch by $\frac{1}{2}$ inch. The proscenium is made of hardboard or plywood, and can be painted in bright fairground patterns and colours. If the puppets are held above the head of the operator, this can be very tiring. A less tiring way is to place a transparent screen of thin thread between the operator and the audience; the operator can then rest his or her elbows on the prop shelf, and because the light is on the audience side the operator can see through the screen without being seen. A simple scene can be painted on the screen with Brusho dyes without obscuring the operator's vision.

Shadow theatre

The opening of any puppet theatre can be used. A screen of thin white cotton stretched over a wooden frame is fitted into the opening. The method of making the screen is the same as that for making a screen for screen printing (see that section). The important thing to remember is that the cloth must be absolutely wrinkle free. Tilt the screen slightly at the top towards the audience, so that the puppets are resting on the screen. The screen is lit from behind the puppets, by a light which is fixed above the operator, so that the operator's shadow is not cast on the screen.

The puppet booth from behind; here the puppets are held above eye level.

Here, a thin cloth screen is placed immediately in front of the puppeteer, who can see what he is doing without being seen.

In the background the cardboard theatre, and in the foreground a drawing of an original print used in Victorian England.

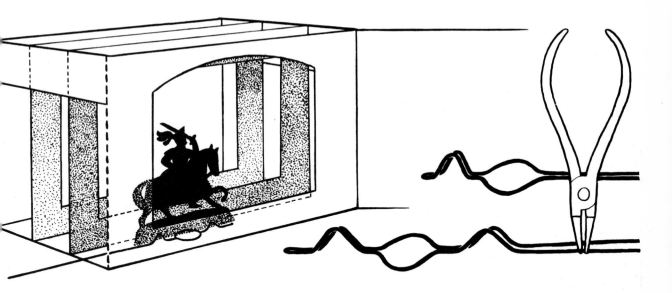

VICTORIAN TOY THEATRE

This originated in England around 1811, as a theatrical souvenir of engravings of the principal actors. They were not intended to be cut out originally, but the practice of cutting them out and sticking them on card soon became widespread. Gradually complete plays were printed, with the characters illustrated in all their main poses, and changes of costume and scenery. A feature of these prints was the very elaborately decorated prosceniums. Soon wire slides were being sold into which the characters could be slotted and by means of which they could be pushed on and off the stage while their words were spoken.

Pollocks Toy Museum, at 1 Scala St, London, W1 (near Goodge Street Station), occasionally put on performances in an upstairs room of toy theatre productions. They also sell the printed stages, characters, slides, etc.

A modern development mechanically is the introduction of magnets. These are attached to the base of the characters, vehicles, etc. (no wires or slides are needed), and are moved by another magnet attached to the end of a rod which is held underneath the stage. This method gives more freedom of movement on stage, and less chaos in the wings. Galts toy shop, 30 Great Marlborough St, London, W1, sell sets of characters.

The construction of the theatre, showing how the figures are moved onto the stage. The wires show the twisting of a loop of wire to hold the figures. Inexpensive plastic slides are also available.

Making the Victorian toy theatre

This is made from card. Reproduction Victorian ones can be bought from Pollock's Toy Museum and are quite inexpensive. The sides of the proscenium and the top are kept very wide in order to hide the characters waiting in the wings. The Victorian ones were very decorative. There are lots of changes in scene, to make up for the lack of movement obtainable in the figures. Various backdrops are slipped in from the top. These are either solid or have openings in them so that two or three can be used, one behind the other, at the same time. Two large cereal packets with one side cut out of each will make a simple toy theatre.

FURTHER READING

BAIRD, B., *The Art of the Puppet* Collier-Macmillan

BATCHELDER, M., *The Puppet Theatre Handbook* Ohio State University Press

BLACKHAM, O., *Shadow Puppets* Barrie & Rockliff

VON BOEHM, M., *Dolls and Puppets* Harrap, 1932

BOHMER, *Puppets Through the Ages* Macdonald

An elaborate Venetian marionette theatre (eighteenth century).

CURRELL, D., *Puppetry in the Primary School* Batsford

FRASER, P., *Introducing Puppetry* Batsford
Punch and Judy Batsford
Puppet Circus Batsford

MCPHARLIN, P., *The Puppet Theatre in America : a History*

SPEAIGHT, G., *History of the English Puppet Theatre* Harrap

Puppetry in the Curriculum, Board of Education, City of New York, Curriculum Bulletin 47–8, series No. 1

A portable marionette theatre seen from the back.

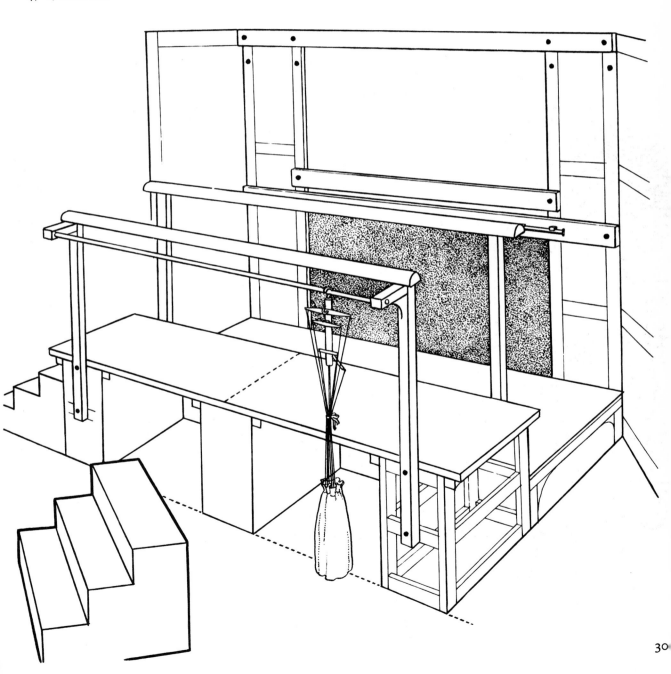

Puppet theatres
The Little Angel
Islington
London N1

The Harlequin
Rhos-on-Sea
Clwyd
North Wales

Pollock's Toy Museum
1 Scala St
London W1

Educational Puppetry Association
23a Southampton Place
London WC1

Arrangements for 'draw' curtains (*above*),
and 'drape' curtains (*below*).

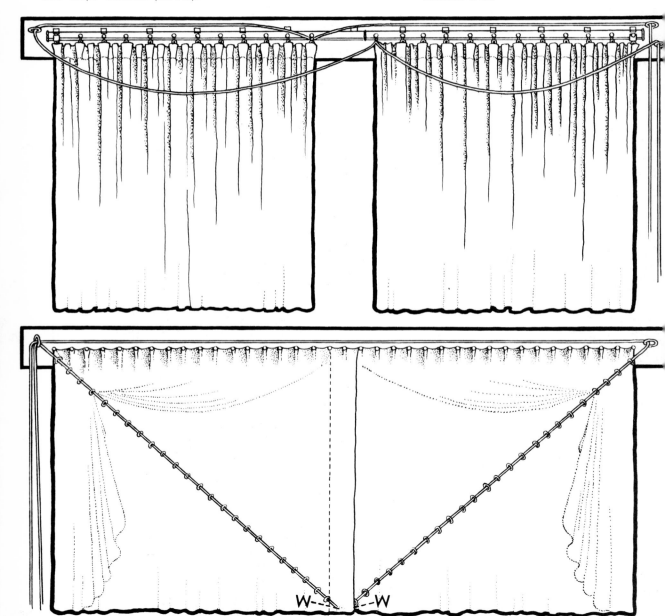

Pyrography (Pyrogravure)

Pyrography is the name given to a certain type of pokerwork (woodburning). By rubbing the tip of a pokerwork tool (woodburning pen) which has an oblique flat end over the surface of wood, all tones from light brown to black can be obtained, depending on how long the tool is held in one place, or how often an area is passed over by the tool. It has much in common with drawing with a thick piece of charcoal. It must have been a very tricky business before the invention of a thermostatically controlled pokerwork tool, and it makes the work of the nineteenth-century pyrographers even more remarkable. The most prolific in England was Ralph Marshall, whose work can be seen at the Pinto Museum in Birmingham, and that of the Comte de Rottermund.

It is very important in pokerwork to have close-grained wood, otherwise the tool tends to skid along the grain lines, or the burning runs along the grain lines. The best woods are sycamore, lime and holly.

The difference between this technique and what is generally thought of as pokerwork lies in the fact that in pyrography the concentration is on tone as opposed to line.

(Right) These examples show a combination of line and tone — a mixture of pyrography and pokerwork. The top example was drawn using only the fine tip by a fourteen year old boy.

305

A wax portrait of Queen Anne, *c.*1710.
(Courtesy of the Lady Lever Art Gallery.)

Quill Work

QUILLING, PAPER FILIGREE, ROLLED PAPER WORK

Simulating gold filigree, and enriched with seed pearls, small shells, metal threads, and miniatures, quill work was used in ecclesiastical art from the fifteenth century to the Reformation. It was revived again in Boston; an advertisement in the Boston Gazette 1755 reads: 'Mrs Hiller still continues to keep school in Hanover St, where young ladies may be taught wax work, filigree, painting on glass, quillwork and featherwork, japanning, and embroidery with gold and silver'.

Stiff paper was cut into strips $\frac{1}{8}$ in. wide, and rolled and glued. One edge was glued and stuck onto the background. It was arranged as formal patterns, or in sprays of flowers or leaves. Complete pictures were made in this way, cabinets were covered in it, but the most common were tea caddies and small workboxes, made specially with recesses in the lids and sides to take the depth of the rolled paper. The backgrounds were sometimes mirrored, sometimes they had tinfoil instead. Occasionally the whole thing was gilded when it was finished. There are some magnificent examples of the work in the Lady Lever Art Gallery, Port Sunlight, and in the Victoria and Albert Museum in London, and a whole gallery is devoted to the paper filigree work of French prisoners-of-war in Peterborough Museum.

Materials and equipment

paper; white glue (PVA); guillotine (paper cutter), or craft knife and steel rule; knitting needle, pencil or cocktail sticks; small brass or plastic curtain rings, small plastic lids; tweezers.

The paper must be firm enough to cut into thin strips and hold its shape when rolled, e.g. typewriting or the thicker sorts of bank paper, writing paper, or cartridge paper are all suitable. The slivers of paper which accumulate after trimming on a guillotine are very useful: you could try your local printer for his waste trimmings. Although traditionally white paper or vellum was used, experiment with coloured paper, or colour the edges of the paper after quilling has been completed. Use a guillotine to cut up the strips of paper, which should be about $\frac{1}{4}$ in. to $\frac{1}{8}$ in. wide, or a Stanley or Exacto knife and cut against a steel rule (making sure that you are cutting on a piece of scrap wood, Formica or thick card to protect the surface on which you are working). Avoid cutting with scissors; it is very difficult to get a smooth edge of any length with a pair of scissors.

The most satisfactory glue is a PVA (Marvin or similar). Apply it with a cocktail stick, and use tweezers to hold the two pieces together while it sets. If you work on a sheet of polythene, plastic, or waxed paper the glued shapes will not stick to these.

The knitting needle is for rolling the paper around, and the curtain rings are for popping the coiled shapes into so that they all expand to the same size (if required).

METHOD

Taking one end of a strip of paper about 4 in. long, roll it around the knitting needle (as you would do for making paper beads). When the paper is all rolled, twist the knitting needle in the opposite direction to the one in which the paper has been rolled, and the coiled shape will slip off easily. At this point you have two alternatives: to make either closed coiled shapes or open coiled shapes.

Open coil shapes

After coiling, the coil is not glued to hold its shape as with the closed coils. Once the paper is taken off the needle it is allowed to spring open. If a length of paper is left uncoiled at the end, this straight piece can be joined with other similar pieces to form a stem, the coils forming tendrils. Alternatively, coil only half the paper, then beginning again from the other end coil the other half. You can make either 'C' scrolls or 'S' scrolls in this way. If the straight part of the 'C' is squeezed, you will have a heart shape; squeeze the other way and you will make a curly 'V'. These are the basic loose coil shapes.

An antique piece of quilling being repaired, showing the recess into which the filigree scrolls were put.

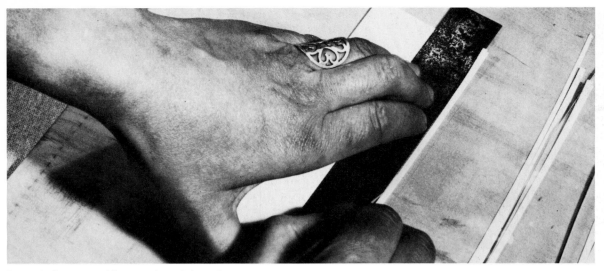

Paper being cut with a steel straight-edge
and a craft knife.

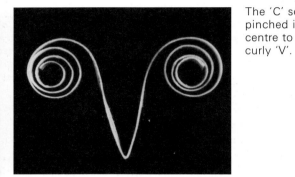

The 'C' scroll
pinched in the
centre to form a
curly 'V'.

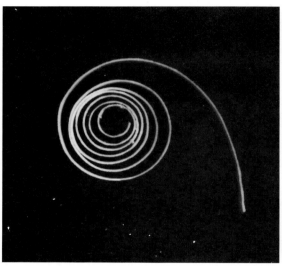

A loose-coiled
shape, the last part
being left uncoiled.

The 'C' scroll.

'S' scroll: both
halves of the strip
were coiled
separately.

Tightly coiled closed shape.

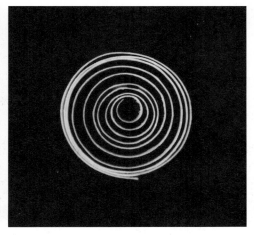

Coiled shape glued after freely expanding.

Leaf or drop shape made by pinching a coil at one end only.

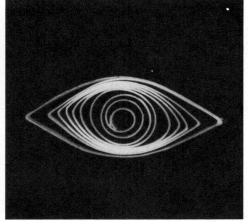

Loose-coiled shape pinched at two opposite ends making an eye shape.

Closed-coil shapes arranged symmetrically.

Closed-coil shapes made into a necklace.
The parts are joined together by jump rings
(see Findings).

Coiling a paper strip around a cocktail
stick.

Popping it into a curtain ring to control the
extent of its expansion.

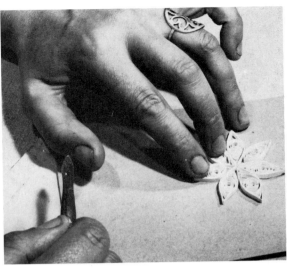

Pinching the two ends to make the eye shape.

Gluing pieces together with a cocktail stick and holding them firmly in place with the tweezers until secure.

A print from a quilled shape.

Closed coil shapes

To make a tightly coiled closed shape, roll the paper around the largest-sized knitting needle or a piece of smooth dowelling of a similar size. Glue the last $\frac{1}{2}$ in. of paper, twist the needle and release the coil. There will be no change of shape when the coil is moved. Larger or smaller circles can be made by varying the diameter of the needle used for wrapping the paper around. For loose closed coiled shapes, do not glue the last $\frac{1}{2}$ in. of paper while it is still on the needle. Take it off, and pop the shape into a shallow plastic lid or curtain ring, or just let it expand on the table. Now glue the last $\frac{1}{2}$ in. of paper (the last part on the outside of the coil).

If you squeeze gently on the outside coils at both ends you will get an eye shape: if you squeeze at only one end, a leaf or drop shape. You can squeeze at three points on the outside coils, in which case you have a triangular shape. Whatever the outside shape becomes, the inside shape is always a spiral. Make several different shapes, and then several of the same shape. The pieces can now be attached to each other, in either symmetrical or asymmetrical arrangements.

When gluing different parts together do so holding them flat on the table: do not try to glue them while holding them in the air. When dry, the shapes can either be used free hanging, as mobiles, or earrings, necklaces, etc., or the whole motif can be glued onto another surface, e.g. hardboard, card, leather, stone, wood. To do this, brush the edges of the quilling with glue on the side to be pressed down. Pictures made of quilling can be set in resin to protect them, as can fingerplates (decorative panels above doorknobs) decorated with quilling. Experiment with quilling on three-dimensional surfaces, such as stone, papier mâché, wood.

Motifs made from quilling can be used for stencil patterns: use an air brush, aerosol paint, or a toothbrush to splatter the paint on. They can also be used as printing blocks (stuck onto hardboard or cardboard), and used for printing on paper or fabric. Water-based ink tends to

Contemporary Christmas tree decorations using the quilling technique with brightly coloured plastic sheeting.

make the paper edges of the quilling go soggy, so use a polymer paint, or oil-based paint, or protect the edges by painting them with a diluted white glue (PVA) first to make them waterproof.

THINGS TO MAKE

Pictures; picture and mirror frame decoration; necklaces, pendants, earrings; small box-lids; valentines, greeting cards; mobiles; Christmas tree decorations; stage jewellery, crowns; printing greeting cards, and small cushions.

RELATED CRAFTS

Coiled paper bead making; finidee (strips of wood veneer); straw stars; string pictures; wire coiling in jewellery; application of thin coils of clay as decoration on pots.

FURTHER READING

AARON, E., *Quilling, the Art of Paper Scroll Work* Batsford

Repoussage (Embossing)

Most of the methods of working with metal are virtually the same as those used since metal was first discovered. All the early metal decorative ware was produced with a hammer, and preceded casting. Before the use of solder was first discovered. The earliest metal decorative ware was produced with a hammer, shape, and then the parts rivetted together; this was how the life-size Egyptian statue of Pepi I, dating from 2300 BC was made. From 2500 BC the process of casting known as lost wax was used in Egypt; this technique had probably been learned from the Sumerians. This became the standard method for casting from then on, but decorative work, and most work in precious metals, continued to be made with the hammer.

The result of hammering metal in one place is to 'stretch' it, i.e. it will appear raised up if the hammering is done in the centre of a sheet. Hammering to produce a decoration on metal is called embossing or repoussage. A drawing is made on a sheet of metal, the lines of the drawing are then hammered gently, producing a fine raised line on the other side. Some form of support is needed for the metal while it is being embossed, and though a sheet of fairly dense rubber is used now, asphalt was the traditional material. Few tools are needed: a round-ended tool for raising curved areas, and a finer tool for chasing and making the detailed linear decoration. A spring tool was used for reaching otherwise inaccessible areas.

Chasing proper is made by hammering punches of various shapes on the front of the metal. It can have the background flattened down by beating flat, which produces an effect similar to that of repoussage, but repoussage has its raised designs pushed up from the reverse side. Engraving incises or cuts a line, actually removing metal in so doing.

Inlaying processes

Damascening was the process for which the goldsmiths of Damascus were famous. The metals on which the damascening is done are steel, bronze, and iron. The gouged lines are cut at an angle to the surface (known as undercutting) then gold (or sometimes silver and copper) wire is forced into the undercut hollow, and held firmly by being hammered along the lines.

Instead of filling the lines with wire, niello is made with a powder which is spread over the metal which has been treated with flux and heated until the powder melts and runs into the engraved channels. The excess is scraped off until the lines appear, and the surface is then polished. The recipe for the powder was given by Cellini in the sixteenth century, and was the same as that given by Theophilus in the eleventh century. Silver, copper and lead were melted together, and the molten alloy was mixed with sulphur. The black alloy that resulted was powdered, and it was this powder that became the niello.

Metals

Metals used for present-day repoussage are obtainable in craft shops. Aluminium foil (domestic) is not suitable because it is already too thin to 'stretch' much. Metal sheet over 0.1 inch (0.4 mm) is too thick for repoussage, but can be hammered; 0.05 inch (0.2 mm) or less is suitable. When buying sheets of metal (it is often sold in packets) pull a sheet out. If it is creased do not buy it: it is too thin. There is a 'rattling' sound as the metal is handled, and the lower the sound the better, so if one has to choose between two thicknesses of unknown weight, choose the one with the lower 'rattle'.

Aluminium is often coloured on one side, gold, copper, blue, green or red, the other side each time being silvery. Copper is a good metal to use, as long as it is not too thick. The best metal is sheet pewter; it is more expensive to buy, but is a joy to work, being more malleable than the other metals and having a softer sheen. To work the metal, use a very large crochet hook, the handle of a teaspoon, an empty biro, or wooden modelling tools. Avoid any tool with a point, because it is very easy to puncture the metal.

When hollowing a large area, work very slowly, starting in the centre of the shape and working outwards. If the shape is small, this can be done in the hollow of the hand. The chasing is done when the embossing is finished, any chased lines on the embossed areas are done while the metal is hollow-side down. The flat areas can be chased on either side. When the work is completed, it might be found useful to fill the hollows on the wrong side with instant papier mâché, or powdered wood. This prevents the work being spoilt later by the hollows being pushed in. Copper can be heated in a butane burner, which alters the colour in patches and also makes it more malleable.

Sheet metal (thin) can also be mechanically embossed, by being pressed into a mould; pressed between dies; or hammered gently over stamps.

This angel was worked on pewter. The particular quality of the sheen of pewter is clearly seen in the soft rounding of all the shapes. There is none of the harsh angularity that occurs in thinner metals. It is very much softer to use than most other metals, and can be pushed out a long way before splitting.

This contemporary Indian piece of repoussage is made by stamping out the design in sheet metal and then cutting it out.

Resin

TYPES OF RESINS

General purpose resin, also called laminating resin, is the one normally used for GRP (glass-fibre reinforced plastics). It is pre-accelerated (quick-drying).

Marine, or heavy duty resin, used for boats, ponds, or anywhere that the resin will be in permanent contact with the water. Expensive, it is about twice the price of general purpose resin.

Thixotropic, or non-drip resins are for use when laying resin on vertical surfaces.

Gel-coat resins are used for the initial coat. They are tough and resilient, but are to be used only for the gel-coat. They have a tendency to remain tacky unless all air is excluded. If the gel-coat is exposed, it must be covered with cellophane.

Clear resins are specially made for decorative panels and the like, and will not yellow with age, as normal resin does slightly.

Casting resins are specially made for casting and embedding. There are many specially formulated resins for specific purposes, but these are not generally available.

Sealers, varnishes, are simple resins to seal the surface or give a better finish, or both. They also contain air-inhibitors to prevent tackiness. They come in two forms: polyester resin-varnish, and polyurethane resin-varnish. The last can be ground and polished if needed. Sealers and varnishes are also useful for sealing casts made of plaster or models of papier mâché, cardboard, etc.

CURING RESIN

There are two methods of curing (setting) resin. One can add a catalyst to the resin, but then one has to apply heat to make the liquid set. The other method does not require the application of external heat. This 'cold cure' method is achieved by adding an 'accelerator', as well as the catalyst. In this case the heat is produced internally (exothermically). The two methods produce a resin of the same characteristics, but the cold cure method is obviously the easier method to use. Do not add the accelerator to the catalyst. It is always best to buy resin which is pre-accelerated. With a pre-accelerated resin, once the catalyst is added the curing process is started.

Catalysts are unstable, and it is possible for them to explode. Any on the skin should be washed off at once. If any gets in your eye it must be washed immediately with plain water. Any rags that have been used to wipe up catalyst should be wetted with water and put in a dustbin (garbage can). If they are left lying around dry, it is possible for them to spontaneously ignite.

FILLERS

This is usually a powder added to liquid resin to give it more bulk, and produce a solid colour. It can also be added to the liquid until it is a paste, and in this state it can be used as a filler on car body repairs. Slate powder is a general purpose bulker, and also gives a grey colour. Metallic flakes give an opalescent metallic finish. Asbestos powder is used for flameproof mouldings. Sawdust produces a surface that is similar to real wood. Vinyl flakes are for 'pearly' effects. Pigments are available in a huge range of colours, and give an opaque colour to the resin. Translucent colours are also available.

RELEASE AGENTS

These are a vital part of the casting process. Resin does not stick to cellophane or cling film polythene or acetate, and although one could cover the mould with polythene before covering with resin, and the resin would come off easily, it would also have followed every crease in the polythene.

Wax polish is the best release agent. Put the polish on the mould, rub off to a high polish, and repeat once more. To make an even more reliable release agent, the wax can be sponged with PVA (white glue).

Wax emulsions are easier to apply than the wax polish: you have to wait until they are dry before polishing. This should be coated with a PVA release agent.

PVA is available in powder, and can be dissolved in hot water. If a little glycerine is added, the film can be stripped off easily in one sheet after the resin has set.

GLASS FIBRE

Glass fibre (fiberglass) is made from glass into various types of cloth. The molten glass is drawn out into continuous filaments, of specific sized diameter. These are either twisted together into a rather loose rope to produce 'rovings', or into 'yarn'. Rovings are used to make the chopped strand mat, which is the common fibre glass cloth used to embed in resin. The chopped up mat is held together with a special binder which dissolves in the resin. The mats are sold by weight per square foot, e.g. 1, 1½, 2 oz mat. Half-way between chopped strand mat and woven cloth is *coiled mat*, made from continuous strand laid randomly, and held with a suitable binder. *Glass fibre tissue* is very fine, and is used to hide the texture of the coarse glass fibre, either in the gel-coat, if that is the important side, or as a final finish.

Glass fibre tape is made as a woven cloth in a narrow strip; it is a convenient size to use when reinforcing corners, or in spiral binding. *Woven glass cloth* produces the strongest laminate, but it is very difficult to 'wet' through with the resin. Because of this, it is often disappointing for beginners to use because the bonding between one layer and the next is frequently poor in places. *Woven rovings* are not as strong as the woven cloth, but are much easier to wet thoroughly with resin, and drape well. They are also cheaper than woven cloth.

GLASS FIBRE CASTS

The basic technique

The mould must be clean, and treated with a release agent. The gel-coat resin is mixed with the catalyst, and brushed onto the mould. Use a wide, soft brush, and sweep it on, distributing it as evenly as possible to a thickness of ·01 in. When the gel-coat has gelled and is no longer sticky to the touch the next stage begins. But, do not touch the gel-coat on the mould. Touch a part of the cast that will eventually be cut off.

Mix up some resin, and paint this over the gel-coat. While this is still wet, lay on the glass mat. If you are using fibre glass tissue, then this goes on first. The fibre glass mat is cut to fit the mould, and if there is any overlapping to be done, tear the fibre glass and then overlap. (A torn edge will almost disappear, whereas a cut edge is difficult to hide.) Place this on the wet resin, and with a stiff brush, dab at the fibre glass until it sinks into the resin. Do this all over the fibre glass until no white patches remain. *Do not 'paint' with the brush.* This only picks up the glass fibres, especially if chopped mat is used, and is the wrong action for pushing down the glass fibre into the wet resin. Make sure that no air bubbles are trapped. If you see any, poke at them with the stiff brush until they disappear.

If you have to join the glass fibre, make the overlap 2 in. wide, and tear the edge. Up to four layers of glass fibre can now be laid onto the wet resin, laying on a coat of resin before the glass fibre each time, making sure that there are no air bubbles, and no white patches of glass fibre. Leave for 24 hours, before trying to release from the mould. It is likely that even though you have used a release agent, the cast will have to be prised away from the mould. Use a wooden knife or plastic spatula for this job, and try to slip it between the cast and the mould. Once air has been introduced between the cast and the mould it is simple to pull the cast away.

PAPIER MÂCHÉ USING RESIN INSTEAD OF PASTE

Make a form out of chicken wire, and securely wire the shapes together, so that there are no sharp bits of wire sticking out. Stuff the inside with crumpled newspaper, so that all the shapes are well supported. Cover the table with polythene (plastic or polyethylene sheeting).

Make up some general purpose resin and into this dip the strips of newspaper, running the strip between two gloved fingers (which removes the excess resin) and bind round the chicken wire form. Continue until the whole wire form is covered (see the section on Papier Mâché).

Depending on the finish required, the next stages are as follows. The newspaper dipped in resin can be the finished surface, or one can use on top of the newspaper strips of coloured paper dipped in resin, to leave a coloured finish. One can also vary the colour of the surface by tearing small pieces of different coloured papers, and after dipping in resin, sticking these all over the surface. Alternatively, one can treat the surface with découpage, again dipped in resin. Sawdust can be added to the resin until the mixture is a thick paste, which can be spread all over the surface with a palette knife. When the surface is cured, it can be sanded and polished.

Many finishes are possible on a fibre glass/resin cast: it can be painted with artist's oil paints; sprayed with car acrylic paints; painted with latex paint; or it can have applied to it any of the things suggested in the section on surface treatments of paper mâché, glued with resin instead of wheat or wallpaper paste. These can be painted over with polyester resin varnish or polyurethane varnish. Experiment with various ideas on small pieces.

SHEET ACETATE MADE RIGID WITH GLASS FIBRE MAT AND RESIN

Using this technique, the shapes arrived at in paper sculpture can be made permanent. Cut the shapes out of sheet acetate. Using the acetate as your pattern cut the same shapes out of fibre glass tissue (two layers). Coat both sides of the acetate with resin, and onto the wet resin lay the matching pieces of glass fibre tissue, dabbing it well into the resin, until it is well soaked. Let the resin cure. Fasten the acetate sheet with a spot of acetone. Hold the two pieces together with a small spring clip while setting. It will be secure in 10 minutes. Perforated zinc can also be cut and bent, and covered with fibre glass mat in resin, and coloured with an opaque pigment. Experiment with polyurethane varnish and fibre glass tissue over foamed polystyrene.

MAKING A FLAT GLASS FIBRE TRANSLUCENT PANEL

Onto a piece of hardboard lay a sheet of cellophane. Paint resin over the cellophane, and onto that lay the sheet of glass fibre mat, and stipple well down into the resin. With a roller, roll all over the sheet of fibre glass, until the mat is really embedded. Lay another sheet of cellophane over the top of the mat, another sheet of hardboard over that, and roll again on top of the hardboard. Leave to cure.

A variation of the above technique embeds fabric or paper, or dried grasses, or other flat objects. Lay a sheet of cellophane on the table. Cut out a piece of cloth, or paper, and a piece of fibre glass mat the same size. Brush a layer of general purpose resin on the cellophane. Place the cloth or the paper onto the resin. Add more resin and into that place the glass fibre sheet. Add more resin and stipple well down until the cloth and the glass mat are well impregnated with resin. Put another sheet of cellophane on the top and roll with a rolling pin until all the air bubbles are squeezed out. Leave between the two sheets of cellophane to harden.

Clean a square of glass and polish with a wax release agent. Stick masking tape all round the edge of the glass in order to hold the resin. Pour some clear catalysed resin onto the glass, and on this arrange pieces of coloured acetate, overlapping them so as to give other colours. Add more resin, into which is pressed a sheet of fibre glass tissue. Stipple with a brush, until well embedded, then cover with a layer of cellophane. Leave to cure.

COLD ENAMELLING ON METAL FOIL

Lay a sheet of aluminium foil onto a pile of newspapers, and draw a design with a biro onto the foil. Turn the foil over, and the drawing will be standing up from the surface on this side. This can now be treated as cloisonné, and the areas between the lines can be filled with different coloured enamels.

CASTING WITH EMBEDDING RESIN

For this technique, one needs a slow setting resin. It is possible to adjust one's resin to make it slow setting, but it is better to buy it ready prepared. It is sometimes called 'potting' resin. The moulds can be made of polythene, glass, or china/pottery. A set of moulds come with the embedding kits. Use these if you have some, if not, smooth glass ash trays, flexible polythene food containers, small cups, etc. can be used. Make sure that the inside is perfectly smooth, dry and clean. Apply a release agent (wax, well polished) and the mould is ready. Forms can also be made out of rigid sheet acetate. The corners can be joined with cement, and the whole made leak-proof. Some very complicated shapes can be constructed in this way. More complicated shapes require the thin acetate sheet, taped at the corners on the outside, and the whole thing should be supported in a box of polystyrene or styrofoam beads or vermiculite. Moulds constructed of acetate or perspex (plexiglass) have the great advantage of needing no release agent.

Pouring the resin

Resin for embedding is mixed up in three or four separate lots as it is required. Bear the following points in mind before you start. Do not let dust fall onto the exposed surface of the resin. As soon as the layer has been poured into the mould, cover the top with some cling film, or anything else to keep the dust out. Beware of bubbles. Pour the resin in very carefully and slowly, and do not stir the resin and catalyst wildly. Do not pour a layer thicker than $\frac{1}{2}$ in. at a time. Any thicker, and you run the risk of marked heating of the resin, and shrinkage, which might make cracks appear. Wait until the last layer has set and cooled before you pour the next layer on.

The number of layers depends on how deep your mould is. Allow $\frac{1}{2}$ in. for each layer poured in, and you can work out how many layers any given mould will need. When the final layer has been poured, cover with a layer of cellophane or cling film. This ensures that the top (it will be the base when the cast is taken out) is hard and not sticky.

Embedding the objects

The objects are placed in after the first layer has set. Whatever is embedded must be absolutely dry. To test whether the resin is set, tilt the mould to one side, and if the resin does not move, it is ready for the next layer. On the small moulds in a kit, setting might only take half an hour; on a larger mould it might take up to 2 hours or more.

If a thin flat object is to be embedded, take care that no air is trapped underneath by putting a blob of resin on it before lowering it onto the resin in the mould. Press well down with a toothpick. If the object is of many layers, like a dried flower, a lot of air can be trapped in it. To get rid of the air, lay the flower down into the resin, but do not cover it in one pouring. Pour a layer up to around half the depth of the flower. Then, when it is set, pour the next layer on. In this way, the air will work its way up to the surface before the next layer is poured on. Fragile seed cases can be filled with resin before they are laid on the layer of resin. Otherwise, they are likely to be crushed in the resin.

Different objects can be placed on each layer of the resin, or threads can be laid onto the first layer, and continued to be laid through all the layers. Experiment: trust your imagination. Remember that the bottom of the mould will be the top of the cast, so that anything placed in the resin should have the 'face' down when it is put in the resin. The final layer can be coloured with the pigment supplied with the kit so that the objects have a 'background' against which to show up. Choose a soft, unobtrusive colour. It is the objects that one is meant to look at, not the background colour. If colour intrigues you, try adding coloured resin in stripes, spots, irregular shapes, on each layer of resin; try cutting shapes out of coloured acetate sheet, and embedding them at different levels.

SLUSH MOULDING

This technique produces a hollow cast. A quick-setting resin is used: it is poured into a hollow mould which is closed. The mould is then firmly held in the hands and rotated rapidly ensuring that the resin is spread all around the inside in an even layer. This is really a commercial technique, and difficult to reproduce at home.

PLIQUE À JOUR

A version of what is really an enamelling technique can be made in resin. Holes must be left in the initial design of the piece of jewellery or plaque. These will be filled with a cold-setting enamel stained with transparent colours. The designs can be made in plasticine, and moulds made from them in plaster of Paris. When it is cured, the inside of the plaster of Paris mould can be treated with a mould release agent such as a wax emulsion. The resin can have aluminium filler added to it if you want a solid-looking cast. When the resin has cured it can be removed and laid on a piece of cellophane or cling film. Cold setting enamel is then coloured and poured into the hole of the design, and left to set hard. The cold setting enamel will stick firmly to the sides of the hole, but will come off the cellophane easily.

MOULDS

MATERIALS SUITABLE	DOMESTIC, EASILY AVAILABLE
Pottery	Ashtray
Polyurethane	Dish
Glass	Egg-cup
Metal	Foil tray
Epoxy resin	Stainless steel bowl
Silicone rubber	
Plaster of Paris	

Do not use polystyrene (styrofoam)

Resist Printing

Historically, resist paste is thought to be the forerunner of wax in the development of the technique of batik. In Japan, it was a folk craft used in the eighteenth and nineteenth centuries to decorate cloth. It is still used by the Yoruba in Nigeria where cassava flour and alum are used to make the paste. It is applied to the cotton with either a brush or a stencil, and the fabric is then dyed in huge vats of Indigo dye.

USING AN IMPROVISED PASTE FOR RESIST

Materials

flour; water; newspaper; dye – Iron Rust or Caledon are recommended for use in schools as they are simple to use and do not need acids in their 'fixing'. Suitable dyes available in the USA are Putnam Fadelen Dyes, Prang Textile Colors Set, and Versatex Water Soluble Textile Colors. For applying paste – a slip trailer, or block (e.g. cork), or brush. The paste can also be squeezed out of a plastic bottle or cake icing tool to achieve a regular line.

METHOD

Mix flour and water to a paste as thick as mayonnaise. Lay the cloth on a newspaper, to absorb excess water from the paste. Apply paste, and leave to dry. Brush the dye over the fabric. If it is immersed in dye, this paste will get soggy, and the dye will creep underneath the paste and dye the whole fabric.

P.R. RESIST AGENT

This is to be used only with Procion dyes. Dilute 1 part Resist Agent P.R. with $\frac{1}{2}$ part water, then stir into 2 parts British Gum thickening. To make British Gum thickening, boil together 4 oz British gum and $\frac{1}{2}$ pint cold water for 20–30 minutes, stirring all the time.

The liquid can be applied either by block printing, or with a brush. When the design is dry, Procion dyes can be either brushed over very lightly, or rolled over. The pattern only appears when the dye has been processed; the areas that have been painted with the P.R. Resist agent will be undyed, or only slightly dyed.

The flour paste being squeezed out onto the fabric. This gives a regular line of equal thickness.

If you want to cover large areas the paste can be applied with a spatula, like spreading butter. This fish has been designed using both areas of paste, and line. It is a two-colour dye, and the dye will have to be cold water dye. Do not attempt to immerse in dye until the paste is absolutely dry.

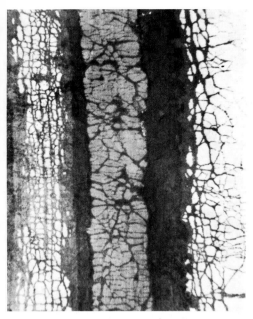

This is a detail of the cracking which inevitably happens when using a paste resist. Compare this cracking with the cracking made by wax in batik.

Rubbings

The three main techniques, frottage (*frotter*, to rub), brass rubbings, and creative rubbings, each use wax rubbed onto a piece of paper.

FROTTAGE

This is a technique developed by Max Ernst when he was working with the Surrealists, and it involves looking at the frottage (rubbing) until you 'see' something in the shapes, lines, and either adding more pieces (to make a collage) or drawing into it with a pen. Essentially, it ignores the subject of the rubbing. A rubbing of a plank of wood would suggest waves in the sea, sunsets, landscapes.

BRASS RUBBINGS

This is a method of reproducing what already exists, and involves little creativity. It has its uses in learning about the history of costume, social history, the history of art, just as the rubbings taken of coins, man-hole covers, tree bark, tombstones, have their place in the study of natural history, numismatology, history, etc.

In Britain, most churches contain medieval brass plate monuments let into the floor, which are excellent subjects for brass rubbings. The earliest extant is at Stoke d'Abernon in Surrey, and dates from A.D. 1277. The London Brass Rubbing Centre at St James' Church, Piccadilly, London W1, is the major brass rubbing centre in Britain.

CREATIVE RUBBINGS

With this technique, the rubbing is constructed by the person doing the rubbing. The technique capitalizes on the delight of an image appearing on a blank sheet of paper (merely by rubbing it with a wax crayon), as if by magic, but at the same time quite complicated aesthetic problems can be dealt with in making the original paper cut from which the rubbing is taken. These are the spatial relationships between the various shapes and between the shapes and the edges of the picture.

METHOD

Cobblers' wax (heelball) or any make of wax crayon is suitable for making a rubbing. Cobblers' wax is a very hard wax which gives particularly even distribution of tone and is excellent for bringing out work done in thin paper on the original, or work using folding (which the coarser waxes fail to reveal) but it gives a very grey rubbing with no strong tone contrasts. Choose a wax which will give strong tone contrasts. Avoid ones which are too greasy and give an uneven build-up of wax on the paper leaving bare patches often unrelated to the original design. Try using gold and copper coloured wax crayons on coloured tissue or wrapping paper. When crayons wear down it will be found difficult to use the small pieces: these can be melted in an old saucepan and poured into a jar lid and used again. The paper on which the rubbing is made should be thin, strong and smooth (such as shelving paper).

Lay the sheet of paper down over the original (whether an engraved brass or a collage of paper cut-outs) and tape it down lightly at the corners so that it does not move during rubbing. Use the whole length of the wax crayon in rubbing, not just the tip. If you rub evenly all over the original, a rather grey picture results, with every part having the same emphasis. A more satisfying result is obtained if certain parts are made stronger in tone by harder rubbing, and other parts understated by only lightly rubbing with the wax. A greater sense of form can be expressed by the general direction and weight of the strokes.

PRINTING FROM RUBBINGS

A heavy rubbing made with black wax crayon can be used to take a print from with a hot iron. To do this, lay the rubbing face down on a clean sheet of paper of the same size as the rubbing. With a warm iron, iron the back of the original rubbing with a medium hot iron. If the paper browns slightly, turn to a lower temperature setting. However the iron must be fairly hot, because the wax has to melt and the excess be absorbed by the lower paper. The quality of the print depends on the surface of the paper used for the print.

FURTHER READING

ANDREW, L., *Creative Rubbings* Batsford

The original paper collage which is the basis of the rubbing. No colour is used when making this so that all concentration is focussed on the shapes used and their disposition on the paper.

The strength of the shape is a distinctive feature of this medium. After the rubbing was made of the cockerel, the background was made by rubbing on strongly grained wood.

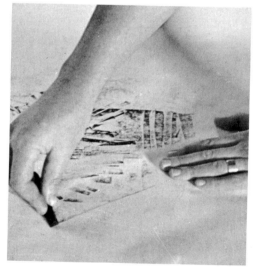

The thin detail paper is held down over the original paper collage and rubbed with the length of the crayon, not the tip.

The ephemeral qualities of paper which has been cut and folded are admirably captured by rubbing.

Note the positive idiosyncratic response by ten-year-old children to identical visual stimuli, in these four rubbings.

A rubbing using two shades of gold wax on a mulberry coloured paper.

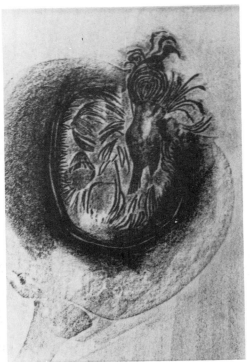

A composition made by direct cutting of a section through a rose hip. Notice the deliberate use of weighting only certain parts of the design with very black rubbing.

Rya

Rya is the name of a stitch used to make shaggy rugs with a needle. The yarn is wound round three fingers between each stitch to establish the length of the pile. This gives a pleasing, slightly irregular finish to the rug, and the irregularity should be further exploited by using different colours.

The Rya canvas is available in widths of 28½ and 48 inches, and the design should first be marked out on it using coloured chalks. The rows are 1⅛ inches apart, giving about 12 knots to 4 inches. It takes some 25 hours to complete one square yard of knotting, so if making a large item, this is an ideal craft to take up when relaxing in the evening.

Rya or Sudan yarn is available in a wide range of colours, and since 3 or 4 strands must be used together in one needle, different coloured strands can be used in each stitch to give a warm, glowing colour effect to the finished rug. The needle should be a large embroidery needle with a blunt end and a large eye, and may be straight or curved.

To achieve a regular pile, a long, flat wooden gauge (about 1½ inches wide) may be used. Make the first knot with two crosses in the fabric with the yarn pulled through them, then (working with the weft of the canvas horizontal) wind the yarn round the gauge from below before forming the next stitch. Cut the loops along the edge of the gauge with a sharp pair of scissors.

To make the edges of the completed canvas secure, oversew the edges with two strands of yarn, working into every hole along the edge of the canvas, then sew flat canvas braid (about 2 inches wide) to the underneath, along the edges, to help the rug keep its shape.

FURTHER READING

KIRSCH, D. & KIRSCH-KORN, J., *Make Your Own Rugs* Batsford

The Rya knot.

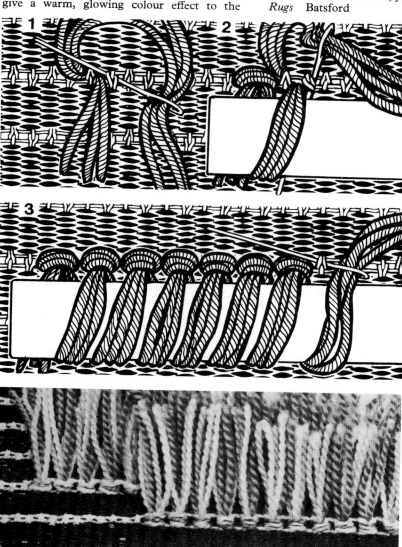

Sand

SAND PICTURES

Sand pictures were introduced into Britain by immigrant craftsmen at the court of George II. Known as 'table deckers', the craftsmen made decorations of coloured sugar, powdered glass, and coloured sand on a cloth tray or board. At the end of the evening, their decorations were swept away. This work was called *marmotinto*. During the 1840s, craftsmen in the Isle of Wight used the naturally-coloured sands that occur there to produce permanent pictures. A painting was roughed out in colour, glue was painted over the whole board, and sand approximating to the colours of the pictures was sifted on. (Coloured sands are available from craft suppliers.)

SAND BOTTLES

These also originated in the Isle of Wight. Narrow bottles are filled with layers of different coloured sand using small amounts at a time, the angle of the sand in the bottle depending on the angle at which the bottle is tilted when the sand is poured in. It is surprising what control one has over the curves and angles made by the different layers, and to what fine limits one can work. When the bottle is as full as possible, press the cork in as far as possible. There must be no gap between the cork and the sand, or when the bottle is turned the right way up, the sand will shift around and the fine detail will be lost.

CARVING WITH SAND

Mixing sand with plaster of Paris produces an interesting material to carve (see the section on Plaster of Paris). Some sandstones are suitable for carving. There is a great variation in the porosity of sandstones, but the harder type is compact and durable, and excellent for sculptural work. The tools required for carving include three chisels: point, claw and flat; a dummy mallet; a rasp and a file for smoothing surfaces, and a riffler (slim curved file) for filing parts that are difficult to reach. The point chisel is used first for large sculptures to remove blocks of stone, and is hit with the mallet at an angle of 45° to the surface. The claw chisel then defines the contours of the sculpture, and the flat chisel smooths away the grooves left by the teeth of the claw chisel; the piece is then filed smooth.

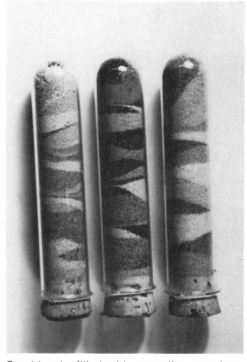

Sand bottle, filled with naturally-occurring coloured sand from the Isle of Wight.

Scraper Board

Scraper (or scratch) board can be bought in a craft shop, but a similar material can be made by painting Indian ink all over a blank white postcard. If the result is patchy, give it a second coat of ink. The black surface is then scratched with a needle, revealing the white underlayer. Home-made board gives a rather furred line, but the proprietary scraper board has a special white coating under the black surface, and the lines scratched on it are very clear, so that one is able to achieve very fine detail. The black is very black and matt, and the white is very white, so it is suitable to use for work that is to be reproduced commercially.

J.L. Hammett Co (USA) supplies Scratchetch Board, on which one can fill the scratched lines with wax crayon or felt marker and wipe the surface clean. This technique resembles the traditional scrimshaw drawings engraved on whalebone objects by American whalers.

Scraperboard drawing of the Thames and Severn Canal by J.K. Ebblewhite.

Screen Printing (Serigraphy)

Although it is supposed that this method was invented by Some-Ya-Yu-Zen in the seventeenth century, it is only in the mid-twentieth century that artists have begun to exploit the technique in any numbers. To transfer an even layer of colour onto either paper or cloth requires a lot of skill, and, in the case of etching, an expensive printing press. The evenness of the print is achieved by scraping viscous ink or dye across a piece of very tightly stretched silk or organdie with a strip of flexible rubber (squeegee). To make the design, parts of the silk are blocked out so that the ink passes through some parts and not others.

Materials and equipment

a frame; organdie (or silk); wax, gum (etc.) to block out parts of the screen; pigment (dye); binder (thickening agent); 2-in. wide sticky brown paper tape; staples and stapler; a squeegee; paper or fabric on which to print.

The frame The frame is made of wood, and there are several ready-made ones available with adjustable sides so that screens of different sizes can be made from the one set. You can make one yourself, but make sure that the corners are rigid. You could use an old picture frame, or an old cardboard box: cut a rectangle out of the bottom and staple a piece of organdie across it. Tape it as well for good measure. A fixed corner frame is the simplest to make. A more useful type of screen frame for someone doing a lot of screen printing is the type that uses half joints secured by a wing nut. If pieces of wood are cut into various lengths, in pairs, then almost any proportion can be made up very quickly, any two lengths being matched by any two others.

The organdie Cut a piece of organdie 2 in. larger all round than the frame itself. Staple

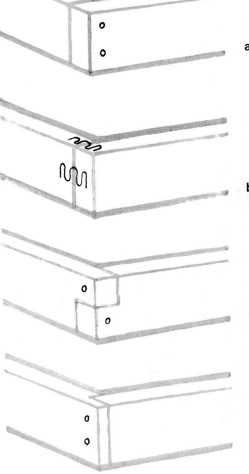

a) A butt joint pinned with a couple of oval nails.
b) A butt joint but instead of nails corrugated dogs (fasteners) are used.
c) A half joint pinned with oval nails.
d) A shoulder joint pinned with oval nails.

this to the sides of the wooden frame, starting in the centre of the side and working a few inches down either side of the centre. Move to the opposite side of the frame, and pulling the organdie as tightly as you can, staple it opposite your first staple. Do not finish either side yet, but do the remaining two sides in the same way. Then work along the sides to the corners, always doing the opposite side to the one just

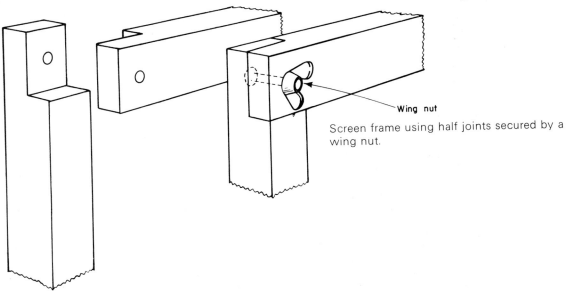

Wing nut

Screen frame using half joints secured by a wing nut.

done. The organdie must be absolutely taut, with no wrinkles anywhere. Besides organdie, experiment with tough nylon lace, or perforated zinc (this would not even require a frame). In America, a wide range of screen fabrics are available: AGB Dacron Screen Cloth, Swiss Organdy, multifilament polyester ('Stencron' polyester), monofilament polyester, and various grades of pure silk.

In America, the screen is not stapled to the frame. It is locked into the underside of the frame by means of a long cord embedded into a groove along all four sides. The cord is pushed into the groove at an even depth with a 'cord applicator'. The underside of the frame is then finished off with a gummed paper tape covering the cord. (Silk screen frames and equipment are available in the USA from Naz-dar, Advance, Speedball and Dick Blick.)

Brown sticky tape This is stuck to the outside of the frame in two strips, one strip being stuck half on the frame (covering the staples or cord) and the other half on the screen. The other strip is wholly on the front. Do this round all four sides. Inside the frame, crease a length of tape and stick it in the corner along the whole length of each side. The gumstrip defines the size and shape of the print, and also holds the pool of pigment/dye before it is squeezed over the screen. If you want to be absolutely certain that no ink seeps through the tape, it can be painted with two coats of shellac.

Pigment (ink/dye) This is always supplied in a concentrated form, and may be diluted. (This does not apply to the fabric dyes sold in craft shops for fabric printing.) The consistency of the dye must stay thick and gelatinous for screen printing, or it will seep along the fibres of the screen and the prints will look smudged. It is diluted and thickened at the same time, with a 'binder'. It is always supplied by the manufacturers of the dyes, and is white and very thick. Into this white paste is stirred the dye/pigment, the amount depending upon the shade required, and the type of dye.

In the absence of 'proper' dyes, make up some wallpaper paste as for wallpapering (half a pack to 3 pints of water), and when the paste has become translucent, add dye. This could be Brusho, or any domestic dye (Dylon), which has been first dissolved in hot water.

The squeegee The squeegee is a strip of stiff rubber held in a wooden strip which is used to squeeze the dye through the organdie. It can be bought ready-made. If you make your own, make sure that you attach a strip of wood so that it overhangs the edge of the screen, otherwise when you let go the squeegee will slide into the ink. A range of squeegees is needed, because the width of the squeegee must fit snugly inside the wooden frame, along the narrow width. The edge of the squeegee must be perfectly flat, otherwise it cannot distribute the ink evenly. Vinyl floor tiles, old rulers and strips of cardboard make suitable substitutes for squeegees.

Covering the screen with organdie.

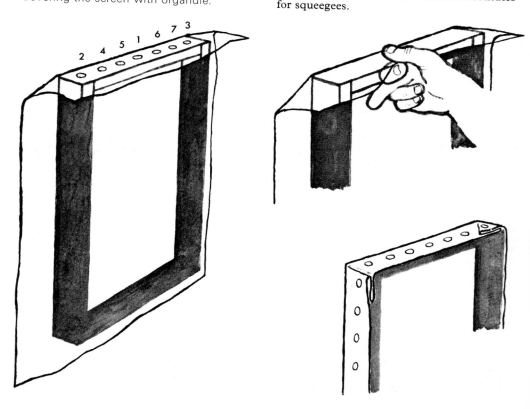

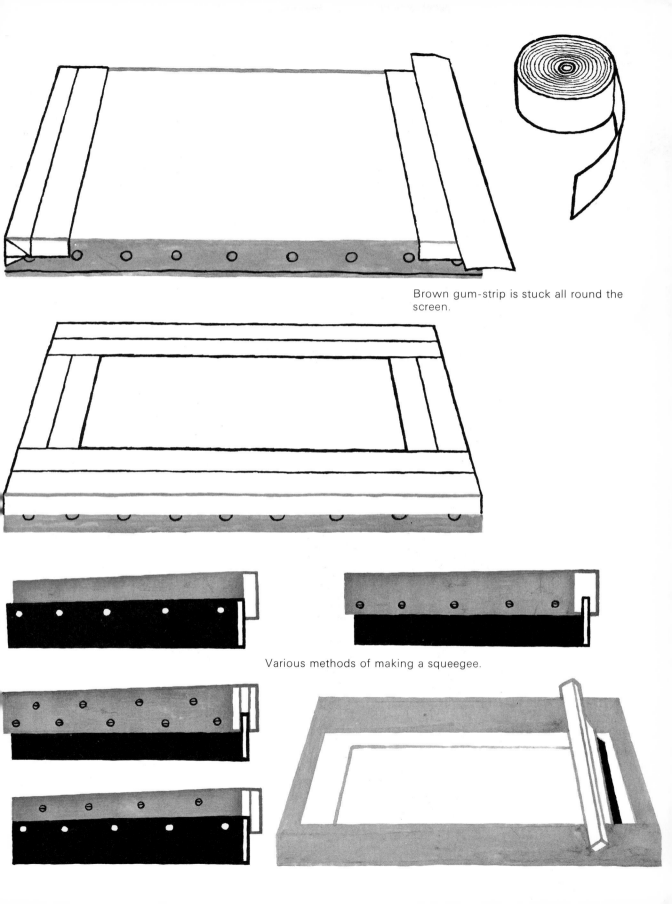

Brown gum-strip is stuck all round the screen.

Various methods of making a squeegee.

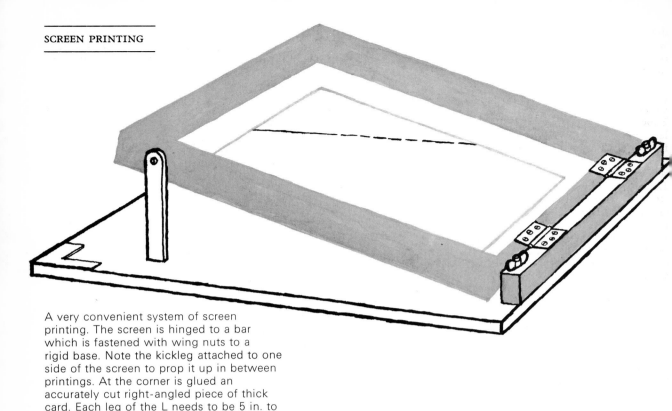

A very convenient system of screen printing. The screen is hinged to a bar which is fastened with wing nuts to a rigid base. Note the kickleg attached to one side of the screen to prop it up in between printings. At the corner is glued an accurately cut right-angled piece of thick card. Each leg of the L needs to be 5 in. to 6 in. long, otherwise they do not really hold the paper firmly.

Another method of propping the screen up — with a strip of wood.

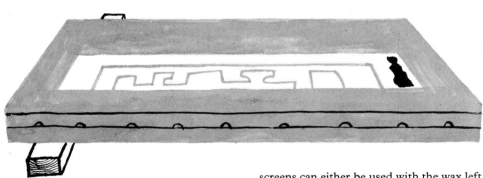

METHODS OF BLOCKING THE SCREEN

Something has to be used to stop the dye going through the organdie and whatever is used has to be applied to the underside of the screen between it and the fabric or paper. This is because if it was on the inside of the frame the squeegee could scrape it off as it was pulled across to take a print. Use a water soluble ink or dye for the following methods.

Wax can be used in various ways to block the screen. It can be melted and painted or dribbled on the screen, or dripped from a lighted candle. A candle can also be used as a crayon and a rubbing made on the organdie instead of on paper. A lot of pressure must be used to get a good thickness of wax onto the organdie. The screens can either be used with the wax left on the organdie, in which case the area covered with wax will appear white on the paper; or the entire screen can be painted over with gelatine/potassium dichromate (see below), and when dry, the wax can be ironed off the organdie, leaving it clear, so that the dye will pass through the areas which were covered by wax. *Gum* can be sponged or dribbled onto the screen to block areas.

Green screen filler (stencil block out) can be spread with a piece of card. Use lacquer filler for water-based inks, and water-soluble filler for oil-based inks.

Cut-film stencils can be applied to the screen by ironing, or adhering fluid.

The pick-up Tear some pieces of absorbent paper (newsprint). Lay them on a table top covered in old newspapers. Place the screen down upon the torn scraps. Load the screen with ink and wipe across the screen. Lift up the screen, and stuck to the underside will be the torn pieces of paper. Remarkable though it may seem, these pieces of paper will stay in position on the screen for many prints until the paper gets too soggy and starts to disintegrate. Experiment with the pick-up technique using lengths of cotton instead of paper; leaves, feathers, pressed flowers, coarse lace, etc.

Transfer lettering pressed onto the inside of the screen can be used to make quick posters. Letraset make reversed letters which can be stuck to the underside of the screen. Letters can also be stuck on with an aerosol fixative, taking care that it does not clog the screen.

Wax stencils for duplicating machines can be used, by drawing onto the stencil with a stylus, or one can type patterns with the letters and symbols of a typewriter. The stencil is picked up as are the torn paper shapes.

Free painting, directly onto the screen, can be done with shellac (button polish), or lacquer, which can be cleaned off afterwards.

POSITIVE PRINTS

The above methods will produce negative prints, i.e. the shapes drawn on the screen are white when printed. Positive prints are made when either stencils are used, or potassium dichromate and gelatine are painted over the screen and the wax drawing ironed off. Add $\frac{1}{2}$ pint of water to 2 heaped tsps of granulated gelatine, and heat in a double boiler, but do not boil. When the gelatine has dissolved, add 1 level tsp of potassium dichromate, and use while still warm. This mixture is a photo-sensitive substance, which is insoluble in water once it is dry and has been exposed to light, which changes it to an amber colour. The wax drawing is removed by laying the screen on old newspapers, laying more on the inside of the screen, and ironing the paper with a warm iron. The wax will melt and be absorbed into the newspaper, leaving the screen 'open'.

Tusche resist Tusche (grease suspended in liquid) is painted on the organdie and allowed to dry. A 50/50 water and glue (Le Page's All-Purpose Glue) solution is painted over the whole screen, and allowed to dry. A solvent (turpentine) for the Tusche is then washed over the screen, which leaves it open where the Tusche drawing was.

Liquid latex solution (E-Z Mask) can also be painted onto the screen with a brush. After the glue resist is applied and dry, the latex is peeled away.

Proprietary stencils (Profilm, etc)

These are sold in sheets, made in two layers; a backing paper or plastic, and a layer of lacquer/shellac. The sheet is laid over the design, and traced through. With a sharp craft knife, the pattern is cut into the lacquer, but not through into the backing. The parts to be printed are then carefully peeled off the backing sheet, and the whole sheet placed lacquer-side to the organdie. Place some newspaper on the inside of the screen and, if using Profilm (British), iron the whole area. This fuses the lacquer to the organdie. The transparent backing is then peeled off. This method produces very crisp edges to a design.

There are many types of cut-film stencils available in the United States: Nu-Film, Pro-film, standard hand-cut films, Ulano films, and presensitized photographic films. These are all applied with an adhering fluid rather than by ironing.

TAKING A PRINT

Take your first one or two prints on some old newspapers. The organdie absorbs quite a lot of dye, and if you take a few trial prints, you will find out how much dye or ink you need to pour out for one print. You need enough dye to make a good print in one movement of the squeegee from one side to the other but not so much that the screen is swimming in dye. You must not stop half-way across the screen and add more dye: it makes a messy print. To begin with you might need a spare pair of hands to hold the screen steady on the paper or cloth while you, holding the squeegee at an angle of 45°, pull the line of dye across the screen. Try and pour a line of dye as evenly as possible at the right-hand end of the screen on the part which is covered by gumstrip on the other side. The perfect print is made in one movement across the screen with the right amount of dye so that there is the same intensity of colour at both ends of the print. A screen with a lot of the organdie blocked out will require less dye than the same screen with only a little blocked out.

Prints using two or more colours

Accurate registration is essential when doing two or more colours. It is also advisable to use a screen of the same size. Make sure that the first prints are absolutely dry before you attempt a second print.

MAKING A SCREEN PHOTOGRAPHICALLY

A silk (or organdie) screen is used for this process, which relies on the fact that potassium dichromate and gelatine form a substance which, after exposure to light, becomes in-soluble in water. Coat the screen with gelatine; let the gelatine dry completely. Very quickly, coat the screen with potassium dichromate solution, and leave in a dark room for 12 hrs.

The design must be completely opaque and the best material for this is black poster paint. Indian ink is not sufficiently opaque. The paper on which the design is drawn must be transparent, so tracing paper should be used. Stack the screen with a board underneath the screen and fitting it exactly. The design is stuck with tape to a piece of plate glass (or heavy window glass), and turned upside down onto the organdie screen, so that the design is between the organdie and the glass. The board underneath the screen must be pressed hard against the organdie. The whole pile is then placed in some strong light, either strong sunlight, or strong artificial light.

The light goes through the transparent parts of the design, hardening the gelatine, but has no effect on the gelatine protected from the light by the poster paint design. The hardening

Taking a print.

process takes about 10 minutes in bright daylight, and 2 hours in dull daylight. Do not put the screen in very bright direct sunlight as this can cause the screen to split. When the colour of the gelatine changes from yellow to brown the process is complete. Lift off the glass, and take the screen to a sink where it can be washed in warm water. This washes away the gelatine from those areas which were covered by the design, and leaves the organdie open.

In the United States there are two methods of making a screen print photographically. The *direct method* uses emulsion and ammonium dichromate. Dichromate emulsions are ready-made emulsions (like Naz-dar's Indicote and Advance's Polycop) which are mixed with ammonium dichromate (supplied in crystal form). Azocol R Direct Emulsion and Sensitizer, made by Colonial of East Rutherford,

NJ, is a nondichromatic sensitized emulsion which requires more light for exposure, but has the advantage of lasting for several weeks. Rockland Superfast Emulsion SC 12 contains silver nitrate, and has to be used in a dark-room.

The *indirect method* consists of using a pre-sensitized film made by Advance Process Supply Co, Naz-dar Co, Ulano, and other major companies. These films are cheaper and easier to use than emulsions, and require only one developer.

MAKING A SCREEN FROM A PHOTOGRAPHIC NEGATIVE

This requires Kodalith translucent printing paper. With an enlarger, project the negative onto the Kodalith paper, and develop it. The Kodalith print is then used in exactly the same way as the poster paint design on tracing paper.

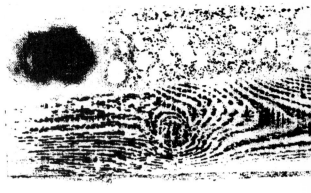

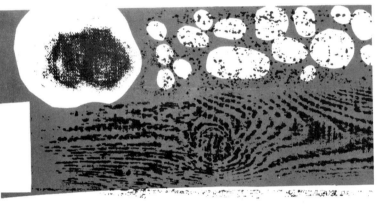

A combination print in two parts. Top right
shows a rubbing which was made directly
onto the organdie of the screen, which was
then coated with gelatine and potassium
dichromate. When dry, the wax was
removed by ironing between sheets of
newspaper. Top left is a paper print,
and at the bottom is the paper print with a
printing of the rubbing superimposed.

A multi-media print.

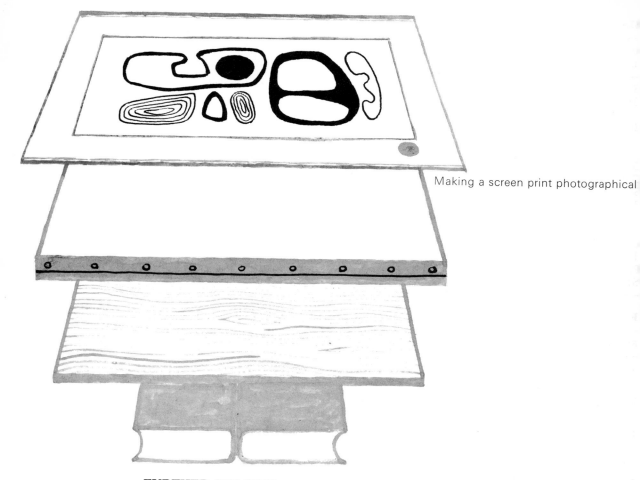

Making a screen print photographical

FURTHER READING

Hand Printed Fabrics Leisurecraft

KINSEY, A., *Introducing Screen Printing* Batsford

ROSS, J. & ROMANO, C., *The Complete Printmaker* The Free Press

TURNER, S., *Screen Printing Techniques* Batsford

SEARLE, V. AND CLAYSON, R., *Screen Printing on Fabric* Studio Vista

WILCOX, J., *Printed Rag Toys* Batsford

EQUIPMENT FOR SCREEN PRINTING

FRAMES	SCREENS	SQUEEGEE	BRITISH DYES
Ready-made	Silk	Ready-made	Printex
Home-made (tradition)	Organdie	Home-made (traditional)	Procion
Corners made rigid by Corrugated dogs	Net/Lace	Ruler	Tinolite
	Perforated zinc (*USA*)	Vinyl tile	Helizarin
Half joint, glued and pinned	AGB Dacron Screen Cloth	Strip of cardboard	Polyprint
Shoulder joint	Swiss Organdy		Binder plus Brusho, dye
Half joint, fixed with wing nuts	Stencron (multi-filament polyester)		Polycell plus Brusho, dye
Butt joint, glued and pinned	Monofilament polyester		USA INKS
Old picture frame	Pure silk		Regular inks
Cardboard box (with window cut in base)	Thrift silk		Fluorescent inks
Piece of card (with window cut out)	Stainless steel 14XX mesh (with photographic film)		Textile inks
			Speedball Acrylic Inks

BLOCKING THE SCREEN

SUBSTANCES FOR BLOCKING THE SCREEN	MIXED WITH, OR SOLUBLE IN	SOLUBLE WHEN DRY, IN	BRUSHES, SCREENS, CLEANED IN
Gelatine	Warm water	Warm water	Warm water
Gelatine plus potass. dichromate	—	Insoluble	—
Emulsion plus ammonium dichromate			
Glue	Hot water	Hot water	Hot water
Gum arabic	Warm water	Insoluble	Warm water
Shellac	Alcohol	Alcohol	Alcohol
Paraffin wax	—	White (mineral) spirits Turpentine	White (mineral) spirits Turpentine
Lacquer/cellulose	Special thinner	—	Special thinner
Tusche	Special thinner	—	Special thinner
Profilm (shellac) Selectasine (lacquer)	(As above for shellac and lacquer)		

RESIST ON THE SCREEN

RESIST ON THE SCREEN	APPROPRIATE PRINTING INK/DYE
Water-soluble glue	Oil base, plastic
Lacquer film stencil	Oil base, water base, dyes plus binder
Photographic stencil	Oil base, any water free ink
Paper pick up	Oil base, binder plus dye, wheat or wallpaper paste (Polycell) plus dye and ink
Shellac, Lacquer	Water base

POSITIVE PRINTS

DRAWING MADE IN	SCREEN AND DRAWING COVERED IN	DRAWING REMOVED BY
Paraffin wax	Gelatine plus potassium dichromate Plastic emulsion paint	A warm iron Washing in warm water
Tusche	50/50 Water glue mixture	Special solvent (Turpentine)
Liquid Latex Solution	50/50 Water glue mixture	Peeling
Glue	Gelatine plus potassium dichromate	Hot water
Proprietary stencils: Profilm, Selectasine	—	Stencil film solvent

NEGATIVE PRINTS

SUBSTANCE	INK/DYE	DRAWING REMOVED BY
Wax	Polycell plus Brusho, dye Binder plus pigment, dye	Ironing off
Paper/gumstrip	Polycell plus Brusho, dye Binder plus pigment, dye	Peeling off
Gum/glue/green filler	Polycell plus Brusho, dye Binder plus pigment, dye	Hot water

All dyes can be made suitable for screen printing by adding a suitable binder.

PROCESSES USED TO ACHIEVE PARTICULAR QUALITIES

HARD EDGE	LINE	TEXTURE (VISUAL)	AREAS
Proprietary stencil (Profilm) Cut paper, gum strip (pick-up) Letraset Wax duplicating stencils	Photographic screen (from a drawing) Pick up of threads *Draw* with: Glue, tusche, wax, direct onto organdie Tjanting tool Duplicating stencil Wax screen all over, draw into it with soldering iron	Wax rubbing direct onto the organdie Rubber solution partly removed Green filler, spread with card Used duplicating stencil Gum, applied with sponge Wax dribbled in multi-directions	Selectasine, Profilm Gum strip Paper pick up Shellac Lacquer Glue
DIRECT IMAGE Photographic screen a) Drawings b) Photographs c) Photograms Pick up of natural objects: leaves, feathers, ferns, grasses, etc., or lace, nets, etc.			

Seed Collage

Seed collage is an effective way of developing perceptual subtlety. The sorting out and arranging of the seeds into various colours and shapes rapidly develops the skill of differentiation, and is therefore a useful learning activity for children. Like mosaic, the units cover the whole of the surface area. Collect as many different types of seeds as possible (e.g. beans, nuts, rice, grass seeds, poppy seed cases), and divide them into categories (round, elliptical, spherical, flat-sided, dull, shiny). Organize them into patterns, contrasting one area of texture with another.

Stick the patterns down onto cardboard, hardboard or insulating board with Dufix glue (which dries transparent) or Evostik Resin 'W'

Here the seeds are used to make a formalized animal.

(Elmer's Glue-All).

When all the seeds have been stuck down varnish the whole picture with Permashine (a polyurethane varnish) to protect it from damp and dust. This also acts as an extra glue, and prevents fading.

Since sticking seeds down is painstaking work, a 12-in. square board is the largest that should be attempted by a child (and a 5-in. square for an infant). A drawing can be made on the board first with a soft pencil to act as a guideline. Placing the seeds is made easier by picking them up with the point of a pencil which has been dipped in glue. Plenty of glue is dabbed onto the back of the seed with a spatula, and when the seed is pressed down onto the board, the pencil comes away easily from the seed.

Note the use of strong tone contrast in this detail, and the use of dull and shiny surfaces.

FURTHER READING

SIMMS, C. & G., *Introducing Seed Collage* Batsford

Shell Work

Delight in the sight and feel of shells is one of the earliest pleasures in the field of natural history. Even primitive man at the end of the Ice Age found delight in shells, for the remains of numerous shells have been found in the limestone caverns of France and Belgium, with holes pierced in them so that they could be fastened to clothing or strung to make a neck-lace. As a basis for decoration, shells have a very long history. Used by the Egyptians and even more by the Minoans as a motif on pottery, they were also used in Crete, Greece, and Rome.

One particular shell, *Murex trunculus*, was specially prized by the Greeks and Romans, because it was from this shell that they obtained the dye known as Tyrian purple. Small shells were crushed (the animals from the larger shells being taken out by hand) and then boiled for 10 days. The colour was a very deep red, and the special quality of the dye was its extra-ordinary fastness: according to Plutarch, the Greeks found in the Persian Royal treasury purple cloth which after 200 years was still a rich purple colour. A similar dye was known in England and Ireland, extracted from the shell *Nucella lapillus*, the common dog periwinkle. The colour was much lighter than the Tyrian purple, and used mainly for staining vellum to set off the gold illuminated capitals of the monks' manuscripts.

PREPARING THE SHELLS

Bleaching

Some small shells bought commercially have already been bleached. Those that have not, both white and coloured ones, and those that you have collected will be much improved if they are soaked in a solution of chlorine bleach. A one-minute soak is enough for thin shells; heavier and larger shells can be left longer until the blemishes disappear. This may take any-thing from 5 minutes to half an hour, so examine them often. After bleaching, wash them thoroughly.

Oiling

To enhance the brightness of both white and coloured shells, rub each one with 2 parts of baby oil to 1 part of lighter fluid. Apply with an artist's camel-hair brush, so as to get into all the crevices. The lighter fluid helps the oil to penetrate the shell, removes grease and then evaporates (apply only the thinnest film, though).

Removing the skin

The skin, or periostracum, can usually be removed with emery cloth, but if it is very tough then stronger measures must be taken. Extreme care must be taken when using the following method; acid can eat holes in metal pans and clothing, and cause severe burns on the skin, so *take care*. First, protect the inner side of the shell by painting paraffin (kerosene) on it. Then use a glass bowl to hold the acid. For medium-size shells, use 4 oz muriatic acid diluted in 1 gallon of water. Small shells are easier to handle if they are placed in a bag. Lay a square of cheesecloth (or similar thin cotton) on the table. Place the paraffin coated shells in the centre of the cloth. Pick up each corner of the cloth and tie with string. Hold onto the string and put the bag in the acid/water for a few seconds. Take out, rinse in cold water, then wash in warm soapy water.

If the periostracum is very thick, one can use chloride of lime. Make a paste with the lime and water, and apply to the shells with a toothbrush. Several hours may be needed before the skin has disappeared, but check frequently, because if it is left too long, the paste will blemish the surface of the shell. When the skin has dissolved, wash thoroughly in warm soapy water, and rinse carefully.

Sorting the shells

When the shells have been cleaned, bleached and oiled they are now ready for sorting. They can be sorted for colour, shape, and size. A very useful container for keeping the sorted shells is one made by Airfix for handymen. It is most important to sort the shells so that when one is making a picture one does not have to stop in the middle and search for 10 minutes to find a shell of the right colour or shape. Discard any shells that are chipped or blemished.

OUTDOOR MOSAICS

The shells are stuck onto a base known as the grout. This can be made using one of three recipes.

First recipe 2 parts of cement; 3 parts of fine white sand; 1 part of slaked lime (the lime makes the cement harden faster).

Second recipe one-third lime; two-thirds cement (by weight). The above is an all-white mixture.

Third recipe 2 parts fine white sand; 2 parts plasterer's lime; 1 part light cement.

Mix all ingredients dry, and add enough water to make a putty-like mix. Add water to a small amount at a time. The shells are pressed into the wet mix rounded side down. If the mosaic is being done indoors, then the shells can be pressed in either way down.

TABLE TOP

Unfinished tables designed to have tiles fitted in are a splendid base. If a table is made specially, it is recommended that a plywood base $\frac{3}{4}$ in. thick be used. Seal the plywood with a waterproofing sealant, and before it dries, sprinkle on it birdcage gravel or coarse sand. This provides a better bond between the mortar and the wood. Make the mortar bed $\frac{3}{8}$ in. thick and wait 2–2$\frac{1}{2}$ hours before setting in the shells. Be sure to make the top level. This can be done by gently pressing a sheet of hardboard the same size as the table gently on the top.

WALL MOSAIC

A shadow box is a picture frame, usually either square or octagonal, with deep sides, to accommodate the depth of the shells. The inside of the frame can be either painted (traditionally pale blue) or covered in velvet. A large variety of small shells, colourful ones, and some larger ones are needed. Use compasses, or cups, plates, etc., to draw the circles and parts of circles, for traditionally the designs are abstract and geometrical. Draw the design onto a piece of paper, then transfer it to a piece of good-quality toned paper with a tracing wheel and carbon paper. Glue the toned paper with the carbon design on it onto the back of the shadow box. All is now ready for filling in the spaces with the shells.

SHELL FLOWERS
Materials

cottonwool (cotton swabs); florists' wire; florists' tape; PVA (white) glue; poppy seed, peppercorns, etc.; jam jar; scraps of polythene (polyethylene); rubber bands; toothpicks, tweezers.

Method

Choose shells in as many different sizes and shapes and colours as you can find. The more variety, the more scope for invention. Cover the top of the jam jar with the polythene, securing it with a strong rubber band, leaving a slight hollow in the surface. The flowers are constructed on this, the polythene supporting the shape as it dries. The flower can be removed quite easily when it is dry because PVA does not stick to polythene. Take a small pull of cottonwool, and soak in PVA. Put this in the centre of the polythene over the jar. Into this press the shells arranging them in a circle, overlapping the 'petals' as you go.

The colouring of shells is very delicate, and the subtlety will be quite lost if a highly decorated or stridently coloured vase is used as a container in which to arrange the 'bouquet'. A sea shell, piece of driftwood, or alabaster vase compliment an arrangement of shells. In using a large shell as the container, choose one that is not strongly marked. Level the shell so that it is stable, gluing two, three or four small shells to the underneath of the shell to prevent it from rocking.

Do not place the bouquet in strong sunlight the colours will fade in a very short time if you do. If it has become dusty, the whole bouquet can be turned upside down and swished around in warm soapy water. Rinse in fresh clear water and leave to dry. If any white spots appear on the shells when they are dry, apply a little baby oil and lighter fluid with a toothpick wrapped in cottonwool to the white spots

The back of the flower showing the cotton wool base. There will be a small piece of cotton wool showing in the centre at the front.

If you have some tiny shells, these can be clustered in the centre. If it is too small for shells you could use peppercorns, poppy seed, etc. Leave the flower nestling in the polythene overnight to support the petals while they dry. To make the stems, coil some millinery wire into a spiral, apply some PVA to it and press the back of the flower to it. Leave to dry.

Victorian articles made from shells. The bottom shells are a needle case; the two shells open out like a book; the 'leaves' are made of fine flannel, in which the needles are kept. The top article is a pin cushion. The two shells are glued to the covering of the wool stuffing with which the shells are filled.

The angle of the wire can be adjusted when the bouquet is arranged.

Arrangement of shells, most of which were attached so that the inside of the shell shows.

Shell flowers wired to stems, and arranged in a three-dimensional table decoration.

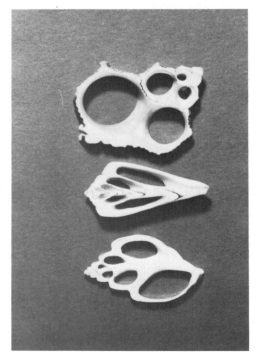

Sections cut through shells.

Silhouettes

The name first appeared in 1798, and was used to describe the paper-cut profiles which were the hobby of an unpopular French Finance Minister, Etienne de Silhouette. Paper-cut profiles had been practised in England for the previous 40 years or more, under the name of shades or profiles. A shade is the shape of a person, building, animal, etc., which is recognizable solely by the outline, the shape itself being traditionally solid black, and giving no clue within the shape to the character of the object presented.

Towards the end of the nineteenth century there was a strong comic element in the work of the silhouettist, exemplified by the work of Phil May and other *Punch* cartoonists. Although there were some full-length profiles made in the eighteenth and early nineteenth centuries, most were profile busts. Profiles were sold framed from the very beginning, and the frames were almost invariably oval, the largest being 7 in. by 5½ in. The eighteenth-century profiles were made using various materials and media. They were painted in black paper, ivory, composition, and under glass: sometimes colour was added, but the face itself was always black, as was the other

Silhouette cut by Augustine Edouart.

n distinguishing feature, be it hat, hair, etc.
he craze for profiles spread to pottery
oration: the potteries at Meissen, Sèvres,
Royal Copenhagen porcelain all used them
ome time as did Worcester in England. A
ous 130-piece dinner service was com-
sion from the Coalport factory by J.J.
erstein (whose bequest of paintings formed
basis of the National Gallery). The
ouettes are full length, the many different
ifs are of a mother in Regency clothes

playing with one, two or three small children.
The artist is unknown. Very similar in style are
some of Arthur Rackham's book illustrations,
which also use pure silhouette. Wedgwood was
also producing portrait plaques, and the
fashion for Bois Durci (see section) followed in
this tradition.

The methods of taking the profiles are either
straightforward observation of the sitter and
free-hand cutting, or using a candle to cast a
shadow onto a piece of paper attached to a wall

339

and tracing round it. This would then be reduced to a miniature size by means of a pantograph and either cut out or traced round and filled in with black paint.

FURTHER READING

VON BOEHM, M., *Miniatures & Silhouettes* Dent

JACKSON, E.N., *The History of the Silhouette*
STODDART, B., *Paper Cutting* Batsford

Silhouette used to decorate an alphabet used in printing at the turn of the century.

Skeleton Leaves

The skeleton of a leaf is the tough structure of veins which remains when the soft cell-structure is removed. This happens naturally when leaves drop off the trees in the autumn, but the process can be speeded up, and can be applied to delicate leaves which totally disintegrate when left to rot naturally. The delicate tracery of veining can be used in collage, with other dried leaves and flowers, or set in resin.

FIRST METHOD
Materials

half a dozen cabbage leaves, plus the perfect leaves you wish to treat; a saucepan; a bucket; water.

Method

Bring the cabbage leaves to the boil, then simmer for half an hour. Strain. Put the liquid into a bucket and into this liquid put the fresh leaves to be skeletonized. Cabbage water is very smelly, so put the bucket with the leaves in it as far away from the house as possible, because the leaves have to be left soaking in the water for 10 days. Then turn them over in the liquid *very* carefully. They are very fragile, so great care must be taken. When the fleshy part of the leaves has become really soft, the leaves are lifted out into a bowl of clean water. With a soft artist's brush (a sable is best) carefully brush the fleshy part away from the veins. Lift and place them, without overlapping, on a piece of clean blotting paper. Place another sheet of blotting paper on top. If there is no blotting paper available, they can be put between the pages of an old telephone directory. Put some heavy books on top. In a few days they will be quite dry and ready for use in a picture.

SECOND METHOD
Materials

2 pints water; 2 dessertspoons washing soda; a saucepan; a bowl.

Method

Heat the water and washing soda until almost boiling. Remove from the heat. Soak the fresh leaves in the liquid for about an hour. Remove leaves from the liquid and proceed as for the first method.

COLOURING THE SKELETONS

When the leaves are dry, they are a brown colour. They can be bleached by immersing them in a very dilute solution of bleach and water. They can be coloured with food colouring once they have been bleached, but subtle colours are more in harmony with the delicacy of the skeleton leaf than the strident colours of the food colouring straight out of the bottle: so mix up a small quantity in a wine-glass of two or more colours, and when satisfied with the colour apply it to the leaf with the sable brush, or a small pad of cottonwool.

Slides made from Natural Objects

To do this you will need to buy some transparency holders from a photographic shop. These are made of two sheets of glass held together with a plastic frame for 35 mm film. Any small objects, parts of feathers, seeds, grasses, can be held between the two sheets of glass and when projected onto a screen the image seems to acquire a new identity. A small drop of oil and coloured ink can also be trapped between the two sheets of glass, which are taped firmly together. When this is projected, the heat from the bulb will cause the oil to move between the sheets of glass, and so produce a coloured moving image on the screen. This sort of projection can be used as a basis for designing.

Slides and filmstrips are also available (J.L. Hammett Co, New York: DIY Slide Making Kit and DIY Filmstrip Kit) on which you can draw directly with coloured pencils, for immediate projection.

Splatter Work

This craft became very popular in Victorian times, when it was used to take 'impressions' of collections of plants and seaweeds that had become part of the summertime holiday activity of Victorian ladies. The plant is lightly pinned onto a piece of paper with dressmaking pins, to keep it as close as possible to the paper while the splattering is done. A more effective method would be to lightly spray it with some spray adhesive which does not have immediate adhesion, so that when the splattering is complete the plant can easily be lifted off. It is easier to splatter if the paper is propped up on the table so that it is vertical. If the paper is flat on the table, it is difficult to avoid getting large drops of colour falling on it. The object of the craft is to produce a fine even distribution of the tiniest drops of colour on the paper. To do it, use either an old toothbrush, nailbrush, or a stencil brush. The more bristles per square inch, the finer the spray. Put some ink, or very dilute water paint, onto a felt or polythene foam pad in a saucer, and press the brush into it. Be careful not to take up too much ink at a time, it will only result in large droplets on the work. Hold the brush a few inches away from the paper and scratch at the ends of the bristles with a finger. As you do so a fine spray of ink will get flicked off the bristles. Continue in this way until there is a dark enough deposit of spray on the paper. It needs to be darkest at the edge of the object. (Really this is another method of stencilling.) Although it is possible to use fresh plants it is easier if you use pressed ones, because they are already flat. This technique was used between 1900 and 1920 to try and revive the declining Scottish souvenir woodware industry, ferns being the most popular decorative motif.

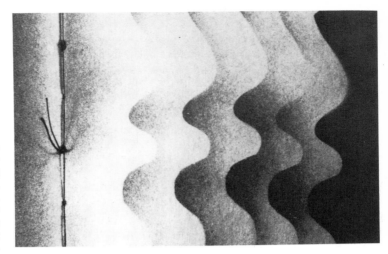

An example of repeated spraying. The initial shape is seen at the extreme right of the page, and the first position was close to the stitching in the centre of the book. It was sprayed, moved along a little, resprayed, moved along and so on across the page.

These dried plants were held down to the paper with Blu-Tack (Plasti-Tack). They must be secured if you use an air-brush or aerosol paint because otherwise they blow away as soon as you begin.

A leaf which had been covered with paint while doing splatter work was carefully pressed painted side down to leave this impression.

Sprang

The leading exponent of sprang weaving in Britain is Peter Collingwood. The pattern is the result of a change in direction of the warps. This is done at the point of the inclusion in the warp of a metal rod, which also weights the work and so makes it hang taut.

Macrogauze 29 by Peter Collingwood (1969).

FURTHER READING

COLLINGWOOD, P., *Sprang* Faber & Faber

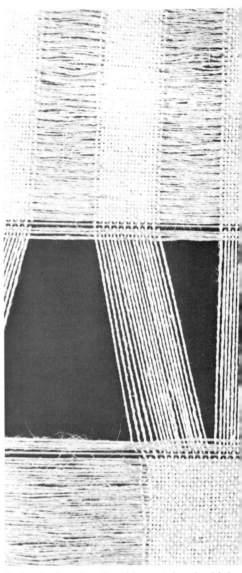

A detail showing the thin metal rod which has been woven into the hanging.

Stencilling

Stencils are a very simple method of making repeats of a given shape with the minimum of equipment. Stencilling was used to decorate floor coverings of heavy cotton sailcloth in America in the early 1800s, and sometimes it was done directly onto the floor. Some of these patterns can be seen in the paintings of eighteenth-century American portrait painters like Stuart, Savage, and Earl. Stencilled bed spreads, tablecloths, and bed hangings were in everyday use in America between 1820 and 1850. Walls would also be stencilled either in a border pattern, or more rarely, as an all-over pattern. Over the mantelpiece, the itinerant decorator might well stencil his *pièce de résistance*, which would be representational

The designs would spread from village to village as the itinerant decorator moved around. Stencils on walls were never shaded as they were on furniture or in theorem painting.

Equipment

stencils: stencil paper (2 weights), or purchased stencils (these can be of paper, rigid plastic or metal); knife: Exacto or similar for cutting stencil paper; piece of Formica or wood on which to cut the paper; tools for applying paint or dye; stencil brush; aerosol spray; old toothbrush; piece of sponge.

Material for stencilling on

paper; cloth; leather; wood; enamel blanks (see Enamelling); light-sensitive paper (see Photograms and glass prints); clay (see Pottery).

Paint

This will vary with the surface being stencilled. For paper use poster paint, gouache, crayon, aerosol. For fabric use fabric dye. For leather and wood use acrylic paint.

The stencil

The stencil needs to be cut from some sort of waterproof material, otherwise the edges will eventually become wet and produce a splodgy print. Special stencil papers are available in two thicknesses. If using card, paint two coats of PVA (white) glue on both sides to waterproof it. Thick clear acetate film, or rigid clear plastic, is possibly the best when experience has been gained, but it is difficult to cut for a beginner. Its main advantage is when using more than one stencil to make a design, because being clear, it is easy to get exact registration.

METHOD

The background onto which you are to stencil must be absolutely flat and rigid. If working on cotton fabric, pin it onto a drawing board, first covering the board with either blotting paper or a piece of old clean ironed cloth, stretching this taut. This is to absorb any excess dye that might seep through (especially important if working on a satin weave, because this is naturally prone to dye 'creep'). The stencil is placed firmly in position, so that it cannot move when the paint or dye is rubbed or stencilled through. It can be secured by using double-sided adhesive paper tabs or strips. The simplest method of applying the paint or dye is with an aerosol, a toothbrush (see ink), or an airbrush.

Traditionally, a stencil brush was used, and still can be. A piece of plastic sponge dipped in the paint is also very effective (though wear a thin plastic glove while doing it). If using bronze powders wrap a piece of velvet round your forefinger, dip in the powder, and gently rub onto the wood, etc. This must first be varnished and almost dry before the bronze powders are applied. The degree of dryness is important: not dry enough and the stencil will stick, too dry and the bronze powder will not.

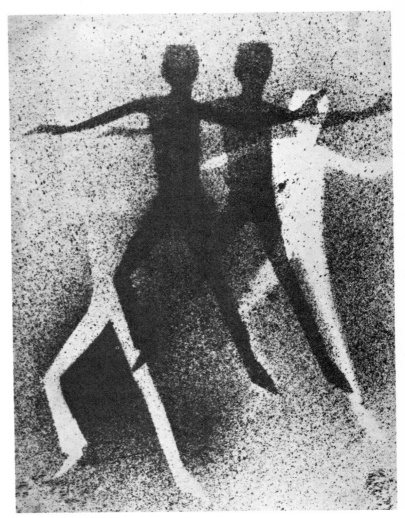

If care is taken in cutting out the shape, the cut out piece can be used also to form a positive/negative image. Here, the inked stencil produced the two dark images, and the cut out piece, with ink splattered over it, produced the two light images.

No double-sided tape is needed to hold the stencil steady, the varnish itself will do that. When the bronze powdering is completed, blow all the excess off. Then lift off the stencil.

When using a sponge or brush, keep them as dry as possible. If too much paint is used, it will seep under the stencil, and a blotchy edge will result. Take care when lifting off the stencil. It must be lifted straight up, do not slide it off or it will smudge the print.

When using a stencil in two parts, stick two lengths of cellophane tape at right angles to each other – strips 4 in. or 5 in. long will be enough. Place the corner of the stencil in the corner made by the tape. Use acrylic paints, not oil paints because they dry too slowly. With fabric, use a hair dryer to speed up the drying of the dye. If you wish to do an

343

all-over pattern with the stencils, or many copies, before you start take two or three rubbings with a black wax crayon, taking care to make rubbings of the edges as well. When the first stencil is worn out, lay the rubbing on some stencil paper, clip the two together with paper clips, and cut your copy.

Clean the stencils after use and between prints by wiping with a rag and clean water. Dry carefully before using again. Wash out with care whatever tool was used to apply the ink, dye or paint at the end of a printing session.

Metal stencils.

Stencils made from mulberry paper said to be part of a shipment from Japan to decorate the clothes for the first London production of the Gilbert and Sullivan opera, *The Mikado*.

Commercial stencils.

Stencilled antique New England trays.

STENCILLING

STENCILS MADE FROM	APPLIED TO	COLOUR APPLIED WITH	USE
Metal	Cloth: Cotton	Stencil brush	Dye
Prepared paper	Velvet	Airbrush	Ink
Celluloid	Satin	Old toothbrush	French enamels
Thin card	Wood	Squeegee	Acrylic paint
Natural objects:	Plaster	Pad of velvet	Poster paint
ferns, feathers, etc.	Tin	Aerosol paint	Smoke
Man-made objects:	Stone	Sponge	Aerosol paint
scissors, paperclips,	Eggshell		Leather dyes
lace, net, paper	Screens (printing)		
doilies, paper	Leather		
cut-outs	Paper		
	Card		
	Fibreglass		

Straw Work

This craft was introduced into Britain by French prisoners-of-war (1765 to 1815). A whole gallery in the Peterborough Museum is devoted to the work of these craftsmen. The straw was split, opened up, cut and glued onto boxes of various sorts, e.g. tea caddies, trinket boxes, silk holders, book covers, etc. The work was extremely fine, and is somewhat like Tunbridge Ware in delicacy, but it has a shimmer and glint which is very attractive and not found in Tunbridge Ware. The straw was often dyed, in pinks and greens, and stuck all over the surface either in the manner of marquetry, with the pieces of straw shaped, or as mosaic. The decorations were geometric, floral and pictorial.

PREPARING THE STRAW

Ideally the straw (the stems of oats, barley, rye, wheat, and bearded wheat) should be picked two weeks before it is ripe for harvesting by the farmer. If it is harvest ripe, the grain of the wheat will fall out when it is being plaited, and you will end up with a very moth-eaten looking straw dolly or favour. Most farmers will be pleased to give or sell you straw: all you need is a small bundle from the edge of the field, but do ask first. Use a pair of shears, and cut it close to the ground. The best sort has a long stalk, and is fat, i.e. has a large hole up the middle. Pull off the outer leaf sheath and the straw is ready to use. Select the most perfect heads of bearded wheat or barley or wheat, and put on one side. Chop the heads off the others just under the head or under the first joint below the head. This is the straw that will be used for straw marquetry, stars, pendants, and favours.

If you have to store it before using it, spread it out on some newspapers and put it in the sun to dry, or in a warm room for two or three days. When it is dry, hang it up in an airy dry place, out of reach of mice and birds. It is important to dry it out, because it can grow mould if it is damp. When ready to use it, soak in warm water for half an hour or so, and then wrap it up in a towel and leave it there for another half hour. Leave it wrapped up in the towel because straw for corn dollies and the like is worked damp.

Art straws (made of thick paper) bought from craft shops may also be used for straw work.

METHOD

For marquetry, on eggs, wood, etc., the straw is split lengthwise, and opened out. With the shiny side uppermost, iron it flat with a warm iron. The straw is then like a ribbon, and can either be used as the wooden strips the Finnish farmers used to make their decorations, or cut up into squares or diamond shapes, and glued down onto the chosen surface with UHU (DuPont's Duco Cement). (See the sections on Egg decorating and Corn dollies.)

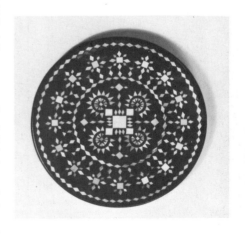

Contemporary Russian straw work plate.

a   b   c   d   e   f

An antique piece of straw work, made on a wooden box. The straw has been coloured and cut to particular shapes.

Contemporary Russian straw work plate. The base is painted black to make the straw work twinkle. Because the straw has a marked grain, the angle at which it is glued on is very important.

Types of corn used to make corn dollies and straw work.
a) Oats.
b) Bearded wheat.
c) Wheat.
d) Rye.
e) Barley.
f) Six-row barley.

Modern Chinese dyed and cut straw work. The actual size is 3 in. by 1½ in.

Paper straws

Paper craft straws are an excellent medium for young children. They are obtainable in bulk from Artstraws Ltd, Bristol, or J.L. Hammett Co, New York. They can be twisted, plaited and tied with thread to form simple animal figures, or woven into boxes and baskets. They can also be cut and glued to form more complex objects, then painted or sprayed.

Paper straws can be used to make fans, mats, mobiles, god's eyes (qv), decorative plaques, and corn dollies (qv).

FURTHER READING

COKER, A., *The Craft of Straw Decoration* Dryad Press

SANDFORD, L., *Straw Work and Corn Dollies* Batsford

String Pictures

Begin by making a large collection of various types of string: sisal, manilla, jute, cotton, linen, hemp, coir, paper string, nylon/terylene, polypropylene, cellophane, wool, and other animal fibres. Each of these have distinctive qualities which make them different from other fibres; explore these by teasing out the fibres, knotting, twisting, weaving. They all have a different texture or 'feel'.

The best glue is PVA (white) glue. It will stick almost anything, and has the advantage of drying transparent. Experiment with various

String, knots and their significance in trade and mythology, are fascinating in their own right, as are these heraldic knots and symbols which use string.

cloths for background, e.g. hessian, satin, towelling, or bases of hardboard, cork, cardboard, polystyrene, styrofoam, wood, etc. Experiment with three-dimensional shapes as well as flat two-dimensional pictures.

FURTHER READING

CAPON, R., *Making Three-Dimensional Pictures* Batsford

SEYD, M., *Designing with String* Batsford

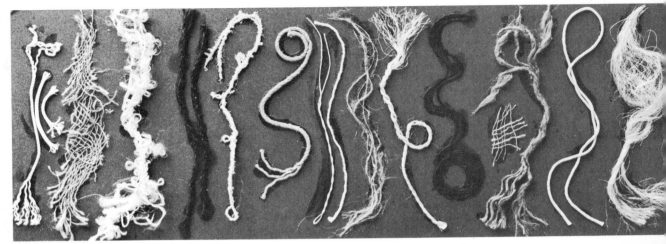

A collection of different types of threads and string, twisted and bent to see what sorts of curves they naturally make, or untwisted to explore the quality of the fibres.

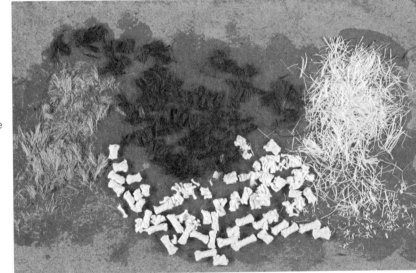

Some threads chopped up to explore the differences between the fibres.

The tense, tight curves of this arrangement are a reflection of the inherent quality of the particular string.

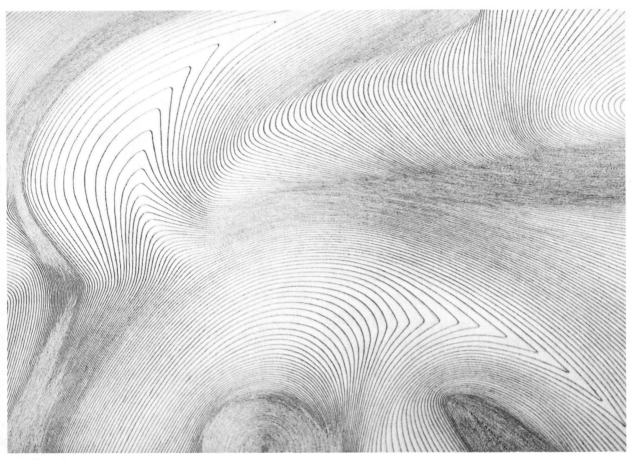

Contrast the tension created in this collage by Gwyther Irvin which is absolutely controlled in each line, with the tension in the previous example which is a personal interpretation of an 'accident'.

Coiling the string emphasises the contrast in colour and thickness.

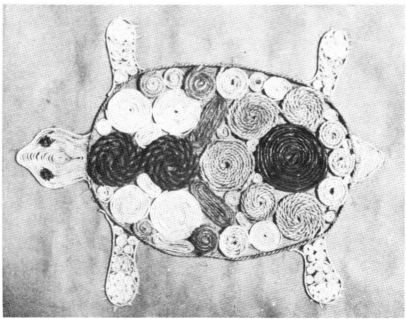

In this highly textured piece, the string is used only in straight lines within the limitation of the horizontal and the vertical. The size and thickness of the line is varied throughout. The difference between the cut end of string and the looped end has been exploited, and knots have been used to create staccato points in the arrangement.

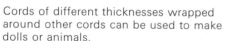

Cords of different thicknesses wrapped around other cords can be used to make dolls or animals.

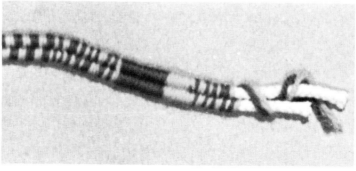

Lengths of cord can be whipped using a figure-of-eight movement, and these whipped cords can be used in hangings or fabric collage. Try using various colour combinations along the length of whipping, and vary the texture of the threads used: dull, hairy, shiny, knobbly.

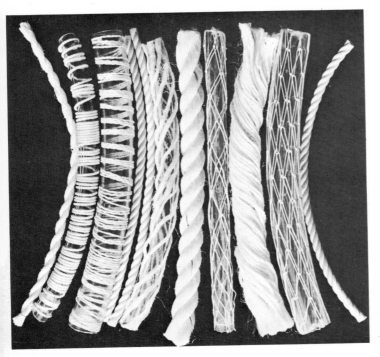

Try wrapping wool and string around twigs, plastic tubing, dowelling, stones, etc.

String can be glued onto a block of wood and after inking the string, a print can be taken from it. Remember that only one thickness of string can be used because the surface used for printing must be level. This example explores the freedom to make all sorts of curves with string.

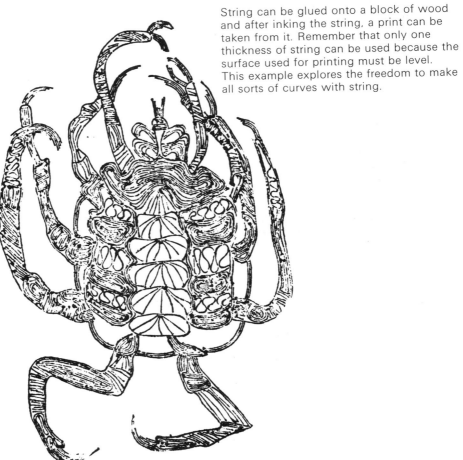

String Prints

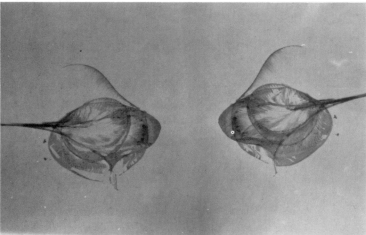

PULLED STRING PRINTS

Materials
string, or thick cotton or wool; writing ink, or Indian ink; paper.

METHOD
Dip a piece of wool or string into some ink or dye. Slowly lower it onto a piece of paper, starting with one end of the string. Fold a piece of paper over the inked string. Press the paper down with one hand, and with the other take hold of one end of the string and pull steadily until all the string is out. Lift off the paper and you will see the very distinctive pattern which results.

ROLLER STRING PRINT
Around the roller normally used for inking up the plate, wind some string, firmly. Roll this roller and string over a glass plate which has been inked up. Roll over a sheet of clean paper. A similar method can be used around an empty food tin.

STRING PRINT THROUGH
Lay a clean piece of string onto a firm surface, avoiding any crossover with the string. On top of this lay a piece of paper. With an inked up roller, run over the paper. Where the string is underneath, a line will appear on the paper.

a) The shapes made by the pulled string print suggested a bird, so the image of a bird was exaggerated by free drawing with pen and ink.
b) The double image that results from a pulled string print.
c) The string was laid in a similar curl each time in this multiple print.

Tablet Weaving

Tablet weaving is one of the earliest forms of weaving. Bodies of the 1st century BC have been found wearing headbands made by tablet weaving. A half-woven braid with 52 wooden tablets was found in the tomb of the Norwegian queen Asa who died about AD 850. The earliest piece of tablet weaving extant is Egyptian, dated between 945 and 745 BC, but it has been inferred from details of clothing depicted in Egyptian paintings that it was practised in 3000 BC. Tablet weaving is still practised in North Africa, where the strips are used to decorate djellabas and harness. The red garters of the Greek national costume are also tablet woven.

Materials and equipment

For the yarn choose a smooth mercerized knitting cotton (Lyscord, Lyscordet, Stalite, or Anchor perle) or a crêpe wool. Do not use a hairy or knobbly wool. With this technique, the colours and texture all come from the warp. The weft is really only to fasten these warp threads together securely and unobtrusively. The colour chosen for the weft should be the colour of the outside warp threads, because this is the only place where it is likely to be seen.

The only equipment needed is something to make the cards from, but for a beginner I recommend buying some plastic ones. It is possible to make your own out of old playing cards, but they tear rather easily in use, and snag the warp at each turn. The cards or tablets are between 2 in. and 3 in. square, with a hole in each corner and a larger one in the centre. They can be three-, four-, five- or six-sided. Each hole at the corners is lettered A, B, C, and D, or numbered 1, 2, 3, 4, in a clockwise direction. Keep a large pattern draft in front of you while you work, with all the details on it. Chenille, raffine, linen, plastic thread, nylon, metallic thread, tubular rayon, and macramé thread can all be experimented with once you have some experience, and one can use up to 50 tablets, or more. For the wider braids you will find it easier to work if the warp is spread out with a small reed (see Weaving).

A SIMPLE DESIGN

Twelve cards are needed for this design. Number these on the side with the numbers 1 to 12. It is then quick to see how a given card should be threaded. There are arrows at the side of the design; this denotes how the card is threaded, up or down. This design needs 18 dark threads, 24 medium, and 6 light threads. To begin, make the warp about 3 ft to 4 ft long. Cut the warp now. Give yourself plenty of room on a table to spread out the yarn. With the pattern draft in front of you, and reading from card no 1, choose four medium threads. Knot them together at the top in twos, and slip them over a metal knitting needle.

Card no 2 needs one dark thread and three medium. Again knot in twos, this time knotting one dark and one medium, and the other two will be medium. Work systematically from 1 to 12, and slip all over the knitting needle. The threads for card no 1 are on the left and on the extreme right are the threads for card no 12. Close to the needle, weave a tape as shown. This is to make sure the groups of four do not get muddled. Look at the illustration showing how to thread for *down*; thread the first card, no 1. Take the first bunch of warp, and thread a medium yarn through each hole. Then take card no 2, and the second bundle of warp, and thread this dark yarn through A and medium through B, C, and D. In this particular pattern all the threads are threaded *down* until no 7, which starts the *up* set.

Card no 3 is threaded dark warp in A and B, medium in C and D, and so on, following the draft very carefully. Leave the card about halfway up the warp. When all the cards are threaded, line them all up together on edge, making sure that the letters are all on the same side. Tie them together with a piece of tape slipped through the hole in the centre for the next stage. Collect up all the warp threads at the untied end, and pull gently so that all the warp threads are equally taut. Pop the needle holding the warp threads into a drawer and close it quite shut. Pull the other end of the warp, and either knot it and tie it to the back of the chair you are going to sit on while you do the weaving, or knot it and fasten it to your belt or waist. When you begin weaving do not expect to see the pattern for the first four or five rows. This is because the warp is bunched together at the knot, and it is only when it flattens out that the pattern really shows.

One word of warning; when you stop for any length of time, make sure that you complete the four turns, and then make a note of the direction to move the cards in on your return. You will never remember which way you had

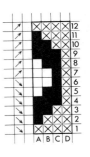

a) This 'Flower' design requires 18 dark threads, 24 medium threads and 6 light threads.

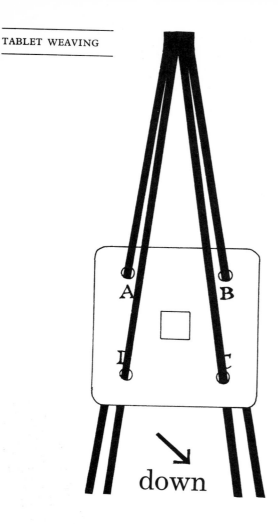

down

up

The different way the cards are threaded for up (away from the weaver) and down (towards the weaver).

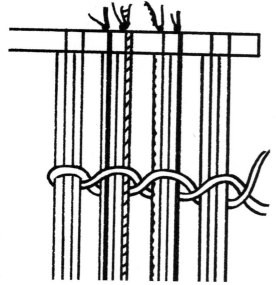

The warp knotted on the knitting needle, and the thread which is woven to separate the bunches according to the particular card.

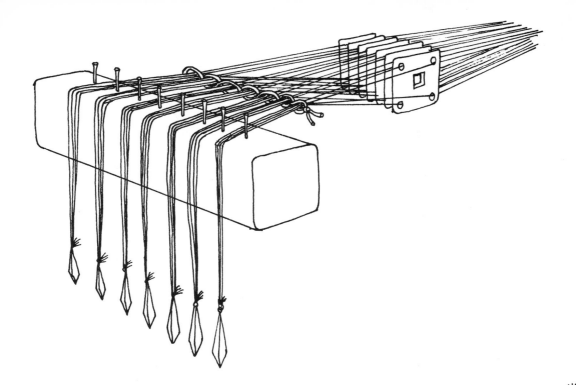

The Luther Hooper system is a device for avoiding the build-up of twist, by weighting the warp at the far end rather than attaching it to a fixed point. The threads are placed between a row of nails (or raddle), and a lead weight is attached to the end of each group, which is then free to spin round as necessary. Patterns can therefore be woven with the tablets being turned in one direction for the whole length of the braid.

The warp gathered up and the cards in place, as they will look when weaving begins, with the tape holding them securely prior to the weaving.

been turning the cards at the beginning, and if you make a mistake you will ruin the pattern.

Wind up the warp on a piece of card, or a shuttle, if possible one known as a Norwegian shuttle. This last holds the weft thread, and the lower edge is designed to be used for 'batting down' the weft, i.e. tapping it so that the thread lies as close as possible to the previous thread. Or one can knock it by inserting a ruler or some such thing in the 'shed' (the gap that is formed between the upper and lower layers of the weft). Leaving a tail of weft hanging loose, pass the dolly (the card onto which the weft has been wound) across the weft.

Holding the whole pack of cards at once (use both hands), turn the whole pack one-quarter turn away from you. As you do this, the warp yarns move up or down and a new set will be on the top. If the letters AD were uppermost when you began, the letters uppermost on the cards now are DC. Check that all the cards have DC on the top. Pass the weft back through the newly formed shed. If you do not have a Norwegian shuttle, use a ruler and pack the warp thread down as described above. Do this after each 'throw' of the weft. Turn the cards a quarter turn away from you again; the letters CB are now on top. Pass the weft across, turn the cards, and BA are on top. Pass the weft across and you are back at the beginning again with AD on top.

The next four turns are made towards the weaver. A check must always be made to see which way the cards are turned. Continue moving the cards four turns towards and four turns away for the rest of the warp. If you did not reverse in this regular way there would be a tremendous build up of twist on the other side of the card. However, this can be used to good advantage if you have a weaving partner who can weave at the other end at the same time. As you move the cards around, the weft is being changed at both sides, and the pattern will be the same at each end.

Another way of moving the cards in one direction and not getting them hopelessly twisted up, is not to knot the far end of the warp. But it has to move freely, and the warp must be kept very taut. Each bundle of four can be weighted with fishermen's weight, or a lead weight as in the Luther Hooper system. A thread woven around the separate bunches of the weft helps to prevent the cards jumping out of place when turning.

Bronze age belt from Borum Eshoj, Denmark (National Museum, Copenhagen). Woven on two-hole tablets: four-hole tablets first made their appearance in the Early Iron Age.

An old tape loom.

The weft here is
carded but unspun
wool.

Various edgings can
be made at the
same time as the
braid is woven.

This pattern
takes 53 tablets and
4 colours. Note
that all the cards are
threaded up in the
same direction.

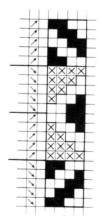

To make a cord with a braided edge, turn
the tablets on each edge with the central
ones, but pass the weft across the central
area only, leaving the edges to twist and
form cords. Weave the cords into the main
body of the braid again at some point
before the reversal of the pattern, and
release them again the same distance after.

On the left, three separate shuttles were used for the last few inches. Above, the warp threads were divided and whipped.

FURTHER READING

ASHLEY, *The Ashley Book of Knots* Faber

ATWATER, *Byways in Weaving* Macmillan, N.Y.

Ciba Review No 117, Nov. 1956, Ciba Ltd, Basle (excellent historical survey)

DILLMONT, *Encyclopaedia of Needlework* D.M.C. Library

Tablet Weaving, Dryad Leaflet 111

GRAUMONT & HENSEL, *Encyclopaedia of Knots & Fancy Rope Work* Cornell Maritime Press

GROFF, *Card Weaving* Robin & Russ Handweavers, Oregon

HARTUNG, *Creative Textile Craft* Batsford

HOOPER, L., *Weaving with a Small Appliance : Tablet Weaving* Pitman

JOHN, *Needleweaving* Batsford

SIMPSON & WEIR, *The Weaver's Craft* Dryad

SUTTON, A. & HOLTOM, P., *Tablet Weaving* Batsford

Finishing the ends

Secure the weft firmly so that it does not unravel by threading it through a needle and turning it back through the weaving, leaving a cut fringe. For a more decorative finish, divide the warp threads into bunches and whip them, or braid them and finish with overhand knots.

Tie and Dye

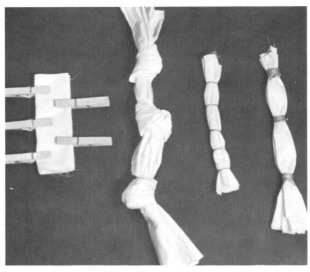

Cloth knotted, gripped with pegs (clothes pins), and tied with thin bands of string.

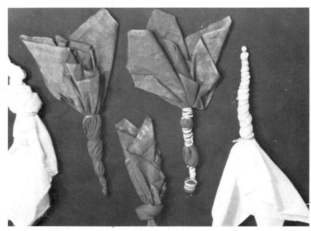

Folding from the centre of a square, and either knotted, or tied in various arrangements with the string.

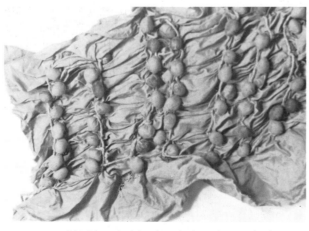

Marbles tied in the cloth, prior to dyeing.

The incredibly fine detail of tie and dye shows up best on silk and very fine cotton. The craft spread from China to India, Cambodia, Java, and Thailand, where it is still the prevailing method of decorating cloth for clothes. In India, where sari lengths are still being tie-dyed, the very fine cotton is laid, damp, over a plank of wood with nails, the pointed side uppermost. The cloth is bound very tightly over the tips of the nails with cotton thread using a long continuous thread. The result is a cloth covered in tiny circles of remarkable fineness. In Malaya, a refinement is made by tie dyeing the warp before a cloth is woven. This is called *ikat*, and is a technique well worth exploring.

The concept behind this craft is really the same as that behind stencilling. A barrier of some sort is placed in the way of the dye, so that it does not reach the cloth, and thus produces a distinctive pattern which is immediately recognizable as being tie-dyed.

Materials and equipment

rubber gloves; plastic tongs; Dylon cold water dyes; Dylon hot water dyes; Procion M dyes; plastic bowls and buckets; large saucepans (for hot dyes); string, pegs (clothes pins); rubber bands; plain white fabric; wooden dowels/wooden spoons; labels; Dylon liquid dyes; marbles, beads, coins, rice, stones, etc.

METHOD

The barrier can be many things: rubber bands, string, pegs, spring paper clips, or one can knot the cloth tightly. For large areas, polythene can be tied securely around the cloth, but only use it when using cold water dyes. Another method is to clamp the area you want preserved between two pieces of wood held together with C-clamps.

There are two variables to explore. One is how the cloth is folded. It can be neatly folded in concertina folds: it can be roughly bunched together: it can be folded from a point in the centre of the square. The other variable is how it is tied, which can be randomly, in regular bands; in irregular bands; with small stones, rice, peanuts, marbles, etc. tied into the cloth, or with nothing.

Plan some arrangements of circles, stripes, etc. Remember that the circles can be almost any size, either concentric, or grouped. More than one colour can be used. All the ties can be taken out before you re-tie and dye in another colour. Or undo some of the ties leaving the rest still tied, and then re-dye in another colour. Another method is to paint on several different colours of dye on the cloth with a brush. When dry, tie up the coloured areas and when they are covered, dye the cloth in a strong dark colour. In this way, although you have only dyed the cloth once, there will be circles or stripes of as many different colours as you painted on initially.

When tie dyeing clothes, pillow cases, or bags, make them up first, and tie the finished article. It is easier to see where best to place the stripes, circles, etc. on the finished article than before it is sewn up. Experiment with potato or stick printing on top of tie dye; try quilting it, or couching threads around it, or machine embroidering over it.

FURTHER READING

MAILE, A., *Tie and Dye as a Present-Day Craft* Mills & Boon

Tie dye can be used on clothes and accessories: this bag has a very large single shape.

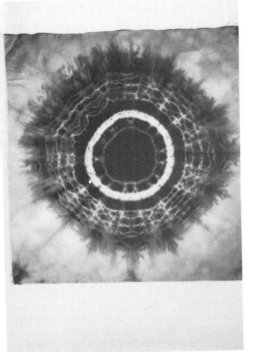

A piece of tie dye where the cloth has been dyed twice. The white circle near the centre is still white, because that string binding, unlike the other first bindings, was kept intact during both dyeings.

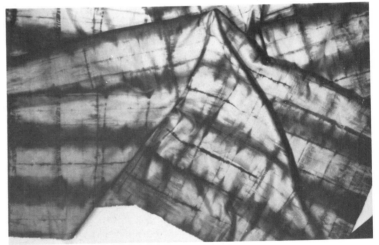

Arrangements of cloth folded at right angles to the edge, in concertina formation.

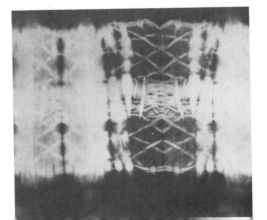

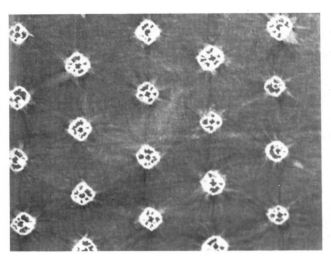

Grains of rice were tied with thread, and a second thread was bound round the point before dyeing.

Peanuts in their brown skins were carefully placed and tied, then dyed in iron rust. The natural tannin in their skins darkens the fabric and leaves a grey shape on the fabric.

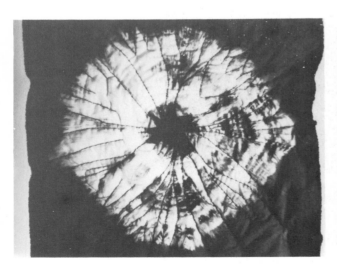

A sample of tie dyeing which has been quilted to exaggerate the lines made in the tie dyeing.

This cushion cover, which uses a single dyed piece, has been hand sewn with a couched thread (laid on top and oversewn onto the fabric) to link the circles together.

Tin-can Craft

The tin cans which are discarded daily in most homes can constitute a very useful craft material, particularly for practising design techniques before tackling more expensive metals. Tin cans consist mainly of steel, with a thin coating of tin on the inside and outside.

TIN-CAN PUNCHING
Tools
For making holes: a nail punch (impact centre punch), a can opener (some openers punch holes, some cut round the top, others cut beneath the rim), an old screwdriver, an old cross-head (Phillips) screwdriver, various nails, hammer.

Method
Support the tin can from the inside with a block of wood padded with newspaper so that the can is not indented by the pounding. Alternatively fill the can with hot wax, which will form a hard core when cold. The various tools when hammered into the can will give different shaped holes. If a pattern of holes is punched completely round the can, it will make an attractive and effective candle shield for evening garden parties. The heat from the candle will create interesting colour effects on painted and unpainted cans. If the can is to hold water, indented designs can be made with the nail punch without piercing the can.

TIN-CAN SOLDERING
Equipment
Medium soldering iron (30 watt); solid wire solder, or acid core solder; flux; industrial-asbestos pad to be used as the work surface.

Method
Experiments using tin cans joined together can produce abstract or figurative three-dimensional structures. Thoroughly clean the metal with a wire brush and detergent. Heat the soldering iron, then apply the flux to the metal and the tip of the iron. (Acid flux is required as an agent to make the solder flow more freely; it is highly corrosive and must be handled with caution.) Melt a droplet of solder (soft solder, a compound of lead and tin) onto the tip of the iron, then heat the metal with the iron. Apply the stick of solder to the joint, and melt away a tiny bead. Rub the iron over the joint to spread the solder into the crevice. When a firm joint has been made, wash it in a soapy solution to prevent the acid flux from discoloring the surrounding metal, then immerse the metal in a weak solution of vinegar and water to remove all traces of the flux.

When sweat-soldering several layers of metal together, paint on the flux with a brush over the whole surface, then heat the metal with a propane torch and dab the solder all over the surface. Heat the surface with the torch again to make the solder spread over the metal, then press the second layer on top.

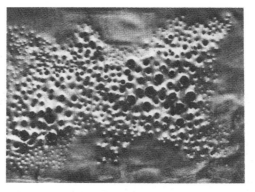

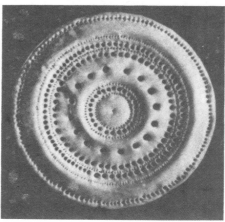

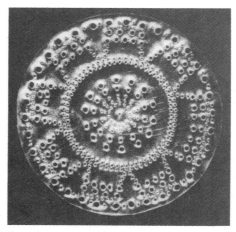

Experiment on a tin can lid arranging the holes in various ways: at random, using various sizes of holes.

CUT TIN CANS
To salvage sheet metal from tin cans, remove the top and bottom with a can opener, and use metal shears to cut off the rims and open the seam. The metal can then be gently uncurled, and hammered flat, and the edges smoothed down with a file. Printed labels can be removed by soaking in water, or blistering with a propane torch and buffing with steel wool. A jeweller's saw can be used to cut motifs in the metal, or several layers can be sweat-soldered

A figurative head. The eyebrows are made from the piece of tin cut from directly over the nose, and bent sideways. Eyelashes are long dressmaker's pins soldered on.

together to form metal blocks. The sheet metal can also be bent with the hands or pliers into curved shapes. The can lids can be snipped and curled to form flower heads, and coathanger wire can be soldered on to form flower stems. Try spraying these flowers with an opaque enamel spray, using cellophane to mask off areas while spraying with each colour.

Decorative ornaments can also be made from lift-top can rings; glued with epoxy cement, these rings constitute a versatile unit for imaginative design.

Chemical oxidation (rusting) can be used to change the colour (patina) of the metal. White (PVA) glue mixed with black water colour or acrylic paint can be used as an oxidiser; paint it across the metal to produce natural rust colours from yellow ochre to rich brown. The oxidation process can be arrested by painting on varnish. Interesting colour effects can also be obtained by playing a low flame over the surface of the metal.

Tissue Paper

Tissue paper has certain very specific qualities. It is thinner than any other paper; it can be folded over and over again into smaller pieces than any other type of paper, and this is a great advantage for the fold and dye method of patterning papers. One can also fold and cut it into very intricate designs. Because it is so thin, when it is stuck down onto a surface, it becomes almost a part of that surface, and can look as though it is printed.

Its transparency makes it perfect for projects which utilize colour and light, e.g. lampshades, imitation stained glass, shadow

puppets, hanging ornaments. It also has a huge range of the most intense colours, but these alas are fugitive, especially the very bright pink. Even this apparent disadvantage can be turned to advantage. Try laying a fern on a piece of bright pink paper and leave in strong sunlight until the paper has noticeably faded. In very strong sunlight this can be a matter of only hours. Take off the fern at the end of this time, and the area covered by the fern will still be bright pink. This piece of paper can only be usefully used on some object which is unlikely to come into contact with sunlight or strong artificial light.

The primary colours and black are much more resistent to fading, and covering the paper with glass or coating the surface with some substance such as a polymer medium and keeping it away from really strong light will minimize the likelihood of fading. It also 'bleeds' when the colours are wet (the colours run). This has creative potential in collage techniques, but if it is undesirable, one can avoid it by using a non-water-based adhesive, such as one of the spray-on adhesives or a diluted white glue.

To prevent the colour from fading, one can colour one's own tissue paper with artists' water colours (which might run with a water-based glue). Polymer paints are the best choice for colouring tissue, as they are both water-proof and resistent to fading. Lay the tissue paper on a sheet of glass and paint with a thick $2\frac{1}{2}$-in. brush. It must be placed on a non-absorbent paper or the paper will stick to it. These paints can destroy the transparency of the paper.

If the paper must be transparent when it is coloured, then dyes are to be used. Water soluble aniline dyes have a large colour range.

Make a concentrated solution of the dye, and pour it into a large shallow tray. Cover the area that you will be working on with newspaper to protect the surface of the table, and wear rubber gloves. Fold the white tissue paper into halves or quarters, and immerse in the dye bath. If there are too many folds in the paper it will not dye evenly. When the paper has been fully penetrated with the dye, lift one edge out of the dye, let the dye slowly run off, and lift right out. Without unfolding, leave it to dry.

Experiment. Lay some tissue onto a sheet of glass. Using an eye dropper, drop coloured dyes onto the sheets and splash with water to make the colours run together. Or drop water onto coloured tissue. The colours will run from one sheet to another and there will be a collection of randomly coloured mottled papers. Try dropping, splattering, printing bleach on the coloured tissue with pipe cleaners. Dip a plastic sponge into bleach and try pressing it onto the paper. You can also paint the tissue paper with melted candle wax. Crumple to crack the wax, then either use bleach to paint over the paper, or dye.

UNUSUAL COMBINATIONS OF MEDIA

A tissue paper collage (picture) can be overlaid with a lino print, a screen print, a frottage, a free cardboard edge print, or a potato print. Natural objects, such as grasses, dried leaves, dead twigs, and seeds, or man-made objects such as string, lace, textured yarns, sand, lentils, and straws, can be added or embedded. Experiment with yarns attached to the surface only at one end, the other end hanging free.

Use a water-based adhesive such as wheat or wallpaper-paste (Polycell) to make the paper 'bleed'. Try peeling off the paper in places when it has lost its colour onto the background paper. Alternatively, ink from a pen can be used to make the colour bleed.

Aluminium foil, or gold and silver paper can also be used as a base on which to glue down the tissue. The reflective nature of the foil surface gives the same luminosity as it does when it is applied to the back of glass paintings.

While the tissue paper is wet, it can be modelled and the surface built up. It can either be soaked in the glue and then crumpled and modelled, or it can be modelled directly onto the background. One would have to use a firm background such as mounting card, cardboard or even hardboard, depending on how thick the impasto is.

Setting tissue paper in waxed paper

Instead of glue one can use candle wax to combine tissue papers. Melt paraffin wax onto white tissue paper on a cardboard base. Lay the piece of coloured tissue on this and top with another layer of white tissue. Add another cut-out and another piece of white paper and so on for four or five patterned cut-outs. Iron with a warm iron, and while still warm peel off from the cardboard base. Trim into the desired shape.

Laminating tissue paper

Lay a sheet of polythene (thin plastic sheeting) on the table and on this place a sheet of tissue paper. With a wide 4-in. brush (a 'brush' of cellulose sponge works very well) paint a thin layer of half water and half white glue (PVA). Lay a piece of tissue on top, and on that lay a second sheet of polythene. With a lino-printing roller, roll very firmly over the two layers. Cover with another layer of dilute white glue, and another layer of tissue. Lay polythene over and roll. Continue until eight to 12 layers are built up. While it is damp, it can be cut and moulded into any shape, and will dry quite hard and resilient. While it is wet it can also be stretched.

Embedding natural objects

Acetate On a sheet of acetate, paint a layer of diluted white glue. Lay on the dried leaves, grasses or feathers. On these paint a layer of dilute paste. Cover with a layer of tissue, then polythene. Roller to remove any trapped air and firmly stick the pieces together. When dry, stick another layer of tissue on the other side.

A fish collage using overlapping shapes, exploring the effects that appear because of the transparency of the paper. It uses only torn pieces of paper; compare with the hard edges of collages which only use cut edges.

Tissue paper moved while still wet with glue to create straight lines suggests a mountain formation.

Freshly picked grasses, powder paint (dry), DIY plaster (Polyfilla), sand are all embedded under two sheets of tissue.

367

Peat was glued down at the bottom edge of the collage, and several layers of tissue were pasted over. Before the tissue was quite dry, some parts were torn back so that the peat was revealed, and the surface of the paper raised by those pieces which were torn and folded back on itself.

This collage combines newspaper cuttings and crumpled tissue.

Cartridge paper Cover a sheet of cartridge (white drawing) paper with dilute white glue. On this lay some dried grasses. Paint some more glue over the grasses, and lay a pale colour tissue torn into small pieces around the edge, and over the grasses stick white tissue. Press well down with the paste brush.

Tissue paper Lay a sheet of white tissue on some polythene, and paint a layer of dilute white glue all over it. Lay a dried grass on the glued paper, cover it with a coat of glue and lay a sheet of white tissue over. Cover with a sheet of transparent plastic cling film (Polywrap) and roller together, removing all air bubbles.

Making parchment

The two methods just described leave the surface ready for writing on without any 'bleeding' of the ink. Without any embedding, one has the technique for making tissue paper 'parchment'. This can be used for making lampshades while the parchment is still damp. It is quite malleable at this stage and can be used on shaped lampshade frames. The metal lampshade frame should first be coated with the white glue undiluted. Cut a piece of the 'parchment' a little larger than the segment to be covered. Allow to dry, and trim off the residue. Repeat until the whole shade is covered.

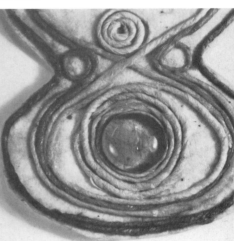

Strips of tissue are pasted with white glue (PVA) then rolled and twisted into a string. Paste the glue over the ground onto which the string is to be placed and lay it on. The centre is a partly melted marble glued on.

The butterfly incorporates areas of aluminium foil and has been glued onto a cork tile with white glue.

ADDITION TO	COLLAGE	EMBEDDING	COLOURING BY

Lino print
Screen print
Frottage
Free card edge print
Potato print
Batik
Line drawing
	Cut paper, reveal
	   other layers
	Folding (shadowing)
	Free collage
	Use aluminium foil
	   as background
	Modelling in low
	   relief
	Add lace, leaves, etc.
		Tissue paper in
		   waxed paper
		Laminating tissue
		Embedding (acetate)
		   on cartridge
		Between two layers
		   of tissue
			Aniline dyes
			Polymer paints
			Bleaching
			Waxing
			Bleeding
			Brusho dyes
			Image produced by
			   paper fading

A dried leaf has been glued onto a piece of card, and two layers of white tissue paper glued on top. A sheet of polythene has been placed on the top, and the paper rubbed firmly to dispel pockets of air.

Small petal shapes can be made from tissue paper pasted over wire shapes to form earrings, or strung together to produce a necklace.

To make a pendant, twist wire into simple shapes, allowing a loop at the top through which a cord can be threaded. Paste a piece of tissue larger than the wire shape, and lay the shaped wire on it. At this stage, any additional shapes can be added to the centre. Coat again with white glue and lay another piece of tissue on top. Leave to dry overnight. Then trim the paper off close to the wire. It is remarkably strong at this stage, but you can paint it with clear nail varnish to strengthen it still further.

Tritik

This is really a version of tie and dye, and is produced by running a long strong thread (bookbinder's linen, or buttonhole thread) along a random line or a precisely designed line, and then pulling the thread very tight when the line is completed. The fabric is then dyed, and patterns are formed where the dye is excluded, just as in tie and dye. The stitch used is not important, though running/tacking are the ones normally used: the important fact to remember is that the cotton has to be pulled very tight as you do the stitch (if you are using whipped stitch) or at the end if you are doing running or tacking stitch. Begin the stitching with a few back stitches; a knot is unlikely to hold the strain that is put on it when the thread is pulled up. None of the running thread must be visible when it is pulled up. See the section on Tie and Dye for the dyeing method.

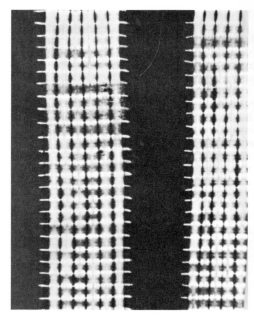

Stitching, by hand or machine, can be used to pinch the cloth together so tightly that the dye cannot penetrate. Here, running stitch has been used on commercially pleated cotton.

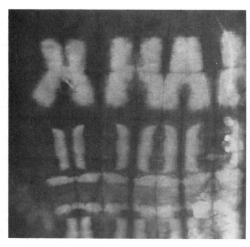

A detail of spring clip tritik on a piece of cloth which had been previously tie-dyed.

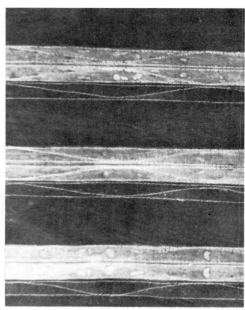

This has been stitched with a sewing machine.

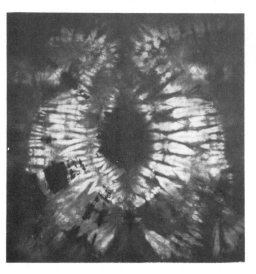

The stitching has been done through two layers of cloth at the same time, thus producing a symmetrical pattern.

Twining

Twining is one of the simplest techniques involved in basketweaving and wickerwork, and can be used to produce soft sculptures and containers.

The warps consist of firm, round reeds, wood or bamboo, and may be attached to a hard circular base (to form a standing container) or curved and shaped into a skeletal structure (to form a carrying basket). A softer material is used for the weft strands: heavy wool yarn, sisal, raffia, jute, seagrass, or willow reeds.

Two weft strands are woven together, one being passed to the front of each warp as the other is passed behind. The resulting surface is strong, highly textured, and stiff enough to hold its own shape. The rows can be spaced so that the warps show as a part of the design, or the warps can be completely covered by the wefts to form a compact structure. In spaced twining, the warps can be curved or crossed over each other between each line of weft to create an openweave pattern, and this looks particularly effective when covering a box or bottle.

FURTHER READING

HARVEY, V., *The Techniques of Basketry* Batsford

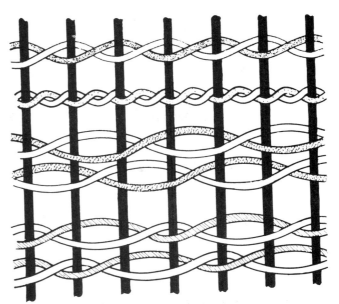

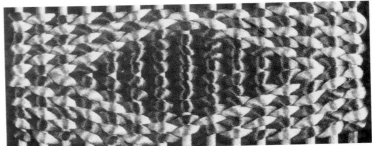

(Top) Various ways of twining the wefts.

(Centre) Two colours were used in this compact twining, and the strands were given a half or full twist to bring each colour to the front.

(Bottom left) Twined reed sculpture by Nichol Kriz.

(Bottom right) Twined reed basket with god's eyes by Vivanna Phillips.

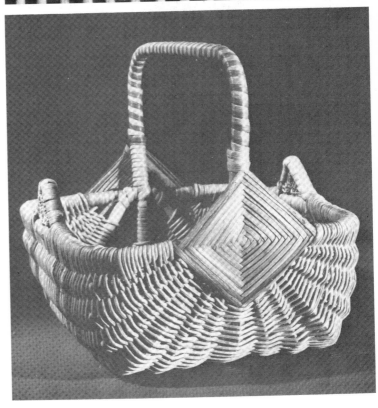

Watermarks

If you hold a blank sheet of paper to the light, it is possible sometimes to see a name appear as if written in white, which disappears as soon as it is put back on the table. This is the watermark, and is made at the same time as the sheet of paper is being made. The examples illustrated are from old books, and are made with fine wire. The design is made exactly as it appears, in wire, and laid on the sieve on which the paper pulp is poured. As the pulp dries, the places where the wire touches the pulp make it more compact (thick) so that when the paper is held up to the light, the thicker impression shows up against the more transparent paper.

FIN DE
M⚜IOHANNOT
DANNONAY
1779

a

A sample of European watermarks:
a) France, 1779.
b) England, 1641.
c) England, 1683.
d) Holland, eighteenth century.
e) Hertford, 1409.
f) Salzburg, 1526.
g) Switzerland, 1560.
h) Munchen, 1490.
i) France, 1593.
j) Cherbourg, 1536.

b

c

e

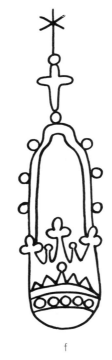

f

g

h

i

j

Wax

Candle and crayon wax can be used in a variety of crafts. For candlemaking, see that section.

Painting with wax
Melt candle wax in a saucepan; dip a brush into the hot wax; quickly dip the brush into powder colour, and paint onto paper. This has to be done very quickly before the wax has become too hard to paint with, and it is only practical on very small pieces of paper.

Cloisonné
Draw enclosed shapes very heavily with a black wax crayon. These can then be filled with different coloured inks (Brusho) in the manner of cloisonné enamelling or stained glass.

Batik
Experiment on paper with a brush or tjanting using coloured inks (Brusho) instead of dyes to experiment with different colour combinations and to discover what colours result from mixing.

Wall plaque
Melt scraps of different coloured wax (candle wax, coloured either by the proper candle dyes or stubs of old candles) in straight-sided metal lids, or pour onto a slab of marble or glass. When cold, break up into small pieces, and arrange on plywood or hardboard. Carefully fill the interstices with plaster of Paris. Insert hairpins before the plaster has dried so that the plaque can be hung up when it is finished, and dry.

Printing onto fabric
Draw very thickly onto hessian, burlap or embroidery canvas, in various colours. Lay it face down onto white paper or fine cotton, and iron off with a medium hot iron. The textured quality of the hessian remains, and if it has been ironed onto fine white cotton, it can be used as a basis for experimental straight stitching either by hand or with a machine. Commercial fabric printing crayons can also be used to draw designs directly onto fabric.

Wax sculpture
Melt coloured candle wax down into sheets. With a knife held in a candle flame to keep it hot, cut the wax into pieces. Weld the pieces together with hot wax to form a three-dimensional construction.

Rubbing
Rubbings can be taken from a paper master (of cut-out shapes), from natural textures, or from man-made textures. Explore the following variations: rubbings in candle wax plus washes of coloured ink; drawings in candle wax plus washes of coloured ink; rubbings in candle wax, washed with waterproof ink, the candle wax then wiped off with methylated spirits (denatured alcohol); heavy wax rubbing, ironed onto a sheet of absorbent paper or tissue collage.

Scraper drawing
Cover card (postcard) thickly with candle wax or a black wax crayon. Scratch through with a pin or nail either a pattern or a drawing. Brush on Indian ink in a contrasting colour.

Melted wax picture
Grate crayons onto a piece of paper, allowing the colours to fall where they will, though trying to keep them separate. Cover with a sheet of paper and iron the paper with a warm iron to melt the wax crayon.

Plaster of Paris engraving
Pour plaster of Paris into a metal lid. Before it has dried, draw into the surface with a stick. When dry, flood with hot coloured candle wax.

Duo prints
Fold a piece of stiff paper or card in half. On one half rub coloured wax crayons or felt-tip pens over the paper. Then cover the whole area with a thick layer of black wax. Fold the paper in half, and on the half that has no wax on it, make a drawing with a tool with a very hard point. When the paper is opened, on one side there will be a drawing in black wax (the reverse side of the paper the drawing was made on) and on the waxed paper the black wax will have been transferred to the other side, revealing a randomly coloured line drawing.

Making carbon paper
Rub black wax crayon thickly on a piece of thin card or cartridge paper. Lay it wax-side down on another piece of paper and draw on it. The drawing will be transferred onto the lower piece of paper. The carbon drawing will have a blurred outline, and this could be used to pleasing effect.

Wax as a mould
Melt candle wax and pour it into a shallow tray. Into the cold wax make a drawing. Use this as a mould in which to cast resin.

A thickly waxed print has been transferred onto a sheet of paper by ironing.

APPLIED TO	APPLY WITH	USES

Paper
Cloth
Card
Polystyrene (Styrofoam)
Plaster of Paris
Wood
Stone
Canvas
Eggshell
Acrylic sheet
	Tjanting
	Hog-hair brush
	Dripped from lit candle
	Pipe cleaners
	Wire
	Cotton buds
	Cellulose sponge held in a
	    wooden peg (clothes pin)
		Fabric decorating: Batik
		                                 Stencil
		Fabric printing crayons
		Grated crayon ironed onto
		    cloth or paper or vilene
		Encaustic
		Frottage
		Creative rubbings
		Duo-prints
		Comb patterns
		Rubbings
		Incised and used as a mould
		    for resin
		Drawing
		Painted onto clay (as a resist)

Weaving

CARDING THE FLEECE

There are two parts to a carding tool (both the same). They are pieces of curved wood with a handle, covered on the convex side in short 'prickles'. Teazles used to be used for this. Small pieces of fleece are laid on the carder to be held in the left hand. The other carder is taken with the other hand and the fleece stroked to get all the fibres in the fleece running in the same direction. The carders are then moved together in the opposite direction and this gathers up all the carded fleece into a long sausage called a rolag. This is what is used for doing the actual spinning.

HAND-SPINNING THE FLEECE

Spindles can be bought ready made, or you can make them yourself. Note the notch in the top of the piece of dowelling used for the shaft. To begin spinning, a piece of spun wool has to be tied on (2- or 3-ply is best), tying the first part just above the whorl; take it under the whorl, round the shaft, then up, and do a half hitch round the notch.

The carded fleece to be spun must be in its original oily condition. A handful of fleece is spun in one length; a piece of fleece is placed between the opened-out end of the wool already on the spindle, then the dangling spindle is given a sharp clockwise twist. The fleece is held in the left hand, and the spinning of the spindle is done with the right hand. More pieces of fleece are added as needed. When a long length has been spun, unfasten the original piece of wool and wind the spun wool round the whorl and the spindle, hitching it round the notch as before.

(Top) Carding the fleece.

(Bottom) Gathering up the carded fleece into a rolag.

Tying spun wool
onto the spindle.

Whorl

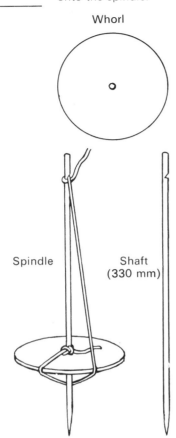

Spindle

Shaft
(330 mm)

WEAVING WITH IMPROVISED LOOMS

In its simplest form, weaving is the construction of a flat compact fabric from two lengths of yarn. The fixed yarn (warp) is held in a zigzag from top to bottom of the loom, and the weaving yarn (weft) is passed in and out of the warp from side to side. Pins or notched card can be used to hold the warp in place, and the weft can be passed through with a large blunt needle.

a) Large headed (glass) pins are pushed into corrugated card at a very shallow angle. It is around these that the warp is wound.

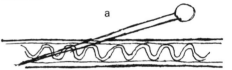

a

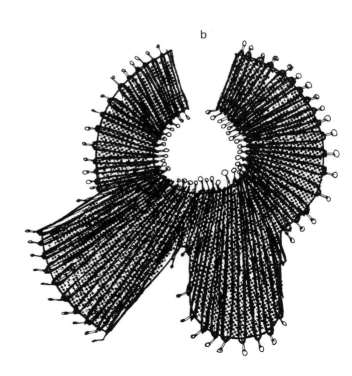

b

b) Free flat shapes can be woven by either cutting out the shape and sticking it onto the corrugated card base or just drawing it. The pins are pushed all round the edge of the shape and the warp wound round them.

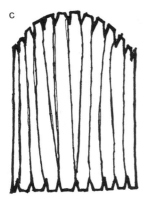

c

c) Pieces of stiff card can have notches cut out of the edge and the warp is held in the base of the 'V' as it is wound round the card.

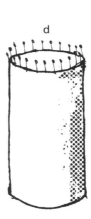

d

d) Pins can be stuck in the top of a thick cardboard tube and the warp wound round the tube from top to bottom.

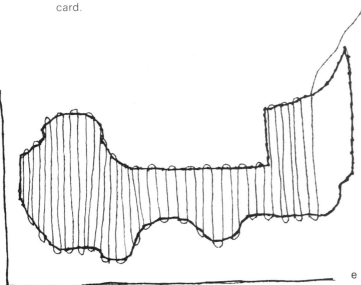

e) Instead of using pins to hold the warp, the shape can be back-stitched and the warp threaded through the individual stitches.

e

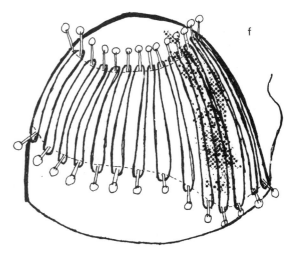

f

f) Polystyrene or Styrofoam wig-stands can be used to fix the pins for making three-dimensional shapes.

377

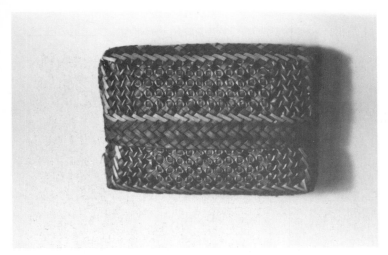

Weaving can be made in many materials: this is made of split bamboo, and very fine straw.

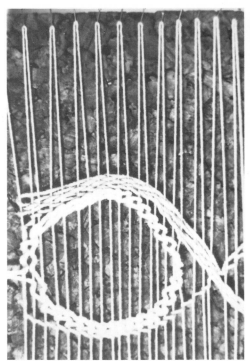

The warp was made on a cork tile, the thread being fastened around pins which were pushed into the cork. With such a warp, one is free to take the weft threads in any direction one wishes.

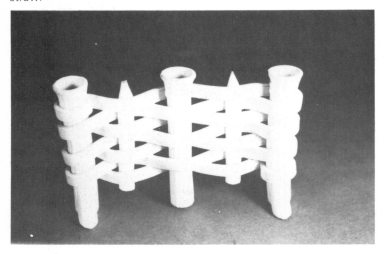

This is weaving with clay!

This paper weaving explores the textural qualities achieved by lifting up the warp.

This warp was set on a thick card base with notches around the edge. These prevent the warp threads from sliding. The traditional under one thread over one thread was used, and notice how the warp thread remains visible.

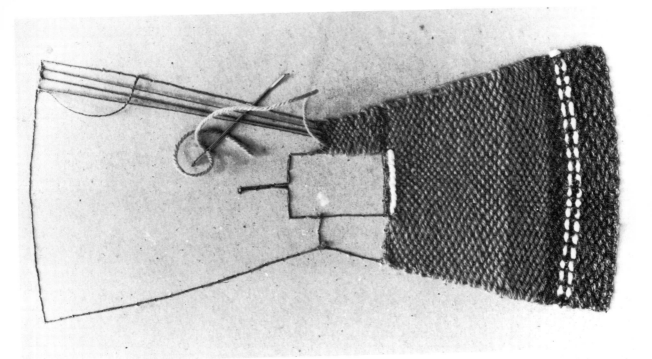

Another method of setting up a warp without the use of pins. The shape is drawn onto card and the outline worked in backstitch. The warps are threaded onto the loops made by the stitches.

This needleweaving is made in natural coloured wools. It was made in Ethiopia and shows the Lion of Judah.

This is an experiment making patches of colours by not weaving right across all the threads but weaving over a few at a time, adding the occasional thread when needed.

LOOMS

Many kinds of looms are used in weaving: card looms, frame looms, roller looms, shaft looms, and rug frames. Roller looms with a rigid heddle cover in a simple way the possibilities of much more complicated looms, and it will be a long time before their possibilities near exhaustion. An unconventional type of weaving which has been revived in the USA with some delightful results is waist weaving. Waist looms or Maya looms are available commercially, or one can do waist weaving without any equipment, simply attaching the warp to a rigid pole. The tautness is achieved by fastening the other end around the waist of the weaver.

The frame loom

The frame loom is the simplest of all looms, and can be made with a picture frame. Staples (the sort used for tacking wire netting, not the sort used for stapling paper) are arranged in a row along two opposite sides. A thick cotton or string warp is wound round the staples and not through them. This is so that when the weaving is finished and has to be taken off the loom it can be lifted up and over the staples. If the warp is threaded through by mistake, all the warp threads will have to be cut, and they are then very difficult to finish off. With the loops however, tassels can be attached to bunches of two or three loops at a time. The beginning of the warp is fastened to the leg of the first staple on the left, and wrapped systematically from the top to the one immediately underneath it, up to the top and so on until the last staple is reached. The thread is then fastened to a leg of the last staple with a knot.

Another type of home-made frame can be made from pieces of wood which are held together with screws. The side pieces are higher than the two end pieces; four cup hooks are screwed in, two at each end, on the raised side pieces, with the openings of the cup hooks pointing away from each other. These hold the two pieces of dowelling on which the warp is fastened. The warp is measured out in pieces which are twice the distance between the dowels, plus 6 in. The extra is to allow for the thread needed for tying. Each warping thread is taken around the far dowel, and knotted over the lower one. One end of the warp is first passed round the dowel twice, once one side of the warp, and once the other. Then make the knot. The extra twists around the dowel are to prevent the warp moving to one side when weaving starts.

The other large frame loom is a rug frame loom; in essence this is the same as the others but with one important difference. It uses a cunning method of tensioning the warp: two wing nuts. The warp for a rug should be of strong twine, three doubles to the inch. For the weft you can either use the ordinary 6-ply rug wool, or (making a total of six) use three shades of a colour in 2-ply rug wool. The

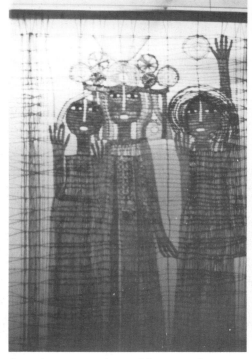

A contemporary piece of free weaving made in Czechoslovakia.

overall effect is much richer if several shades of one colour are used. Before embarking on a large project, experiment on a small frame loom until you find exactly the right combinations of colours and threads. Mistakes on a large scale are disappointing to have to live with.

For schools, a wide range of looms are available from educational suppliers: 2-harness and 4-harness table or floor looms; inkle looms (for making long belts and strips over a succession of racks); and foot-powered looms (Dryad, UK; Dick Blick, Craftool and Hammett's, USA).

The shuttle

There comes a point in weaving when the needle will not reach all the way across the warp in one go. So something else has to be used. This is called a shuttle, and is a piece of wood rather like a ruler, with a deep notch cut out at each end. The yarn is wound round and round this until the notch is full.

The heddle

To avoid the tedium of lifting every single warp thread on every single row, a heddle is used; these are available in many different widths and should be chosen to fit the warp width. The heddle is made out of metal, with alternate slits and eyes. The warp is threaded through this after the warp is fastened round the far roller, but before it is fastened to the near roller. A special warp hook is needed to thread the warp threads through the heddle. Starting at the left-hand side, thread the first

A simple ridge heddle.

The heddle in use.

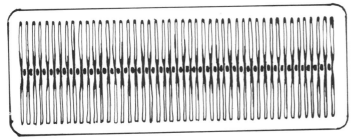

warp through the eye, the next through the slit, and so on until all the warp threads are threaded. Now tie the warps onto the roller.

If you now lift the heddle, holding it at the top, you will see that all the threads through the eyes have come up too, while those in the slits have stayed where they were because they could move freely in the slits. There is now a gap in the warp from one side to the other, this is called the shed. Pass the shuttle through and one row of weaving is done with one movement. Press the heddle down so that those threads through the eye of the heddle are below the others now. Pass the shuttle back and another row is done, and so on.

FURTHER READING

Atlas Leaflet 62, *Handloom Weaving* Atlas Handicrafts, Manchester, 4

BAINES, P., *Spinning Wheels* Batsford

Dryad Leaflet 89, *Hand-weaving on Four-way Table Looms*

Dryad Leaflet 91, *Hand-weaving on Two-way Looms*

DUCHEMIN, M., *Handweaving* Batsford

KREVITSKY & ERICSON, *Shaped Weaving* Van Nostrand Reinhold

RHODES, M., *Small Woven Tapestries* Batsford

SHILLINGLAW, P., *Introducing Weaving* Batsford

TOVEY, J., *The Technique of Weaving* Batsford

A simple frame
loom.

A home-made
frame.

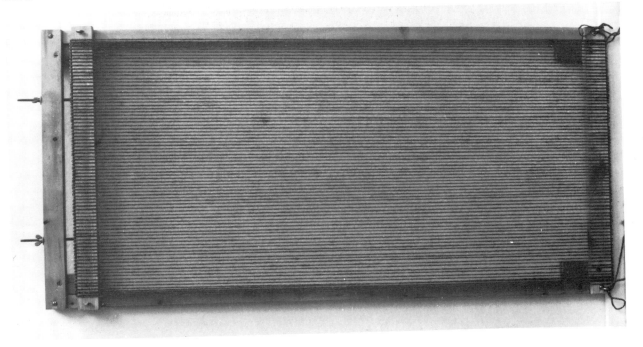

A rug frame loom.

A four-shaft table loom, Harris model. A shaft acts like a heddle and with four, the warp threads are arranged in four possible 'layers', so that by altering the order in which they are lifted up, different patterns are made. These particular shafts are lifted from the right-hand side by means of a wooden rod with a chain attached.

Paper has been wound round the warp on this small roller loom to make the unwinding during the weaving easier. If the wool is hairy, without paper it can easily get tangled. Any length of weaving longer than the actual loom must have some method of rolling up the unused warp.

A waist loom with a rigid heddle.

...ist weaving in progress. The warp is
...tened round a piece of dowelling or a
...er. Tie a piece of strong string to each
...d of the dowelling and fasten securely to
...hair. Thread the warp through a heddle
...the appropriate size, tie the other end of
... warp into a loose knot and fasten it to
...r belt.

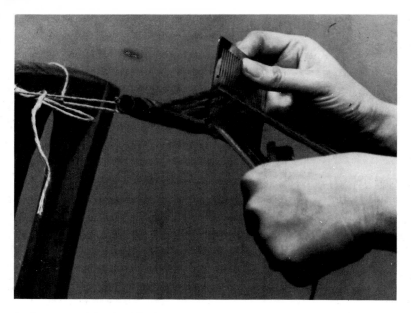

A close-up of the heddle in use,
separating the warp and making plenty of
room to pass the shuttle through.

WEAVING

USING	ACROSS
Wool and other animal fibres	A loom warp (all sorts)
Raw, unspun	Chicken wire
All thicknesses	Across twigs
Ikat dyed	Across bicycle wheel
With beads threaded on	Card looms, cut edge, notched edge
Vegetable dyed	Free weaving over cut paper shape
Cotton and other vegetable fibres	(applied to a firm base)
(as above)	Picture frame
Paper	Metal mesh
Cellophane	Perforated hardboard
Tissue	
Metallic papers	
Foil	
Marbled	
(crushed, plaited, twisted, rolled,	
knotted, etc.)	
Sticks, rushes, reeds, wickerwork	
Clay	
Plastic	
Sheeting	
Tubing, wrapped with wool, stuffed with	
coloured papers, etc.	
Metal rods (Sprang)	
Wooden dowelling (all sizes)	

Well Dressing

This is a very ancient English craft of making pictures out of overlapping flower petals pressed into wet clay. It was used to decorate wells for special church processions and services to give thanks for the supply of water. The pictures continue to be made around midsummer in a few villages in Derbyshire, the most well-known being Tideswell, Youlgreave, Tissington, and Eyam.

The pictures are made in large (up to 10 ft high) shallow wooden boxes, which are soaked in water and then filled with very wet clay. The design is drawn out on tracing paper, then pricked through the paper into the clay. The design is then outlined with berries, seeds or black wool. The shapes are filled in petal by petal, each slightly overlapping the previous one, and each row slightly overlapping the previous row. Only certain flowers are suitable for this treatment: buttercups, pansies, and hydrangeas stand up without curling or changing colour for the week the pictures are on view. By then the petals will have deteriorated, the clay begun to dry out, and the ceremony is over for another year.

Wire

The following examples all use straight pieces of wire as the unit, yet the results are quite different.

Wire can be bent into units by pliers or round a jig, and joined with wire links to form jewellery.

Wire can be drawn through a jeweller's drawplate (through specially-shaped holes) to change its shape, or hammered at intervals along its length to form flat decorative shapes. Several wires can be twisted together by means of a vice and pliers (or a bent nail held in a hand-drill). Regular shaped units can be obtained by bending wire round a jig, made either of nails protruding from a block of wood, or grooves made in the top of a block of wood. (See the jewellery section for these techniques.)

Wire can be wound round a core (a cardboard tube) to form a spiral, or cut with cutting pliers and soldered to make sculptures (see the Tin-can craft section for soldering techniques). Fine wire can be glued together with epoxy cement. Use wire or chicken wire to make armatures which can be covered with papier mâché or plaster of Paris. Wooden human models or mannikins are available for copying figurative postures and proportions.

Aluminium, copper and brass wire are suitable for jewellery. Galvanised wire is rustproof (iron wire is liable to rust). Coat-hanger wire is a useful scrap material for junk sculpture, and can be soldered to sheet metal.

FURTHER READING

ULLRICH, H. & KLANTE, D., *Creative Metal Craft* Batsford

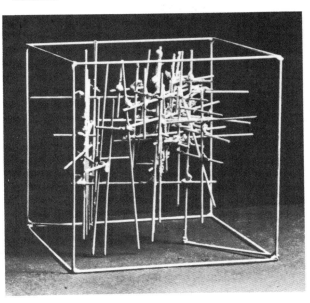

Wood Engraving

This technique requires an end grained block of wood, because only on this can one cut in any direction without splintering the wood. Boxwood is the traditional medium, but it is expensive. Maple is much cheaper and works very well. Tools for engraving on wood are called burins. Different names are given to tools making particular sorts of lines, but the main ones are the lozenge, spitsticker, scorper, and the velo which makes many lines at the same time.

If you paint the block black with poster paint before you start, then the line you see as you cut is the one you will see when you print. Traditionally the difference between wood engravings and woodcuts is that the former were seen as a white line drawing on black, and the latter as black lines on a white ground. Ink up as for woodcuts, and take a print by laying a damp piece of paper over the block and burnishing.

One of England's greatest wood engravers was Thomas Bewick, 1753–1828. His most important works were his *General History of Quadrupeds*, 1785, and in 1797 and 1804 he published the two volumes of *The History of British Birds*. Bewick perfected the technique during the last 40 years of his life, and from his death until the introduction of photography, book illustration continued to use wood engravings, instead of the copper engravings which had been employed previously. Wood engraving blocks proved very durable in the printing presses, some of Bewick's blocks being used for as many as 900,000 prints.

William Blake also used wood engraving, and in this century Eric Gill is one of its best known exponents. In America, Alexander Anderson was among the first to use the technique and the engravings of Rockwell Kent were very popular in the 1930s. In France, wood engravings held their own in the nineteenth century even against lithography. De Luxe editions of the French 'romantic illustrated book' illustrated with vignettes in wood engraving first appeared in 1835. Giroux, Doré, Monnier, and Gradville are some of the artists who worked in this field.

This type of engraving is a vignette, which means that the design is embedded in an irregularly shaped background, usually of foliage. Thomas Bewick constantly varied the arrangement of the animals and birds he illustrated, by altering the degree of 'embedding' of the subject.

This Bewick engraving has (apart from the branch) no background at all.

Woodcuts

This technique developed from the use of wooden stamps to make decorative or ideographic impressions in clay or wax by the Chinese. Paper was known in China in the second century, and when the Chinese took Buddhism to Japan in the sixth century, they also took wood-cutting, where the woodcut reached unmatched heights. (The earliest surviving printed texts in the world are Japanese eighth century Buddhist charms.) In Europe the woodcut was first used on fabric (and still is in India), the earliest known being fourteenth century.

METHOD

Almost any scrap wood can be used for wood cuts. To cut the wood use a penknife, Stanley, or Exacto knife, or a traditional V-cutting tool. Take care not to under-cut the line left standing. If you do, the least pressure on it when taking a print will snap it off. So make sure that the base of the line is wider than the line on the surface. Make a cut at an angle of 45° into the wood. Turn the wood round, and make another cut at 45° into the first cut.

The ink for woodcuts, litho prints and wood engravings is very thick and stiff. One has to 'work' it for quite a while on a slab of glass before it is in a state fit for rolling up. One does this with a flexible putty knife. If it is very stiff, add a little Vaseline to soften it. One can apply the ink to the wood block with a roller, a leather dabber, a sponge, or a stiff brush. A thin even film of ink is what you are aiming for.

Coloured Japanese woodcut.

Indian woodcut blocks, used for printing fabric.

Lay a sheet of damp paper over the block. With the back of a dessertspoon, gently rub the paper all over the block. If you are using a thin paper you will see the shapes of the wood appearing on the paper as you rub. If the paper is very thick peel back the edge every now and then to see how it is progressing.

When you have taken enough prints, clean the equipment and block with turpentine substitute. It is easy while the ink is still wet; but becomes impossible once it has dried.

FURTHER READING

DANIELS, H., *Printmaking* Hamlyn

Title page of the English edition of Gesner's *Historia Animalium* published in 1658. This particular design was still alive and being used to provide a base for glass paintings on clocks made in Connecticut in the second half of the nineteenth century.

Appendices

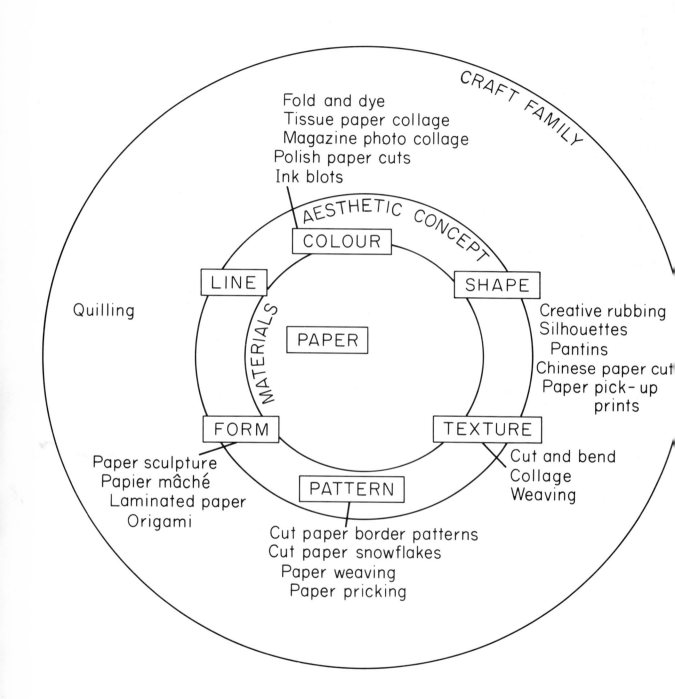

CRAFT FAMILY

Fold and dye
Tissue paper collage
Magazine photo collage
Polish paper cuts
Ink blots

AESTHETIC CONCEPT

COLOUR

LINE

SHAPE

Quilling

MATERIALS

PAPER

Creative rubbing
Silhouettes
Pantins
Chinese paper cut
Paper pick-up
prints

FORM

TEXTURE

Paper sculpture
Papier mâché
Laminated paper
Origami

PATTERN

Cut and bend
Collage
Weaving

Cut paper border patterns
Cut paper snowflakes
Paper weaving
Paper pricking

The Structure of Craft Processes

Of the special kinds of experience and thinking processes involved in visual art, the most important are exploration, perception, creative techniques and evaluation.

Exploration

Exploration covers materials, mechanics and aesthetics. In exploring materials one should experience them for what they are rather than what one thinks they should be. To do this, one must shed all preconceptions about the normal use to which a material is put; natural curiosity about a material will lead to problems in its use, and hence to possible solutions. In exploring the mechanics or techniques for a given craft, one encounters mechanics which have a general application across many crafts, such as joining, melting, threading, etc. Exploring the aesthetics of a craft involves the systematic experiencing of the concepts of line, shape, colour, texture, pattern, form and kinetics (real or implied).

Draw a series of concentric circles, and place a different craft family (such as printing, pottery, or puppetry) in each centre hub; do the same with different materials, then with different aesthetic concepts. In the middle circle place, respectively, aesthetic concept/aesthetic concept/materials; and in the outer circle place, respectively, craft subsections/craft family/craft subsections. This will allow you to recognize how things are related, and will offer flexibility of sequence in exploration and project work. The three examples shown (centred on 'paper', 'colour' and 'puppetry', pages 392, 394 and 395 respectively) are not complete, but illustrate how these concentric charts may be constructed.

Perception

The process of perception has to be focussed onto some particular concept so that it does not become an unwieldy collection of unrelated visual input. Focus, for example, on colour, mood evoked by different light sources and quantities, the differences in growth and decay, the young and the old, reflected surfaces, and distorted images.

Creative techniques

The practical techniques which are taught for each craft are those which have evolved over the years as the best way of achieving particular results: a known route towards a known goal. When the student or craftsman comes to experiment, it is important that he understands the reasons for a given technique, so that he can apply this knowledge to his chosen medium of expression. How well a technique is performed is the result of practice; the success of a work depends upon the successful expression of the original aesthetic concept by means of those techniques.

Evaluation

Evaluation of a product of art or craft should not rely solely on the judge's personal taste. The most important things to take into consideration are: the creativity 'type' (whether divergent, spontaneous, or academic), and the historical and social group-culture of the artist; what he set out to achieve, and the success with which he solved the problem; and his skills in aesthetic organization and mechanical techniques. No one can justifiably evaluate a work of art without knowing the series of problems to which any end product is merely one of a continuing series of answers.

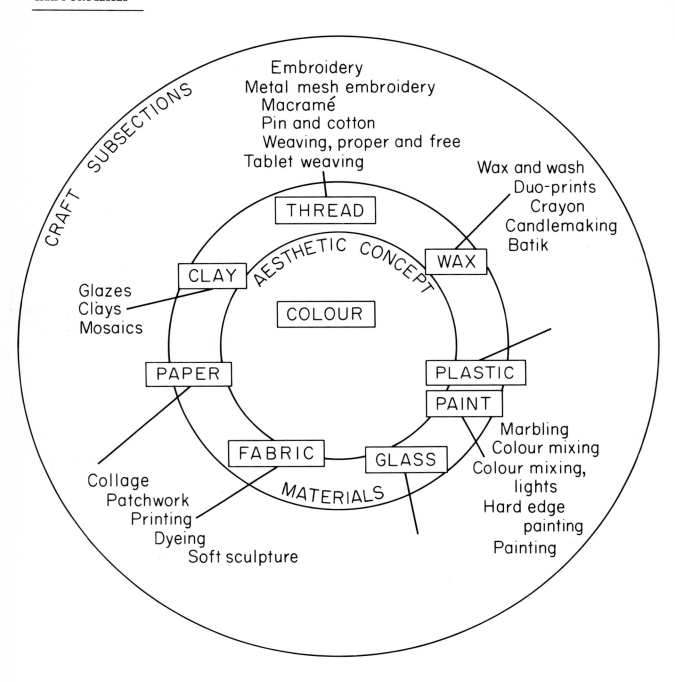

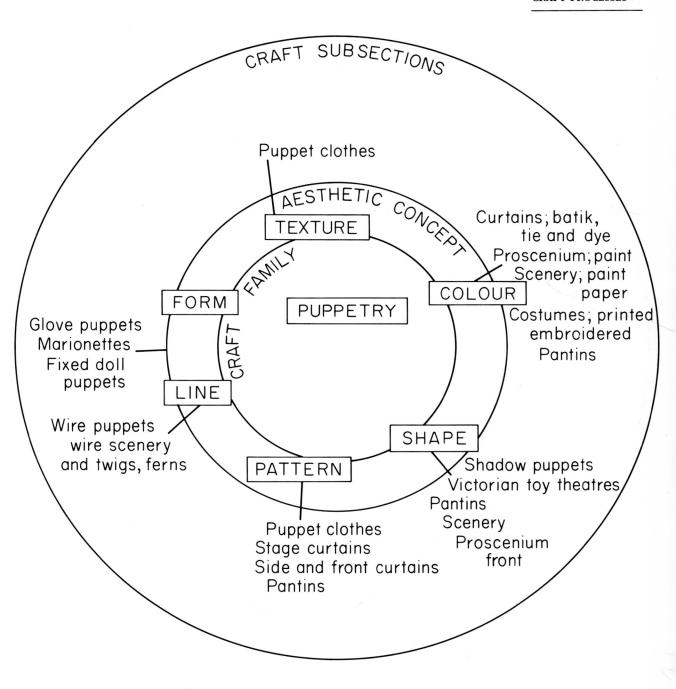

CRAFT SUBSECTIONS

Puppet clothes

AESTHETIC CONCEPT

TEXTURE

Curtains; batik,
tie and dye
Proscenium; paint
Scenery; paint
paper
Costumes; printed
embroidered
Pantins

FAMILY

FORM

COLOUR

CRAFT

PUPPETRY

Glove puppets
Marionettes
Fixed doll
puppets

LINE

SHAPE

Wire puppets
wire scenery
and twigs, ferns

PATTERN

Shadow puppets
Victorian toy theatres
Pantins
Scenery
Proscenium
front

Puppet clothes
Stage curtains
Side and front curtains
Pantins

Further Reading

Abercrombie, *The Anatomy of Judgements* Penguin

Arnheim, *Art & Visual Perception* Faber

de Bono, *Beyond Yes and No* Penguin

de Bono, *Children Solve Problems* Penguin

Carraher & Thurston, *Optical Illusions and the Visual Arts* Studio Vista

Dennison, *The Lives of Children* Penguin

Dewey, *Art as Experience* Capricorn Books

Eisner, *Educating Artistic Vision* Macmillan

Eisner & Ecker, *Readings in Art Education* Xerox College Publishing

Entwistle & Nisbet, *Educational Research in Action* Unibooks

Evans, *Planning Small Scale Research* NFER

Frière, *Cultural Action for Freedom* Penguin

Goodman, *Compulsory Miseducation* Penguin

Gordon, *Synectics : The Development of Creative Capacity* Macmillan

Gordon & Wyman, *Primer of Perception* Reinhold

Gregory, *The Intelligent Eye* World University

Henry, *Essays on Education* Penguin

Hogg (ed.), *Psychology of the Visual Arts* Penguin

Holt, *How Children Fail* Penguin

Holt, *How Children Learn* Penguin

Holt, *The Underachieving School* Penguin

Hudson, *Contrary Imaginations* Penguin

Illich, *Deschooling Society* Penguin

Jones, *Fantasy and Feeling in Education* Penguin

Kepes, *Education of Vision* Studio Vista

Kohl, *Children* Penguin

Kris, *Psychoanalytic Explorations in Art* IUP

McKim, *Experience in Visual Thinking* Brooks/Cole, Monterey, California

Moles, *Information Theory & Esthetic Perception* Illini Books

Pateman, *Counter Course* Penguin

Pickering, *Visual Education* Batsford

Plutchik, *Foundations of Experimental Research* Harper & Row

Reimer, *School is Dead* Penguin

Richardson, *Mental Imagery* R.K.P.

Soltis, *An Introduction to the Analysis of Educational Concepts* Addison Wesley Pub. Co., Menlo Park, California

Spiller (ed.), *Paul Klee, the Thinking Eye* Lund Humphries

Jack Vernon, *Inside the Black Room : Studies in sensory deprivation* Penguin

M.D. Vernon, *Experiments in Visual Perception* Penguin

M.D. Vernon, *The Psychology of Perception* Penguin

Weingarten & Postman, *Teaching as a Subversive Activity* Penguin

TEACHING

Barker, *Experiments with Shapes* Evans (4 booklets)

Craig, *Creative Art Activities* International Textbook Co., Scranton, Pennsylvania

Lark-Horovitz, *Understanding Children's Art for Better Teaching* Prentice Hall

Lindsay, *Art for Spastics* Mills & Boon

Marshall, *Aspects of Art Work with 5–9-year-olds* Evans

Marshall, *Experiment in Education* Cambridge University

Melzi, *Art in the Primary School* Blackwell

Myers, *Art & Civilization* Hamlyn

Richardson, *Art and the Child* U.L.P.

Sauboa (ed.), *Introduction to the Visual Arts* Harrap

Publishers who carry a list of books on art and craft are:

(UK)

B.T. Batsford Ltd
4 Fitzhardinge St
London, W1H 0AH

G. Bell & Sons Ltd
6 Portugal St, London, WC2A 2HL

J.M. Dent & Sons
26 Albemarle St, London, W1X 4QY

Croom Helm Ltd
2/10 St John's Rd, London, SW11

Mills and Boon Ltd
17/19 Foley St, London, W1A 1DR

George Allen and Unwin Ltd
40 Museum St, London, WC1 1LU

Search Press Ltd
2–10 Jerdan Place
London, SW6 5PT

Studio Vista
35 Red Lion Square, London, WC1R 4SG

(USA)

Arco Publishing Co Inc
219 Park Avenue South
New York 10003

Charles T. Branford Co
28 Union St
Newton Centre, Mass. 02159

Crown Publishers Inc
One Park Avenue, NY 10016

Dover Publications Inc
180 Varick St, NY 10014

Charles Scribner's Sons
597 Fifth Avenue, NY 10017

Taplinger Publishing Co Inc
200 Park Avenue Sth, NY 10003

Van Nostrand Reinhold Co
450 West 33rd St, NY 10001

Conversions and Translations

Metric Conversion Chart

in.	cm
$\frac{1}{8}$	0.3
$\frac{1}{4}$	0.6
$\frac{3}{8}$	1.0
$\frac{1}{2}$	1.3
$\frac{5}{8}$	1.5
$\frac{3}{4}$	2.0
$\frac{7}{8}$	2.2
1	2.5
2	5.0
3	7.5
4	10.0
5	12.5
6	15.0
7	18.0
8	20.5
9	23.0
10	25.5
11	28.0
12	30.5
13	33.0
14	35.5
15	38.0
16	40.5
17	43.0
18	46.0
19	48.5
20	51.0
21	53.5
22	56.0
23	58.5
24	61.0
25	63.5
26	66.0
27	68.5
28	71.0
29	73.5
30	76.0
31	79.0
32	81.5
33	84.0
34	86.5
35	89.0

YARDS TO METRES

yd	m
$\frac{1}{8}$	0.15
$\frac{1}{4}$	0.25
$\frac{3}{8}$	0.35
$\frac{1}{2}$	0.50
$\frac{5}{8}$	0.60
$\frac{3}{4}$	0.70
$\frac{7}{8}$	0.80
1	0.95
$1\frac{1}{8}$	1.05
$1\frac{1}{4}$	1.15
$1\frac{3}{8}$	1.30
$1\frac{1}{2}$	1.40
$1\frac{5}{8}$	1.50
$1\frac{3}{4}$	1.60
$1\frac{7}{8}$	1.75
2	1.85
3	2.75
4	3.70
5	4.60
6	5.50

PINTS TO LITRES

pt	lit
$\frac{1}{4}$	0.1
$\frac{1}{2}$	0.3
1	0.5
2	1.0
3	1.7
4	2.3
5	2.8
6	3.4
7	4.0
8	4.5

GALLONS TO LITRES

gall	lit
1	4.5
2	9.0
3	13.6
4	18.2
5	22.7
6	27.3
7	31.8
8	36.4
9	41.0
10	45.5

FLUID OUNCES TO CUBIC CENTIMETRES

fl oz	cc
1	28.4
2	56.8
3	85.2
4	113.6
5	142.1
6	170.5
7	198.9
8	227.3
9	255.7
10	284.1
11	312.5
12	340.9
13	369.3
14	397.8

OUNCES TO GRAMMES

oz	gm
$\frac{1}{2}$	14
$\frac{3}{4}$	21
1	28
$1\frac{1}{2}$	42
$1\frac{3}{4}$	50
2	56
3	85
4	113
5	141
6	170
7	198
8	226
9	255
10	283
11	311
12	340
13	368
14	396
15	425
16	453

(All figures have been rounded off to simplify the tables.)

USA MEASURES AND EQUIVALENTS

USA Dry Measure Equivalents

1 pint	=0·9689 UK pt	=0·5506 litres
1 bushel	=0·9689 UK bu	=35·238 litres
	(64 pints)	

USA Liquid Measure Equivalents

1 fluid ounce	= 1·0408 UK fl oz	=0·0296 litres
1 pint (16 fl oz)	=0·8327 UK pt	=0·4732 litres
1 gallon	=0·8327 UK gal	=3·7853 litres
	(8 pints)	

TEMPERATURE

°C	°F
250	432
150	302
100*	212*
90	194
80	176
70	153
60	140
50	122
40	104
30	86
20	68
10	50
0**	32**
—10	14

* Boiling point of water
** Freezing point

To convert Fahrenheit to Centigrade, deduct 32, multiply remainder by 5 and divide by 9.
To convert Centigrade to Fahrenheit, multiply by 9, divide by 5 and add 32.

Translations of Artists' Colours

List supplied by Rowney & Co Ltd, UK

ENGLISH	FRENCH	GERMAN
Blacks and Greys		
26 Black	Noir	Schwarz
33 Blue Black	Noir de Vigne	Blauschwarz
30 Bone Black	Noir Animal	Knochenschwarz
54 Deep Grey	Gris Foncé	Dunkelgrau
345 Green Grey	Gris Vert	Grüngrau
56 Grey	Gris	Grau
34 Ivory Black	Noir d'Ivoire	Elfenbeinschwarz
35 Lamp Black	Noir de Bougie	Lampenschwarz
59 Light Grey	Gris Clair	Hellgrau
37 Medium Black	Noit Moyen	Mittelschwarz
60 Mushroom Grey	Gris Champignon	Pilzgrau
65 Payne's Grey	Gris de Payne	Payne's Grau
39 Velvet Black	Noir Velours	Samtschwarz
68 Yellow Grey	Gris Jaune	Gelbgrau
Blues		
100 Blue	Bleu	Blau
102 Blue Lake	Bleu de Lac	Seeblau
144 Brilliant Azure	Bleu Azur Brillant	Brillantazur
109 Cobalt Blue	Bleu de Cobalt	Kobaltblau
111 Coeruleum	Bleu Caeruleum	Conlinblau
123 French Ultramarine	Outremer Français	Französiches Ultramarin
107 Indanthrene Blue	Bleu d'Indanthrène	Indanthrenblau
127 Indigo	Indigo	Indigo
136 Monestial Blue	Bleu de Phtalocyanine	Phthalocyaninblau
137 Permanent Blue	Bleu Permanent	Permanentblau
135 Prussian Blue	Bleu de Prusse	Preussischblau
115 Sky Blue	Bleu de Ciel	Himmelblau
116 Slate Blue	Bleu Ardoise	Schieferblau
145 Turquoise	Turquoise	Türkisblau
123 Ultramarine	Outremer	Ultramarin

Browns

	English	French	German
11	Brown Ochre	Ocre Brune	Dunkelocker
15	Brown Pink	Stil de Grain Brun	Stil de Grain Braun
21	Burnt Sienna	Terre de Sienne Brûlée	Gebrannte Siena
23	Burnt Umber	Terre d'Ombre Brûlée	Gebrannte Umbra
07	Madder Brown (Alizarin)	Laque de Garance Brun	Krapplack Braun
33	Mars Brown	Brun de Mars	Marsbraun
47	Raw Umber	Terre d'Ombre Naturelle	Umbra
51	Sepia	Sépia	Sepia
60	Transparent Brown	Brun Transparent	Transparentbraun
63	Vandyke Brown	Brun Van Dyck	Vandykbraun

Greens

	English	French	German
01	Alizarin Green	Vert Alizarine	Alizaringrün
08	Bright Green	Vert Brillant	Hochgrün
05	Brilliant Cyprus Green	Vert de Chypre Brillant	Brillantcypergrün
06	Brilliant Emerald Green	Vert Véronèse Brillant	Brillantsmaragdgrün
09	Brilliant Green	Vert Brillant	Brillantgrün
10	Cadmium Green	Vert de Cadmium	Kadmiumgrün
12	Chrome Green	Vert de Chrome	Chromgrün
24	Cobalt Green	Vert de Cobalt	Kobaltgrün
34	Deep Green	Vert Foncé	Dunkelgrün
38	Emerald Green (Hue)	Vert Véronèse Imit	Smaragdgrün Imit
40	Fir Green	Vert de Sapin	Tannengrün
52	Hooker's Green	Vert de Hooker	Hooker's Grün
55	Leaf Green	Vert Feuille	Blattgrün
48	Light Green	Vert Clair	Hellgrün
58	Lime Green	Vert Tilleul	Lindengrün
59	Middle Green	Vert Moyen	Mittelgrün
60	Mimosa	Mimosa	Mimosa
62	Monestial Green	Vert de Phtalocyanine	Phtalocyaningrün
63	Olive Green	Vert Olive	Olivengrün
67	Opaque Oxide of Chromium	Oxyde De Chrome	Chromoxydgrün
68	Pale Olive Green	Vert Olive Clair	Hellolivengrün
69	Prussian Green	Vert de Prusse	Preussischgrün
71	Rowney Emerald	Veronese de Rowney	Rowney Smaragdgrün
72	Rowney Olive	Olive de Rowney	Rowney Olive
75	Sap Green	Vert de Vessie	Saftgrün
76	Sea Green	Vert Marine	Meergrün
80	Terre Verte	Terre Verte Naturelle	Grüne Erde
81	Viridian	Vert Emeraude	Chromoxydgrün, Feurig

Reds

	English	French	German
45	Bordeaux Red	Rouge Bordeaux	Bordeauxrot
48	Bright Red	Rouge Brilliant	Hochrot
49	Brilliant Rose	Rose Brillant	Brillantrosa
01	Cadmium Red	Rouge de Cadmium	Kadmiumrot
02	Cadmium Red Deep	Rouge de Cadmium Foncé	Dunkles Kadmiumrot
06	Cadmium Red Light	Rouge de Cadmium Clair	Helles Kadmiumrot
07	Cadmium Scarlet	Ecarlate de Cadmium	Kadmiumscharlach
09	Carmine (Alizarin)	Carmin (Alizarine)	Karmin (Alizarin)
13	Crimson	Cramoisi	Karmesin
15	Crimson Alizarin	Cramoisi d'Alizarine	Alizarinkarmesin
14	Crimson Lake	Laque Cramoisie	Karmesinlack
78	Flesh Tint	Teinte Chair	Fleischfarbe
19	Geranium Lake	Laque Géranium	Geraniumlack
23	Indian Red	Rouge Indien	Indischrot
27	Light Red	Rouge Clair	Gebrannter Lichter Ocker
33	Mars Red	Rouge de Mars	Marsrot
35	Permanent Red	Rouge Permanent	Permanentrot
37	Permanent Rose	Rose Permanent	Permanentrosa
41	Poster Red	Rouge Affiche	Plakat Rot
60	Rose Doré Alizarin	Rose Doré (Alizarine)	Rose Doré (Alizarin)
64	Rowney Red	Rouge de Rowney	Rowney Rot
65	Rowney Rose	Rose de Rowney	Rowney Rosa

ENGLISH	FRENCH	GERMAN
566 Rust Red	Rouille	Rostrot
567 Scarlet	Ecarlate	Scharlach
569 Scarlet Alizarin	Ecarlate D'Alizarine	Alizarinscharlach
571 Scarlet Lake	Laque Ecarlate	Scharlachlack
573 Scarlet Vermilion	Vermillon Ecarlate	Scharlachzinnober
583 Venetian Red	Rouge de Venise	Venezianischrot
587 Vermilion	Vermillon	Zinnober

Violets and Purples

402 Brilliant Garnet	Grenat Brillant	Brillantgranat
410 Brilliant Lilac	Lilas Brillant	Brillantlilak
404 Brilliant Magenta	Magenta Brillant	Brillantmagenta
407 Brilliant Violet	Violet Brillant	Brillantviolett
405 Cobalt Violet	Violet de Cobalt	Kobaltviolett
408 Deep Violet	Violet Foncé	Dunkelviolett
418 Lilac	Lilas	Lilak
409 Magenta	Magenta	Magenta
411 Mars Violet	Violet de Mars	Marsviolett
414 Middle Violet	Violet Moyen	Mittelviolett
415 Mineral Violet	Violet Mineral	Mineralviolett
413 Permanent Mauve	Mauve Permanent	Permanentmalvenfarbe
430 Permanent Violet	Violet Permanent	Permanentviolett
433 Purple	Pourpre	Purpur
437 Purple Lake	Laque Pourpre	Purpurlack
439 Purple Madder (Alizarin)	Garance Pourpre (Alizarine)	Purpurkrapplack (Alizarin)
441 Red Violet	Rouge Violet	Rotviolett
450 Violet	Violet	Violett
453 Violet Alizarin	Alizarine Violet	Alizarinviolett

Whites

1 Chinese White	Blanc de Chine	Chinesischweiss
5 Flake White	Blanc de Plomb	Bleiweiss
9 Titanium White	Blanc de Titane	Titanweiss
11 White	Blanc	Weiss
1 Zinc White	Blanc de Zinc	Zinkweiss

Yellows and Oranges

601 Aureolin	Auréoline	Aureolin
605 Brilliant Orange	Orange Brillant	Brillantorange
606 Brilliant Primrose	Primevère Brillante	Brillantprimelgelb
607 Brilliant Yellow	Jaune Brillant	Brillantgelb
615 Cadmium Orange	Orange de Cadmium	Kadmiumorange
612 Cadmium Yellow	Jaune de Cadmium	Kadmiumgelb
613 Cadmium Yellow Deep	Jaune de Cadmium Foncé	Dunkles Kadmiumgelb
624 Chrome Orange	Orange de Chrome	Chromorange
625 Chrome Orange Deep	Orange de Chrome Foncé	Chromdunkelorange
622 Chrome Yellow	Jaune de Chrome	Chromgelb
627 Corn Yellow	Jaune Blé	Korngelb
628 Deep Orange	Orange Foncé	Dunkelorange
629 Deep Yellow	Jaune Foncé	Dunkelgelb
639 Gamboge	Gomme-Gutte	Gummigut
641 Golden Ochre	Ocre d'Or	Goldocker
642 Green Yellow	Jaune Vert	Grüngelb
643 Indian Yellow	Jaune Indien	Indischgelb
645 Italian Pink	Stil de Grain Jaune	Stil de Grain Gelb
650 Lemon	Citron	Zitron
651 Lemon Yellow	Jaune Citron	Zitronengelb
652 Marigold	Souci	Sonnenblumengelb
654 Mars Orange	Orange de Mars	Marsorange
655 Mars Yellow	Jaune de Mars	Marsgelb
656 Middle Yellow	Jaune Moyen	Mittelgelb
634 Naples Yellow	Jaune de Naples	Neapelgelb
660 Orange	Orange	Orange

ENGLISH	FRENCH	GERMAN
664 Permanent Yellow	Jaune Permanent	Permanentgelb
665 Primrose	Primevère	Primelgelb
667 Raw Sienna	Terre de Sienne Naturelle	Terra di Siena
673 Rowney Golden Yellow	Jaune d'Or De Rowney	Rowney Goldgelb
674 Rowney Yellow	Jaune de Rowney	Rowney-gelb
677 Transparent Gold Ochre	Ocre d'Or Transparente	Transparenter Gold Ocker
680 Yellow	Jaune	Gelb
663 Yellow Ochre	Ocre Jaune	Lichter Ocker

Degree of Permanence of Artists' Colours

List supplied by Rowney & Co Ltd, UK

Colour	Degree of permanence					Transparency (T) Opacity (O)	Composition
	Artists' Water Colours	Artists' Oil Colours	Georgian Oil Colours	Cryla Acrylic	Cryla Flow Formula		
441 Red Violet	—	—	—	★★★	★★★	T	Quinacridone
441 Rowney Red Violet	—	★★★	—	—	—	T	Quinacridone
453 Violet Alizarin	★★	—	—	—	—	T	Rubine Lake
Blues							
109 Cobalt Blue	★★★★	★★★★	—	★★★★	★★★★	T	Cobalt Aluminate
110 Cobalt Blue (Hue)	—	—	★★★	—	—		Essentially a compound of Silica, Alumina Sulphur and Soda
111 Coeruleum	★★★★	★★★★	—	★★★★	—		Mixture Copper Phthalocyanine and Aluminate with Titanium Dioxide
112 Coeruleum (Hue)	—	—	★★★	—	★★★		Mixture Copper Phthalocyanine with an Earth
123 French Ultramarine	★★★	★★★	★★★	★★★	★★★		Compound of Silica Alumina, Sulphur and Soda
127 Indigo	★★	★★	—	—	—	T	Indigo (synthetic)
136 Monestial Blue	★★★	★★★	★★★	★★★	★★★	T	Copper Phthalocyanine
137 Permanent Blue	★★★	★★★	★★★	—	—		Similar to Ultramarine
135 Prussian Blue	★★	★★	★★	—	—	T	Potassium Ferric-ferrocyanide
107 Rowney Indanthrene Blue	—	★★★	—	★★★	★★★	T	Indanthrene
145 Turquoise	—	—	—	★★★	★★★		Mixture Phthalocyanines with Titanium Dioxide

Greens

No.	Name							Composition
301	Alizarin Green	*	**	—	—	—	T	Mixture Halogenated Copper Phthalocyanine and a Tartrazine Lake
308	Bright Green	—	—	—	***	***		Mixture Phthalocyanine and Arylamide Yellow
310	Cadmium Green	—	***	—	—	—		Viridian and Cadmium Yellow
312	Chrome Green	—	—	**	—	—	O	Potassium Ferric-ferrocyanide and Lead Sulphochromate co-precipitated
324	Cobalt Green	****	****	—	—	—		Compound of Cobalt and Zinc Oxide
338	Emerald Green (Hue)	—	—	***	—	—		Mixture Phthalocyanine and Arylamide Yellow
352	Hookers Green	—	—	—	***	***	T	Mixture Phthalocyanine and Arylamide Yellow shaded with Carbon Black
353	Hookers Green No. 1	**	—	—	—	—	T	Mixture Phthalocyanines and Tartrazine Lake
354	Hookers Green No. 2	**	**	—	—	—	T	Phospho-Tungsto-Molybdic acid complex of a basic dye
362	Monestial Green	—	***	***	***	***	T	Halogenated Copper Phthalocyanine
363	Olive Green	**	**	—	—	—	T	Tartrazine Lake mixed with Anthraquinone Lake and shaded with Phthalocyanine
367	Opaque Oxide of Chromium	—	****	—	****	****	O	Oxide of Chromium
368	Pale Olive Green	—	—	—	—	***	T	Nickel complex of an organic pigment dyestuff shaded with Phthalocyanine and Titanium Dioxide
369	Prussian Green	—	—	***	—	—	T	Permanent Organic Pigments
371	Rowney Emerald	—	—	—	***	***		Mixture Arylamide Yellow and a Halogenated Copper Phthalocyanine
371	Rowney Emerald	—	***	—	—	—		Mixture Cadmium Sulphide and Halogenated Copper Phthalocyanine
372	Rowney Olive	—	***	—	—	—	T	Nickel complex of an organic pigment dyestuff
375	Sap Green	**	**	**	—	—	T	Tartrazine Lake/Phthalocyanine
380	Terre Verte	****	****	****	—	—	T	Complex Natural Earth
381	Viridian	****	****	—	—	—	T	Hydrated Oxide of Chromium
382	Viridian (Hue)	—	—	***	—	—	T	Mixed Phthalocyanines
368	Pale Olive Green	—	—	—	***	—	T	Nickel complex of an organic pigment dyestuff

Browns

No.	Name						T/O	Composition
207	Brown Madder (Alizarin)	**	***	—	—	—	T	Mixture Anthraquinone Lake with Natural Earths
211	Brown Ochre	—	****	—	—	—		Natural Earth containing Iron Oxide
215	Brown Pink	*	**	—	—	—	T	Mixture of Tartrazine and Anthraquinone Lakes shaded with Carbon Black
221	Burnt Sienna	****	****	****	****	****	T	Calcined Natural Earth containing Iron Oxide
223	Burnt Umber	****	****	****	****	****	O	Calcined Natural Earth containing Iron and Manganese
207	Madder Brown	—	—	***	—	—	T	Alizarin Lake and Burnt Umber
233	Mars Brown	—	****	—	—	—		Synthetic Oxide of Iron
567	Raw Sienna	****	****	****	****	****	T	Natural Earth containing Iron Oxide
247	Raw Umber	****	****	****	****	****		Natural Earth containing Oxides of Iron and Manganese
260	Rowney Transparent Brown	—	***	—	***	***	T	Quinacridone
251	Sepia	***	****	—	—	—		Mixture of Natural Earth with Carbon Black
263	Vandyke Brown	**	**	**	—	—	T	Bituminous Earth

Blacks and Greys

No.	Name						T/O	Composition
26	Black	—	—	—	****	****	O	Iron Oxide
33	Blue Black	—	****	—	—	—	O	Vine Charcoal
34	Ivory Black	****	****	****	—	—	O	Bone Black
35	Lamp Black	****	****	****	—	—	O	Hydrocarbon Black
65	Paynes Grey	***	***	***	—	—	O	Ultramarine and Black

Whites

No.	Name						T/O	Composition
1	Chinese White	***	—	—	—	—		Zinc Oxide
5	Flake White	—	***	***	—	—	O	Basic Lead Carbonate
9	Titanium White	—	***	***	—	—	O	Mixture Titanium Dioxide with Zinc Oxide
11	White	—	—	—	***	***	O	Titanium Oxide
1	Zinc White	—	***	***	—	—	O	Zinc Oxide

Further information on the properties and availability of artists' colours may be obtained from major art suppliers: Rowney, Reeves, Winsor & Newton (UK) and Grumbacher, Winsor & Newton, and Weber (USA).

CRAFTLINE

The Brigh
Series Fro

Batsford has sold over 1,000,000 c
A selection of best selling titles h
an outstanding new list – CRAFTI

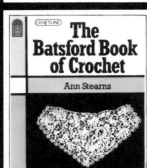

The Batsford Book of Crochet
Ann Stearns

'Expertly done, this is a necessary encyclopaedia on crochet art which any long-time crocheter, as well as novice, will find both helpful and enjoyable.'
Crochet World

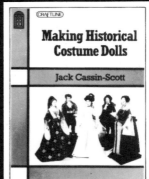

Making Historical Costume Dolls
Jack Cassin-Scott

'Clear instructions cover all stages of making the model ar dressing it.'
Pins and Needles

'Anyone interested in jewellery will find everything they could possibly want to know about how to make and design it…(the book) is not only a must for a beginner, but is an important must for the advanced craftsman as well.'
The Artist

The Technique of Jewellery
Rod Edwards

'Very comprehensive and highly recommended.'
Family Circle

Making Pressed Flower Pictures
Margaret Kennedy Scott
Mary Beazley

Machine Patchwork
Technique and design
Dorothy Osler

'…not just another book of patchwork, but a concise useful reference book, which I am sure will give many people encouragement and inspiration as well as practical help.'
Quilter's Guild Newsletter

Bobbin Lace Making
Pamela Nottingham

'…presents an interesting modern approach and maintains Pamela Nottingham very high standard'
The Lacemaker

Batsford Ltd., 4 Fitzhardinge St., London W1 0AH

Batsford Embroidery Titles

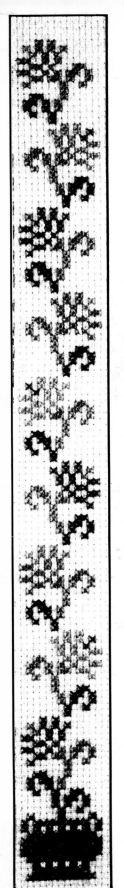

Blackwork Embroidery
Design & Technique
Margaret Pascoe
'This book which has much to recommend it both for those who have not tried blackwork and the
more experienced. A welcome addition to any embroiderer's library.'   *Embroidery*
152 illustrations   144 pages   0 7134 5145 9   hardback

The Children's Book of Embroidery
Tess Marsh
'It will, I am sure, be most useful in schools and YES groups for giving teachers and group leaders
ideas for projects and methods.'
Embroidery
102 illustrations   68 pages   0 7134 5142 4   hardback

Cross Stitch Samplers
Jane Kendon
'. . . an encouraging book suitable for the beginner . . . charts are especially clear and I like the way
the author tells us just which bit to embroider first.'   *Embroidery*
45 illustrations   15 charts   128 pages   0 7134 4917 9   hardback

Landscape in Embroidery
Verina Warren
'. . . stimulating and practical . . . The book is a mine of excellent advice and good value for money.'
202 illustrations   152 pages   0 7134 4567 X   hardback   *Embroidery*

Metal Thread Embroidery
Tools, Materials and Techniques
Jane Lemon
'The sumptuous illustrations in this fascinating and comprehensive volume should inspire even the most
ham-fisted stitcher, with Jane Lemon's detailed and informative text to guide them along the way.'
370 illustrations   232 pages   0 7134 5577 2   hardback   *The Journal, Salisbury*

Stumpwork
Historical and Contemporary Raised Embroidery
Muriel Best
'The methods and stitches can be used in so many ways, which makes it a very useful and
informative book to possess.'   *West Country Embroiderers*
148 illustrations   128 pages   0 7134 5572 1   hardback

White Work Embroidery
Barbara Dawson
'This is an interesting book to browse through and one that could help identify the various
techniques that come under the name of whitework.'   *Pins & Needles*
350 illustrations   192 pages   0 7134 3950 5   hardback

Machine Embroidery
Lace and See-through Techniques
'A very exciting book, bursting with ideas, that will have anyone interested in embroidery dashing
to their sewing machine.'   *Pins & Needles*
168 illustrations   124 pages   0 7134 4485 1   hardback

FROM THE BLUE EMBROIDERY PAPERBACK SERIES:
Embroidered Boxes
Jane Lemon
Step-by-step instructions for constructing boxes from fabric-covered card and enhancing
them with appliqué, quilting, canvas work and many other forms of embroidery.
311 illustrations   192 pages   0 7134 4587 4

Embroidery in Religion and Ceremonial
Beryl Dean
'. . . likely to be the standard work for a lifetime's reference and she has made sure that such
reference is quick and easy.'   *Embroidery*
Over 300 illustrations   296 pages   0 7134 5280 3

Samplers and Stitches
Mrs Archibald Christie
'Many books have been written on this fascinating subject, but we cannot remember coming
across any more comprehensive and complete work than Mrs Christie's. Indeed, so exhaustive
(and at the same time exhilarating) is it in its treatment that a careful study would teach as
much as any number of practical lessons. In the name of all needlewomen, there should be
accorded to Mrs Christie a very grateful vote of thanks.'   *Country Life, 1920*
278 illustrations   192 pages   0 7134 4796 6

Write to us for a complete list of all Batsford embroidery titles at:
B.T. Batsford Ltd, Fitzhardinge Street, London W1H 0AH